T0214691

Lecture Notes in Computer Science   12580

Ioana Boureanu · Constantin Cătălin Drăgan ·
Mark Manulis · Thanassis Giannetsos ·
Christoforos Dadoyan · Panagiotis Gouvas ·
Roger A. Hallman · Shujun Li ·
Victor Chang · Frank Pallas ·
Jörg Pohle · Angela Sasse (Eds.)

Computer Security

ESORICS 2020 International Workshops,
DETIPS, DeSECSys, MPS, and SPOSE
Guildford, UK, September 17–18, 2020
Revised Selected Papers

 Springer

Editors
Ioana Boureanu (iD)
University of Surrey
Guildford, UK

Mark Manulis (iD)
University of Surrey
Guildford, UK

Christoforos Dadoyan (iD)
Ionian University
Kerkira, Greece

Roger A. Hallman
Dartmouth College and Naval Information
Warfare Center
Hanover, NH, USA

Victor Chang
Teessside University
Middlesbrough, UK

Jörg Pohle
Alexander von Humboldt Institute
for Internet and Society
Berlin, Germany

Constantin Cătălin Drăgan (iD)
University of Surrey
Guildford, UK

Thanassis Giannetsos (iD)
Technical University of Denmark
Kongens Lyngby, Denmark

Panagiotis Gouvas
UBITECH Ltd.
Chalandri, Greece

Shujun Li
University of Kent
Canterbury, Kent, UK

Frank Pallas (iD)
Technical University of Berlin
Berlin, Germany

Angela Sasse (iD)
Ruhr University Bochum
Bochum, Germany

ISSN 0302-9743   ISSN 1611-3349 (electronic)
Lecture Notes in Computer Science
ISBN 978-3-030-66503-6   ISBN 978-3-030-66504-3 (eBook)
https://doi.org/10.1007/978-3-030-66504-3

LNCS Sublibrary: SL4 – Security and Cryptology

This Springer imprint is published by the registered company Springer Nature Switzerland AG
The registered company address is: Gewerbestrasse 11, 6330 Cham, Switzerland

DETIPS 2020 Preface

This book contains revised versions of the papers presented at the Interdisciplinary Workshop on Trust, Identity, Privacy and Security in the Digital Economy (DETIPS 2020). The workshop was co-located with the 25th European Symposium on Research in Computer Security (ESORICS 2020) and was held in Guildford during September 18, 2020.

The DETIPS 2020 workshop aims to bring together researchers solving real problems in cross-disciplinary aspects of trust, identity, privacy and security in the context of digital economy and its applications. Topics of interest address various aspects of the core areas in relation to Digital Economy: Trust (e.g. risk management, trust models, reputation systems, trustworthy AI, trust perception, human and societal aspects of trust in technology, technology acceptance, etc.), Identity (e.g. identity management, web authentication, access control, online fraud, etc.), Privacy (e.g. policies/GDPR, data protection, data sharing, anonymity, privacy-enhancing technologies, privacy for DLT applications, AI and privacy, etc.), and Security (e.g. digital transactions, cloud/IoT security, usability, legal aspects, socio-technical aspects, DLT security, security and AI, etc.). This workshop is supported by the UKRI EPSRC Digital Economy theme.

DETIPS 2020 attracted 16 high-quality submissions, each of which was assigned to 3-4 referees for review; the review process resulted in six full and two short papers being accepted to be presented and included in the proceedings. We would like to express our thanks to all those who assisted us in organizing the events and putting together the programs. We are very grateful to the members of the Program Committee for their timely and rigorous reviews. and to all the authors who submitted their work to the workshop and contributed to an interesting set of proceedings.

November 2020

Ioana Boureanu
Constantin Cătălin Drăgan
Mark Manulis

DETIPS 2020 Organization

Program Committee Chairs

Ioana Boureanu	University of Surrey, UK
Constantin Cătălin Drăgan	University of Surrey, UK
Mark Manulis	University of Surrey, UK

Program Committee

Arosha Bandara	The Open University, UK
Colin Boyd	NTNU, Norway
Jo Briggs	Northumbria University, UK
John Collomosse	University of Surrey, UK
Mauro Conti	University of Padua, Italy
Kovila Coopamootoo	Newcastle University, UK
Alexandra Dmitrienko	University of Würzburg, Germany
Karen Elliott	Newcastle University, UK
Simone Fischer-Hübner	Karlstad University, Sweden
Duncan Hodges	Cranfield University, UK
Mark W. Jones	Swansea University, UK
Sokratis Katsikas	NTNU, Norway
Alptekin Küpçü	Koç University, Turkey
Shujun Li	University of Kent, UK
Wendy Moncur	University of Dundee, UK
Cristina Onete	University of Limoges, France
Olivier Pereira	UCLouvain, Belgium
Delphine Reinhardt	University of Göttingen, Germany
Peter Roenne	University of Luxembourg, Luxembourg
P. Y. A. Ryan	University of Luxembourg, Luxembourg
Kouichi Sakurai	Kyushu University, Japan
Joerg Schwenk	Ruhr University Bochum, Germany
Aad Van Moorsel	University of Newcastle, UK
Wim Vanderbauwhede	University of Glasgow, UK
Melek Önen	EURECOM, France

DeSECSyS 2020 Preface

Information security and privacy have already been established as some of the most crucial aspects of technology especially in a world that is migrating to digital applications by the day. This has inevitably led to the emergence of technologies that support the safety and dependability of the ever-increasing sensitive data handled by these applications. Additionally, besides these technologies which target security by their design, there are other technologies, such as machine learning, which could potentially be applied to security in innovative schemes. Towards this direction, security is about balancing several trade-offs, e.g. security vs privacy, security vs trust, security vs usability, security vs cost, research vs standardization, academic research vs real applications, just to name a few. For example, while artificial intelligence provides the ability to efficiently analyze massive data streams to detect patterns of anomalous behavior, it also threatens user privacy by enabling the analysis of individual behaviors, and democratic government by subverting opinions via electronic media. Likewise, the use of trustworthy computing and trusted hardware: while it fortifies systems by providing stronger security and operational assurance guarantees, it also allows attackers to perform stealthy attacks and could be used to damage user privacy.

The DeSECSyS 2020 workshop had the objective of fostering collaboration and discussion of these issues and the various facets and trade-offs of cyber-security among cyber-security researchers and practitioners, in particular, applications, opportunities and possible shortcomings of novel security technologies and their integration in emerging application domains. The goal was to produce a collection of state-of-the-art research about emerging security technologies, their applications, their shortcomings and their verification with a focus on their uncompromised integration, in terms of security, safety and dependability.

The first edition of the International Workshop on Dependability and Safety Emerging Cloud and Fog Systems (DeSECSyS) took place in September in collocation with the ESORICS 2020 conference and collected inputs from various security research fields that can be applied towards the strengthening of fog and cloud security posture. The workshop lasted a full day and received seven valid submissions, of which four papers were selected as full papers after a double-blind review by our program committee. Submissions arrived from researchers in six countries, from a wide variety of academic and corporate institutions. The format of the workshop included technical presentations followed by presentations of preliminary project results from five H2020 projects: FutureTPM, INCOGNITO, SECONDO, ASTRID, and CUREX. The workshop was attended by around 50 people on average.

This volume contains the research outcomes of the DeSECSyS 2020 workshop by including the camera-ready versions of all the scientific works that were presented during the workshop, as well as extended abstracts of the two keynote talks, which were given by Prof. Feng Hao, University of Warwick, UK (*"SEAL: Sealed-Bid Auction without Auctioneers"*) and Dr. Nikoloas Loutaris, IMDEA Networks, Spain

(*"Measuring Online Behavioural Advertising and Other Adventures in Data Protection & Data Economics"*).

Putting together DeSECSyS 2020 was a team effort. We first thank the authors for the quality of their submissions. We are grateful to the Program Committee, who worked hard in reviewing papers and providing valuable feedback to the authors. In addition, we would like to thank the General Chairs, Prof. Liqun Chen from University of Surrey, UK, and Prof. Christos Xenakis from University of Piraeus, Greece, for their valuable support and help with the planning and organization of the workshop. Finally, special thanks to the ESORICS 2020 Organizing Committee for (virtually) hosting both the main conference and its affiliated workshops.

November 2020   Thanassis Giannetsos
                                                                   Christoforos Dadoyan
                                                                   Panagiotis Gouvas

DeSECSyS 2020 Organization

Supporters

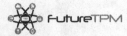

FutureTPM

INCOGNITO

SECONDO

ASTRID

CUREX

MPS 2020 Preface

This book contains the revised papers presented at the 3rd International Workshop on Multimedia Privacy and Security (MPS 2020), which was co-located with the 25th European Symposium on Research in Computer Security (ESORICS 2020). ESORICS 2020 and its affiliated workshops were originally to be held from 14–18 September, 2020 at the University of Surrey in Guildford, UK but instead became a virtual event due to the COVID-19 pandemic.

The MPS 2020 Workshop brought together researchers interested in the security and privacy of multimedia systems, which have become ubiquitous, especially with respect to multimedia data generated by the Internet of Things and Web 2.0. Indeed, topics related to the security and privacy of multimedia systems are of unprecedented importance as the COVID-19 pandemic has led to a sudden mass adoption of Internet-based video conferencing systems (e.g., Zoom, Microsoft Teams, Google Meet), online chatrooms (e.g., Slack), as well as other services to support telework capabilities as offices have been vacated around the world. Furthermore, the proliferation of misleadingly edited or fake multimedia through online social networks has the potential to severely impact social events and electoral processes around the world. Other topics of interest address various aspects of security and privacy as they apply to multimedia systems: Privacy (e.g., bystander privacy, biometrics, location-based privacy, crowdsensing, etc.), Security (e.g., multimedia encryption, malware in multimedia, multimedia forensics, side channel attacks, adversarial AI, access control and authentication), and Multimedia Systems (e.g., cloud-based multimedia systems, multimedia integration into IoT and online social networks, augmented and virtual reality, multimedia application of distributed ledger technologies and cryptocurrencies).

MPS 2020 received 10 high-quality submissions, each of which was reviewed by at least two expert referees. After reviewing referee comments and criticisms, we selected two Regular Papers and one Short Paper to be presented and included in the proceedings. Additionally, we hosted two keynote addresses:

- Jana Dittmann and Christian Kraetzer, *Forensics in the Encrypted Domain: Analysis of Network Stream to Detect Keystrokes and Audio-Video User Behavior*;
- Frederik Temmermans, Deepayan Bhowmik, Bernando Pereira, and Touradj Ebrahimi, *Fake Media – the JPEG Stake.*

We would like to express our deepest gratitude to the ESORICS 2020 Organizing Committee and the University of Surrey for their assistance and support in organizing this workshop, as well as the members of our Program Committee and referees who volunteered their time and expertise to review submissions. Finally, we must thank the authors for submitting their manuscripts to the MPS 2020 Workshop and for contributing to the proceedings.

November 2020   Roger A. Hallman
                                                    Shujun Li
                                                    Victor Chang

MPS 2020 Organization

SPOSE 2020 Preface

Over the past decades, a multitude of security- and privacy-enhancing technologies have been developed and brought to considerable maturity. However, the design and engineering of such technologies often ignores the organizational context in which the respective technologies are to be applied. A large and hierarchical organization, for example, calls for significantly different security and privacy practices and respective technologies than an agile, small startup. Similarly, whenever employees' behavior plays a significant role for the ultimate level of security and privacy provided, their individual interests and incentives as well as typical behavioral patterns must be taken into account and materialized in concrete technical solutions and practices. Even though research on security- and privacy-related technologies increasingly considers questions of practical applicability in realistic scenarios, implementation decisions are still mostly technology-driven, and existing technical limitations and notions of "this is how we've always done it" hamper innovation.

On the other hand, a substantial body of organization-related security and privacy research already exists, incorporating aspects like decision and governance structures, individual interests and incentives of employees, organizational roles and procedures, organizational as well as national culture, or business models and organizational goals. However, there is still a large gap between the generation of respective insights and their actual incorporation in concrete technical mechanisms, frameworks, and systems.

This disconnection between rather technical and rather organization-related security and privacy research leaves substantial room for improving the fit between organizational practices on the one hand and the engineering of concrete technologies on the other hand. Achieving a better fit between these two sides through security and privacy technologies that soundly incorporate organizational and behavioral theories and practices promises substantial benefits for organizations and data subjects, engineers, policy makers, and society as a whole.

The aim of the second Workshop on Security, Privacy, Organizations, and Systems Engineering (SPOSE) therefore was to discuss, exchange, and develop ideas and questions regarding the design and engineering of technical security and privacy mechanisms with particular reference to organizational contexts. We invited researchers and practitioners working in security- and privacy-related systems engineering as well as in the field of organizational science to submit their contributions. Besides regular and short papers, we also invited practical demonstrations, intermediate reports, and mini-tutorials on respective technologies currently under development to stimulate forward-looking discussions.

The papers included in the following pages demonstrate the possible spectrum for fruitful research at the intersection of security, privacy, organizational science, and systems engineering: Karen Renaud opened the Workshop with a brilliant keynote on the ongoing trend towards "Cyber Security Responsibilization of Citizens" and – given the contagious nature of security threats as well as the high level of expertise required to address them properly – argued for a more supportive policy approach to security with less responsibility being offloaded on individuals, employees and citizens alike.

The theme of responsibilization set the stage for the accepted-papers sessions: Jake Weidman, Igor Bilogrevic, and Jens Grossklags presented an empirical study on minimum security standards gathered from 29 US universities both in 2017 and in 2020. They found a high diversity between these documents in length and content as well as in matters of readability, language tone, and actionability. This lack of consistency across minimum security standards even for very similar organizations raises questions about the necessity of more coordinated and/or standardized efforts. Dimitri Van Landuyt, Laurens Sion, Pierre Dewitte, and Wouter Joosen, in turn, explored the implementation of data protection impact assessments in the light of prevailing, largely interconnected organizational structures and systems architectures. They identified and discussed two conceptually different approaches for conducting such assessments in the context of complex, inter-organizational data processing activities: a centralized and a federated one.

Two papers then closed the circle back to the responsibilization of individual users: Vera Hazilov and Sebastian Pape report on their experiences in the systematic creation of personas and scenarios for a serious game used in the context of security awareness training. They highlighted the importance of tailoring such personas and scenarios to the domain they are to be applied in and demonstrated how they did so for the context of consulting companies. Melanie Volkamer, Martina Angela Sasse, and Franziska Boehm finally shared their experiences from simulated phishing campaigns, an instrument often used in practice to assess and raise individual staff's capabilities for identifying and appropriately reacting to phishing mails. In contrast to common belief, they particularly highlighted the costs associated with successfully running such campaigns and the possibility of adverse effects on employees' self-efficacy and trust in the organization. They thus highlighted that for many organizations (a combination of) other approaches might better serve the goal of lowering the impact of phishing.

Altogether, these papers, complemented by an open-minded, keen-to-debate, and constructively thinking audience made the second iteration of the workshop another success, even though participant interaction was unquestionably somewhat constricted by the special conditions under which ESORICS 2020 had to take place. For nonetheless making SPOSE 2020 a success, we would like to thank everybody who contributed – authors, presenters, participants, reviewers, and, of course, the whole organizing team of ESORICS 2020. We are definitely looking forward to the next – and hopefully again face-to-face – iteration of SPOSE.

November 2020

Frank Pallas
Jörg Pohle
Angela Sasse

SPOSE 2020 Organization

Organizers

Frank Pallas	TU Berlin, Germany
Jörg Pohle	Humboldt Institute for Internet and Society, Germany
Angela Sasse	Ruhr-University Bochum, Germany

Program Committee

Zinaida Benenson	Friedrich-Alexander University Erlangen-Nürnberg, Germany
Athena Bourka	ENISA, Crete
Seda Gürses	TU Delft, The Netherlands
Marit Hansen	ULD, Germany
Heleen Janssen	Cambridge University, UK
Gabriele Lenzini	University of Luxembourg, Luxembourg
Sebastian Pape	Goethe University Frankfurt/Main, Germany
Simon Parkin	UCL, UK
Burkhard Schäfer	Edinburgh University, UK
Jatinder Singh	Cambridge University, UK
Max-R. Ulbricht	TU Berlin, Germany
Tobias Urban	if(is), Germany
Melanie Volkamer	KIT, Germany

Additional Reviewers

Lukas Aldag	KIT, Germany
Patricia Arias Cabarcos	KIT, Germany
Huseyin Demirci	University of Luxembourg, Luxembourg
Verena Distler	University of Luxembourg, Luxembourg
Russel W. F. Lai	Friedrich-Alexander University Erlangen-Nürnberg, Germany

Sealed-Bid Auctions Without Auctioneers
(DeSECSyS 2020 Workshop Keynote)

Feng Hao

Department of Computer Science, University of Warwick, UK
feng.hao@warwick.ac.uk

Abstract. In this talk, I will present our recent work on verifiable e-auction [1], which is done in collaboration with Samiran Bag, Siamak Shahandashti and Indranil Ray. Vickrey auction is a second-price sealed-bid auction scheme, named after William Vickrey who among many other contributions first developed the theory for this scheme and won a Nobel prize in 1996. However, despite the extreme importance in the auction theory, Vickrey auction has rarely been used in practice. One key obstacle concerns the trustworthiness of the auctioneer. The auctioneer can trivially learn all bid inputs which may contain trade secrets. Furthermore, a dishonest auctioneer may secretly modify the second-highest price in order to increase the auction revenue without bidders noticing it. In this talk, we resolve this fundamental trust problem by designing a publicly verifiable e-auction scheme that completely removes the need for auctioneers. This represents a paradigm change from previous schemes. Our solution is called Self-Enforcing Auction Lot (SEAL). It does not require any secret channels between bidders; all communication is public and everyone including the third party observers can verify the integrity of the auction outcome; the system allows bidders to jointly compute the winning bid while preserving the privacy of losing bids, as well as effectively resolving any tie in the contest if it exists; it supports both first-price and second-price sealed-bid auctions; most importantly, it occurs only a linear computation and communication complexity with respect to the bit length of the bid price, which is probably the best one may hope for. All these make SEAL a practical solution to deploy in a real-world application, e.g., as a smart contract on a blockchain platform.

Keywords: Sealed-bid auction · Vickrey auction · Multi-party computation

Reference

1. Bag, S., Hao, F., Shahandashti, S., Ray, I.G.: SEAL: Sealed-bid Auction without Auctioneers. IEEE Trans. Inf. Secur. Forensics 15, 2042–2052 (2020)

Biography

Feng Hao is a Professor of Security Engineering, and Head of the Systems and Security (SAS) research theme at the Department of Computer Science, University of Warwick. He received his PhD in 2007 in Computer Science from the University of Cambridge. Being a security engineer, he has a mixture of industrial and academic experiences. Prior to starting his academic career, he worked in the security industry for 6 years. With colleagues, he designed a few cryptographic protocols: AV-net, OV-net, J-PAKE, YAK, DRE-i and DRE-ip, some of which have been used in real-life applications. In particular, J-PAKE has been adopted by the Thread Group as a de facto standard to perform the IoT commissioning process (used in Google Nest, ARM mbed, NXP, OpenThread, D-Link, Qualcomm, Samsung, and Texas Instruments IoT products, etc) and internationally standardized in ISO/IEC 11770-4. DRE-ip has been successfully trialed in Gateshead during the UK local elections on 2 May 2019. His first paper during PhD on "combining crypto with biometrics effectively" (IEEE Trans. Computers 2006) was ranked the top in 2017 Google Classic papers in the category of "cryptography & computer security". His work on "self-enforcing e-voting" has led to a € 1.5 m ERC starting grant and an ERC proof-of-concept grant.

Cyber Security Responsibilization of Citizens A Paradigm Mismatch? (SPOSE 2020 Workshop Keynote)

Karen Renaud (iD)

Abertay University, UK
e-mail: cyber4humans@gmail.com
https://www.karenrenaud.com
Rhodes University, South Africa
University of South Africa, South Africa

Abstract. Responsibilization can be seen as "a reduction in direct government intervention with respect to a particular issue, trending towards less intervention" [5]. Tsinovoi and Adler-Nissen [7] explain that where previously governments embraced a 'duty of care', the mind-set is now one of "citizens as resources'" p. 3. Governments have shifted from considering themselves to be shepherds protecting their flocks, towards a view that citizens need to take care of themselves i.e. they are responsibilized. Governments focus primarily on building capabilities [7]. Many governments cyber responsibilize their citizens [5], providing advice but no direct support. Citizens are thus vulnerable: soft targets for cyber criminals [2, 3].

If we look at the history of risk management, we see that risks have two characteristics that influence the extent to which governments responsibilize their citizens to manage these risks, or provide explicit support. These are:

(1) **Potential Contagion/Catastrophe:** If a risk is contagious, such as COVID-19, or can lead to catastrophe, like fire, governments tend to provide significant support.

(2) **Whether Specific Expertise is Required:** If risk management requires significant expertise that is not possessed by the majority of the population, governments will step in to assist citizens. If they do not do this, the contagion will be uncontained and a bigger catasrophe might result, leading to even greater losses.

Figure 1 shows how other risks fit into a two-by-two grid based on these characteristics, with Cyber Security currently appearing bottom left (no contagion, no expertise). Now, consider that cyber security infections actually demonstrate contagion [1], can lead to catastrophes [6], and require specific expertise [4]. That being so, Cyber Security should be situated in the upper right-hand quadrant.

Hence, the cyber responsibilization of citizens by governments needs to be reconsidered. Given the nature of the cyber risk, more support should be provided to citizens. This is the only way that millions of private citizens are going to be able to resist the increasing numbers of cyber attacks targeting them.

Keywords: Responsibilization · Cyber Security

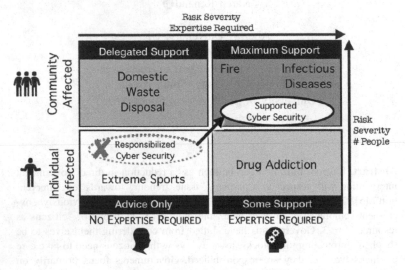

Fig. 1 Situating the cyber risk

References

1. Camp, L.J., Grobler, M., Jang-Jaccard, J., Probst, C., Renaud, K., Watters, P.: Measuring human resilience in the Face of the global epidemiology of cyber attacks. In: Proceedings of the 52nd Hawaii International Conference on System Sciences (2019)
2. Hughes, K.: Coronavirus fraud warnings as Britons lose $800,000 since outbreak arrived (2020). https://www.independent.co.uk/money/spend-save/fraud-scams-coronavirus-phishing-tricks-malware-refund-push-payment-a9405846.html. Accessed 25 Mar 2020
3. I-Team: Wired away: Couple loses life savings during home purchase (2017). https://abc7chicago.com/realestate/wired-away-couple-loses-life-savings-during-home-purchase/2630496/. Accessed 29 Oct 2019
4. Nthala, N., Flechais, I.: "If It's urgent or it is stopping me from doing something, then i might just go straight at it": a study into home data security decisions. In: Tryfonas, T. (eds.) HAS 2017. LNCS, vol. 10292, pp. 123–142. Springer, Cham (2017). https://doi.org/10.1007/978-3-319-58460-7_9
5. Renaud, K., Orgeron, C., Warkentin, M., French, P.E.: Cyber security responsi- bilization: an evaluation of the intervention approaches adopted by the five eyes countries and China. Public Adm. Rev. 80(4), 577–589 (2020)

6. Scroxton, A.: German authorities probe ransomware hos pital death (2020). https://www.computerweekly.com/news/252489247/German-authorities-probe-ransomware-hospital-death. Accessed 21 Sept 2020
7. Tsinovoi, A., Adler-Nissen, R.: Inversion of the 'duty of care': Diplomacy and the protection of citizens abroad, from pastoral care to neoliberal governmentality. Hague J. Dipl. **13**(2), 211–232 (2018)

Contents

MPS 2020

SPOSE 2020

DETIPS 2020

IMC: A Classification of Identity Management Approaches

Daniela Pöhn(✉) and Wolfgang Hommel(✉)

Research Institute CODE, Bundeswehr Universität München, Munich, Germany
{daniela.poehn,wolfgang.hommel}@unibw.de

Abstract. This paper presents a comprehensive classification of identity management approaches. The classification makes use of three axes: topology, type of user, and type of environment. The analysis of existing approaches using the resulting identity management cube (IMC) highlights the trade-off between user control and trust in attributes. A comparative analysis of IMC and established models identifies missing links between the approaches. The IMC is extended by a morphology of identity management, describing characteristics of cooperation. The morphology is then mapped to the life cycle of users and identity management in a further step. These classifications are practically underlined with current approaches. Both methods combined provide a comprehensive characterization of identity management approaches. The methods help to choose suited approaches and implement needed tools.

Keywords: Security · Identity management · Model · Taxonomy

1 Introduction

Thousands of web applications around the world provide different services via the internet. These services require the user to present an identity for authentication, otherwise the user is not able to access them. To manage different users with their identities, identity management (IdM) was introduced as a paradigm more than two decades ago. It focuses on managing usernames, which are used as identifier assigned to users, some sort of credential, usually a password, and further information, like email address and postal address, called user attributes.

Different evolving requirements led to the creation of different models of and protocols for identity management systems (IdMS). While stand-alone organizations run a *centralized* Identity & Access Management (I&AM) system, many organizations with collaboration, especially in academia, introduced *Federated Identity Management* (FIM). FIM is an arrangement between multiple entities in order to let users use the same identification data as in their home organization. By FIM, users obtain access to the services provided by partners, called service providers (SPs), within organizational trust boundaries called federations. The often-used Security Assertion Markup Language (SAML) [11] is rather static, whereas OAuth and OpenID Connect (OIDC) [14] provide a dynamic approach,

© Springer Nature Switzerland AG 2020
I. Boureanu et al. (Eds.): ESORICS 2020 Workshops, LNCS 12580, pp. 3–20, 2020.
https://doi.org/10.1007/978-3-030-66504-3_1

known for example from Google. Limitations of FIM led to different approaches, like inter-federations (e.g. eduGAIN [5]), the use of the Domain Name System (DNS) for discovery and trust, e.g., LIGHTest [13], different assurance frameworks and components. In parallel, *user-centric solutions* were developed. User Managed Access (UMA) [8], an OAuth-based standard, enables the user to control the authorization of data sharing and other protected resources. The user of *Self-Sovereign Identities* (SSIs) is the ultimate owner of the identity. SSIs are typically realized by decentralized networks, like distributed ledger technologies (DLTs) [2]. Decentralized Identifiers (DIDs) [12] often make use of DLTs.

IdM is one crucial pillar of security frameworks. Several different models and approaches are currently developed and run. Not all approaches fit into one single model, making a categorization challenging. This paper contributes the following improvements: The developed identity management cube (IMC) categorizes different IdM approaches. The cube is broadened by a morphology describing aspects of collaboration within the life cycle. Both categorizations are applied to different protocols and applications. This helps to identify fitting approaches and missing tools for interoperability. It also provides an overview of important aspects during the life cycle, helping stakeholders.

This paper is organized as follows. We discuss related work in Sect. 2. In Sect. 3, we present a new categorization of IdM and provide a brief classification of current approaches. Additionally, we present a morphology in Sect. 4, which is then mapped to the life cycle of identities and identity management. The newly developed IMC and the morphology are applied to current approaches and then discussed in Sect. 5. The paper is concluded in Sect. 6 by a summary of the results achieved so far and an outlook to ongoing work.

2   Related Work

Yuan Cao and Lin Yang [16] identify three core components for IdM: user, service provider (SP), and identity provider (IdP). The authors further describe the three models isolated, centralized, and federated. According to them, the IdM paradigms can be classified into network-centric paradigm, service-centric paradigm, and user-centric paradigm. Sovrin [15] sees SSI as next step after isolated, centralized, federated, and user-centric IdM models. In other papers, either the models isolated, centralized, federated, and user-centric or centralized, federated, and decentralized are used.

Boujezza et al. [1] describe a taxonomy for Internet of Things (IoT) by adapting the paradigms and requirements. The authors classify user model, service provider model, and hybrid model, combining user and SP, and further submodels. In contrast, Pal et al. [10] relate IoT identities to things-centric identities. Gao et al. [3] describe an IdM model for big data based on authorization, authentication, identification, and audit modules. Habiba et al. [7] use the IdM requirements taxonomy to classify cloud IdMS. Further approaches have been developed, leading to different directions, which we integrate into our model.

3   Identity Management Models

The main functionalities of IdM are identification, authentication, and authorization. In most cases, a password is provided for authentication, which fulfills a required complexity or entropy. Second factor, multi-factor, and anonymous are also possible. The authorization is based on policies, which describe whether the user is allowed to access a certain functionality or data. With collaborations, the information about the user is stored at the IdP. The user wants to access a service of the entity SP. Minor entities are trusted third parties (TTPs), attribute authorities (AAs), having additional information about the user, and federation operators, if IdPs and SPs form trust boundaries. As new requirements are evolving, different approaches for IdM have been developed and will be emerging in the future. The existing IdM models do not work for several use cases. Therefore, new models are developed and applied in the following.

3.1   Analysis of Identity Management Models

In order to distinguish different IdM approaches, models have been established. These models were updated for user-centric models and partly for SSI. As described in Sect. 2, the following IdM models are mostly used.

Isolated: I&AM per service.
Centralized: Network-centric. I&AM per entity, e.g., with single sign-on (SSO).
Federated: Application-centric. I&AM per federation, which is a set of IdPs
  and SPs. Possible protocols are, e.g., OIDC and SAML.
Decentralized: User-centric. I&AM, where the user is in control. Used for FIM
  in many cases. Possible approaches are UMA and SSI. Decentralized is partly
  divided into user-centric and SSI.

The models are seen as evolution with almost no intersection, displayed in Fig. 1a. The models describe the topology and the source of truth, i.e., the user or another entity. Approaches can fit into two models at the same time, see Fig. 1b, e.g., if the IdM is user-centric but the SPs form a federation. In this case, SSI respectively UMA belong to two models.

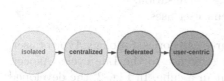
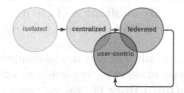

(a) Evolution of Identity Management   (b) Orthogonality of Identity Manage-
Models   ment Models

Fig. 1. Identity management models

3.2   The Identity Management Cube (IMC)

In order to distinguish the approaches, we use the following dimensions.

Topology: Topology of the IdM approach.
Type of User: Type of user, using the approach.
Type of Service: Type of service featured by the approach.

The *topology* is orthogonal to user-centric and can be used as one category. Based on existing approaches, the topology can be described as follows. Isolated is left out of the category as it disappears due to the management overhead.

Centralized: I&AM per entity.
With TTP: I&AM with several entities, where at least one TTP is involved. This applies to many cases of FIM and is, therefore, similar to federated.
Without TTP: I&AM with several entities, where no TTP is involved. As it describes a distributed, completely decentralized structure, it addresses different approaches. Most cases of SSI belong to this category.

User-centric describes two things: a human user and user as source of truth. Other user types are computers, like servers, and IoT devices. Therefore, the second category is *type of user*. The human user is further divided into user-centric and provider-centric, describing attribute handling.

User: Divided into user-centric and provider-centric. This includes cases of UMA, SSI, but also SAML and OIDC.
Computer: Machine to machine (M2M) communication, for example.
IoT Device: IoT devices usually have less computing power, which restricts computationally intensive cryptographic operations.

Although an increasing number of web services are used, like Office 365, several services are non-web-based. In order to distinguish the *type of service*, the following characteristics are set.

Non-Web Service: M2M communication, but also local services.
Background Web Service: Services, which are need for interactive web services, like localization of the user's home organisation.
Interactive Web Service: Services the end-user uses.

As a result, the new model comprises three categories, topology, type of user, and type of service, displayed as axes. In reference to the Life cycle, Aspect, Layer (LAL) Brick [4], the categories result in a cube. In Fig. 2, the developed IdM cube including the labels of the different axes is shown. User-centric and provider-centric are thus left out for clarity reasons.

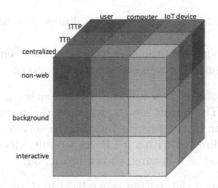

Fig. 2. Identity management cube

3.3 IMC Applied to Current Approaches

In order to depict the IMC, different IdM approaches are classified by the categories described above. As examples, centralized IdM with SAML federations in research and education (R&E), OIDC in the web, UMA for private users, and SSI as new approach are chosen. In addition, IdM for servers, IoT, and with Active Directory (AD) are explained.

SAML is used in R&E to let users access web services at research partners. It is based on lightweight directory access protocol (LDAP), databases, or even AD with the add-on federation. The entities form a federation, which relies on contracts with the federation operator. As a result, it has the following characteristics, as shown in Fig. 3a.

Topology: With federation tools as TTPs.
Type of User: User are humans, but the type is provider-centric.
Type of Service: Interactive web services for end users.

OIDC is used in web as well, but is a more dynamic protocol without a TTP, based on OAuth. UMA is also developed on top of OAuth, but more user-centric. This can be seen in the characteristics, shown in Fig. 3b.

Topology: Using Webfinger technology is without a TTP, but can be centralized in some use cases.
Type of User: Human end user in most cases, which can be either provider-centric (OIDC) or user-centric (UMA).
Type of Service: Typically interactive web for end users, but others types are also possible.

SSI is seen as the new step in evolution of IdM, as the user is in control of everything. The concept is without a TTP, but it evolves to a topology with a TTP for scalability and performance reasons. Most approaches concentrate on interactive web services, though the concept could be applied to other services as well. SSI, therefore, has the following characteristics, displayed in Fig. 3c.

Topology: Originally, SSI is without a TTP, but is evolving to centralized services.

Type of User: SSI focuses on the user, therefore, user-centric.

Type of Service: Interactive web services for end users.

Besides web application, *servers* are run at the backend, which are normally access through keys. The public key is stored at the server, while the administrator is in possession of the private key. So, the service is non-web and it is typically either centralized or with a TTP. As a result, identity management for servers can be described as following, shown in Fig. 3d.

Topology: Either centralized, with a centralized IdM, or with a TTP.

Type of User: Both, computer in M2M or human users are possible.

Type of Service: The services are typically non-web.

Centralized IdM with AD is used in companies to enable employees to login at their computer, provision folders and shares, but also to access web services with single sign-on (SSO). It has the following characteristics, shown in Fig. 3e.

Topology: The AD itself is centralized.

Type of User: The human user is in focus, but the IdM is provider-centric. Additionally, Windows computer can be a user.

Type of Service: All types of services are possible, as it relies on Windows.

IoT devices often communicate with Constrained Application Protocol (CoAP) instead of Hypertext Transfer Protocol (HTTP). The devices, which either lack a browser to perform user-agent based authorization or are input constrained, cannot make use of typical web protocols, like OAuth or SAML. One option is, e.g., to utilize shared keys, another is ACE-OAuth. ACE-OAuth maps OAuth methods to Authentication and Authorization for Constrained Environments (ACE). The characteristics are shown in Fig. 3f.

Topology: IoT networks are typically centralized managed, which can be with or without a TTP.

Type of User: The type is IoT device.

Type of Service: IoT devices are mainly background services.

The selected approaches can be merged in one IMC. The colors are used as in the figure above: AD dark green, SAML yellow, OIDC dark blue, SSI light blue, servers orange, IoT light green. The cube illustrates that many approaches are used for interactive web and human users, while the protocols themselves could be used for other user cases as well. The figure at the same time visualizes the differences between the approaches. While AD is focused on centralized topology, SAML typically uses a TTP, while OIDC, UMA, and SSI tend to work without TTP. The most common type of service are used in Fig. 4a, while Fig. 4b adds also unusual use cases. Both figures show that the selected approaches do not cover all aspects of the IMC. SSI with a centralized party would partly fulfill the application of SAML, as it would double to with a TTP from the

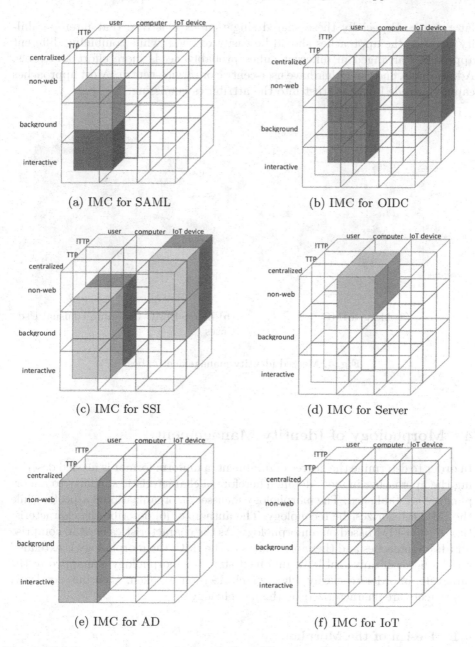

Fig. 3. Identity management cubes applied to different use cases (Color figure online)

later figure. Especially these shared single cubes illustrate that interoperability between the approaches should be easily reached, while combining different approaches arranged in different cubes probably needs more effort and tools. Additionally, one can either have user-centric or service-centric. Most approaches cannot provide both, as trust into the attributes is missing.

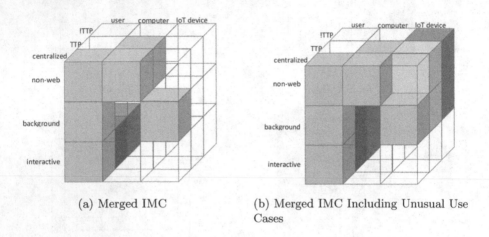

(a) Merged IMC

(b) Merged IMC Including Unusual Use Cases

Fig. 4. Merged identity management cubes

4   Morphology of Identity Management

In order to determine the degree of fulfilment, a uniform format is needed describing the approaches in more detail. Therefore, a characteristic similarly to a morphology is established. The morphology focusses on organizational aspects, while the IMC categorizes the technology. The authors of [6] describe the characteristics of Inter-FIM based on a morphology. As the characteristics need to comprise all IdM approaches and therefore relates to the IMC, the morphology is extended for the needs of universal IdM. In a next step, the morphology is mapped to the life-cycle, in order to clarify when which decision is taken. Last but not least, approaches are characterized by the morphology.

4.1   Design of the Morphology

The morphology describes the characteristics of the cooperation. [6] uses cooperation structure, members, group structure, federation dimension, organizational dimension, duration, sort of collaboration, coordination, establishment, circle of trust, degree of commitment, and trust relationship. As this approach concentrates on Inter-FIM, the following characteristics can be left out or need changed.

Structure of Cooperation: The structure described topology and cooperation customized for federations. The topology is described by the cube, while different aspects of the cooperation are part of the morphology.

Cooperation: Instead of FIM, Projects, and Communities, this characteristic is now described in "Reason for Joining" as well as "Order".

Formalization: Differentiates between "limited contract" and "cooperation agreements", in order to describe the distinction of contracts.

Dynamic of Joining: Broader scope with "stable" and "unstable".

To describe different organizational aspects, other characteristics need to be added. Several characteristics relate to the IdM architecture.

Reason for Joining: In order to differentiate between private usage and business reasons, this characteristic was included.

Connectivity: Describes the interaction between involved parties, which might have consequences for the architecture.

Direction of Cooperation: Broadens the scope.

Administration: Degree of automation, which relates to the architecture.

Cooperation Structure: Either "hierarchical" or "heterarchical".

Level of Trust: Trust between involved parties.

Identities: Included as it has implications for the architecture.

4.2 Identity Management Morphology

This results in a morphology, which includes more and broader characteristics. The morphology has the following categorize, as shown in Table 1.

Initiation: Initiation of the cooperation.

Cooperation: Settings of the cooperation.

Coordination: Settings of the coordination.

Trust: Trust between participating entities.

Identities: Settings of the identities.

Initiation comprises of reason for joining and dynamic of joining. The *reason* can be "personal", "social", like in social media, "by law" or "economic". Economic reasons can further be split into "time", "risk", "earnings", "competence", "costs", "pressure", and "protection". Another distinction could be "planned", if necessary, and "spontaneously event-driven". The *dynamic* is either "stable" or "unstable", i.e., it is either predictable or not.

The *cooperation* itself is described by degree of integration, connectivity, professional limits, factual limits, direction of cooperation, order, locality, organizational, and formalization. Both, the degree of integration and the connectivity between partners, are part of the networking between partners. The *degree of integration* can either be "autonomous", "coordinated" or "integrated". This means that either the partners work autonomous, coordinated towards a goal. Integrated can be a fusion of organizations. The *connectivity* has two steps: "low" and "high". It partly relates to integration. The next category are both limits,

Table 1. Morphology for identity management in detail

Initiation				
Reason for joining	Personal	Social	Economic	Law
Dynamic of joining	Stable		Unstable	
Cooperation				
Degree of integration	Autonomous	Coordinated	Integrated	
Connectivity	Low		High	
Professional limits	User	R&D	Department	Value chain
Factual limits	Short	Medium	Long	Permanent
Direction of cooperation	Vertical	Horizontal	Diagonal	
Order	Strategy	Project	R&E	Region
Locality	Local	Regional	National	International
Organizational	Micro	Meso	Macro	
Formalization	Arrangement	Limited contract	Cooperation agreement	Capital interweaving
Coordination				
Administration	Manual	Supported	Automated	
Number of participants	Bilateral	Simple	Complex	
Group structure	Open	With limitations	Closed	
Cooperation structure	Hierarchical		Heterarchical	
Sort of coordination	Implicit		Explicit	
Trust				
Directness	Direct		Transitive	
Circle of Trust	Static	Dynamic	Virtual	
Level of Trust	Zero	Low	Medium	High
Identities				
Transparency	Low	Medium	High	
Controllability	Low	Medium	High	
Identification	Internal	External	Combination	
Authentication Method	Anonymous	Simple	2FA	MFA
Authentication organization	Internal	External	Combination	
Authorization	Internal	External	Combination	

professional and factual. *Professional limits* describe which organization part is involved in the cooperation. It can be "research", a "department", the complete "value chain", or just one or more "users". *Factual limits* are described by "permanent" or "restricted". Restricted can further be split into "short", "medium", and "long". The *direction of cooperation* depicts how close both economic levels are related. "Horizontal cooperation" describes the cooperation of companies of the same business or same level of the value chain, while "vertical cooperation" is a cooperation between organizations of different economic levels, like retail company and production company. A cooperation is "diagonal", if all involved companies are neither on the same economic level nor business, e.g., travel company and food company. The *order* characterizes the reason for the cooperation, which is "strategic", a "project", "R&E", or based on the "region". Both, the locality and the organizational are dimensions of the cooperation. The *locality* of the cooperation is either "local", "regional", "national", or "international". A national federation are the R&E federations, like SWITCHaai in Switzerland. eduGAIN is the international umbrella federation for the national pendants.

The *organizational* dimension describes the viewing plane of the cooperation. Terminology from economics is used. "Micro" plane consists of one single entity, while the "meso" plane comprises of several organizations, e.g., in a federation. The "macro" plane shows the cooperation of cooperation, e.g., an inter-federation. The *formalization* classifies the kind of formality between the entities. While an "arrangement" can be oral or somehow written, a "contract" is divided into limited length and cooperation. The last step is a "capital" interweaving of the involved entities. An example for an arrangement is the usage of social media for end users, while contracts are typical for projects. The formalization also describes the binding intensity, which is the degree by with the involved entities give up their autonomy.

The *coordination* explains the management of the cooperation, which consists of administration, number of participants, group structure, order, and sort of coordination. The number of participants is related to the group structure. Open cooperation do not have a firm number of participants. Closed cooperation allow simple as well as bilateral structures. The coordination further relates to trust. The *administration* can be "manual", "supported" or "automated". The *number of participants* is strongly related to cooperation. The participating entities can either have a "bilateral" agreement, the cooperation can have a "simple" structure, or it can be "complex". While bilateral cooperation still work with duplicated user bases, this is not possible with more entities involved. Simple networks can be realized with security assertion markup language (SAML) federations, while complex structures are also more complex for technical realization. OpenID Connect (OIDC) can be used for it. The *group structure* is either "open", "with limitations" or "closed". OIDC is typically open, while SAML federations have limitations in R&E or are closed in industry. The *cooperation structure* is "hierarchical" or "heterarchical", when all partners are more or less of the same level. The *sort of coordination* has two possible values: "implicit" or "explicit".

With an explicit coordination, the integration of an institutional coordination instance is supported. An implicit coordination needs a local coordination.

Trust between entities is the result of several different factors, like recommendation or past experience. Within the morphology, only the basics for the cooperation are described, which includes directness, dynamics, and the average level of trust. The circle of trust (CoT) relates to the sort of cooperation. If the group structure is limited, then the CoT can be static. If the number of participants is complex, is the CoT virtual as not all the information about all participants cannot be fully known. Direct trust implicates static or dynamic CoT. *Directness* describes how the trust between two entities is derived. The trust is either "direct" or "transitive/indirect", via another entity. The *dynamics* characterize the trust over time, which is either "static" or "dynamic". Last but not least, the *level of trust* can be "zero", "low", "medium", or "high".

As final category, *identities* are classified. Identities especially describe factors of trust and also user-centric features. This includes transparency, controllability, identification, authentication, consisting of methods and organizational factors, as well as authorization. The *transparency* is either "low", "medium" or "high". The same characteristics can be applied to *controllability*. The *identification, authentication,* and *authorization* can be done "internally", "externally", or in a "combination" of different entities. The *authentication methods* describe the sort of credentials used, which is either "anonymous", "simple" (like a password), "second-factor authentication (2FA)" or "multi-factor authentication (MFA)". In order to reduce the complexity of the morphology, suited characteristics can be left out. In the next step, special characteristics for the use case, like topology of federation can be added. This depends on the specific use case.

4.3   Morphology Mapped to Life Cycle

The morphology can be mapped to the life cycle of IdM, helping starting cooperation to identify their framework. The life cycle is similar to the Deming Cycle [9], which has the phases plan, do, check, act. The Deming Cycle is an iterative four-step management method used in business to control improvements of processes and products. It can be applied to service management, security management, and many other, like identity management. The life cycle of IdM has the phases initiation, agreement, cooperation, reconsideration and improvement, and termination. Reconsideration can either lead to improvement or termination. The phases of the *IdM life cycle* have the following characteristics.

Initiation: A purpose leads to the initiation of the cooperation.

Agreement: After discussions, an agreement is signed, describing the framework of the cooperation. IdM should be a part of the agreement. Otherwise, the parties need to agree on IT aspects outside of the agreement.

Cooperation: The cooperation is starting. In many cases, the cooperation is starting slowly, setting everything in place. Then there is a hype of cooperation, where everything is running and the original purpose is hopefully met. In IT, the start requires work, setting up the infrastructure.

Reconsideration: It describes if the cooperation is proceeded and if changes need to be made. The same appears for IdM.

Improvement: The changes lead to improvements, which are implemented.

Termination: If the purpose is met or other reasons lead to the end of the cooperation, the IdM is also terminated for the project.

The morphology, described in the previous section, can be mapped to the life cycle. This helps to gain a better picture of the required decisions, as shown in Fig. 5a. The *initiation* phase comprises both characteristics of the morphology of initiation, which means "Reason of Joining" and "Dynamics of Joining". *Cooperation* and *coordination*, have characteristics in "Agreement" and "Cooperation". This is the case as some characteristics are decided at the agreement, while others have more impact on the cooperation. The agreement thereby features: "Formalization", "Limitations", "Direction of Cooperation", "Cooperation Structure", "Dimensions", "Number of Participants", and "Group Structure". The cooperation as a result includes "Trust", "Identity", "Degree of Integration", "Connectivity", "Administration", and "Sort of Cooperation". During *reconsideration* every aspect is re-evaluated. Some aspects are enhanced during *improvement*. The life cycle is terminated, if the cooperation ends.

The IdM life cycle includes the user life cycle, because users change throughout a project or life cycle. During a project, users leave, while others join. This is also the case for IdM in organizations. In the end, every user account needs to be closed. The *life cycle of the user* includes the following phases.

Request: The user requests an account at an IdMS.

Provisioning: The account is provisioned (attributes, roles, and permissions).

Identification: The user identifies himself.

Authentication and Authorization: First authentication, then authorization.

Self-Service: The user can access the self-service.

De-Provisioning: In the end, the user account is de-provisioned.

The life cycle of the user has only few interactions with the morphology: trust into the service provider during *request*, then identification, authentication, authorization themselves as well as transparency in the *self-service* phase. This is also visualized in Fig. 5b.

As a result, IdM models describe the approaches in general, while the morphology details aspects of the cooperation. The mapping of morphology with the life cycles explains the order of the actions, which need to be taken. This can guide projects and organizations to identity management processes. Nevertheless, a decision matrix for choosing the best fitting approach is missing, although the cube gives a first hint. Additionally, interfaces to already established processes, like service management and security management, are needed.

4.4 Morphology Applied to Current Approaches

Following, the morphology is applied to centralized IdM with AD and the differences for SAML, OIDC, SSI, server, and IoT devices are described. *Centralized*

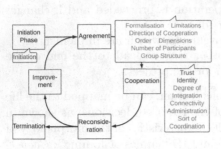

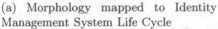

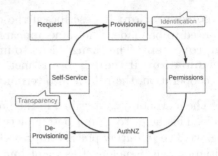

(a) Morphology mapped to Identity Management System Life Cycle

(b) Morphology mapped to User Life Cycle

Fig. 5. Morphology mapped to life cycles

IdM with AD is typically used in companies. Depending on whether they have cooperation, several branches or not, the complexity is different. Also depending on the point of view, e.g., user or company, different properties can be coloured. Let us assume the company in this example just uses AD for its users, while they have other methods for cooperation. Therefore, the following morphology can be formed, see Table 2. The reason for joining is economic, while the dynamic is stable. AD was introduced at some point in time. When regarding the cooperation, the cooperation within the company is considered. The integration is therefore integrated. The connectivity is high as all participants work together. AD was introduced for the complete value chain of the company. It should be a permanent solution, though technologies and decisions change. The direction of cooperation cannot be described by the categorization. The order was based on a strategy, while the company is local. The organizational factor is micro. The cooperation within the company depends on contracts with its employees. The administration is hopefully supported, while the number of participants can be described with bilateral. The group structure is at least currently closed, while the coordination is hierarchical and explicit. The trust is direct, rather static, with medium trust, as all employees needed to submit papers. The identities are managed within the company, with simple and second factors.

The entities of *SAML* in R&E form federations, which are spread over regions, countries, and the world. The entities have contracts with federation operators, which have contracts with the inter-federation operator. The coordination between the entities is rather low. As the identities are managed by the home organization, trust is lower. Therefore, the following morphology can be seen.

Initiation: Individuals join for R&E, while companies have economic reasons. The dynamic is rather stable, as entities have to sign on contracts.

Cooperation: The cooperation is autonomous, only little coordinated by the federation and inter-federation operators. The connectivity between the entities is low, as there are many different services within a federation and only a small percentage of users will use the specific service of a service provider.

Table 2. Morphology for centralized identity management with AD

	Initiation			
Reason for joining	Personal	Social	Economic	Law
Dynamic of joining	Stable		Unstable	
Cooperation				
Degree of integration	Autonomous	Coordinated	Integrated	
Connectivity	Low		High	
Professional limits	User	R&D	Department	Value chain
Factual limits	Short	Medium	Long	Permanent
Direction of cooperation	Vertical	Horizontal	Diagonal	
Order	Strategy	Project	R&E	Region
Locality	Local	Regional	National	International
Organizational	Micro	Meso	Macro	
Formalization	Arrangement	Limited contract	Cooperation agreement	Capital interweaving
Coordination				
Administration	Manual	Supported	Automated	
Number of participants	Bilateral	Simple	Complex	
Group structure	Open	With limitations	Closed	
Cooperation structure	Hierarchical		Heterarchical	
Sort of coordination	Implicit		Explicit	
Trust				
Directness	Direct		Transitive	
Circle of trust	Static	Dynamic	Virtual	
Level of trust	Zero	Low	Medium	High
Identities				
Transparency	Low	Medium	High	
Controllability	Low	Medium	High	
Identification	Internal	External	Combination	
Authentication method	Anonymous	Simple	2FA	MFA
Authentication organization	Internal	External	Combination	
Authorization	Internal	External	Combination	

Mostly, the entities have contact with the federation operators. The cooperation is limited to research, while the time depends on several reasons. The cooperation can be vertical as well as horizontal. The locality is national or international in most cases. Also regional federations are established. The organization form is either meso or macro, depending on the type of federation. Federations are formalized by contracts with the federation operator and partly arrangements between entities.

Coordination: The administration is supported with manual steps needed. As contracts need to be signed, the number of participants is simple and the group structure is with limitations. The order is more heterarchical than hierarchical, while the coordination is more implicit than explicit.

Trust: Trust is transitive via federation or inter-federation operator. With a static number of participants, the circle of trust is also static with little dynamics. The level of trust is low or medium, depending on separate means.

Identities: Since communities with additional attribute authorities were formed and other means of identification are in use, authorization and identification are either internal or a combination, while authentication is internal. Transparency and controllability are rather low as a result of the structure.

IdM with *OIDC* distinguishes from SAML as the protocol is dynamic and the widely known use case is web authentication. For OIDC, the initiation can have several reasons, therefore, the dynamic is unstable. The cooperation is loose, which is true for the coordination as well. Trust is rather low, but can be stepped up with a second factor. The different constellations also have impact on the identities. *SSI* is different as the user is in control of the attributes, which then impacts trust and identities. If a company hosts their *servers* in-house, then the cooperation is within the company and maybe with other offices. *IoT devices* can be used at home as well as at organizations. The trust into the devices is typically low, as others might manipulate the device without notice.

5   Discussion

We characterized IdM approaches in two ways: the IMC describes the technical aspects, followed the morphology for organizational aspects. In order to compile an overview of IdM approaches, we noticed intersections between existing IdM models. These intersections helped us to identify categories, which are needed to differentiate IdM approaches. The three categories topology, type of user, and type of service are arranged in a cube, the IMC. IMC clarifies the characteristics type of user and topology. Additionally, the perspective is made clear, i.e., user-centric or provider-centric. While an approach could belong to two models used beforehand, it can be clearly classified by the IMC. With the flexibility of the three categories in mind, future approaches should be able to be characterized. In the next step, we applied different IdM approaches to the cube. These approaches were typical web services for end users, but also servers and IoT, resulting in a colourful IMC. Some use cases are more typical than others. Besides this fact, the application was straight forward and showed us similarities and differences between the approaches. These findings might indicate a possible combination of approaches. It is noticeable that trust and user-centric are not featured together in the shown examples. The IMC can, therefore, help to combine different IdM approaches and explore missing tools.

In a next step, a morphology for IdM was developed. The morphology describes different aspects of a cooperation. In this case, the categories initiation, cooperation, coordination, trust, and identities with their categorizations need to be regarded. The relationship between morphology and the different life cycles were shown in a next step. For guidance, the morphology can be used to speed up the implementation and evaluation in a later step. The morphology was then mapped to different approaches. A certain variance is seen, which depends on the actual implementation. Nevertheless, organizational settings are made clear. This does not include internal processes, which will be regarded in future work.

Both, the IMC and the morphology, do not describe IdM in all aspects, but help to categorize different approaches, use cases, and their implementation. The categorization helps within the life cycle of IdM to mix different approaches, see missing tools, and to regard all relevant aspects.

6   Conclusion and Future Work

Identities are everywhere nowadays. With the growing number of internet users and accounts, more servers are used. With new opportunities, also new use cases come into sight. The IdM model was developed before the hype of blockchain. New approaches were established since then.

In this paper, we introduced a broad classification of IdM. The existing IdM modes were extended to an IMC with three axes. Topology, type of user, and type of environment describe the IdM approach in more details while still being vague about the actual protocols. The IMC was applied to different approaches, showing silos as well as approaches, which should be comparably easy to interoperate with additional tools. This showed that many aspects rely on the actual implementation within the organization. Also, it visualizes a trade-off between user control and trust into attributes. The IMC was extended by a morphology of IdM, which describes the characteristics of cooperation. This morphology was mapped to the life cycle of users and IdM in a further step. The result of the mapping can help to distinguish relevant questions during a cooperation. Both methods, the IMC and the IdM morphology, combined provide a comprehensive characterization of IdM approaches. This helps to choose suitable approaches for an organization or cooperation. Furthermore, needed tools for interoperability can be explored. An integration into processes and a guide to choose the best fitting IdM approach were left out and will be further work. The methods also reveal that interesting features for a holistic IdM have not been designed yet.

In order to create one holistic IdM framework, integrating different IdM approaches, an architecture is being developed. This architecture is extended by service models, visualizing needed processes. As a another step, processes interacting with already established management processes are investigated. To decide for the best fitting IdM approach, a decision matrix is created, all helping to ease the use and improve the quality of IdM.

References

1. Boujezza, H., AL-Mufti, M., Ayed, H.K.B., Saidane, L.: A taxonomy of identities management systems in IOT. In: 2015 IEEE/ACS 12th International Conference of Computer Systems and Applications (AICCSA), pp. 1–8, November 2015. https://doi.org/10.1109/AICCSA.2015.7507266
2. Ferdous, M.S., Chowdhury, F., Alassafi, M.O.: In search of self-sovereign identity leveraging blockchain technology. IEEE Access **7**, 103059–103079 (2019). https://doi.org/10.1109/ACCESS.2019.2931173
3. Gao, F., Zhang, F., Xia, J., Ma, Z.: General identity management model for big data analysis. In: 2016 18th International Conference on Advanced Communication Technology (ICACT), p. 1, January 2016. https://doi.org/10.1109/ICACT.2016.7423325
4. Garschhammer, M., Roelle, H.: Requirements on quality specification posed by service orientation. In: Sahai, A., Wu, F. (eds.) DSOM 2004. LNCS, vol. 3278, pp. 1–14. Springer, Heidelberg (2004). https://doi.org/10.1007/978-3-540-30184-4_1
5. GÉANT: edugain technical site (2020). https://technical.edugain.org/status.php. Accessed 25 Nov 2020
6. Grabatin, M., Hommel, W., Metzger, S., Pöhn, D.: DAME: on-demand internet-scale SAML metadata exchange. Int. J. Adv. Syst. Meas. **8**, 156–167 (2015)
7. Habiba, U., Masood, R., Shibli, M.A., Niazi, M.A.: Cloud identity management security issues & solutions: a taxonomy. Complex Adapt. Syst. Model. **2**(1), 2194–3206 (2014). https://doi.org/10.1186/s40294-014-0005-9
8. Kantara Initiative: Home - WG - User Managed Access (2020). https://kantarainitiative.org/confluence/display/uma/Home. Accessed 25 Nov 2020
9. Milgram, L., Spector, A., Treger, M.: Chapter 21 - Plan, Do, Check, Act: The Deming or Shewhart Cycle, vol. Managing Smart. Gulf Professional Publishing (1999)
10. Pal, S., Hitchens, M., Varadharajan, V.: Modeling identity for the internet of things: survey, classification and trends. In: 2018 12th International Conference on Sensing Technology (ICST), pp. 45–51, December 2018. https://doi.org/10.1109/ICSensT.2018.8603595
11. Ragouzis, N., Hughes, J., Philpott, R., Maler, E.: Security assertion markup language (SAML) V2.0 technical overview. Technical report, OASIS (2008)
12. Reed, D., et al.: Decentralized identifiers (DIDs) v1.0 - core architecture, data model, and representation. Technical report, W3C (2020)
13. Roßnagel, H.: A mechanism for discovery and verification of trust scheme memberships: the lightest reference architecture. In: Fritsch, L., Roßnagel, H., Hühnlein, D. (eds.) Open Identity Summit 2017, pp. 81–92. Gesellschaft für Informatik, Bonn (2017)
14. Sakimura, N., Bradley, J., Jones, M.B., de Medeiros, B., Mortimore, C.: OpenID connect core 1.0. Technical report, OpenID Foundation (2014)
15. Tobin, A., Reed, D.: The Inevitable Rise of Self-Sovereign Identity (2017). Accessed 25 Nov 2020
16. Cao, Y., Yang, L.: A survey of identity management technology. In: 2010 IEEE International Conference on Information Theory and Information Security, pp. 287–293, December 2010. https://doi.org/10.1109/ICITIS.2010.5689468

Keeping it Human: A Focus Group Study of Public Attitudes Towards AI in Banking

Mhairi Aitken[1]([✉]) [ID], Magdalene Ng[2], Ehsan Toreini[3] [ID], Aad van Moorsel[2] [ID], Kovila P. L. Coopamootoo[2], and Karen Elliott[1] [ID]

[1] Newcastle University Business School, Newcastle University,
1 Science Square, Newcastle upon Tyne NE4 5TG, UK
{Mhairi.aitken,Karen.Elliott}@newcastle.ac.uk
[2] School of Computing Science, Newcastle Newcastle University,
1 Science Square, Newcastle upon Tyne NE4 5TG, UK
{Magdalene.Ng,aad.vanmoorsel,Kovila.Coopamootoo}@newcastle.ac.uk
[3] Department of Computer Science, Durham University, Lower Mountjoy,
South Road, Durham DH1 3LE, UK
ehsan.toreini@durham.ac.uk

Abstract. While there is substantial interest in ethical practice relating to Artificial Intelligence (AI), to date there has been limited consideration of what this means in the banking sector. This study aimed to address this gap in the literature through a qualitative study of public attitudes and perceptions of current and potential future uses of AI in banking. A series of focus groups were conducted with diverse members of the public. Focus group participants were largely positive about the role of AI in speeding up financial processes and increasing efficiency. Yet, they also expressed a number of concerns around potential negative impacts on society and consistently emphasized the importance of human judgement or oversight. The findings suggest a potential cognitive dissonance where people use new services due to perceived convenience or immediate benefits, while disliking or distrusting those services or holding concerns about their impacts on society. The findings illustrate that participants' concerns did not typically relate to private or individual interests but more often to wider ethical and social concerns. The focus groups demonstrated the value of qualitative, deliberative methods to explore the nuances of public responses and highlighted the importance of taking account of conditions for public acceptability - rather than just customer uptake - in order to develop ethical practice and establish a social licence for uses of AI in banking.

Keywords: FinTech · Artificial Intelligence · Public acceptability

1 Introduction

Innovation in artificial intelligence (AI) is underpinning the development of new products and services across a wide range of industries. This is particularly true in banking where

© Springer Nature Switzerland AG 2020
I. Boureanu et al. (Eds.): ESORICS 2020 Workshops, LNCS 12580, pp. 21–38, 2020.
https://doi.org/10.1007/978-3-030-66504-3_2

digital innovation and new data practices are fuelling interest and investment in FinTech (financial technology) and changing the banking sector as a whole [1].

AI in banking is used for a number of purposes including developing automated chatbots for customer services, efficient processes for detecting fraud and money laundering and improving automated processes that utilise large volumes of data (e.g. client risk profiling or credit scoring [2]).

While, there is substantial interest in ethical practice relating to AI and growing consideration of what it means for AI to be trustworthy [3, 4], as well as some evidence of growing interest in what this means in the financial sector[1]. The existing literature typically does not engage with public – rather than professional stakeholder – views and experiences. Studies which have examined public attitudes or responses have typically focused on customer uptake of FinTech products (e.g. 5–7). In doing so they have tended to focus on customers' motivations for using FinTech services, and largely neglected non-customers' reasons for not using FinTech services, or the reasons why some FinTech offerings have been unsuccessful [8]. Where studies have considered trust relating to FinTech (e.g. 5, 6) they have typically focused on customer trust and willingness to use FinTech services and largely overlooked considerations of what it means for a FinTech to be trustworthy.

While there is a rapidly growing literature relating to social and ethical dimensions of AI (e.g. 9, 10) across both industry and academia. There is a lack of research examining the extent to which FinTech practices align with public values and interests, in particular there is very limited evidence relating to public acceptability of uses of AI in banking [1]. Therefore, this study aims to address this important gap in the literature through a qualitative study of public attitudes and perceptions of digital innovation in banking with a particular focus on current and potential future uses of AI in banking.

The research was undertaken through a series of focus groups which engaged with diverse members of the public. Focus group participants are referred to as members of the public rather than customers or consumers since the study aimed to engage broad perspectives rather than solely those of current or potential FinTech customers. Indeed, the aim was not to identify customer experiences or reasons for using/not using FinTech services, but rather to understand public attitudes, concerns and interests relating to uses, and potential uses of AI in banking. This is important since finance is an area that affects most – if not all – members of society and therefore digital innovation in this field is likely to have broad, and diverse, impacts. Such impacts might be positive (e.g. opening up financial services to unbanked or underbanked populations [11]) or negative (e.g. creating new opaque systems through which access to finance is determined or increasingly necessitate citizens' participation in the Big Data society [1]). Therefore, ethical practice requires considering broader social acceptability – not just customer uptake - of innovation.

---

[1] For example, through the work of organisations such as the Finance Innovation Lab: financeinnovationlab.org or industry oriented publications on developing ethical AI.

2 Methods

A series of five focus groups were held between September and November 2019. Participants were recruited through pre-established groups including students, meetup groups for senior citizens and young professionals, and via community centres. Focus group participants were sampled through purposive sampling focused on maximising diversity across the focus groups to access a broad range of viewpoints and perspectives. The aim was to have a diverse, rather than statistically representative, sample [12]. It was important that individuals within each of the groups shared common traits or interests as this meant that they felt comfortable and able to discuss the issues freely [12].

A semi-structured approach was taken. A topic guide was developed to ensure a level of consistency between the focus groups. This was very flexible and allowed participants to raise issues and/or concerns which they considered to be relevant. The semi-structured design also meant that topics of discussion did not always arise in a pre-determined order, and that the focus groups were able to explore unanticipated areas of interest. As is recognised to be an advantage of focus group research, this approach allowed for a responsive, conversational style resulting in open and frank discussions and enabled individuals to engage with aspects of the topic which were previously unfamiliar to them [12].

The focus groups began by asking participants about the ways in which they currently access banking services and their experiences using digital banking and mobile banking. Following this the focus groups then focused on digital innovation in banking. A series of vignettes were introduced to engage the participants in discussions of the ways in which digital innovation is used in banking and how this may change banking services in the future. Through these discussions participants were encouraged to reflect on how they felt about these areas of innovation, whether they would be interested in using them and what potential benefits or risks they anticipated relating to these. Following the focused discussions on each of the vignettes the focus groups then led into broader discussions of attitudes, preferences and concerns around future directions of digital innovation in banking and, in particular, the role of AI in banking.

The focus groups typically lasted around one hour. They were audio-recorded with consent from participants. The recordings were professionally transcribed. The transcripts were reviewed and corrected by MA and any potentially identifying information was removed (e.g. any names or details about workplaces) before the transcripts were analysed.

The transcripts were coded in NVivo. This coding process identified key themes in the focus group discussions and highlighted emerging areas of interest and/or concern. Following an inductive approach the coding focused on bringing out high level themes which emerged from the data, to structure a narrative account of the discussions. The themes were mapped to illustrate their interconnections and the ways in which different topics discussed related to one another. The mapping exercise then informed the process of writing up the findings by indicating the connections between different areas of interest.

2.1 Sample

Five focus groups were conducted these are referred to in the following discussion by reference to the common characteristics of the participants in each group:

1. Seniors (members of a meetup group for senior citizens)
2. Rural (a focus group held in a rural town 20 miles outside Newcastle)
3. Young Professionals (recruited via a meetup group for young professionals)
4. International Students (recruited via student forums at Newcastle University)
5. Postgraduate Students (recruited via student forums at Newcastle University)

The focus groups all took place in Newcastle, except for one which was held in a rural town 20 miles outside of Newcastle. It was important to hold a focus group in a more rural location as it was anticipated that rural residents may be likely to have different experiences relating to accessibility of banking services and digital connectivity.

A total of 23 participants took part in the focus groups. While the majority of participants were under the age of 40, the focus groups engaged a diverse range of age groups (the youngest participants being in their early 20 s and the oldest over 75). Participants came from a range of professional backgrounds, the largest group were students (39 per cent), 13 per cent of participants were employed full-time and equally 13 per cent were employed part-time, 13 per cent were jobseekers, 9 per cent of participants were self-employed and equally 9 per cent were retired. Sixty per cent of the sample identified as white, 21 per cent identified as Asian or Asian British, 4 per cent identified as Black or Black British, 4 per cent as mixed and 8 per cent as other.

While the focus groups were conducted with a range of groups which were non-gender specific, in all instances female members were more likely to volunteer to participate in the study. This resulted in the sample being almost 75 per cent female (17 women, 6 men). This is a limitation of the present study which will be addressed in future research.

In the following discussion individual participants are identified by the name of the group they participated in followed by either F or M (to indicate Female of Male) and a number which remains the same for each participant throughout.

3 Findings

While the focus groups discussed a variety of forms of digital innovation in banking, this paper reports findings relating to responses to AI in banking. Across the focus groups participants discussed current and potential roles of AI in banking. In particular this was explored in relation to: virtual money coaches, chatbots and algorithmic decision-making.

3.1 Virtual Money Coaches

Virtual money coaches was introduced as a vignette to spark discussions on potential uses of AI in banking. Participants were given some brief information about current applications (apps) which can track customers' spending habits and provide advice on how to meet savings goals and/or which banking services would be most suitable (e.g. credit cards, loans, savings accounts). The information given noted that these apps may use AI to process customers' information and give advice and that AI can be used to create personalised "virtual money coaches" which can track spending habits and offer advice.

Participants had mixed responses to this vignette. Some reported already using apps that had these functions, or potentially being interested to use them in the future. However, a common area of concern was the frequency of alerts that such apps send, and that they can become a nuisance.

Other participants were strongly opposed to using virtual money coaches. A key factor distinguishing responses of participants who were enthusiastic about virtual money coaches from those who were opposed to using them was whether they were perceived to give customers more or less control over their personal finances, for example in one discussion a participant described virtual money coaches as being useful for people who "want to have their lives run for them":

F1: I think it's quite a good idea, because my stepdaughter- I always withdraw cash a couple of times a week £40 here or there, but she just uses her card for everything and she's got no track of what she spends, so I think that for someone like her it would be good
F2: She doesn't even keep her statements does she?
F1: No she puts her statements straight on the fire, she's terrible! So I think something like that for her, people like her, would be really good
F2: If they want to have their lives run for them it's ideal
F1: But I like to keep track of my own money
F2: I do as well
(SENIORS)

Some participants felt that such tools relinquished personal control or decision-making:

"I think it's good but I always have the opinion you should do something yourself about it and not have others influence you. If it's a virtual money coach or your mum or whatever, you should have you own control and find your own ways of how to use your money because this is not really a way to learn how to deal with money or how to spend your money or how to save money. It's just literally someone in the back always coaching you so you're never really independent in whatever you do." (INTERNATIONAL STUDENTS: M2)

Conversely, other participants felt that virtual money coaches gave individuals more control over their finances:

F2: I think it's a good idea more so than getting alerts on you're reaching your limit or whatever, but getting coaching on right you've been to Costa coffee twice already this week, did you know that if you swapped that for something else you could save this much

F1: Yeah, if it was kind of helpful like that. Maybe not just an alert like you've spent this much. If you're spending this much eating out this week, maybe just make a sandwich! (RURAL)

A number of participants were concerned that data collected through virtual money coaches could be used for marketing or commercial purposes. Therefore, they would be more inclined to use the service when it was provided by a trusted organisation or a non-profit third party.

> "I'd feel a lot happier if the virtual money coach is set by the government or by Watchdog or somebody that's fully impartial like Citizen's Advice Bureau type thing. If it was just giving sound financial advice, that's brilliant. If it's a start-up and it's minor information that you're giving to it selling that to third parties or if it's sold through a bank and they have a vested interest and say, "You'll save £100 if you buy this financial product," then I think that's a lot murkier but then I also think that if it was done by the government, the artificial intelligence might not develop quite as quickly" (POSTGRADUATE STUDENTS: M2)

Another area of concern relating to virtual money coaches was the extent to which an automated, AI-powered process could take account of the personal, emotional nature of finances:

> "the money coach doesn't really know your own situation. It doesn't know I have 500 Euros cash, someone else is going to pay me something, someone else has to pay me something back or these kind of things they are not taking into consideration your own situation for when I'm like I have, I don't know, 30 Euros in cash so I'm paying 30 Euros from my savings, they're like, "You can't touch that kind of thing." I'm like, "I have cash," and those kinds of things. That's what I think." (INTERNATIONAL STUDENTS: M2)

M1: I think it's good to have the human touch behind it, because sometimes if you're going through some sort of vulnerability or problem and you're trying to discuss with this money coach, it doesn't understand that vulnerability
F1: yeah, I would like to speak to a person if I was having money problems
F2: Yeah I would definitely
M1: Yeah
MA: Is that because a person has empathy?
F2: You're not talking to a machine
M1: It could make things worse talking to a machine when you've got problems
(SENIORS)

This emphasis on human involvement to take account of personal and emotive factors is a theme which was also salient in relation to chatbots.

3.2 Chatbots

In discussing the role of technology in banking, participants frequently raised examples of experiences with chatbots in customer services. Chatbots were not introduced as a vignette in the focus groups but were frequently referred to by participants, suggesting this was a topic that participants had some familiarity with and were comfortable discussing. Typically participants discussed this in relation to experiences with automated telephone services and reflected on their experiences and frustrations with current automation in customer services. In particular, participants frequently reported frustrations relating to trying to get answers to questions that were not routine queries, resulting in slower processes with calls eventually being redirected to human handlers:

F1: but you could ask it something that it doesn't understand
F2: does not compute
F1: when you do telephone banking and you get the press 1, 2, 3 sort of thing sometimes they don't understand what you're asking. If it's anything that deviates from what they're programmed to do
F2: yeah, yeah I've had problems like that. I think I had to do that when I was making enquiries about my card possibly being scammed, I didn't answer with so many words
F1: and then they don't understand
F2: they don't understand
F1: They do put you through to somebody eventually
F2: am I going to get somebody real on this phone
F1: yeah, I want to speak someone real
(SENIORS)

> "every time we need to call to the customer service centre to say, "Okay, my card is lost, please freeze." So it takes time because by the time you want to reach them, you go through, I don't know, ask you, "Okay, you have to press one, press two," so it takes a lot of time. Then you're worrying at that time so it's very frustrating." (INTERNATIONAL STUDENTS: F1)

These same frustrations were also reported in relation to participants' experiences with chatbots. The majority of participants reported disliking chatbots:

> "One of the reasons I said I left M&S is because of their customer service and one of it is because it's a chat bot. It looks like you're going to be speaking with a human and it's not. You ask it a question and it just gives obviously this default standard answer which is really frustrating when you've got an actual question that needs answering. Then you have to ring up, doubling the time. That's not for me. I can't stand chat bots. I like to speak to a real person" (RURAL: F1)

F1: I always get frustrated by chatbots because every time they just ask you one question and then you click the answer and then they pop up other things. Then you go through... at the end it doesn't really solve my problem so it's very frustrating I could save my time and talk to someone else.

M2: You sometimes also have very specific questions that can be answered, like they would analyse it as this is a general question and you're like, "Yes, it is a general question but it has a completely different context," which the machine wouldn't really understand. That's the problem I have a lot.
(INTERNATIONAL STUDENTS)

"I'm not a lover of chat bots and stuff because I think if you've got a query that's not, what's the word, not ordinary, it's complex in some way, they don't always have the right answer so you end up ringing up and speaking to somebody anyway"
(POSTGRADUATE STUDENTS: F2)

Many participants did not like to use chatbots as they felt it was important to speak to a human when discussing personal finances. This was in part because the data disclosed was sensitive and also because participants considered human judgement and empathy to be important when providing advice on financial matters.

M2: I totally agree because it's such sensitive data, it's such a personalised thing, I don't want to talk to a robot about my finances. I'd rather have a person who has experience with it and can basically react to my specific case because the chat bots are only there to take all these questions that can easily be answered from the service team, which is a good idea for the bank because it saves time but I would still…
F3: It saves them money for customer care.
(INTERNATIONAL STUDENTS)

M2: I would still prefer to talk to someone in person because you know who is sitting there, you know the person who is telling you this, who is behind it. If you just talk to the machine then it's like you have no point of relation to the machine or to the bank or anything. It's more trustworthy to just go to the person who is representing the bank as well.
M1: I think at the end of the day, even if you physically talk to a person, the person is only looking at the information on the screen. He is just interpreting that in a human friendly way. So at the end of the day it is machines and I think all of those systems are, in one way or the other, linked to artificial intelligence so I'm not sure. Even for example for the loan side or anything, even if you explain to him for example about the credit score, if the machine says no, if the system says no, I don't think he physically can do anything about it so he's just saying it maybe in a nicer way.
F4: I think for me myself, I prefer talking to a person because somehow a person has more emotion and can consider the consequences, he can tell you more things than the artificial intelligence can do. Some people just like to have this relationship where you just want to talk to that person face to face and then they can consider you and they can sympathise with you. They give you the best solution and all that. People can take advice and they will tend to follow what the other person is advising them.
M2: Because otherwise you're just a case, like the case opens, they analyse you, the case closes, okay next one. You're like, "Okay, can I have this?" "No," where else to go or

what else to do or who to talk to or whatever. That's what I'm missing with this human connection.
(INTERNATIONAL STUDENTS)

However, there were a small number of participants who preferred speaking with chatbots compared to human customer service operatives. For those who preferred chatbots the primary reason was being able to get answers to questions quickly and easily:

M2: I find the online chat really useful. It's outsourced to people but you can get to meet to have a look over your history and any questions that you've got or if something isn't quite right, I can go into the actual bank itself.
F3: Yes. For me it's anything that I can avoid. If I can avoid going into the bank, I will. I think now, I can only speak for myself but I think I've got quite a lot of trust even if it's not a person behind, even if it's a bot, especially with machine learning and there's such advanced AI capabilities I'm okay speaking with a robot as long as I get my answer quickly. So any services that prevent me from going out to stand in a queue or to the bank is a bonus for me.
(POSTGRADUATE STUDENTS)

While most participants felt that the sensitive nature of personal finances required human consideration, these participants felt more comfortable disclosing sensitive – or potentially embarrassing – information to a machine:

"For me, if we get the security sorted and all of that sorted, I would probably use it just because I think I'd feel a bit more confident saying things which I don't want to say to a human being or person. For example if nowadays you go on to Google and you search anything, sometimes silly questions or anything which you wouldn't be able to go to someone and ask them, you just don't feel confident whereas with Google you know it's a machine. It will give you the right things you are looking for, probably better than a human being but even give you that confidence that no one is going to know about it but it gives you that more privacy I'd say." (INTERNATIONAL STUDENTS:M1)

However, even participants who were more positive about using chatbots had concerns. In particular, some participants felt uneasy with the idea of "talking to a robot" or with AI imitating human emotions:

"It sounds a bit strange, like as if you're talking to a robot. So I don't know if it's that trust that it's not a human you're talking to, but if they're intelligent. I guess it would just be like getting an alert but they're speaking to you. I mean maybe because people do really like Alexa and stuff" (YOUNG PROFESSIONALS: F1)

The discussions around experiences and perceptions of chatbots revealed the importance of human involvement. Participants who did not like chatbots typically stressed the importance of human judgement and human relationships in providing appropriate, responsive and empathetic customer service. Conversely, participants who were happier using chatbots typically did not feel that such human features were necessary, indeed in some cases a chatbot was preferred if it did not imitate human interaction (e.g. people may feel more confident to disclose information to a machine which does not have human judgement or emotional responses).

3.3 Algorithmic Decision-Making

Participants were told that algorithms – or computer programmes – are increasingly being used to quickly process large amounts of financial information and that these can identify patterns in the information and identify which loan applications are high risk or low risk. Participants were told that at the moment algorithms are used to assess suitability of loan applicants but the final decision is overseen by a human member of the bank's staff.

Some participants were fairly ambivalent about algorithmic decision-making:

"I think as long as there is some kind of appeals process I'd be fine with it because if you could see all of the information they have access to and you can say, "Yes, that is my credit card. Yes, that is the thing that I did there," as long as that's there, as long as there is a way to say, "I think something is not right, can I speak to a human being," I think it's fine. A lot of cases are quite simple and some cases are complicated. So the complicated situations might just be escalated but as a general thing, I think they're just taking numbers and data anyway. It's not like they're doing a personality assessment. So I think it's generally fine, in my opinion." (POSTGRADUATE STUDENTS: F5)

Most participants felt that automated processes could be positive in increasing speed and efficiency of decision-making processes and were satisfied provided that final decisions were taken by humans:

M1: for me I think it's good the way it is, to have the algorithm assisted by the humans
F1: yeah
M2: because then in a way you've got two different opinions whereas if you had just the human they could make a biased or prejudiced decision, or even the algorithm itself. So I like it how it is
F2: yes, I suppose if you wanted a loan or a mortgage it would be helpful so long as there was a backup
F1: yeah, it would be quicker
F2: yeah, I suppose it would be a good idea so long as someone is keeping an eye on things
(SENIORS)

Across all the focus groups human oversight was described as a vital condition for acceptability of algorithmic decision-making. Participants typically stressed that they would not be comfortable with final decisions being made by an algorithm. This was largely due to a sense that algorithms cannot fully take account of people's individual circumstances or the complexities of people's lives:

F1: People freelance as well, they work for themselves, you have to show the last three months. Your income might be one thing for three months, huge amounts for the previous but an algorithm is not going to pick up whereas you can see it in person, however in the last year I earned this. There is no way to do that when it's all just done on algorithms. I think you need a human person making the ultimate decision.
F3: Exactly. I don't like this. It's very black and white. Like you say, life is not black and white. You do need to have that human interaction to make decisions and to look outside of the digital box. People don't just tick boxes everyday because life isn't like that. So I disagree.
(RURAL)

> "I would be scared if it's completely automatic in the future because [...] the algorithm can't say, "Is this good? What is the reason for this?" and so on. So I would always prefer to have a human overseeing the whole process because algorithms can also be completely faulty like with You Tube where they just recommend completely old videos or videos you've already watched. It's just complete mistakes, the evaluation of the video or anything like that. So I don't think I would like to have it completely. Maybe as a help but always have a human before you with that kind of thing" (INTERNATIONAL STUDENTS: M2)

It was frequently acknowledged that all systems – whether based on human judgement or algorithms – contain bias and as such neither automated nor human decision-making were considered to be free of bias. However, it was largely suggested that it was easier to deal with and address human biases, either through discussion or by seeking a different person:

> "I think you do find biases in algorithms in certain things, whereas a person can have biases but that may vary person to person. So if you try to get a different person, you might get a different result, whereas I hate technology and I think personally I would prefer it to be a person who made the final decision rather than an algorithm." (POSTGRADUATE STUDENTS: M2)

Participants also felt that automated processes would reduce the opportunities for customers to discuss their needs and circumstances, appeal decisions or ask for advice:

F1: I think it's kind of good that there's a human still involved
F2: Yeah
F1: because people might have previously been in bad financial situations and a computer – I don't know how smart these computer are – they might not then look at it from a human perspective and say well they were like this, but look at them now this is their salary and they're doing a lot better, they can kind of prove that they can afford a mortgage or whatnot. But an automated system might just say no, they were bad previously, so they're bad. But I don't know how smart they are about it.
F2: I think when you've still got a human like at the moment, that kind of fall back to know the particular circumstances, so you can go back and say I know I was rejected

for these particular terms but this is what I need them for, this is what I want them for and I don't think a computer could do that

F1: Or you can ask what do you recommend. What are the options. You can't really talk about that with a computer.

(YOUNG PROFESSIONALS)

> "I think it depends what the algorithm looks at because if it's a physical person, they can weigh up the pros and cons whereas an algorithm, it's either yes, no dependent upon your credit score or whatever. But I know somebody who had entries from somebody else's credit file on there so bringing their credit score down. So with the computer they wouldn't have gotten anywhere" (POSTGRADUATE STUDENTS: F2)

In summary, while some participants were positive about the potential for algorithmic decision-making to speed up processes, there was considerable concern about automated decision-making. In particular, it was widely agreed that human judgement and oversight are essential to ensure that decisions adequately take account of individuals' circumstances and needs.

3.4   Broader Themes

Through discussion of particular examples a number of broader themes emerged. In particular there were some key areas of concern that emerged consistently across the focus groups.

Pace of Change

Across the focus groups there was considerable discussion of the rapid rate at which technological innovation is advancing. For many this was an area of concern:

> "urgh. It's too much, it's like sci-fi. All these stories you read. Don't laugh: it could happen! Machines taking over and running the world. Everything's moving so fast" (SENIORS: F1)

> "Things are maybe moving a little bit too far [...] So it really is about, I think I'm being a Luddite as well in pushing back against technology a little bit with banking. I have a feeling people are going to do that a bit more, even the younger generation when they figure it out, will be doing that as well." (RURAL: M1)

> "I think probably banking technology has gone as far as I need it to go because maybe I'm traditional or old fashioned but a lot of this is just a bit of a step too far, for me personally. I don't know. I don't want everything to be, all the decisions, I don't want that all to be by computer and not people" (RURAL: F3)

> "I think it is quite scary how things are evolving now in the future but I think there is no stopping it. Things are constantly being evolved and companies are constantly evolving to be easier and better which is to the detriment of, this is

maybe pessimistic but it takes out that human to human interaction of a bank and stuff which maybe some elderly people, it's the only interaction they have in a week or whatever." (POSTGRADUATE STUDENTS: F6)

However, it was frequently mentioned that while new technologies can be unnerving, typically when they are convenient or beneficial people adapt to using them relatively easily:

F1: I mean probably in the next twenty years everybody will be computer literate
M1: it's about easing people into change, because we're all afraid it, but 9 times out of 10 it's ok so there needs to be something that makes us all feel-
F2: safe
M1: yeah, safe
(SENIORS)

"But everyone for example in this room said at the beginning that all of us use the banking apps but then when we talked about it everyone didn't like it. But when you just see the final product, everyone likes it. I think they probably didn't like the journey or when it was developed. People probably 15-20 years ago they didn't like it but us, we're just born with it, we think everyone just enjoys it. We wouldn't imagine life without it." (INTERNATIONAL STUDENTS: M1)

"I think it really depends heavily on the context you grow up in and the time period because some of the things that we use every day like mobile banking, if we pitched that idea to our parents and grandparents they would say, "Well no, I'm going to go into a bank for the rest of my life. That's a crazy, stupid idea." If we have this conversation in ten years, all of these things that are hypothetical now could be part of everyday practice." (POSTGRADUATE STUDENTS:F5)

Slippery Slopes
Related to discussions of the pace of change, there were significant concerns about potential "slippery slopes". A number of participants were concerned about the ways in which data used in financial apps such as virtual money coaches might potentially be reused in the future. Beyond particular data uses, there was also concern about potential "slippery slopes" around the role of AI and impacts on society. Participants expressed concern that increasing reliance on AI in automating decision-making processes could erode human capacities and expertise:

F1: I think it's kind of worrying if now we have this one and then we depend on AI to give us advice. Say AI is getting better and then everyone can, let's say AI can really does the job and then everyone just talks to AI and then no more human interactions and then we are all relying on this AI to give us whatever advice. It's going to take over our thinking. We cannot think as a human but it's like we let them think and then they tell us. I'm just worried.

M2: Yes, that's what I meant especially with teenagers and people who grew up then in that time because they don't know anything else.
F1: They will always think, "Okay, there is an app, AI, that can always give me that."
M2: They depend on it.
M1: At the same time, these apps, these systems need humans behind the scenes developing them. They wouldn't just happen from nowhere. You'd need so many brains behind the scenes developing, debugging, expanding those systems.
F3: When they take over, suppose we are asking finance questions, obviously finance people are only in the development phase, they are only telling them, "You have to advise this." […] I think if I'm not using my brain for ten years and suddenly, even if I'm a finance person and for example you come and ask me and I'm like I don't know, I don't remember
(INTERNATIONAL STUDENTS)

This related to concern that AI could "take over":

"If this did come about, how long would it before artificial intelligence takes over the whole thing?" (SENIORS: F2)

The risks of AI and automation increasingly replacing human judgement and oversight was a major theme which emerged consistently across all the focus groups and which was articulated in relation to each of the examples discussed above.

"I think personally that there's got to be some sort of human interaction no matter how far the technology goes because a human can spot if there's something wrong, whether it's through feeling or patterns or whatever, which technology might not. Say someone has got dementia and they've applied for five credit cards, is the algorithm going to spot that or is someone physically looking at stuff going to be like, "Well something is not right here"?" (POSTGRADUATE STUDENTS: F2)

"I also believe that no matter what we should rely on ourselves. Technology is good but human connection is actually important in our life I think." (INTERNATIONAL STUDENTS: F4)

Related to this a number of participants discussed the potential for increasing use of AI to result in job losses and bank branch closures:

F1: they're going to put people out of work aren't they?
F2: yeah, that's a good point. They do away with all- oh you can laugh but it's true! They're doing away with lots of jobs. I mean there's banks closing all over the place. I think my local one will be next
(SENIORS)

"It's also like because people will just get lazier and lazier and lazier. Also if everything they can do with AI and then humans will have no job at all so in society they will do nothing and they will have no earning, no income and all that." (INTERNATIONAL STUDENTS: F4)

"I think it's just becoming more convenient, isn't it, to everybody. I love my banking app because I can do stuff while I'm on the move and you're not standing in queues all the time but is that necessarily a good thing because you're taking jobs off people." (POSTGRADUATE STUDENTS: F2)

These discussions indicated tensions between people's concerns about societal impacts of AI in banking, and their own willingness to use technologies which were perceived as increasing convenience. The discussions also highlighted that ethical concerns were most often raised not in relation to impacts on individual service users or bank customers, but rather on wider society. This has important implications for the ways in which ethical considerations may be conceptualized and addressed.

4 Discussion

The focus groups covered a wide range of topics relating to digital innovation in banking. Throughout the focus groups, and in conversations after the groups had formally ended, participants often remarked that these were not topics they typically gave much consideration to, yet many participants said that they enjoyed the discussions and that it had been helpful to consider these areas and develop their own views. Moreover, focus group participants remarked that they did not generally think about banking in their day-to-day lives and indeed they did not want to have to think about banking. As one participant said they "don't want to be too involved with [their] bank" (RURAL: F1). Where people described current frustrations with banking these typically related to inconveniences or friction in accessing services. Therefore, digital innovation was more likely to be viewed positively if it increased convenience and resulted in faster or smoother experiences. As has been observed previously [13], this suggests that new technologies or data practices which lead to frictionless banking services have a high chance of being adopted.

However, this points to a tension in the focus group findings. On the one hand, participants want faster, frictionless services and do not want to have to think about those services in their day-to-day lives: they want banking just to "fit in" with their lives. Yet on the other hand, there was considerable concern across the focus groups that increasing automation of services has negative impacts for both individuals and society. In particular there was concern about the potential for reliance on automated processes and AI to erode human capacities and skills. There was quite significant concern that this might reduce future generations' abilities to make sound financial decisions, or to make decisions independently, as well as reducing the skills, expertise and authority of employees in the banking sector. As such there was a clear tension between participants' desire for greater convenience and their concerns for potential negative societal impacts of increasing automation. This may suggest a potential cognitive dissonance [14] where people use new services due to perceived convenience or immediate benefits, while disliking or distrusting those services or holding concerns about their impacts on society.

Concern about a lack of human judgement or oversight was a major theme which emerged consistently across all the focus groups. Participants typically stressed the importance of human judgement and interaction in relation to financial decision-making (e.g. determining loan applications), customer services (e.g. in contrast to chatbots) and advice (e.g. in contrast to virtual money coaches). AI, or automated processes, were largely perceived as unable to take account of the complexities of real lives or the particularities of individuals' financial circumstances. There was a preference for human interaction in order to enable decision-making and/or advice which engaged more fully with these dimensions. Additionally, human involvement was seen to enhance accountability and trustworthiness which gave focus group participants more confidence to discuss financial matters or access services.

Many of the concerns raised reflect what Taddeo and Floridi [9] have described as the invisibility of AI. This relates to the scope for AI to exert increasing, but imperceptible influence over our lives and identities and to undermine individual or society's control. These concerns were consistently expressed throughout the focus groups in discussions of the ways in which AI might reduce human capacities or individual's ability to make sound decisions. This highlights that public concerns were not limited to short-term or immediate impacts of new technologies, rather they reflected an awareness of – and concern about – long-term societal impacts.

Nevertheless, most participants were not opposed to automated processes or AI in banking. Automation was widely recognised to have a valuable role to play in increasing efficiency and convenience of banking services. Yet, across the focus groups human oversight was consistently articulated as a vital condition for acceptability of AI and automation. In particular, where algorithms are informing decision-making processes, focus group participants expressed a clear preference for final decisions to be made by humans. Similarly, while automated processes were recognised to be useful at answering frequently asked questions, human interaction was considered important when customers had unusual queries or sensitive matters to discuss.

5 Conclusions

The focus group discussions demonstrated participants' enthusiasm to engage with the subject of AI in banking. The topic guide for the focus groups was intentionally flexible to allow unanticipated areas of interest to emerge, while particular examples presented worked well as catalysts for discussions, across the focus groups this typically led into broad discussions raising considerations of impacts on society and future generations. This illustrates that participants' concerns did not typically relate to private or individual interests but more often to wider ethical and social concerns, highlighting the importance of taking account of conditions for public acceptability - rather than just customer uptake - in order to develop ethical practice and establish a social licence [1] for uses of AI in banking.

Parallels can be drawn with research into public attitudes towards data-intensive innovation in other sectors. For example, research into public responses to uses – and reuses – of patients' health data has found that members of the public are primarily concerned with the extent to which data will be used in ways which bring public benefits and conversely the possibility for indirect negative, societal impacts of data use [15]. There may be some value in looking at the wider literature around public attitudes to data practices in order to reflect on conditions which need to be met in order to establish a social licence for data-intensive innovation in FinTech and banking.

Pursuing a social licence recognises that there can be meaningful differences between what is legally permissible and what is socially acceptable [1]. Therefore, establishing and maintaining a social licence requires going beyond legal compliance in relation to safeguarding customer's data and instead taking steps to align with public values and expectations. This research has indicated that doing so may necessitate a focus on long-term, indirect impacts of innovation and taking approaches which are aimed at societal – rather than just individual – benefits.

The focus groups demonstrated the value of qualitative, deliberative methods to explore the nuances of public responses. In particular, they revealed a potential cognitive dissonance whereby individuals are concerned about new areas of innovation and yet use these services due to perceived convenience or immediate benefits for individuals. This highlights the importance of considering wider public responses - rather than simply reasons for customer uptake of new FinTech services – in order to identify and address ethical concerns.

Further research is needed in this field to inform emerging practices in the fast-paced industry and to ensure public concerns and interests are addressed. To date, the limited literature around public, or customer responses to FinTech and/or digital innovation in banking has tended to focus on individual concerns (e.g. regarding privacy and security) or perceived benefits to individual customers. However the focus groups have demonstrated that such matters form only a small proportion of the concerns held by members of the public. This suggests that establishing a social licence for AI in banking [1] requires much more than consideration of privacy and security or direct customer experiences, but rather necessitates attending to broader social considerations.

As is a common feature of focus group research, this study enabled a deep understanding of the nuances of public attitudes and the conditions for public acceptability. However, the focus on depth of understanding meant that the number of participants in the study was small and it cannot claim to be representative of wider public views. This represents an important first step in building the evidence base in this field. Further, qualitative and deliberative research is needed to build on this study and further explore wider public attitudes towards AI in banking.

Acknowledgement. This research was funded by the EPSRC, grant reference: EP/R033595/1.

References

1. Aitken, M., Toreini, E., Carmichael, P., Coopamootoo, K., Elliott, K., van Moorsel, A.: Establishing a social licence for Financial Technology: reflections on the role of the private sector in pursuing ethical data practices. Big Data Soc. **7**(1) (2020). https://doi.org/10.1177/205395 1720908892
2. Maskey, S.: How Artificial Intelligence is Helping Financial Institutions. Forbes (2018)
3. Floridi, Luciano: Establishing the rules for building trustworthy AI. Nat. Mach. Intell. **1**(6), 261–262 (2019)
4. Toreini, E., Aitken, M., Coopamootoo, K., Elliott, K., Zelaya, C.G., van Moorsel, A.: The relationship between trust in AI and trustworthy machine learning technologies. In: Proceedings of the 2020 Conference on Fairness, Accountability, and Transparency, pp. 272–283 (2020)

5. Chuang, L.-M., Liu, C.-C., Kao, H.-K.: The adoption of fintech service: TAM perspective. Int. J. Manag. Adm. Sci. **3**(7), 1–15 (2016)
6. Gulamhuseinwala, I., Bull, T., Lewis, S.: FinTech is gaining traction and young, high-income users are the early adopters. J. Financ. Perspect. **3**(3) (2015)
7. Gulamhuseinwala, I., Hatch, M., Lloyd, J., Bull, T., Chen, S.: EY FinTech Adoption Index 2017: The rapid emergence of FinTech. Ernst & Young Global Limited (2017)
8. Kavuri, A.S., Milne, A.: FinTech and the future of financial services: What are the research gaps? (2019)
9. Taddeo, M., Floridi, L.: How AI can be a force for good. Science **361**(6404), 751–752 (2018)
10. Mittelstadt, B.: Principles alone cannot guarantee ethical AI. Nat. Mach. Intell. **1**, 1–7 (2019)
11. Demirguc-Kunt, A., Klapper, L., Singer, D., Ansar, S., Hess, J.: The Global Findex Database 2017: Measuring financial inclusion and the fintech revolution. The World Bank (2018)
12. Barbour, R.: Doing focus groups. Sage (2008)
13. King, B.: Bank 4.0: Banking Everywhere, Never at a Bank. Wiley, Hoboken (2018)
14. Festinger, L.: A Theory of Cognitive Dissonance, vol. 2. Stanford University Press, Redwood City (1957)
15. Aitken, M., de St Jorre, J., Pagliari, C., Jepson, R., Cunningham-Burley, S.: Public responses to the sharing and linkage of health data for research purposes: a systematic review and thematic synthesis of qualitative studies. BMC Med. Ethics **17**(1), 73 (2016)

Creative Toolkits for TIPS

Helen Collard$^{(\boxtimes)}$ ⓘ and Jo Briggs ⓘ

School of Design, Northumbria University, Newcastle-upon-Tyne, UK
{h.collard,jo.briggs}@northumbria.ac.uk

Abstract. We present a survey of toolkits employed in research workshop approaches within TIPS (Trust, Identity, Privacy and Security) domains. Our survey was developed within wider design research to develop digital service prototypes that support people in evaluating whether to trust that an online actor's identity is not recently faked, and that a service they are registering personal information with is legitimate; and a subsequent project involving a tool that invites people to reflect on the cumulative risks of sharing apparently harmless personal information online. The radically multidisciplinary nature of both these TIPS projects has determined that we create a research space to promote exchange to, as design researchers, better understand the 'opaque' immediate and longer term implications of our proposed services and invite cross-disciplinary discussion towards interdisciplinary understandings. This paper is intended as an at-a-glance resource for researchers from a range of disciplinary backgrounds working on TIPS research to inform on various different material engagements, with research stakeholders, through creative workshop approaches. Our survey focused on the literature from Design (especially Participatory Design or PD, and Codesign), Human Computer Interaction (HCI) and cyber related security research. It comprises 30 papers or toolkit examples organised across: review papers; example toolkits; case studies reporting relevant toolkit use; applied toolkits for learning/knowledge exchange; research toolkits focused on demonstrating a methodological-conceptual approach (some problematising emergent or near-future technologies); and two papers that straddled the latter two categories, focusing on future practical application. We begin with an overview of our rationale and method before presenting each group of texts in a table alongside a summary discussion. We go on to discuss the various material components, affordances and terminology of the toolkits along with core concerns often left out of the reporting of research; before going on to recognise toolkits not so much as things that diagnose and fix things, but as a loose collection of readily available material and wider resources, used in particular participatory approaches, which together help account for techno-relational differences and contingencies in TIPS-related fields.

Keywords: Toolkits · Creative workshops · TIPS · Interdisciplinarity · Participatory design

TAPESTRY is funded by EPSRC Grant Ref: EP/N02799X/1; Cumulative Revelations is funded by EPSRC Grant Ref: EP/R033870/1, both under the UKRI Digital Economy Programme.

I. Boureanu et al. (Eds.): ESORICS 2020 Workshops, LNCS 12580, pp. 39–55, 2020.
https://doi.org/10.1007/978-3-030-66504-3_3

1   Introduction

Our motivation was to synthesise the rapidly growing body of research that use-fully demonstrates workshop-based design techniques drawn particularly from Participatory Design approaches. If not always explicitly presented as involving toolkits, the design tools and techniques reported employ a form of making—from storytelling and 3D modelling to role play and map making. The literature mostly presents a workshop setting involving a toolkit, or toolbox of materials and processes that facilitate creative and reflective processes to unfold. Fur-thermore, the workshops are conducted across collaborative (multidisciplinary), and cross-sectoral (involving stakeholders) settings. This collection of creative toolkits employs various materials, and their inherent affordances, to prompt critical thinking and identify aspects of user/stakeholder/security practitioner understandings and assessments of trust, identity, privacy and security, typi-cally within the context of a particular digital technology. The TIPS acronym has been taken up as a neologism in UK research following two respectively named funding calls in 2015 and 2017. These invited:

> co-created, novel, interdisciplinary projects that solve real problems in aspects of trust, identity, privacy and security (TIPS) in the digital econ-omy in a responsible way. We also want to engender a sustained and col-laborative approach so that these projects engage with the wider relevant sectors and disciplines ... [19]

We have been involved in projects enabled through both rounds, primarily due to their rationale of cocreating research and possible solutions with stakehold-ers, and their underlying synergy to research design involving participation and cocreation. These provided a unique opportunity to design, prototype and trial creative methodologies across sustained multidisciplinary research also involving ideating, prototyping and trialing a digital technology service. Our survey has uncovered earlier, including foundational, work (also generated from a EPSRC call in 2008 and a 2012 EPSRC sandpit). We position this paper as having par-ticular relevance for early career researchers and those new to large multidisci-plinary collaborative research involving participatory and generative workshops involving stakeholders in the broad area(s) of TIPS.

2   Survey of Papers

The term toolkit may suggest an off-the-shelf solution to enabling TIPS related learning or data generation. We think the term is over and often uncritically used, if nonetheless a convenient catch-all reference to a wide spectrum of practically applied and cocreative (socio)material approaches or principles. We unpick and identify these in the following sections.

2.1   Method

We discussed a number of potentially relevant papers informed by earlier work [32]. The first author conducted a broad search for papers published since 2011 focusing on, but not limited to HCI, Computer Supported Cooperative Work (CSCW), New Security Paradigms Workshop (NSPW) and Designing Interactive Systems (DIS) in the ACM and IEEE Xplore Digital Libraries, using keyword search term 'toolkit', extended variously through companion terms: 'toolbox', 'tools', 'techniques', 'physical modelling', 'physicalisation' etc., to widen the scope of the search. We then filtered the results to focus our inclusion criteria on 'workshop' activities, and then in turn to focus on TIPS domains: 'trust', 'identity', 'privacy' and 'security'. The first author then conducted similar 6-word keyword searches to the SOUPS archives (again from 2011 to 2020). Crucially, we identified relevant texts referenced in our corpus and also used some creative licence in our final selection, to include two papers that we consider of particular methodological interest due to demonstrations of and reporting on a PD approach with an individual [31] and an apparently silly approach to critically engaging with concerns around current and near-future technologies [5]. Our final survey comprises 26 papers and four exemplar practical toolkit manuals (one is reported upon within workshop use and all four are intended for such). We categorised the papers accordingly: Review Toolkit papers (offering a broad snapshot of toolkits in the disciplinary fields relevant to our multidisciplinary research); Example Toolkits (created for application to other similar projects); Case Study Papers That Include Toolkits; Applied Research Toolkits (that address specific problem spaces); Conceptual/Methodological Research Toolkits (that offer methodological insight) and finally; Conceptual Future Application Toolkits (that, although primarily methodological, demonstrate a workshop and toolkit that is easily transferable to another application). We acknowledge that other creative toolkit papers of relevance to TIPS may exist. However, we claim that our sample serves as a representative, useful and readily applicable review of demonstrated approaches of particular use to this broad and rapidly growing field of research.

2.2   Review Papers

We selected six toolkit review papers (Table 1) that straddle the range of disciplinary fields relevant to our multidisciplinary research across HCI/CSCW, PD and cybersecurity research and practice. Two are firmly HCI: toolkits within HCI [28] and IoT in HCI [4]. The combined scope of these reviews demonstrates the substantive nature of toolkit related research in HCI, primarily in enabling and influencing foci, design and deployment of technologies and interactions. Ledo et al. [28] synthesised 68 toolkit papers to propose strategies for a toolkit evaluation and classification system, and offers insights into toolkits' relative value, potential for bias and various trade-offs. This is technically focused work, following earlier interface design concept toolkits for designer-developer teams – updated as more "generative platforms ...provid(ing) easy access to complex

Table 1. Review papers.

Reference	Field/Toolkit	Toolkit review
Brandt *et al.* 2012 [8]	PD review of toolboxes for co-creation in multiple domains	Widely recognised approach using probes, models, games, workbooks, scenarios and mapping techniques – demonstrates availability of tools/techniques and opportunity for various combinations, adaptation and extensions
Berger *et al.* 2019 [4]	IoT evaluation and analysis of 3 IoT toolkits for co-designing design stories	IoT Un-Kit experience comprises hybrid and analogue methods; proposes framework to compare/assess design stories generated
Fox *et al.* 2018 [20]	Cybersecurity; reviews 41 public facing security- related toolkits to help achieve online security	Focuses on articulating "differential vulnerabilities" to promote understanding on security as socio-culturally situated and group specific
Ledo *et al.* 2018 [28]	HCI overview and discussion of evaluation methods for HCI toolkits	Analysis of 68 HCI toolkits proposing they comprise 4 categories: novel examples; replicated examples; case studies and exploration of a design space
Sanders *et al.* 2010 [37]	PD framework for organising the proliferation of PD tools, techniques and methods	Framework provides tools and techniques for engaging non-designers; suggests three dimensions of form, purpose and context for designing new PD methods
Sanders *et al..* 2014 [38]	Co-design overview of cultural probes, toolkits and prototypes in design research/practice	Offers perspectives across: approach (probes, generative toolkits, design prototypes); mindset (designing for/with people); temporal aspects (design for now, near/speculative futures) and variations in intent (to provoke, engage or serve)

algorithms, enable fast prototyping of software and hardware interfaces, or enable creative exploration of design spaces." (p. 2) Berger *et al.* [4] focused on more creative narrative approaches involving IoT toolkits, synthesising work reporting on cocreated design scenarios, fictions and stories. These authors found that some approaches enable immediately functioning scenario development while others involve more speculative notions. Pragmatically they recommend questioning and adapting toolkit materials to support creation of under-explored design stories. The HCI literature is important in demonstrating different forms of engagement with the users of TIPS research; [33] and [45] advocate the field's relevance for considering and improving system use for the intended user.

From CSCW we included a review of practical public-facing toolkits [20] due to its critical review of 41 toolkits available online to promote cybersecurity; defined as "online collections of tools, tutorials, and tips aimed to help individuals or groups improve their security online." (p. 2) Two overlapping categories of security toolkit are identified; toolkits in the first group address those for general use amongst nonspecific populations, such as Electronic Frontier's Surveillance Self-Defense toolkit [1]. Those in the second group support people with a conflict or distrust of institutions (governments, device manufacturers, service providers), for example produced by grassroots, activist or other organisations to support members' particular online security practices and to address the unique threats and harms directed at those who are on political and social peripheries. The evaluation revealed many comprised bolt-on functionality to meet specific needs of certain groups, due to the inadequacy of mainstream tools. Institutional tools (e.g. provided by manufacturers, governments) aimed to promote neutral socio-political stances and in so doing so failed to meet many groups' needs, meanwhile also stigmatising them as "(in)secure users" (p. 1). The authors build on Dourish's and Anderson's 2006 [14] work that called for better contextual understanding around safety, security and privacy as not primarily technological, but rather, socio-politically "entangled" (p. 319).

The other three review papers represent foundational PD literature as a resource for TIPS. PD considers the socio-political contexts of technological development and deployment, with its roots in Scandinavian cooperative design—an approach engaging all stakeholders (e.g. employees, customers, trade union officials) to enable robust input into technological system design to ensure that all perspectives are considered and needs met. PD also provides a methodological foundation for toolkits within TIPS alongside practical guidance especially when approaching enhancement of usability outcomes (by improving the functional design and evaluation of user facing security technologies). Additionally PD concerns sociopolitical contexts of intended toolkit use – or technology outcomes of use. Interestingly, whilst HCI borrows heavily (if to varying levels of credit) from PD, PD is criticised from amongst its own community for its ambivalence [8] in failing to promote wider take up and use of its own tools and techniques elsewhere. This is particularly telling in areas such as TIPS with dichotomous and often competing aims and objectives (compare with [9]).

2.3   Toolkits

From the vast number of practical toolkit examples available for general use we selected four for inclusion in our sample. We considered these as exemplars, worthy of mention due to being specifically on-topic and/or comprehensive; and they are also critically framed. They are: a manual of toolkits to support the design of

Table 2. Example toolkits.

Toolkit name	Overview	Application
You Shape Security, Coles-Kemp *et al.* 2018 [12] – TIPS	Three manuals outlining toolkit principles, materials and processes	Security practitioners; designers and managers of technical security approaches in organisations
Unbias Fairness Toolkit, Lane *et al.* 2018 [26] – TIPS	Handbook, awareness cards, trustScape, metaMap, value perception worksheets, facilitator booklet	Promotes awareness of algorithms, trust, bias and fairness to stimulate civic dialogue
Co-Creative Methodology Workshop Handbook, Stembert. 2017 [40] – TIPS	Bring together multiple stakeholders to co-create IoT in a couple of hours	End-user engagement toolkit on how to organise, facilitate, analyse and document a co-creative Workshop
Participatory Methods Toolkit Slocum. 2003 [39] – PD Methods	Manual includes 10 in-depth fiches and overviews 38 participatory methods and techniques	For starting up/managing participatory projects in organisations

digital security, You Shape Security [12], which emphasises in its detailed series of user manuals the importance of collaborative "creative engagement" (p. 4) to enable people within organisations to discuss their individual situations, security focus and protection practices, and to develop shared understandings of their wider security landscape. The approach assists the generation and exchange of learning around the hazards and risks of day-to-day information security. This represents a "radical departure [from] affirming the principles of technological security through compliant practice" [13] (p. 10) and provides a platform that enables participating communities, and indeed those who do not engage in security programmes, to enter a dialogue of security concerns. The second example is a toolkit of participatory methods – a comprehensive document of PD methods and materials aimed more at practitioners [39]. Third is a co-creative toolkit and handbook to help IoT teams and end users identify and discuss TIPS barriers to IoT adoption [40]. And finally, the Fairness Toolkit [26], from an EPSRC funded project "UnBias: Emancipating Users Against Algorithmic Biases for a Trusted Digital Economy" uses cards, mapping and facilitation techniques to promote awareness and civic dialogue about algorithmic systems, trust, bias and fairness. All four toolkits have been structured and compiled to be used beyond the workshops they were created for, each having application beyond the specific problem space applied to. All four also provide off-the-shelf guidance on workshop facilitation, toolkit materials and frameworks to support others' use; one comprises a PD guide [39] with the other three [12,26,40] more focused towards supporting research within TIPS domains.

Table 3. Case study papers that include toolkits.

Ref. – TIPS	Toolkit overview	Toolkit findings
Dunphy *et al.* 2014 [17] – Trust – Identity – Privacy – Security	Focuses on under-represented groups: 80 somethings; an international women's centre and an under-resourced community	Introduces notion of experience-centered privacy and security; advocates engaging users in sharing experiences of privacy and security; demonstrates a range of mixed creative methods
Jensen *et al.* 2020 [23] – Trust – Security	Geographically, socially and culturally diverse communities of: seafarers; Geenland residents and North East unemployed; uses a wide range of creative methods and information gathering	Ethnographic/conversational approach to solicit plurality of voices/experiences (around liminality and social isolation linked to security and technological innovation)

2.4 Case Study Papers

Further, we selected two papers that report on a number of different case studies – some of which are more relevant to TIPS than others, but which valuably synthesise, analyse and contribute critical insights into methodological approaches, with particular [17] or broad [39] relevance to TIPS (Table 3).

2.5 Applied Research Toolkits

The remaining papers in our survey report on a focused study involving one or series of related workshops/participatory activities involving to different extents design, demonstration and evaluation of toolkit approaches in a particular TIPS problem space. We further clustered this large group between reported research that was explicitly applied to exchanging knowledge, encouraging critical reflection on personal or collective practices towards supporting safety amongst particular participating groups; these papers are discussed in this section; the others are primarily methodological and conceptual (despite some claiming practical application/impact). A further three papers fall somewhere in between, in that they clearly offer future applicability to addressing a particular area of concern. These three groups of papers are discussed in turn below (Table 4).

The applied toolkit texts focus on sharing principles, guidelines and frameworks, grounded in empirical work that demonstrates particular creative approaches used in specific user contexts. Coles-Kemp and Ashenden are leaders in devising novel creative approaches to engaging stakeholders in debates and knowledge exchange about online security, including to humanise what otherwise is often highly technical, while also emphasising finding practical ways to vitally enable different voices and points of view. This marked a paradigm shift towards human centredness for privacy and security research. Early VOME

Table 4. Applied research toolkits.

Ref. – TIPS	Applied toolkit/workshop	Guidance/application
Bowyer *et al.* 2018 [7] – Trust – Privacy – Security	For system designers and policy makers on range of privacy, security and social justice issues relating to family-oriented data; involving cross-generational families	Offers principles on rights, control and visibility over civic data handling and involvement of families in decision-making
Coles-Kemp *et al.* 2012 [11] – Privacy	Support privacy and consent decision-making and promotes methodology in future oriented privacy and online awareness; focuses on hard to reach groups excluded from privacy design	Offers a range of domain specific participatory methods guides
Coles-Kemp *et al.* 2020 [13] – Security	Security design for security practitioners and healthcare service providers	User guides comparing top down and bottom up perspectives with related discussion aiming to share understanding from alternative security perspectives
Heath *et al.* 2019 [22] – Trust – Security	Security focused offering guidance for smart technology adoption amongst community/resident groups	Suggests actions towards enabling a successful community-focused outcome

(Visualisation and Other Methods of Expression) work over a 4-year period applied and demonstrated its 'community-centric engagement' approach, which informed contribution towards a multi-disciplinary methodological framework. The specific papers included here consider designed interventions to promote privacy awareness both on and off-line [11] (Table 5).

2.6 Conceptual/Methodological Research Toolkit

The conceptual and methodological texts demonstrate, trial, evaluate and critique various multi- and interdisciplinary research design approaches or methodologies. In total these comprise 11 papers, by some measure our largest category within the review. Some of the research reported is intended to challenge and provoke thinking and discussion around current, emerging and future technological systems and our attitudes as both designers and users of these systems. Blythe *et al.*, used an imaginary design workbook [6] approach with industry partner Mozilla and a social work professional to promote critical envisioning around (post) privacy and the surveillance potential of home-hub technologies "that record the minutia of our lives" (p. 10). The experimental design workshop process demonstrated one approach to enabling HCI to better "engage with political, ethical and legal issues" (p. 10), yet also questioned whether HCI design researchers actually want to engage or not. Blythe and colleagues also

Table 5. Conceptual/methodological research toolkits.

Ref. – TIPS	Toolkit and workshop overview	Approach
Blythe et al. 2016 [5]	Demonstrates participatory critical design fiction approach informed by Magic Machines [2]; with interdisciplinary research team and older community	Critical design and unuseless designs towards an anti-solutionist methodology
Blythe et al. 2018 [6] – Privacy – Security	Constructive criticism through practical provocations approach to data post-privacy, with HCI specialists (Mozilla) and a social work professional	Exploration and creative design with/in post-privacy space
Clarke et al. 2019 [10] – Trust	Critically investigates sociomaterial trust in design workshop methods to investigate trust-related perspectives towards particular people or institutions; with a low-resource community organisation	Articulates significance of material use not just as a workshop topic but in building or unsettling trusted relations between researchers and participants; broadly based beyond digital contexts
Durrant et al. 2018 [18] – Identity	Investigates how UK citizens at 3 life-transitions create and manage their online identities with young adults; new parents and recent retirees	Ethnography/experience-centred design to "inform policy-making and service innovation for enhancing digital literacy in online self-representation" (p. 122)
Gatehouse et al. 2018 [21] – Trust – Security	Creative HCI design approach to enable and communicate trust/mistrust and LGBTQ identities in the context of hate crime reporting with young people and community police	Informed by Magic Machine approach [2] to challenge conceptualisations of LGBTQ young people's vulnerability by designers, and to lesser extent, criminal justice workers
Khairuddin et al. 2019 [25] – Trust	HCI tool to engage participants in designing trust protocol in blockchain with experienced bitcoin users	A toolkit for visually materialising and discussing non-visual blockchain phenomenon relating to transactions and trust
Light et al. 2011 [31] – Identity	HCI approach to investigating user vulnerability focusing on one older person's experiences	Improvisation performance experiment to investigate personal transformation through experiential learning through participation
Maxwell et al. 2015 [34] – Trust	Design-HCI approach to informing blockchain enabled platform service design using peer-to-peer validation with students, designers, tech start up reps. and bitcoin users	A 'tangible interactive workshop' invited participants to enact trusted transactions as though on a Blockchain, with Lego
Mathiasen et al. 2011 [33] – Security	Participatory and experience-driven design using prompted exploration workshops/acting out security techniques with professional typesetters and senior citizens	Explores space between security experience and expectation and participants' changing strategies different security situations.
Sturdee et al. 2016 [42] – Identity	HCI approach to exploring value of creating fictional research worlds involving conference Workshop participants	Design fiction, imagined future interactions and online identity
Vines et al. 2012 [44] – Trust	PD workshops soliciting older olds' experiences of banking	Concept cards, design sketches and brief outlines of concepts to solicit ideation around new financial services with/for the older old

adopt 'silly' design fiction magic machine-making [5] to unsettle researchers' relationship to technological solutionism – the critique of trends towards delegating human agency and morality to technology – as posited by Evgeny Morozov [35]. The resulting "unuseless, partial or silly objects" [5] (p. 4977) created are illustrated in the paper to problematise surveillance by stealth potential of urban data capture. Blythe is one of a number of UK and wider researchers extending Design Fiction – associated with Critical Design and typically accredited to Bruce Sterling in 2005 (see [41]) to envision plausible near-futures. This body of work aims to provoke a sense of discomfort through recognition of one's role in co-constituting unwelcome technological outcomes.

Several of the papers clearly demonstrate a particular methodological approach within or that came out of TIPS research with particular user groups; 80-somethings and trusted banking using 'questionable concepts' [44]; investigating older people learning about the potential of digital technologies through props and performance over several sessions [30]; making workshops with LGBTQ young people and community police to surface attitudes from both groups on aspects of hate crime and hate crime reporting, to inform design for particular groups and their needs; workshop outcomes were then adapted as design materials in a public intervention [21]; a generative workshop approach, "Blockit", to support understanding of blockchain and cryptocurrency [25]; socio-material aspects of workshop materials and their interpretation and use (or non-use) by particular groups building or negotiating mis/trust, both amongst researchers and workshop participants and between participants and (in this specific case) local officials [10]; didactic approaches to understanding 'opaque technologies' [34]; and using an illustrated guide in supporting people undergoing life transitions [18]. Some of these involve different user groups while others, as with [5] and [43], involve hosting conference or university workshops to explore and/or demonstrate an approach for take up and use by others. Mathiasen *et al.* is worth noting in that [33] explores the spaces between participants' security experiences and their expectations of a new working system for typesetters.

2.7   Conceptual Future Application Toolkit

This final group of three papers highlights the potential future application of creative making workshops in knowledge exchange activities with end-users [16] (one toolkit from this wider study is included in Table 2 Example Toolkits [40]) of InfoSec practitioners [29] and cybersecurity practitioners and policy makers [3]. These papers fell between our conceptual and applied categories, yet are clearly motivated to provide a workshop method of clearly explicated relevance to TIPS practitioners towards their understanding the operational context of different professional roles and related stakeholders, such as policy makers. We suggest these three toolkits are adaptable or easily re-appropriated to future projects in related fields (Table 6).

Table 6. Table of conceptual future application toolkits.

Ref. – TIPS	Toolkit and workshop overview	Approach
Ashenden *et al.* 2013 [3] – Privacy – Security	Toolkit and approach to expand the boundary of the currently held mental models of risk and security; with cyber security practitioners and policy makers	Critical design - creating speculative scenarios suggested as a research technique for imagining future cyber security risk
Drajic *et al.* 2019 [16] – Trust – Privacy – Security	To engage end-users in large scale pilot design. Living Labs, Games, co-creative workshops for end-user engagement and personal data protection	To improve the effectiveness, trust and adoption barriers of IoT development processes.
Lewis *et al.* 2014 [29] – Security	Toolkit for InfoSec practitioners to better understand other user communities and their security practices; with InfoSec practitioners	Suggested as an approach for security training and awareness programmes to understand operational contexts of differing professional roles, for planning exercises around professional roles needed for particular security tasks

3   Discussion

Socio-technical design is increasingly concerned with critically considering the impacts on society, citizens and non-human actors of current or near-future technologies. While current and emerging technologies have enormous societal potential, including through providing enhanced online privacy and security, their design involves many operational challenges including their immaterial illegibility; challenging understanding by even technologists that help create them [32]; but certainly the multiplicity of stakeholders who commission, promote, benefit or otherwise from uptake and use. Concerns include the increasing 'reach' of data-generating technologies as they encroach across every aspect of our everyday lives [15, 24, 32, 36].

So, across multiple intersecting concerns and contexts; what makes a good toolkit? The survey covers a number of creative participatory workshop approaches – designed for a specific purpose and group(s) of participants. Our review papers comprise many materials, devices and props as described by their authors and available in Appendix A (see link at the end of the paper). Crucially, these are used in particular research approaches in different ways, with different groups. We have categorised approaches broadly across five themes: storytelling and reflective annotation; visual and 3D modelling; improvisation, performance and roleplay; games and cards and finally; landscaping, problem setting and mapping. These are available in Appendix B as a set of creative approaches for soliciting research information.

We caution, however, that there are crossovers and overlaps between the approaches; Lego bricks are readily assembled into physical interpretative mod-

els that in turn invite articulation and dialogue. Storyboarding [29] lends itself –
beyond soliciting and giving form to immaterial ideas, understandings or experiences of its creator – to the visual construction of narrative, which in turn can be
shared and made sense of, including through discussion. Often, the narrative arc
afforded by provision of particular individual or combinations of toolkit assets
invited or scaffolded particular approaches to storytelling. Landscaping, problem setting and mapping were all used in various combination of the selected
papers to explore a problem space, promote participants' ideation and envisioning and collectively organising new approaches that went beyond researchers'
expectations. And it is often mentioned that in tandem, toolkit development was
informal and/or iterative involving a pick and mix of materials and approaches.

Analysis of applicability of the toolkits and methods to specific TIPS design
projects is difficult. This largely relies on the participants and facilitation process, along with the contextual and problem space setting. Coles Kemp advises
amongst her four principles of creative engagement to:

> Cede control to the participants to create a form of engagement where
> participants are able to negotiate the terms on which the engagement
> takes place. [12] (p. 3)

One vital component involves pre-engagement in order to select relevant toolkit
materials and identify topics and benefits for participant engagement. Therefore, while this paper offers a list of previously used materials and categories of approaches, meaningfully expediating any of the toolkits and workshop approaches involves research workshop design and appropriate participant
engagement and facilitation. However as previously outlined in Table 2 Example Toolkits, [12,26,40] offer facilitation guidance, and are intended to be used
off-the-shelf by other researchers in focused TIPS domains.

Essentially, workshop facilitated toolkits used in TIPS problem spaces can provide a vehicle to displacing singular viewpoints. The toolkits reported here often
identify and bolster 'ground up', multi-perspectival, experience-centered information and thus insights. The benefit is this avoids, and challenges a generic, univer-
salising mind-set. Notably [35] offers a collection of tools – in order to question the
meanings of security within a given setting, alongside an opportunity to converge
on, and then respond to that set of understandings. We suggest the applicability
and strength of the toolkit approach is a resource for creative questioning and a
useful 'off the road' addition to the rigour and testing of compliant practice.

4   Summary and Conclusion

It is apparent from the survey that this multiplicity of different and largely
inexpensive and readily available materials have different physical affordances.
LEGO bricks afford their assemblage. Similarly, pieces of clothing invite role play,
individual expression and the trying on of possible future identities. Following
Le Guin [27] we suggest that these various toolkits are not about their physical
properties, but about their collective and generative afforances. Le Guin argues

that our technology should not be discussed and understood in terms of its techno-heroism, as she puts it:

> We've all heard all about the sticks and spears and swords, the things to bash and poke and hit with, the long, hard things, but we have not heard about the thing to put things in, the container for the thing contained. [27] (p. 151)

Tools and technologies have historically invited narratives based on weaponry, that poke and prod and potentially maim. Le Guin goes on to suggest technology is better and more accurately conceptualised as a container into which often mundane necessities are collected; the humdrum but essential function of many technologies remain largely absent from technology's dominant *heroic* narrative. Relatedly, the survey comprises a container of toolkits; we are not prescribing a toolkit's contents but demonstrating how a range of associated materials and approaches can be brought together in research design to address human challenges of TIPS research. Crucially, we have selected papers that include the quite technically focused [28] while also offering a richness of demonstrated creative design methodologies.

We research in interesting times when the perception of technological complexity raises many salient societal questions. Le Guin highlights it is not about promoting compliance amongst citizens and users of technologies, but also taking better care to understand different groups' characteristics, abilities, needs and values. Containers, or toolkits, within this mindset could be more fully exploited. We consider them at their best as a pre-production or engagement resource that facilitates exploration, ideation and negotiation of trust, identity, privacy and security within the research process itself, not merely its final object(ive), enabling multiple different realms of social, relational contingencies and dependencies. These toolkits comprise a pragmatic design resource or approach for current and continuing TIPS researchers to not so much aim for others' compliance but through which to engage critically, offering a vantage point from which to consider the unstable, unseen, and differently-abled experience-centred factors; all much needed in TIPS research.

Survey Spreadsheet with Additional Detail Appendices A and B at https://doi.org/10.25398/rd.northumbria.12854888.

References

1. Electronic Frontier's Surveillance Self Defence Kit. https://ssd.eff.org/enfoundational
2. Andersen, K., Wakkary, R.: The magic machine workshops: making personal design knowledge. In: Proceedings of the 2019 CHI Conference on Human Factors in Computing Systems, CHI 2019, New York, NY, USA, pp. 1–13. Association for Computing Machinery (2019). https://doi.org/10.1145/3290605.3300342

3. Ashenden, D., Benque, D., Houldsworth, A.: 'It fauna' and 'crime pays': using critical design to envision cyber security futures. In: Praxis & Poetics, Research Through Design, RTD 2013 (2013)
4. Berger, A., Ambe, A.H., Soro, A., De Roeck, D., Brereton, M.: The stories people tell about the home through IoT toolkits. In: Proceedings of the 2019 on Designing Interactive Systems Conference, DIS 2019, New York, NY, USA, pp. 7–19. Association for Computing Machinery (2019). https://doi.org/10.1145/3322276.3322308
5. Blythe, M., Andersen, K., Clarke, R., Wright, P.: Anti-solutionist strategies: seriously silly design fiction. In: Proceedings of the 2016 CHI Conference on Human Factors in Computing Systems, CHI 2016, New York, NY, USA, pp. 4968–4978. Association for Computing Machinery (2016). https://doi.org/10.1145/2858036.2858482
6. Blythe, M., Encinas, E., Kaye, J., Avery, M.L., McCabe, R., Andersen, K.: Imaginary design workbooks: constructive criticism and practical provocation. In: Proceedings of the 2018 CHI Conference on Human Factors in Computing Systems, CHI 2018, New York, NY, USA, pp. 1–12. Association for Computing Machinery (2018). https://doi.org/10.1145/3173574.3173807
7. Bowyer, A., Montague, K., Wheater, S., McGovern, R., Lingam, R., Balaam, M.: Understanding the family perspective on the storage, sharing and handling of family civic data. In: Proceedings of the 2018 CHI Conference on Human Factors in Computing Systems, CHI 2018, New York, NY, USA, pp. 1–13. Association for Computing Machinery (2018). https://doi.org/10.1145/3173574.3173710
8. Brandt, E., Binder, T., Sanders, E.: Tools and techniques: ways to engage telling, making and enacting, pp. 145–181. Routledge International Handbooks, Routledge (2012)
9. Bratteteig, T., Verne, G.: Does AI make PD obsolete? Exploring challenges from artificial intelligence to participatory design. In: Proceedings of the 15th Participatory Design Conference: Short Papers, Situated Actions, Workshops and Tutorial - Volume 2, PDC 2018, New York, NY, USA. Association for Computing Machinery (2018). https://doi.org/10.1145/3210604.3210646
10. Clarke, R.E., Briggs, J., Armstrong, A., MacDonald, A., Vines, J., Flynn, E.,Salt, K.: Socio-materiality of trust: co-design with a resource limited community organisation. CoDesign (0), 1–20 (2019). https://doi.org/10.1080/15710882.2019.1631349
11. Coles-Kemp, L., Ashenden, A.: Community-centric engagement: lessons learned from privacy awareness intervention design. In: The 26th BCS Conference on Human Computer Interaction (HCI), pp. 1–4, September 2012. https://doi.org/10.14236/ewic/HCI2012.65
12. Coles Kemp, L., Heath, C., NCSC: You Shape Security Toolkit. https://www.ncsc.gov.uk/collection/you-shape-security
13. Coles-kemp, L., Holloway, R., Holloway, R., Heath, C.P.R., Arts, M., Holloway, R.: Too much information: questioning security in a post-digital society. In: Proceedings of the CHI 2020 Conference on Human Factors in Computing Systems, pp. 1–14 (2020)
14. Dourish, P., Anderson, K.: Collective information practice: exploring privacy and security as social and cultural phenomena. Hum. Comput. Interact. 21(3), 319–342 (2006). https://doi.org/10.1207/s15327051hci2103_2
15. Dove, G., Halskov, K., Forlizzi, J., Zimmerman, J.: UX design innovation: challenges for working with machine learning as a design material. In: Proceedings of the CHI 2017 Conference on Human Factors in Computing Systems, pp. 278–288 (2017)

16. Drajic, D., et al.: User engagement for large scale pilots in the Internet of Things. In: Proceedings of TELSIKS 2019 14th International Conference on Advanced Technologies, Systems and Services in Telecommunications, pp. 46–53 (2019). https://doi.org/10.1109/TELSIKS46999.2019.9002017

17. Dunphy, P., et al.: Understanding the experience-centeredness of privacy and security technologies. In: Proceedings of the 2014 New Security Paradigms Workshop, NSPW 2014, New York, NY, USA, pp. 83–94. Association for Computing Machinery (2014). https://doi.org/10.1145/2683467.2683475

18. Durrant, A.C., Kirk, D.S., Moncur, W., Orzech, K.M., Taylor, R., Trujillo Pisanty, D.: Rich pictures for stakeholder dialogue: a polyphonic picture book. Des. Stud. **56**, 122–148 (2018). https://doi.org/10.1016/j.destud.2018.01.001

19. EPSRC: Trust, Identity, Privacy and Security in the Digital Economy 2.0 (2017). https://www.epsrc.ukri.org/funding/calls/tips2/

20. Fox, S., Merrill, N., Wong, R., Pierce, J.: Differential vulnerabilities and a diversity of tactics: what toolkits teach us about cybersecurity. In: Proceedings of the ACM on Human-Computer Interaction (2 CSCW) (2018). https://doi.org/10.1145/3274408

21. Gatehouse, C., Wood, M., Briggs, J., Pickles, J., Lawson, S.: Troubling vulnerability: designing with LGBT young people's ambivalence towards hate crime reporting. In: Proceedings of the 2018 CHI Conference on Human Factors in Computing Systems, CHI 2018, New York, NY, USA, pp. 1–13. Association for Computing Machinery (2018). https://doi.org/10.1145/3173574.3173683

22. Heath, C.P.R., Crivellaro, C., Coles-Kemp, L.: Relations are more than bytes: rethinking the benefits of smart services through people and things. In: Proceedings of the 2019 CHI Conference on Human Factors in Computing Systems, CHI 2019, New York, NY, USA, pp. 1–12. Association for Computing Machinery (2019). https://doi.org/10.1145/3290605.3300538

23. Jensen, R.B., Coles-Kemp, L., Wendt, N., Lewis, M.: Digital liminalities: understanding isolated communities on the edge. In: Proceedings of the 2020 CHI Conference on Human Factors in Computing Systems, CHI 2020, New York, NY, USA, pp. 1–14. Association for Computing Machinery (2020). https://doi.org/10.1145/3313831.3376137

24. Kelly, K.: The Inevitable: Understanding the 12 Technological Forces That Will Shape Our Future. Viking Press, USA (2016)

25. Khairuddin, I.E., Sas, C., Speed, C.: Blockit: a physical kit for materializing and designing for blockchain infrastructure. In: Proceedings of the 2019 on Designing Interactive Systems Conference, DIS 2019, New York, NY, USA, pp. 1449–1462. Association for Computing Machinery (2019). https://doi.org/10.1145/3322276.3322370

26. Lane, G.: UnBias Fairness Toolkit (2018). https://unbias.wp.horizon.ac.uk/fairness-toolkit/

27. Le Guin, U.K.: The Carrier Bag Theory of Fiction, the Ecocriticism Reader: Landmarks in Literacy Ecology. University of Georgia Press, Athens (1996)

28. Ledo, D., Houben, S., Vermeulen, J., Marquardt, N., Oehlberg, L., Greenberg, S.: Evaluation strategies for HCI toolkit research. In: Proceedings of the 2018 CHI Conference on Human Factors in Computing Systems, CHI 2018, New York, NY, USA, pp. 1–17. Association for Computing Machinery (2018). https://doi.org/10.1145/3173574.3173610

29. Lewis, M.M., Coles-Kemp, L.: Who says personas can't dance? The use of comic strips to design information security personas. In: CHI '14 Extended Abstracts on Human Factors in Computing Systems, CHI EA 2014, New York, NY, USA, pp. 2485–2490. Association for Computing Machinery (2014). https://doi.org/10.1145/2559206.2581323

30. Light, A., Luckin, R.: Designing for social justice: people, technology, learning (2008)

31. Light, A.: Democratising technology: making transformation using designing, performance and props. In: Proceedings of the SIGCHI Conference on Human Factors in Computing Systems, CHI 2011, New York, NY, USA, pp. 2239–2242. Association for Computing Machinery (2011). https://doi.org/10.1145/1978942.1979269

32. Manohar, A., Briggs, J.: Designing in with black box technologies and PD, pp. 2294–2307. Design Research Society (2018). https://doi.org/10.21606/drs.2018.296

33. Mathiasen, N.R., Bødker, S.: Experiencing security in interaction design. In: Proceedings of the SIGCHI Conference on Human Factors in Computing Systems, CHI 2011, New York, NY, USA, pp. 2325–2334. Association for Computing Machinery (2011). https://doi.org/10.1145/1978942.1979283

34. Maxwell, D., Speed, C., Campbell, D.: 'Effing' the ineffable: Opening up understandings of the blockchain. In: Proceedings of the 2015 British HCI Conference, British HCI 2015, New York, NY, USA, pp. 208–209. Association for Computing Machinery (2015). https://doi.org/10.1145/2783446.2783593

35. Morozov, E.: To Save Everything, Click Here: The Folly of Technological Solutionism. Public Affairs (2013)

36. Pasquale, F.: The Black Box Society. Harvard Universty Press (2015). https://doi.org/10.4159/harvard.9780674736061

37. Sanders, E.B.N., Brandt, E., Binder, T.: A framework for organizing the tools and techniques of participatory design. In: Proceedings of the 11th Biennial Participatory Design Conference, PDC 2010, New York, NY, USA, pp. 195–198. Association for Computing Machinery (2010). https://doi.org/10.1145/1900441.1900476

38. Sanders, E.B., Stappers, P.J.: Probes, toolkits and prototypes: three approaches to making in codesigning. CoDesign 10(1), 5–14 (2014). https://doi.org/10.1080/15710882.2014.888183

39. Slocum, N.: Participatory Methods Toolkit: A practitioner's manual. King Baudouin Foundation and the Flemish Institute for Science and Technology Assessment (viWTA) (UNU/CRIS) (2003). www.kbs-frb.be

40. Stembert, N.: Co-Creative Workshop Methodology. U4IoT Consortium, Horizon 2020 European research project. https://u4iot.eu/pdf/U4IoT_CoCreativeWorkshopMethodology_Handbook.pdf

41. Sterling, B.: Shaping Things. MIT Press, Cambridge (2005)

42. Sturdee, M., Coulton, P., Lindley, J.G., Stead, M., Ali, H., Hudson-Smith, a.: design fiction: how to build a Voight-Kampff machine. In: Proceedings of the 2016 CHI Conference Extended Abstracts on Human Factors in Computing Systems, CHI EA 2016, New York, NY, USA, pp. 375–386. Association for Computing Machinery (2016). https://doi.org/10.1145/2851581.2892574

43. Sturdee, M., Lindley, J.: Sketching and drawing as future inquiry in HCI. In: Proceedings of the Halfway to the Future Symposium 2019, HTTF 2019, New York, NY, USA. Association for Computing Machinery (2019). https://doi.org/10.1145/3363384.3363402

44. Vines, J., Blythe, M., Lindsay, S., Dunphy, P., Monk, A., Olivier, P.: Questionable concepts: critique as a resource for designing with eighty somethings. In: Conference on Human Factors in Computing Systems - Proceedings, pp. 1169–1178 (2012). https://doi.org/10.1145/2207676.2208567

45. Zurko, M.E., Simon, R.T.: User-centered security. In: Proceedings of the 1996 Workshop on New Security Paradigms, NSPW 1996, New York, NY, USA, pp. 27–33. Association for Computing Machinery (1996). https://doi.org/10.1145/304851.304859

Post-quantum Certificates for Electronic Travel Documents

Gaëtan Pradel[1,2(✉)] and Chris J. Mitchell[2(✉)]

[1] INCERT, Luxembourg, Luxembourg
gpradel@incert.lu
[2] Information Security Group, Royal Holloway, University of London, London, UK
me@chrismitchell.net

Abstract. Public key cryptosystems play a crucial role in the security of widely used communication protocols and in the protection of data. However, the foreseen emergence of quantum computers will break the security of most of the asymmetric cryptographic techniques used today, including those used to verify the authenticity of electronic travel documents. The security of international borders would thus be jeopardised in a quantum scenario. To overcome the threat to current asymmetric cryptography, post-quantum cryptography aims to provide practical mechanisms which are resilient to attacks using quantum computers. In this paper, we investigate the practicality of employing post-quantum digital signatures to ensure the authenticity of an electronic travel document. We created a special-purpose public key infrastructure based on these techniques, and give performance results for both creation and verification of certificates. This is the first important step towards specifying the next generation of electronic travel documents, as well as providing a valuable test use case for post-quantum techniques.

Keywords: Post-quantum cryptography · Electronic travel document · PKI · Certificates

1 Introduction

Like many modern systems, the security of electronic passports and other electronic travel documents relies on public key cryptography. The idea of making travel documents *electronic*, i.e. by adding a chip, emerged in 1988 [14], although it wasn't until the late 1990s that electronic travel documents started to appear. A few years later, the International Civil Aviation Organization (ICAO) released design specifications to enable their authenticity to be verified worldwide [23], and shortly after, in 2004, the first ICAO compliant electronic travel document was issued [4]. Initiatives such as the US Visa Waiver Program (VWP) [45] helped their adoption by forcing member states to implement these specifications for their citizens' travel documents.

Starting with the work of Juels et al. [31], since 2005 a range of security analyses of the ICAO standards have been performed [21,39]. The feature in the

© Springer Nature Switzerland AG 2020
I. Boureanu et al. (Eds.): ESORICS 2020 Workshops, LNCS 12580, pp. 56–73, 2020.
https://doi.org/10.1007/978-3-030-66504-3_4

ICAO specifications which has gone through the most changes because of security issues covers access control to the chip – see Avoine et al. [4] and Chaabouni and Vaudenay [10]. Versions of the ICAO access control protocol include the 2005 Basic Access Control (BAC) and the 2009 Extended Access Control (EAC) versions 1 and 2 [4].

Quite separately from the known issues with the ICAO protocols, the potential advent of large-scale, general-purpose, quantum computing will radically change the situation. Quantum computers can solve mathematical problems that classical computers cannot. Over the past few years, much effort has been devoted to building such a device, although experts in the field suggest that it will be one or two decades before large scale quantum computers are a reality [12]. In the post-quantum era, the currently used asymmetric cryptographic techniques, i.e. integer factorization-based schemes (such as RSA [42]) and discrete logarithm-based schemes [15]), will become breakable [40,43]. This threatens the security of a wide range of systems, including the authenticity of electronic travel documents (the main focus of this paper).

In order to address this issue, as summarised by Bernstein and Lange [7], much recent effort has been devoted to developing post-quantum cryptographic schemes, i.e. schemes secure against attacks using both quantum and classical computers. In parallel with this research effort, a number of major standardisation bodies have inaugurated projects to develop standards for post-quantum algorithms. Perhaps the most important of these is the standardisation process led by the *National Institute of Standards and Technology (NIST)* [12]. So far, from an initial 82 submissions, after Round 3 of this process only 15[1] schemes remain in the running for adoption[2].

Besides having a portfolio of cryptographic algorithms resilient to cryptanalysis using quantum computers, it is also necessary to ensure that they are practical and can interoperate with current applications and protocols based on asymmetric cryptography. For example, Kampanakis et al. [32] showed that post-quantum X.509 certificates are viable for TLS-like communication protocols for use in a "post-quantum Internet". X.509 certificates are also commonly used to protect the authenticity and integrity of data inside electronic travel documents, namely the owner's data.

The focus of this paper is on a practical trial designed to test the feasibility of using currently available post-quantum cryptographic techniques in electronic travel documents. We have implemented a post-quantum *Public Key Infrastructure (PKI)* for electronic travel documents, and have also obtained results on its performance. Since this PKI is fundamental to the operation of security for electronic travel documents, the work described here can be seen as both preliminary research for the next generation of travel documents and also a testbed for evaluating post-quantum cryptographic techniques.

---

[1] More precisely, 7 schemes are finalists and the other 8 are kept as alternatives.

[2] The results of Round 3 of the process were published on July 22, 2020, https://csrc.nist.gov/projects/post-quantum-cryptography/round-3-submissions.

In Sect. 2 we describe how security is implemented for electronic travel documents. We then explain the development of the prototype post-quantum PKI in Sect. 3 and present the challenges we encountered in Sect. 4. Finally, we discuss our results in Sect. 5 and draw conclusions in Sect. 6.

2   Security for Electronic Travel Documents

2.1   Electronic Travel Documents

For the last couple of decades, digital signatures have been used to protect electronic travel and national identity documents. The ICAO started work on *Machine Readable Travel Documents* (*MRTDs*) as long ago as the late 1960s [23]. More recently, in 1998, work commenced on *electronic MRTDs* (*e-MRTDs*), resulting in a set of specifications covering the issue and border verification of such documents [23].

The specifications include protocols and mechanisms designed to protect the data inside the contactless chips embedded in the documents and allow border controllers to securely authenticate an issued e-MRTD. In order to verify an e-MRTD, the *inspection system* (*IS*) used by border controllers for validating the authenticity of an e-MRTD, must:

1. access the contactless chip (see Sect. 2.4), where the IS proves to the chip that it is authorised to access it;
2. authenticate the card data (see Sect. 2.5), where the IS verifies that the data inside the chip (including the information in the data page[3]) is digitally signed by an appropriate authority;
3. (optionally) authenticate the contactless chip (see Sect. 2.6), where the chip proves to the IS that it is a genuine chip belonging to a genuine e-MRTD;
4. (optionally) perform extended security protocols, e.g. to gain access to specific biometric data such as fingerprint or iris information.

2.2   Public Key Infrastructures

The security of e-MRTDs rests on an underlying PKI, the operation of which is the main focus of this paper. For our purposes a PKI (see, for example, Barak [5]) is a means of distributing trusted copies of public keys for asymmetric cryptographic techniques, and relies on the use of digital signatures. It involves a collection of *public key certificates*, digitally signed by *Certification Authorities* (*CAs*), where each certificate contains a public key and associated information including the name of the owner, who is usually assumed to have the private key corresponding to the public key in the certificate. Certificates which are no longer trusted are called revoked certificates, and are listed in a *Certificate Revocation List* (*CRL*) digitally signed by a CA.

---

[3] The document data page is the page containing personal information of the document owner, such as photograph, name, date of birth, etc.

The entities participating in a PKI can be arranged as the vertices in a directed graph, where an edge goes from A to B if the certificate for B (Cert_B) was signed using A's private signature key, i.e. so that the public key of A can be used to verify Cert_B. Typically, a PKI will be arranged hierarchically, so that there is always a direct path (a *certificate chain*) from the *Root CA* to every *end-entity*.

That is, if an entity has a trusted copy of the Root CA public key (typically distributed as a self-signed *Root CA certificate*), then a trusted copy of every end-entity's public key can be obtained in the following way. First construct a certificate chain from the Root CA to the end-entity, and then verify all the certificates in the chain in turn, at each stage verifying a certificate using the public key obtained by verifying the previous certificate and the status of the certificate using the corresponding CRL.

2.3 PKI for Electronic Travel Documents

The PKI for e-MRTDs, including e-passports, typically has three levels. The Root CAs are known as *Country Signing Certification Authorities* (*CSCAs*), and, as the name suggests, are typically operated on behalf of a government department such as the Ministry of Foreign Affairs. Each country will operate a Root CSCA, and each such Root CSCA will have a digital signature key pair and a (self-signed) certificate for its public key, i.e. a public key certificate signed using the corresponding private key. A Root CSCA uses its private signing key to sign *Document Signer* (DS) *Certificates* (DSCs), containing public keys of e-MRTD manufacturers. The corresponding private signature keys are used by the manufacturers to sign information held inside an e-MRTD.

In order to prove the authenticity and integrity of an e-MRTD at a border control, the self-signed root CSCA certificates are shared among states by bilateral exchanges, through states' *Master Lists*[4] or soon using the ICAO *Public Key Directory*[5].

In a typical PKI, the Root CA is kept offline in order to diminish the risks of a potential security breach that might lead to the leakage of its private signing key, whereas the Intermediate CAs are kept online. The reason is operational, as requests are sent on a daily basis to the CAs for issuing and revoking end-entity certificates. If and when an Intermediate CA certificate needs to be revoked/renewed because of a potential compromise or expiry of its private signing key, the Root CA is activated and its private signing key is used locally to issue a new Intermediate CA certificate or revoke the current one. In a PKI for e-MRTDs, the Root CSCA is also kept offline, in line with a recommendation by ICAO [26]. There are no Intermediate CSCAs because, from an operational point of view, this role is managed by the DSs, who receive all requests for signing e-MRTD data sets.

---

[4] For example the German Master List: https://www.bsi.bund.de/SharedDocs/ Downloads/DE/BSI/ElekAusweise/CSCA/GermanMasterList.html.

[5] See https://pkddownloadsg.icao.int/.

2.4   Access to the Contactless Chip

The first step for an IS is to gain authorised access to the e-MRTD's chip. It proves to the chip that it has the necessary authorisation using one of the following two ICAO-specified protocols[6] [26]. To perform them, the IS shall have access to the *Machine Readable Zone* (*MRZ*) of the e-MRTD and be equipped to acquire it from the data page, requiring the passport to be physically opened to be read optically.

We only very briefly sketch the two protocols here, since they are not the main focus of this paper. As noted above in Sect. 1, the shortcomings of the first scheme have been widely discussed.

Basic Access Control. Basic Access Control (BAC) is based on symmetric cryptography, and consists of a three-pass challenge-response protocol in accordance with Key Establishment Mechanism 6 of ISO/IEC 11770-2 [30] using two-key Triple-DES (see ISO/IEC 18033-3 [28]). A Message Authentication Code (MAC) is appended to the ciphertexts, computed using MAC algorithm 6 of ISO/IEC 9797-1 [29].

Password Authenticated Connexion Establishment. Password Authenticated Connexion Establishment (PACE) [27] is based on asymmetric cryptography, and consists of a password-authenticated Diffie-Hellman key agreement protocol (see [9]) which supplements and enhances BAC. The chip verifies that the IS is authorised to access its data and a secure communications channel is established.

2.5   Authentication of the Data

This step, i.e. authentication of the chip-resident data, forms the main focus of this paper; verifying the validity of the e-MRTD data is probably the most important security function. This step includes a single protocol called Passive Authentication (PA) [25], so called because it does not require any computational capabilities (such as performing cryptographic operations) from the chip.

However, the storage capacity of the chip is of paramount importance for executing PA, since the chip needs to keep certain key data. In particular, all the data related to the owner, such as the data page information, owner's photo and fingerprints, etc., are stored in *Data Groups* (*DGs*) on the chip [24]. Also stored is the *Document Security Object* (SO_D), which contains the hash values of the DGs and is digitally signed with the private key of a manufacturer. The corresponding manufacturer public key is in a DSC signed with the private key associated with a root CSCA certificate (belonging to the government agency on whose behalf the manufacturer is acting). The DSC must be placed in the SO_D

---

[6] Since January 2018, states have been permitted to implement PACE but not BAC, given the known security issues with BAC; previously both protocols had to be implemented for interoperability reasons.

so that the IS can retrieve it and use it to help verify this digital signature in order to verify the integrity and authenticity of the chip data [25].

In this paper, a key focus is the size of these data elements (see Sect. 5). Post-Quantum Digital Signature Algorithms (PQDSAs) usually involve longer keys and signatures than currently used techniques [7], and thus we need to investigate the limited storage capacity of current chips to discover if they are adequate for the post-quantum era.

The PKI described in Sect. 2.3 is used in the following way to support data authentication. The IS retrieves the signed data and the DSC from the chip. The IS determines which CSCA signed the DSC, and constructs a certificate chain from the appropriate Root CSCA certificate and the DSC. Verifying this chain (using the appropriate stored trusted Root CSCA public key) enables the appropriate DSC public key to be authenticated. Finally, this public key can be used to verify the signature on the chip data.

2.6 Authentication of the Contactless Chip

The third step for the IS is to authenticate the contactless chip, although this is not mandatory. This step enables the IS to verify that the chip is genuine, preventing copying and/or substitution; it uses one of the following three protocols.

As in Sect. 2.4, the protocols for this step are only briefly sketched, since they are not the main focus of this paper.

Active Authentication. Active Authentication [25] is based on asymmetric cryptography and requires the chip to sign a challenge sent by the IS with a private key held by the chip. This means that the chip must have the computational power to perform a digital signature. The associated public key is accessible by the IS, and its authenticity has already been verified during PA (see Sect. 2.5). After verifying the signed challenge, the IS is assured of the authenticity of the chip. This technique can raise a privacy issue under specific conditions [31], as each generated signature could be logged. The owner of an e-MRTD (and thus the owner of the private key used to sign the challenges) could then be traced using the logged signatures. The Chip Authentication protocol (see below) has been devised as a replacement in order to mitigate this risk.

Chip Authentication. Chip Authentication [25] is based on asymmetric cryptography, more precisely on a variant of the Diffie-Hellman key agreement protocol [15]. In addition to guaranteeing the authenticity of the chip, it also provides authentication of the data inside the chip and a secure communication channel between chip and IS. Moreover, as the exchanged keys are ephemeral, it prevents any tracing of the e-MRTD's owner [25]. The static key pair used in the protocol is stored inside the chip; the private key is held in secure memory whereas the public key is accessible to the IS. However, Chip Authentication is subject to reset and transferability attacks [8].

PACE with Chip Authentication Mapping. PACE with Chip Authentication Mapping is a combination of PACE (Sect. 2.4) and Chip Authentication (Sect. 2.6), optimised for performance.

3   Building a Post-quantum PKI for Electronic Travel Documents

As discussed in Sect. 2.5, the authenticity of e-MRTD chip data is verified using the PA protocol. This protocol relies on the PKI established by states through their networks of CSCAs. Thus, to ensure that PA continues to provide security in the post-quantum world, a *post-quantum PKI* (*pqPKI*), i.e. a PKI based on the architecture presented in Sect. 2.3 but using post-quantum cryptography, is needed. To verify the practicality of building and operating such a PKI, we have built a proof-of-concept implementation which we next describe.

3.1   Design

For the purposes of this proof-of-concept, the PKI architecture for e-MRTDs as described in Sect. 2.3 can be simplified without loss of generality. The proof-of-concept PKI is composed of one CSCA certificate and one DSC.

Both types of certificate follow the standard structure for an X.509 certificate, signed using a PQDSA, e.g. as presented in [32], although the certificates must also be compliant with the relevant ICAO specification [26]. This latter specification defines the extensions and the associated values for each type of certificate in the e-MRTD PKI, with the details depending on their role in this structure, i.e. their *certificate profile*.

The CSCA certificate is self-signed and the associated private key is used to sign the private key associated with the DSC. The DSC is then normally used to sign an e-MRTD document; in our case this involves signing data of any type, ideally an SO_D (see Sect. 2).

3.2   Algorithm Selection

Quantum computers pose a great threat to public key cryptography, including digital signature algorithms. Signature schemes usually use a hash function, which must remain secure in a post-quantum scenario [7]. We used the hash function that the designers included in their implementation, typically SHA-3 [46].

To enable a comparison, we incorporated seven different PQDSAs into our prototype, all of which were candidates in Round 2[7] of the NIST standardisation process [12]. We chose these particular algorithms from the set of candidates for two main reasons: the cryptographic library we used (see Sect. 3.3) provides

---

[7] The experiments were run before the publication of Round 3, which was announced on July 22, 2020.

implementations of these schemes, and as their security is not based on the same mathematical properties, they cover a broad range of the hard problems underlying post-quantum cryptography. The chosen algorithms[8] are as follows:

- qTESLA [3], which is a lattice-based digital signature scheme. The hardness assumption on which the security of qTESLA is based is the R-LWE problem [35,41].
- CRYSTALS-Dilithium [17], referred simply as Dilithium here, which is also a lattice-based digital signature scheme. The hardness assumption on which the security of Dilithium is based is the M-LWE problem [2,41].
- Picnic [11], whose security is not directly based on hardness assumptions, as is usually the case in public key cryptography. Its security is rather based on a zero-knowledge proof [20] and symmetric key primitives, which makes the scheme very different from the other examples.
- FALCON [18] is also a lattice-based digital signature scheme, based on the work of Gentry et al. [19]. Its hardness assumption is based on the Short-Integer-Solution (SIS) [1] problem over NTRU lattices [22].
- MQDSS [13] is based on the hardness of the multivariate quadratic problem.
- Rainbow [16] is also based on the hardness of the multivariate quadratic problem.
- SPHINCS+ [6] is a set of three stateless hash-based signature schemes. The three schemes differ by the hash function used. We decided to use only two of the schemes, one instantiated with SHAKE256 (which is part of the SHA-3 family [46]) and the other with Haraka [34].

3.3   Implementation

To implement the prototype, we used a fork of OpenSSL combined with the library liboqs from the *Open Quantum Safe (OQS)* project [44]. OpenSSL is an open-source implementation of the Transport Layer Security (TLS) and Secure Sockets Layer (SSL) protocols, and incorporates a widely used cryptographic primitives library. It was not designed to establish PKIs, such as a PKI for e-MRTDs; however, despite this we decided to use this software because of its wide use and flexibility.

liboqs is an open-source library in C of post-quantum algorithms, which has been integrated into prototype forks of OpenSSL and OpenSSH. liboqs includes algorithms from the NIST Post Quantum Standardization Project. To generate the PKI for e-MRTDs described in Sect. 3.1, we implemented an OpenSSL configuration file that caused it to issue certificates with the appropriate extensions. The configuration file included all the certificate components and extensions needed by each certificate type, as defined in the relevant certificate profile, i.e. a CSCA certificate or a DSC, as specified in ICAO Doc 9303 Part 12 [26].

---

[8] Some of the chosen algorithms did not advance to Round 3 of the NIST competition. The results are published on the following website: https://csrc.nist.gov/projects/post-quantum-cryptography/round-3-submissions.

3.4 Overview of Experiments Performed

For each of the selected PQDSAs (together with two currently used schemes for comparison purposes), we performed the following steps.

1. We generated a key pair to be associated with the root CSCA certificate, with the parameter sets corresponding to the highest NIST security level available [38].
2. We generated a *Certificate Signing Request* (*CSR*) with the previously generated key pair and the CSCA certificate profile in order to create a (self-signed) CSCA certificate.
3. We generated a key pair to be associated with the DSC, with the parameter sets corresponding to the lowest NIST security level available [38].
4. We generated another CSR with the key pair generated in step (3) and the DS certificate profile to create a DSC signed using the CSCA private key generated in step (1).
5. We hashed and signed a random data string using the private key associated with the DSC to complete the chain.

The two key pairs generated in step (1) and (3) do not have the same parameter sets because their role is quite different (see [26] for more details). The key pair from step (1) has a long lifespan (it can be as much as one to two decades) and is used from time to time to verify or renew DSCs; thus a high NIST security level is required. The key pair from step (3) however has a much shorter lifespan (it can be days, weeks or months depending on the configuration chosen by the relevant state) and is used to sign the chip data of many e-MRTDs (during their production) in order to ensure their authenticity. To optimize performance, a lower NIST security level seems adequate.

4   Challenges

OpenSSL is an implementation of SSL/TLS, and is not designed to generate and manage a PKI producing certificates for signing e-MRTDs according to the relevant ICAO specifications [25,26]. For example, extensions such as *Private Key Usage period*, which are required by ICAO, cannot be set up with OpenSSL, although they can be displayed. To overcome this difficulty, we took advantage of the fact that OpenSSL allows integration of ad hoc extensions created by the user via the Arbitrary Extension module[9]. This allows an implementer to encode arbitrary extensions in created certificates[10].

A problem was encountered when trying to create a certificate chain. Although the software produced chains using well-established digital signature schemes, it refused to produce them for the chosen post-quantum algorithms. We reported the problem to the authors of the `liboqs` library, and simultaneously

---

[9] https://www.openssl.org/docs/manmaster/man5/x509v3_config.html.

[10] An example of such an ad hoc extension is given at: http://openssl.6102.n7.nabble.com/Private-Key-Usage-Period-td28401.html.

worked on a resolution. The issue has been resolved and the documentation for the software has been updated[11].

5 Results

We generated certificates according to the two certificate profiles described in Sect. 3 (CSCA certificate and DSC) for ten algorithms and two parameter sets, and in each case measured the memory needed to store them and their generation time. To perform the operations we used an Ubuntu 18.04.2 LTS $x86\_64$ machine with 8GB of RAM and a four-core Intel(R) Core(TM) i5-3470 CPU @ 3.20GHz. Two of the ten algorithms used were long-established signature schemes (RSASSA-PSS [37] and ECDSA [33] with the Brainpool parameters [36]), which were included for comparison purposes. We chose these algorithms because they are currently used by governments in their CSCAs[12] (see [4] for more details). The eight other algorithms were the PQDSAs presented in Sect. 3. Note that in the results reported below, certificate generation included both key pair generation and signing of the certificate, apart from Fig. 1a, b and c for which the different steps of the certificate issuance process have been clearly separated. Table 1 summarises the algorithms and key lengths used for the two certificate types.

Table 1. Algorithms and key lengths by certificate type

	CSCA certificate	DSC
RSASSA-PSS	4096 bits with SHA-256	2048 bits with SHA-256
Brainpool	384 bits with SHA-256	224 bits with SHA-256
qTESLA	qTESLA-p-III with SHAKE256	qTESLA-p-I with SHAKE128
Dilithium	Dilithium-4 with SHAKE256	Dilithium-2 with SHAKE128
Picnic	Picnic2-L5-FS with SHAKE256	Picnic2-L1-FS with SHAKE128
FALCON	FALCON-1024 with SHAKE256	FALCON-1024 with SHAKE256
MQDSS	MQDSS-31-64 with SHAKE256	MQDSS-31-48 with SHAKE256
Rainbow	Rainbow-Vc with SHA-512	Rainbow-Ia with SHA-256
SPHINCS+	SPHINCS-Haraka-256f-robust	SPHINCS-Haraka-128f-robust
SPHINCS+	SPHINCS-SHAKE256-256f-robust	SPHINCS-SHAKE256-128f-robust

To construct a post-quantum PKI, we separated certificate generation into three steps, according to the process described in Sect. 3.1, as follows:

1. generation of the key pair;
2. generation of the CSR; and

---

[11] See resolution in https://github.com/open-quantum-safe/openssl/issues/68.

[12] In particular, the CSCA certificate from Luxembourg is signed using RSASSA-PSS. See https://repository.incert.lu/ for more details.

3. generation of the certificate (including the digital signature of the CSR generated in step (2) using the key generated in step (1)).

To be consistent with the associated certificate profile, the CSCA certificates were all self-signed and the DSCs were signed with a CSCA private key from the same algorithm family, e.g. a DSC including a qTESLA-p-I public key was signed with a qTESLA-p-III private key. We measured the execution time for 1000 iterations. The results are shown in Figs. 1a, b and c respectively for each generation step. Figure 1d shows the total execution time for the three steps.

Overall, Dilithium is the best performing PQDSA, and even has a slightly better performance then Brainpool. The most secure version of Rainbow gave the worst performance, since key generation is very slow. Similar remarks apply to RSASSA-PSS. However, the less secure version of Rainbow performed better for the DSCs, as SPHINCS-SHAKE was slower. In particular, for SPHINCS-SHAKE and also Picnic, as expected their key generation is quite fast, although computing signatures is much slower than for their counterparts. All the other PQDSAs give results that are of the same order of magnitude, except qTESLA which gave similar results to Dilithium and Brainpool, but still performs much better than RSASSA-PSS.

In addition, we generated as many certificates as possible during a five-second period for each certificate profile, algorithm and key length. The results are exactly as expected based on Fig. 1d. Again, Dilithium shows on average better performance than all the other schemes, with Brainpool and qTESLA almost as good. Because of slow key pair generation or signature computation, we managed to generate on average only a few CSCA certificates and DSCs with the four worst performing algorithms: Rainbow, Picnic, SPHINCS-SHAKE and RSASSA-PSS.

With respect to computation, the performance of several post-quantum schemes was actually superior to that of the existing algorithms. However, we also examined the memory space necessary to store the various certificates. This is a crucial point to consider in practice because of the limited memory capacity of contactless chips.

The certificates based on the two classical algorithms were significantly smaller than all of those based on post-quantum algorithms (see Fig. 3a), although Falcon and Dilithium yielded much shorter certificates than their peers. When considering the sizes of the generated key pairs (see Fig. 3b), we obtained heterogeneous results. PQDSAs based on symmetric cryptography such as Picnic and SPHINCS+ have extremely short keys. Brainpool has similar key sizes. As for Rainbow, both certificate and key sizes are much greater than any of the other algorithms. Figures 3a and b suggest that, as far as storage is concerned, Falcon is the best post-quantum candidate, with Dilithium not far behind.

Over and above these somewhat abstract performance results, we wanted to consider how a switch to post-quantum algorithms would affect the "real world". That is, we wanted to assess the impact of a move to the post-quantum world on the generation and management of CSCA certificates and DSCs for government authorities (Fig. 2).

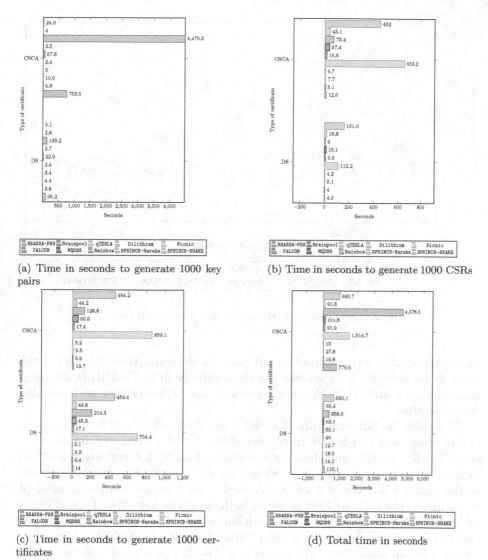

(a) Time in seconds to generate 1000 key pairs

(b) Time in seconds to generate 1000 CSRs

(c) Time in seconds to generate 1000 certificates

(d) Total time in seconds

Fig. 1. Performance results

We used as an example Luxembourg, in which the management of the PKI for generating the digital signatures of e-MRTDs has been assigned to a public agency[13] under the authority of the Ministry of Economy and the Ministry of Foreign Affairs.

We did not consider the computational power of the contactless chips inside the e-MRTDs, but rather the memory space available in those chips (see Sect. 2).

---

[13] https://www.incert.lu.

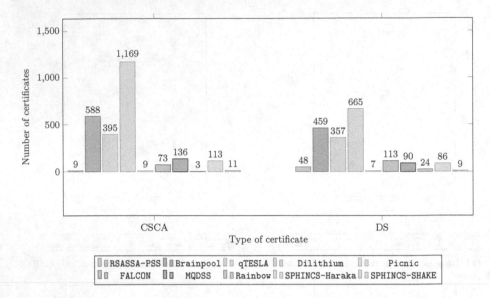

Fig. 2. Throughput of certificates in a five-second period

As explained above, the computational power of the contactless chips is not the main focus here. Such issues are the responsibility of the e-MRTD and chip manufacturers, and a CSCA, as a purchaser, has little say over such detailed design matters.

Typically, the infrastructure of a PKI is based on servers and hardware security modules, and can be arbitrarily expanded. CSCA certificates are re-issued every 3 to 5 years [26], and thus any cost change for CSCA certificate generation in terms of performance and memory will not be an issue. Two criteria are used to determine when DSCs must be renewed: their lifespan and the number of signatures performed. As best practice, both should be kept low. Typical limits might be a lifespan of at most one month and a limit of 100 000 e-MRTDs. In the case of Luxembourg, with only around 600 000 inhabitants of which only half are citizens, we can assume that the production of e-MRTDs is much less than many other countries. With this number of citizens, each DSC is most unlikely to reach the threshold of 100 000 digital signatures. For the algorithms we examined, we have disparate results. For some PQDSAs, both key generation and signing are faster than for the classical schemes, although this was not universally true.

When considering the memory space capacities of the contactless chip inside e-MRTDs, we only check that the chip provides enough memory space to store the post-quantum certificates and signatures necessary to perform PA, a protocol which does not require any computational power from the chip (see Sect. 2.5). Current chips[14] for e-MRTDs can have as much as 160 Kbytes of EEPROM

---

[14] See for example these contactless cryptocontrollers: https://www.infineon.com/cms/en/product/security-smart-card-solutions/security-controllers/sle-78/.

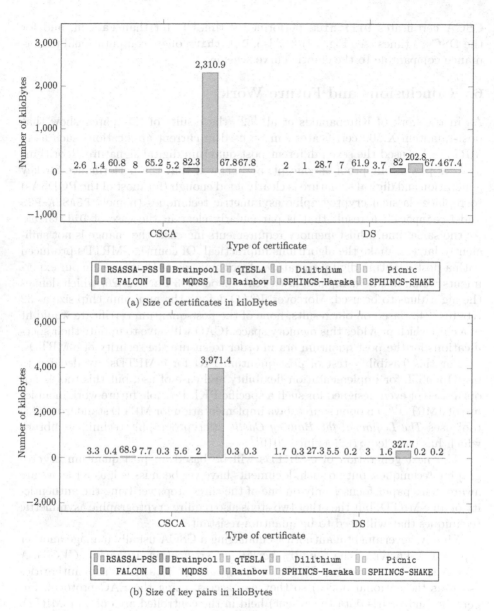

(a) Size of certificates in kiloBytes

(b) Size of key pairs in kiloBytes

Fig. 3. Memory space results

memory and 280 Kbytes of User ROM. This would be large enough to store a post-quantum certificate and digital signatures for all of the PQDSAs we studied except Rainbow.

If we consider both computational and storage requirements, Dilithium offers the best performance overall. Falcon has very low storage requirements, but performs worse than Dilithium computationally. In particular, for the

CSCA certificates `Dilithium` performed 7 times faster than `Falcon`, and for the DSCs, 4 times (see Fig. 1d)[15]. Also, `Dilithium` offers computational performance comparable to the elliptic curve scheme.

6   Conclusions and Future Work

As in the work of Kampanakis et al. [32], the results of this paper show that post-quantum X.509 certificates can be used in current applications such as e-MRTDs. We used the seven different post-quantum digital signature algorithms as examples in our proof-of-concept, and showed that the performance for key generation and digital signature is clearly good enough (for most of the PQDSAs) to replace classical cryptographic asymmetric techniques (namely `RSASSA-PSS` and `Brainpool`), a result that is particularly clear in the case of `Dilithium`. At the same time, whilst memory requirements increase, the change is not sufficiently large to make the algorithms impractical. Of course, e-MRTDs produced with a post-quantum digital signature algorithm such as those used in our experiments would not be compliant with ICAO Doc 9303 Part 12 [26] which defines the algorithms to be used. Moreover, ICAO defines the minimum chip size as 32 Kbytes [24]. Based on our results, none of the post-quantum certificate would fit in a chip which provides this memory space. ICAO will have to update their specifications for the post-quantum era in order to ensure the security of e-MRTDs.

For this feasibility test of post-quantum PKI for e-MRTDs, we decided to use OpenSSL for implementation flexibility and ease of use, but this tool is not optimised or even designed for such a specific PKI. Possible future work includes use of JMRTD[16], an open source Java implementation for MRTD standards. This tool uses *The Legion of the Bouncy Castle*, a cryptographic techniques library which has included `qTESLA` since 2019[17].

The next generation of e-MRTDs will be based on post-quantum cryptographic techniques, but no such documents have yet been issued, as far as we are aware. This paper focuses only on one of the three steps verifying the authenticity of an e-MRTD, but the other two steps also require cryptographic asymmetric techniques that will need to be quantum-resistant.

Finally, governmental authorities managing a CSCA usually manage another type of CA, known as the *Country Verifying Certification Authority* (*CVCA*). A CVCA is used to issue *Card Verifiable Certificates* (*CVCs*) to control authorities (such as the national police) so they can access, using the EAC protocol, fingerprint and/or iris data (if present) held in the controlled area of an e-MRTD. Further experiments will also be required to check possible post-quantum migration paths for this class of lightweight certificates.

Acknowledgements. Supported by the Luxembourg National Research Fund (FNR) (12602667).

---

[15] These results are in line with the NIST Round 3 statement: https://nvlpubs.nist.gov/nistpubs/ir/2020/NIST.IR.8309.pdf.

[16] https://jmrtd.org/.

[17] Please see https://www.bouncycastle.org/releasenotes.html.

References

1. Ajtai, M.: Generating hard instances of lattice problems (extended abstract). In: STOC, pp. 99–108. ACM (1996)
2. Albrecht, M.R., Deo, A.: Large modulus ring-LWE $\geq$ module-LWE. In: Takagi, T., Peyrin, T. (eds.) ASIACRYPT 2017, Part I. LNCS, vol. 10624, pp. 267–296. Springer, Cham (2017). https://doi.org/10.1007/978-3-319-70694-8_10
3. Alkim, E., Barreto, P.S.L.M., Bindel, N., Longa, P., Ricardini, J.E.: The lattice-based digital signature scheme qtesla. Cryptology ePrint Archive, Report 2019/085 (2019)
4. Avoine, G., Beaujeant, A., Hernandez-Castro, J., Demay, L., Teuwen, P.: A survey of security and privacy issues in ePassport protocols. ACM Comput. Surv. **48**(3), 471–4737 (2016)
5. Barak, B.: The complexity of public-key cryptography. Tutorials on the Foundations of Cryptography. ISC, pp. 45–77. Springer, Cham (2017). https://doi.org/10.1007/978-3-319-57048-8_2
6. Bernstein, D.J., Hülsing, A., Kölbl, S., Niederhagen, R., Rijneveld, J., Schwabe, P.: The sphincs$^+$ signature framework. In: ACM Conference on Computer and Communications Security, pp. 2129–2146. ACM (2019)
7. Bernstein, D.J., Lange, T.: Post-quantum cryptography – dealing with the fallout of physics success. Cryptology ePrint Archive, Report 2017/314 (2017)
8. Blundo, C., Persiano, G., Sadeghi1, A.R., Visconti, I.: Resettable and non-transferable chip authentication for e-passports. In: Workshop on RFID Security (RFIDSec 2008) (2008)
9. BSI: Elliptic curve cryptography. Technical guideline, Federal Office for Information Security, Bonn, Germany (2018)
10. Chaabouni, R., Vaudenay, S.: The extended access control for machine readable travel documents. In: BIOSIG. LNI, vol. P-155, pp. 93–103. GI (2009)
11. Chase, M., et al.: Post-quantum zero-knowledge and signatures from symmetric-key primitives. In: ACM Conference on Computer and Communications Security. pp. 1825–1842. ACM (2017)
12. Chen, L., et al.: Report on post-quantum cryptography. Report, US Department of Commerce, National Institute of Standards and Technology (2016)
13. Chen, M., Hülsing, A., Rijneveld, J., Samardjiska, S., Schwabe, P.: From 5-pass MQ -based identification to MQ -based signatures. In: ASIACRYPT (2). LNCS, vol. 10032, pp. 135–165 (2016)
14. Davida, G.I., Desmedt, Y.G.: Passports and visas versus IDs. In: Barstow, D., et al. (eds.) EUROCRYPT 1988. LNCS, vol. 330, pp. 183–188. Springer, Heidelberg (1988). https://doi.org/10.1007/3-540-45961-8_16
15. Diffie, W., Hellman, M.E.: New directions in cryptography. IEEE Trans. Inf. Theory **22**(6), 644–654 (1976)
16. Ding, J., Schmidt, D.: Rainbow, a new multivariable polynomial signature scheme. In: Ioannidis, J., Keromytis, A., Yung, M. (eds.) ACNS 2005. LNCS, vol. 3531, pp. 164–175. Springer, Heidelberg (2005). https://doi.org/10.1007/11496137_12
17. Ducas, L., et al.: Crystals-dilithium: a lattice-based digital signature scheme. IACR Trans. Cryptogr. Hardw. Embed. Syst. **2018**(1), 238–268 (2018)
18. Fouque, P.A., et al.: Falcon: Fast-fourier lattice-based compact signatures over NTRU (2017)
19. Gentry, C., Peikert, C., Vaikuntanathan, V.: Trapdoors for hard lattices and new cryptographic constructions. In: STOC, pp. 197–206. ACM (2008)

20. Goldwasser, S., Micali, S., Rackoff, C.: The knowledge complexity of interactive proof-systems (extended abstract). In: STOC, pp. 291–304. ACM (1985)

21. Hoepman, J.-H., Hubbers, E., Jacobs, B., Oostdijk, M., Schreur, R.W.: Crossing borders: security and privacy issues of the european e-passport. In: Yoshiura, H., Sakurai, K., Rannenberg, K., Murayama, Y., Kawamura, S. (eds.) IWSEC 2006. LNCS, vol. 4266, pp. 152–167. Springer, Heidelberg (2006). https://doi.org/10.1007/11908739_11

22. Hoffstein, J., Pipher, J., Silverman, J.H.: NTRU: a ring-based public key cryptosystem. In: Buhler, J.P. (ed.) ANTS 1998. LNCS, vol. 1423, pp. 267–288. Springer, Heidelberg (1998). https://doi.org/10.1007/BFb0054868

23. International Civil Aviation Organization (ICAO): Doc 9303 – Machine Readable Travel Documents – Part 1: Introduction. Technical report, 7th Edn. ICAO, Montréal, CA (2015)

24. International Civil Aviation Organization (ICAO): Doc 9303 – Machine Readable Travel Documents – Part 10: Logical Data Structure (LDS) for Storage of Biometrics and Other Data in the Contactless Integrated Circuit (IC). Technical report, 7th Edn. ICAO, Montréal, CA (2015)

25. International Civil Aviation Organization (ICAO): Doc 9303 – Machine Readable Travel Documents – Part 11: Security Mechanisms for MRTDs. Technical report, 7th Edn. ICAO, Montréal, CA (2015)

26. International Civil Aviation Organization (ICAO): Doc 9303 – Machine Readable Travel Documents – Part 12: Public Key Infrastructure for MRTDs. Technical report, 7th Edn. ICAO, Montréal, CA (2015)

27. International Civil Aviation Organization (ICAO): Supplemental Access Control for Machine Readable Travel Documents. Technical report, Version 1.01. ICAO, Montréal, CA (2015)

28. ISO Central Secretary: Information technology – Security techniques – Encryption algorithms – Part 3: Block ciphers. Standard ISO/IEC 18033–3:2010, International Organization for Standardization, Geneva, CH (2010)

29. ISO Central Secretary: Information technology – Security techniques – Message Authentication Codes (MACs) – Part 1: Mechanisms using a block cipher. Standard ISO/IEC 9797–1:2011, International Organization for Standardization, Geneva, CH (2011)

30. ISO Central Secretary: IT Security techniques – Key management – Part 2: Mechanisms using symmetric techniques. Standard ISO/IEC 11770–2:2018, International Organization for Standardization, Geneva, CH (2018)

31. Juels, A., Molnar, D., Wagner, D.A.: Security and privacy issues in e-passports. In: First International Conference on Security and Privacy for Emerging Areas in Communications Networks, SecureComm 2005, Athens, Greece, 5–9 September 2005, pp. 74–88. IEEE (2005)

32. Kampanakis, P., Panburana, P., Daw, E., Geest, D.V.: The viability of post-quantum x.509 certificates. Cryptology ePrint Archive, Report 2018/063 (2018)

33. Kerry, C.F., Secretary, A., Director, C.R.: FIPS PUB 186–4 Digital Signature Standard (DSS) (2013)

34. Kölbl, S., Lauridsen, M.M., Mendel, F., Rechberger, C.: Haraka v2 - efficient short-input hashing for post-quantum applications. IACR Trans. Symmetric Cryptol. **2016**(2), 1–29 (2016)

35. Lyubashevsky, V., Peikert, C., Regev, O.: On ideal lattices and learning with errors over rings. In: Gilbert, H. (ed.) EUROCRYPT 2010. LNCS, vol. 6110, pp. 1–23. Springer, Heidelberg (2010). https://doi.org/10.1007/978-3-642-13190-5_1

36. Merkle, J., Lochter, M.: Elliptic Curve Cryptography (ECC) Brainpool Standard Curves and Curve Generation. RFC 5639, March 2010
37. Moriarty, K.M., Kaliski, B., Jonsson, J., Rusch, A.: PKCS#1: RSA Cryptography Specifications Version 2.2. RFC 8017, November 2016
38. National Institute of Standards and Technology: Submission requirements and evaluation criteria for the post-quantum cryptography standardization process. Report, US Department of Commerce, December 2016
39. Pasupathinathan, V., Pieprzyk, J., Wang, H.: Security analysis of Australian and E.U. e-passport implementation. J. Res. Pract. Inf. Technol. 40(3), 187–206 (2008)
40. Proos, J., Zalka, C.: Shor's discrete logarithm quantum algorithm for elliptic curves. Quantum Inf. Comput. 3(4), 317–344 (2003)
41. Regev, O.: On lattices, learning with errors, random linear codes, and cryptography. In: STOC, pp. 84–93. ACM (2005)
42. Rivest, R.L., Shamir, A., Adleman, L.M.: A method for obtaining digital signatures and public-key cryptosystems. Commun. ACM 21(2), 120–126 (1978)
43. Shor, P.W.: Polynomial-time algorithms for prime factorization and discrete logarithms on a quantum computer. SIAM J. Comput. 26(5), 1484–1509 (1997)
44. Stebila, D., Mosca, M.: Post-quantum key exchange for the internet and the open quantum safe project. In: Avanzi, R., Heys, H. (eds.) SAC 2016. LNCS, vol. 10532, pp. 14–37. Springer, Cham (2017). https://doi.org/10.1007/978-3-319-69453-5_2
45. United States Department of Homeland Security: United states customs and border protection: Visage waiver passport requirements, October 2006
46. U.S. DoC/NIST: Sha-3 standard: Permutation-based hash and extendable-output functions. Standard, National Institute for Standards and Technology (2015)

Development of Trust Infrastructures for Virtual Asset Service Providers

Thomas Hardjono[✉]

MIT Connection Science and Engineering, Massachusetts Institute of Technology,
Cambridge, MA 02139, USA
hardjono@mit.edu

Abstract. Virtual asset service providers (VASPs) currently face a
number of challenges, both from the technological and the regulatory
perspectives. In the context of virtual asset transfers one key issue is the
need for VASPs to securely exchange customer information to comply to
the Travel Rule. We discuss a VASP *information sharing network* as one
form of a trust infrastructure for VASP-to-VASP interactions. Related to
this is the need for a trusted *identity infrastructure for VASPs* that would
permit other entities to quickly ascertain the legal business status of a
VASP. For customers of VASPs there is a need for seamless integration
between the VASP services and the existing consumer identity management infrastructure, providing a user-friendly experience for transferring
virtual assets to other users. Finally, for regulated wallets, an *attestation
infrastructure* may provide VASPs and insurance providers with better
visibility into the state of wallets based on trusted hardware.

Keywords: Virtual assets · Blockchains · Trust · Infrastructure

1 Introduction

It has been over a decade since the advent of the Bitcoin cryptocurrency system [34] based on the hash-chain model of Haber and Stornetta [15]. Considerable interest, hype and speculative investments have gone into various projects
on blockchains aimed at developing decentralized virtual asset ecosystems. At
the same time, there has been a growing trend of theft and misappropriation of
virtual assets [36,43]. Additionally, crypto-currencies are still being exploited for
money-laundering [4,40], raising significant concern on the part of regulators.

The FATF Recommendation No. 15 [8] that was finalized in mid-2019 provided a definition of virtual assets and virtual asset service providers (VASP).
This places VASPs under the same Anti-Money Laundering (AML) regulations
as that of traditional financial institutions, notably the Travel Rule in the case
of asset transfers. In short, the Travel Rule requires a VASP to obtain, validate
and retain their customers' personal information as part of compliance to the
AML regulations. In the case of virtual asset transfers between an originator
and a beneficiary, their corresponding VASPs must share validated information
about the originator and beneficiary.

© Springer Nature Switzerland AG 2020
I. Boureanu et al. (Eds.): ESORICS 2020 Workshops, LNCS 12580, pp. 74–91, 2020.
https://doi.org/10.1007/978-3-030-66504-3_5

Today many users possessing virtual assets (e.g. cryptocurrencies) expect asset transfers through VASPs to be confirmed or settled in a matter of seconds or minutes. However, the need for VASPs to exchange validated customer information prior to asset transfers may impose delays on the settlement of transfers. Furthermore, VASPs currently do not as yet have a standard mechanism (protocol) to exchange their respective customer information in a secure and reliable manner.

We believe that this lack of a standard information exchange mechanism points to a more fundamental challenge facing the VASP community worldwide: namely the lack of *trust infrastructures* that are highly scalable and interoperable, which permit business-trust and legal-trust to be established for peer-to-peer transactions of virtual assets across different jurisdictions.

In the current work we discuss three forms trust infrastructures relevant to the VASP industry as a whole. The first is an *information sharing infrastructure* specifically for VASPs (Sect. 3). The main purpose of a VASP information sharing infrastructure is to securely and confidentially share customer information in the context of virtual asset transfers. Related to this information sharing network is the VASP *identity infrastructure* that permits VASPs and other entities to quickly ascertain the business legal status of other VASPs (Sect. 4).

Most users will seek to re-use their current Internet identifier (e.g. email address) as a means to identify each other. Most end-users will not remember the public-keys of friends and colleagues, and thus will resort to using their Internet identifiers. As such, there is a need for VASP services to integrate seamlessly into the existing consumer digital identity infrastructure (Sect. 5).

Finally, if wallets become a popular means for consumers and enterprises to holds cryptographic keys and to initiate (or sign) transactions, then there may be a need for these wallets to have device-attestations capabilities. This permits an entity (e.g. asset insurance provider) to obtain assurance that a key truly reside within a given device and that a copy of the key has not been extracted (copied out) by the user. However, this capability on the side the of wallets can only be meaningful if an *attestation infrastructure* exists on the part of VASPs and insurance providers – namely an infrastructure that permits the correct appraisal of the attestation-evidence yielded by a wallet device. This is the topic of Sect. 6. We close the paper with some conclusions in Sect. 7.

2   The Travel Rule and VASP Customer Information

With the emergence of blockchain technologies, virtual assets and cryptocurrencies, the FATF recognized the need to adequately mitigate the money laundering (ML) and terrorist financing (TF) risks associated with virtual asset activities. The *Financial Action Task Force* (FATF) is an inter-governmental body established in 1989 by the ministers of its member countries or jurisdictions. The objectives of the FATF are to set standards and promote effective implementation of legal, regulatory and operational measures for combating money laundering, terrorist financing and other related threats to the integrity of the international financial system.

The FATF Recommendation 15 [8,9] defines a *virtual asset* as a digital representation of value that can be digitally traded, or transferred, and can be used for payment or investment purposes. Virtual assets do not include digital representations of fiat currencies, securities and other financial assets that are already covered elsewhere in the FATF Recommendations. The FATF defines a *virtual asset service provider* (VASP) to be any natural or legal person who is not covered elsewhere under the Recommendations, and as a business conducts one or more of the following activities or operations for or on behalf of another natural or legal person: (i) exchange between virtual assets and fiat currencies; (ii) exchange between one or more forms of virtual assets; (iii) transfer of virtual assets; (iv) safekeeping and/or administration of virtual assets or instruments enabling control over virtual assets; and (v) participation in and provision of financial services related to an issuer's offer and/or sale of a virtual asset.

The implication of the Recommendation 15, among others, is that VASPs must be able to share the originator and beneficiary information for virtual asset transactions. This process – also known as the *Travel Rule* – originates from under the US Bank Secrecy Act (BSA - 31 USC 5311 - 5330), which mandates that financial institutions deliver certain types of information to the next financial institution when a funds transmittal event involves more than one financial institution. This customer information includes (i) originator's name; (ii) originator's account number (e.g. at the Originating-VASP); (iii) originator's geographical address, or national identity number, or customer identification number (or date and place of birth); (iv) beneficiary's name; (v) beneficiary account number (e.g. at the Beneficiary-VASP).

It is important to emphasize that a VASP as a business entity must be able to respond comprehensively to legitimate inquiries from law enforcement regarding one or more of its customers owning virtual assets (e.g. legal SAR inquiries/warrants). More specifically, both the Originator-VASP and Beneficiary-VASP must possess the complete and accurate *actual* personal information (i.e. data) regarding their account holders (i.e. customer). This need for actual data, therefore, precludes the use of advanced cryptographic techniques that aim to prevent disclosure while yielding implied knowledge, such as those based on Zero-Knowledge Proof (ZKP) schemes [14].

Although beyond the scope for the current work, one of the key challenging issues related to the Travel Rule is the privacy of customer information [7] once it has been delivered between VASPs. More specifically, if a Beneficiary-VASP is located under a different legal jurisdiction (e.g. foreign country) observing weaker privacy regulations than the originator's jurisdiction, there are no means for the originator to ensure her customer information is not leaked or stolen from that Beneficiary-VASP.

As such, operating standards for customer data retention and data privacy protection – and the means to evaluate their implementation – need to be developed for the VASP industry globally. The lack of assurance regarding the handling of customer data may deter consumers from using VASP services for virtual asset transfers.

3   Information Sharing Infrastructure for VASPs

A core part of an information sharing infrastructure is a network shared among VASPs to exchange information about themselves and their customers. The notion of an *out-of-band* (off-chain) TCP/IP based network for VASPs to share information was first proposed in [18] as part of the broader discussion within the FATF Private Sector Consultative Forum leading up to the finalization of Recommendation 15 in mid-2019. The TCP/IP Internet has achieved technological maturity and today provides connection resilience and speed for various applications. The idea of a customer information sharing network is in itself not new, and the banking community established such a network over two decades ago (i.e. the SWIFT network [11]). Today this network is the backbone for global correspondent banking.

There are several fundamental requirements for an information sharing network for VASPs (Fig. 1):

- *Security, reliability and confidentiality of transport*: The VASP information sharing network must provide security, reliability and confidentiality of communications between an Originator-VASP and Beneficiary-VASP. Several standards exist already that may fulfill this requirement (e.g. IPsec VPNs, TLS-based secure channels [38], etc.).
- *Strong end-point identification and authentication*: VASPs must use strong endpoint identification and authentication mechanisms to ensure source and destination authenticity and to prevent (reduce) man-in-the-middle types of attacks. Mechanisms such as X.509 certificates [5,25] have been used for over two decades across various industries, government and defense as a practical means to achieve this goal [18].
- *Correlation of customer information with on-chain transactions*: There must be a mechanism to permit a VASP to accurately correlate (match) between customer information (exchanged within the VASP information sharing network) and the blockchain transactions belonging to the respective customers. This must be true also in the case of *batch transactions* performed by a VASP (e.g. in the commingled accounts business model) [21].
- *Consent from originator and beneficiary for customer information exchange*: Unambiguous consent [7] must be obtained by VASPs from their customers with regards to the transmittal of customer personal information to another VASP. Additionally, a Beneficiary-VASP must obtain consent from its beneficiary customer to receive asset transfers into the customer's account.

Efforts are currently underway to begin addressing the need for a VASP information sharing network to support VASPs in complying to the various aspects of the Travel Rule (see [26,39]). A standard customer information model has recently been developed [24] that would allow VASPs to interoperate with each other with semantic consistency.

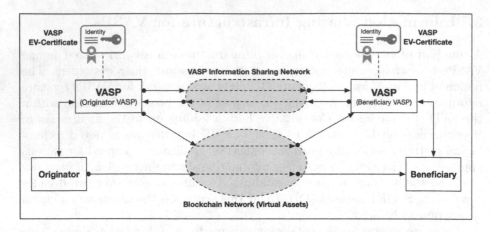

Fig. 1. Overview of VASP information sharing network (after [18,26])

4   A Trusted Identity Infrastructure for VASPs

Related to the information sharing infrastructure is a VASP *trusted identity infrastructure* that permits VASPs to prove their identity, public-key(s), and legal business information.

A trusted identity infrastructure must address the various challenges around VASP identities and provide the following types of mechanism:

- *Discovery of VASP identity and verification of business status*: Mechanism are needed to permit any entity on the Internet to ascertain whether a virtual asset service provider is a regulated VASP within a given jurisdiction. An Originator-VASP must be able to easily locate the identity information for Beneficiary-VASP and to rapidly determine the business and legal status of that Beneficiary-VASP (vice versa).
- *Discovery and verification of VASP public-keys*: Mechanism are needed to permit any entity on the Internet to ascertain whether a given public-key legally belongs to (operated by) a given VASP.
- *Discovery and verification of VASP service endpoints*: Mechanisms are needed to permit a VASP to ascertain whether it is connecting to the legitimate service endpoints (e.g. URL) of another VASP (and not a rogue endpoint belonging to an attacker).
- *Discovery of VASPs using customer identifiers*: Mechanisms are needed to permit a VASP to search and discover a binding (association) between a customer user-friendly identifier (e.g. email address) and the VASP (one or more) that may hold an account for that customer.

4.1   Extended Validation Certificates for VASP Business Identity

The problem of discovering and verifying service provider public-keys and service endpoints was faced by numerous online merchants nearly two decades ago.

For the end-user (i.e. home consumer) it was increasingly difficult to distinguish between a legitimate service provider (e.g. online merchant) from rogue web-servers that mimic the look-and-feel of legitimate merchants. In response to a growing trend of man-in-the-middle attacks, a number of browser vendors established an alliance in the late 2000s – called the *CA/Browser Forum* (CAB Forum) – that brought together browser vendors and X.509 certification authorities (CA). The CAB forum, as an industry standards-defining organization, published a number of industry technical specifications for *Extended Validation* (EV) identity certificates [2]. The overall goal was to enhance the basic X.509 certificate [5,25] with additional business related information regarding the subject (i.e. the online merchant). The CA that issues EV-certificates must perform the various information background checks regarding the subject, to ensure that the subject was a legitimate business. Correspondingly, the browser vendors supported EV-certificates by pre-installing a copy of the root CA certificate of all compliant CAs into their browser software.

We believe a similar approach is suitable for fulfilling a number of the VASP requirements discussed above. Some of the subject (VASP) business information to be included in the VASP identity EV-certificate could be as follows [26]:

- *Organization name*: The Organization field must contain the full legal name of the VASP legal entity controlling the VASP service endpoint, as listed in the official records in the VASP's jurisdiction.
- *VASP Alternative Name Extension*: The Domain Name(s) owned or controlled by the VASP and to be associated with the VASP's server as the endpoint associated with the certificate.
- *VASP Incorporation Number or LEI* (if available): This field must contain the unique Incorporation Number assigned by the Incorporating Agency in the jurisdiction of incorporation. If an LEI number [13] is available, then the LEI number should be used instead.
- *VASP Address of Place of Business*: This is the address of the physical location of the VASP's Place of Business.
- *VASP Jurisdiction of Incorporation or Registration*: This field contain information regarding the Incorporating Agency or Registration Agency.
- *VASP Number*: This is the globally unique VASP number, if available (see OpenVASP [39]).
- *EV Certificate Policy Object Identifier*: This is the identifier for the policies that determine the certificate processing rules. Such policies could be created by the organization using the certificate, such a consortium of VASPs (see Sect. 4.3 below).

4.2 VASP Transactions-Signing and Claims-Signing Certificates

For assets in commingled accounts managed by a VASP, the asset transfer on the blockchain is performed by the VASP using its own private-public key pair on behalf of the customer. The customer holds no keys in the commingled cases. We refer to these private-public keys as the VASP *transactions signing-keys*, and we refer to corresponding certificate as the *transactions signing-key certificates*. The purpose of signing-key certificates is to certify the ownership of the private-public keys as belonging to the VASP. A given VASP may own multiple transactions signing-keys and therefore multiple signing-key certificates.

Because a VASP must stand behind the customer information it provides to other VASPs, any *claims* [42] or *assertions* [35] that a VASP produces about its customers must be digitally signed by the VASP. We refer to these private-public keys as *claims signing-keys*, and we refer to corresponding certificate as the *claims signing-key certificates*.

It is crucial for a VASP that these three (3) key-pairs be distinct. This is because the key-usage purpose of the keys are different, and each key may have differing lifetime durations. Depending on the profile of a transactions signing-key certificate and the claims signing-key certificate, they may include the serial number (or hash) of the identity EV-certificate of the VASP. This provides a mechanism for a recipient to validate that the owner of these two certificates is the same legal entity as the owner of the VASP identity EV-certificate.

4.3   Consortium-Based VASP Certificate Hierarchy

In order for VASPs to have a high degree of interoperability – at both the technical and legal levels – a *consortium* arrangement provides a number of advantages for the information sharing network. Members in a consortium are free to collectively define the common *operating rules* that members must abide by. The operating rules become input material into the definition of the *legal trust framework* which expresses the contractual legal obligations of the members.

A well-crafted set of operating rules for a VASP information sharing network provides its members with the several benefits. First, it provides a means for the members to *improve risk management* because the operating rules will allow members to quantify and manage risks inherent in participating within the network. Secondly, the operating rules provides its members with *legal certainty and predictability* by addressing the legal rights, responsibilities, and liabilities of participating within the network. Thirdly, the operating rules provides *transparency* to the members of the network by having all members agree to the same terms of membership (i.e. contract). Since the operating rules is a legal contract, it is legally enforceable upon all members. Finally, a set of operating rules which define common technical specifications (e.g. APIs, cryptographic functions, certificates, etc.), for all the members provides the highest chance of technical interoperability of services. In turn, this reduces overall system-development costs by allowing entities to re-use implementations of those standardized technical specifications. Several examples of consortium-based operating rules exist today (e.g. NACHA [33]). Business interoperability can only be achieved if all members of the information sharing network observe and implement these common operating rules, and if there is legal and monetary liability for not doing so.

The consortium arrangement lends itself to its membership sharing a common *certificate hierarchy* that is rooted at the consortium organization. This

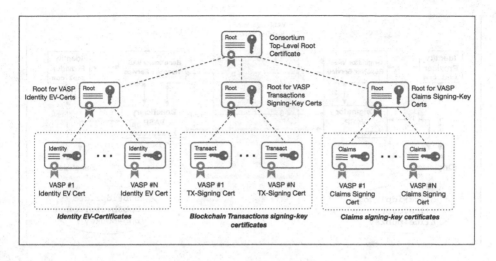

Fig. 2. Overview of a certificate hierarchy for VASP consortium

is shown in Fig. 2, where the consortium becomes the Root-CA for the certificates issued to all VASPs in the consortium organization. This permits a high degree of interoperability across VASPs. All VASPs in the consortium holds a copy of the Root-CA certificate of the consortium, and can therefore immediately validate whether another VASP is also a member. An Originator-VASP can quickly validate the identity EV-certificate of a Beneficiary-VASP (and vice versa) by validating whether the certificate *chain of issuance* goes up to the same Root-CA certificate. If the certificate of a Beneficiary-VASP cryptographically "chains-up" to the same Root-CA certificate, it means the Beneficiary-VASP is also a member of the same consortium.

Certificate hierarchies have been successfully deployed in numerous organizations, ranging from government organizations [28], to financial networks [11], to mobile devices and networks [1], to consortiums of cable-device manufacturers [3]. An example of a consortium that brings together device manufacturers (i.e. Cable Modem manufacturers) and service operators (i.e. cable TV access providers) is an organization called Cable Laboratories (CableLabs). The fact that device manufacturers and cable service providers operate under a common Root-CA certificate (rooted at CableLabs) permits cable service providers to detect counterfeit devices (e.g. hacked modems) and provide end-to-end protection (encryption) for valuable content (e.g. latest movies) to the consumer's home.

This combined hierarchy – VASP identity EV-certificates and its customer device-certificates – will be useful in dealing with various aspects of customer wallets. VASPs should have the capability to issue *customer identity certificates* that is cryptographically bound to the *wallet device certificates* of the trusted hardware in the wallet. This topic is beyond the scope of the current work and is discussed further in [22].

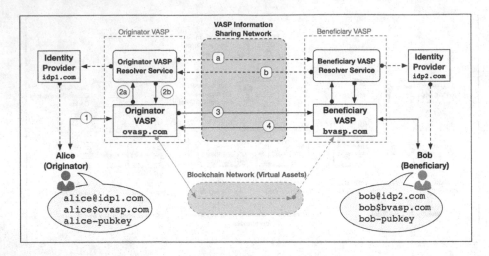

Fig. 3. VASP identifier resolver services

5   Customer Identity and Key Management Infrastructure

From the customer usability perspective, crypto-asset management systems need to be integrated seamlessly with existing consumer identity management infrastructure functions, including identity authentication services, authorization services, and consent management services.

5.1   Customer Identities and Digital Identifiers

Currently most users employ their email address as a form of user *identifier* in the context of obtaining services on the Internet. Many of these identifiers do not represent the user's full person (core) identity [17], and have short-term or ephemeral value (i.e. identifier can be replaced with a new one). Typically the entities who issues the identifiers are email providers and social media platform providers. The industry jargon used to describe them (rather inaccurately) is *Identity Provider* (IdP). Besides providing email-routable identifiers to users, the identity provider's role in the identity ecosystem is to provide mediated authentication services and credential-management on behalf of the user [19]. Mediated authentication – such as single sign-on (SSO) – provides convenience for the user by obviating the need for them to authenticate multiple times to each online service provider (e.g. online merchant) they visit. The online merchants redirects the user temporarily to the IdP for user-authentication, and upon success the user is returned back to the merchant.

The predominance of email-identifiers for users is a matter of consideration for VASPs because many users may wish to use their email address as the main identifier for account-creation at the VASP. Users may also seek to use email-identifiers to identify beneficiaries in the context of asset transfers, instead of public-keys. Furthermore, a user may have multiple accounts, each at different

VASPs and each employing different email-identifiers obtained from different IdPs.

An interesting approach is used in the PayID scheme [32] where the user is identified using a string similar to the *addr-spec* identifier (RFC5322), but with the "@" symbol replaced by the dollar sign ("$") while retaining the local-part and the domain-part. For example, if Alice has an account at the PayID provider (e.g. ACMEpay.com) then her PayID identifier would be `alice$acmepay.com`.

5.2   Identifier Resolvers

The matter of user identifiers is important not only from the customer usability perspective, but also from the need for interoperability of services across VASPs within the information sharing network. An Originator-VASP and Beneficiary-VASP must share the same syntactic and semantic understanding of the identifier scheme used for originators and beneficiaries. In the case of asset transfers both VASPs must be identifying the same pair of originator and beneficiary customers. As such, there is need for VASPs to employ *Identifier Resolver Services* (server) that maps, for example, from the off-chain beneficiary identifier scheme to the correct beneficiary public-key used on-chain.

We argue that the VASP information sharing network discussed in Sect. 3 should in fact be used for interconnecting or federating the identifier resolver services among VASPs. Figure 3 illustrates the message flows (a) and (b) between two identifier resolver services belonging to an Originator-VASP and a Beneficiary-VASP.

Some of the general requirements for a VASP identifier resolver service are as follows (non-exhaustive):

- *Support for multiple user-identifiers*: The identifier resolver service must permit multiple types of user-identifiers to be associated with the customer of the VASP.
- *Fast lookup for VASP determination*: The identifier resolver service must support fast look-ups or searches (e.g. by other VASPs in the network) based on an identifier string. The identifier string may be supplied by a customer (originator) of a VASP who is seeking to validate the user-identifier of a beneficiary.
- *Protected APIs*: The service endpoints (e.g. RESTful APIs) of the identifier resolver service must be access-protected. This is to protect against attacks from external entities (e.g. non-VASPs). The intended caller to the service endpoint should be another VASP, and therefore should be authenticated and validated as being a VASP (e.g. using the identity EV certificates discussed in Sect. 4.1).
- *Validation of user-identifier to IdP*: Optionally, for every user-identifier string submitted (added to) by a customer to their account at the VASP, the resolver service of the VASP should validate the string to its original issuer (if it was not the VASP). Thus, if customer Alice wishes to employ her email address `alice@idp1.com` then the resolver service should validate that Alice is known to identity/email provider IdP1.

Figure 3 illustrates that both Alice and Bob can be recognized using three different means: (i) their email address issued by an IdP (e.g. `alice@idp1.com`); (ii) their PayID address managed by a VASP (e.g. `alice$ovasp.com`); or (iii) their bare public-keys (e.g. `alice-pubkey`).

Using Fig. 3, consider the example of Alice who wishes to transfer virtual assets to Bob, but who only knows Bob's email address (e.g. `bob@idp2.com`). Alice does not know Bob's public-key or Bob's VASP. This means that Alice's Originator-VASP must query its resolver service – as shown in Step 2(a) and Step 2(b) of Fig. 3 – to discover which other VASPs in the network may know of the string `bob@idp2.com` (i.e. uses the string in an account). Assuming the resolver service returns a positive response (i.e. VASP-identifier or VASP-number found), the Originator-VASP can begin inquiring to that VASP about Bob (per the Travel Rule), as summarized in Step 3 and Step 4 of Fig. 3.

Note that the resolver service of the Originator-VASP may return more than one possible Beneficiary VASP-identifier or VASP-number. This could mean that Bob has an active account at each of these VASPs (each possibly using a different private-public key pair). In such cases, the Originator-VASP may need to request further information (regarding Bob) from Alice.

It is worth noting that that identifier resolvers are not new, and several resolver protocols have been standardized and have been in wide deployment for over two decades now (e.g. Domain Name Service (RFC1035), Handle System (RFC3650), etc.). As such, the nascent VASP industry should consider using and extending these well-deployed systems.

In deploying identifier resolver services, VASPs need to maintain the privacy of its customer – namely the privacy of the binding between a user-identifier and a public-key. The information (metadata) about the customer relationship between a user-identifier and a VASP is less revealing than information about the association between a user-identifier and a public-key. User-identifiers (e.g. email addresses) belonging to a customer at an account at a VASP can be changed by the customer at anytime without impacting the virtual assets bound to the customer's public-key. In contrast, a change to the customer's public-key may have privacy implications because it may be visible on the blockchain.

5.3   Federation of VASP Identifier Resolver Services

In order for VASP resolver services to scale-up, the VASPs must *federate* their resolver services under a common legal framework (i.e. the consortium model discussed above). A federation agreement allows VASPs to share customer identifier information (as known to the VASP) over the information sharing network (discussed in Sect. 3). Indeed, this is one of the main purposes of the network.

For example, using the information sharing network, VASPs can regularly (e.g. overnight) exchange knowledge about each other's customer identifiers. This is shown in Fig. 3 in Step (a) and Step (b) that runs between the VASP resolver services.

Although the precise protocol is beyond the scope of the current work, in the simplest form the exchange of customer identifier information between VASP resolver services can consists of pairs of VASP-identifier value and customer-identifier values (i.e. list of customer-identifiers as known to the VASP):

`VASP-identifier, Customer-id-1, Customer-id-2, ... Customer-id-N`

This approach is akin to IP route Link State Advertisements (LSA) used within some link-state routing protocols (e.g. OSPF (RFC2328)). In this case, a VASP is "advertising" its knowledge of customers bearing the stated identifiers.

The exchange of customer identifier information between two VASP resolver services must be conducted through a SSL/TLS secure channel established using the VASP X.509 EV-certificates to ensure traffic confidentiality and source authenticity.

5.4 Customer Managed Access to Claims

In some cases, static attributes regarding a customer (e.g. age, state of residence, driving license, etc.) can be obtained from authorized entities (e.g. government departments) in the form of asserted claims in one format or another [35,42], with a fixed validity period. Within the identity and access management (IAM) industry, an entity who issues authoritative signed assertions or claims about a subject is referred to as the *Claims Provider* (CP). A given customer of a VASP may already be in possession of a signed claim (e.g. driving license number) from an authoritative CP (e.g. Department of Motorized Vehicles), where the claim signature is still valid. The customer may keep a copy of the signed claim in the customer's personal *Claims Store* (e.g. mobile device, home server, cloud storage, etc.). The customer could provide its VASP with a copy of the claims, or the customer may provide its VASP with access to the customer's claims store.

There are several requirements and challenges for VASP access to claims store managed by the customer:

- *Customer-managed authorization to access claims-store*: Access to the a customer's claims-store must be customer driven, where access policies (rules) are determined by the customer as the claims owner.
- *Notice and consent from customer to use specific claims*: The customer as the claims owner must determine via access policies (i) which claims are accessible (readable) to the VASP, (ii) the usage-purpose limitations of the claims, (iii) and the right for the customer to retract (withdraw) the consent [7]. The customer's claims store must provide notice to the VASP, and the VASP must agree to the terms of use.
- *Consent-receipt issuance to VASP*: The customer's claims-store must issue a *consent-receipt* [30] to the VASP which acts exculpatory evidence covering the VASP.

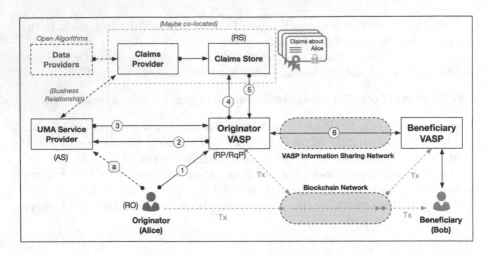

Fig. 4. Overview of originator authorization for VASP to retrieve claims

An extension to the OAuth2.0 authorization framework called the *User Managed Access* (UMA) protocol [16,31] can be the basis for customer-managed access to the claims store. In the example of Fig. 4, the Originator-VASP is seeking to obtain signed claims regarding the originator customer (Alice) located in her claims store. Access polices have been set by Alice in Step (a). In Step 1 Alice provides her VASP with the location of this service provider. When the VASP reaches the UMA Service Provider (Step 2) – which acts as the authorization server in the OAuth2.0 and UMA context – the VASP is provided with authorization-token that identifies the specific claims the VASP is authorized to fetc.h (Step 3). The VASP wields the authorization-token to the claims-store (Step 4). The VASP obtains access to the relevant claims and is provided with a consent-receipt by the claims-store (Step 5).

A claims store can be implemented in several ways. For example, it can be a Resource Server under the control of the CP, it can reside on Alice's own mobile device, it can be placed in a cloud-based Trusted Execution Environment (TEE) [6], or it may implemented in a decentralized file system such as IPFS/Filecoin [29] based on a decentralized identifier (DID) scheme [37].

6 Attestations Infrastructures for Regulated Wallets

With the increase in the number of individuals and organizations holding private-public keys bound to virtual assets on a blockchain, there is an increase risk of the loss and/or theft of private-keys. VASPs who are custodians of a customer's private-public keys and VASPs who employ their own keys to transact on behalf of customers face the problem of key management. As such, the use of *electronic wallets* based on *trusted hardware* – such as the Trusted Platform Module (TPM) chip [44] – that offers key-protection may increasingly become a necessity for VASPs for their own business survival. Funds insurance providers [27] may seek to obtain evidence of the use of trusted hardware by VASPs and their customers. This brings to the foreground the challenge of establishing an *attestation infrastructure* for VASPs that assists them in obtaining greater visibility into the state of wallets implemented using trusted hardware.

In the following we use the term *regulated wallet* to denote a wallet system (hardware and software) that is in possession of a customer of a supervised (regulated) VASP [12]. We use the term *private wallet* to denote a wallet system belonging to an *unverified entity* [10].

6.1   Attestation Evidence Relevant to VASPs & Asset Insurers

We use the term *attestation* to mean the capability in some trusted hardware to yield evidence that a device (built using the trusted hardware) can be trusted to correctly and truthfully report the internal state of the device [41]. The information reported is signed by the trusted hardware using an internal private-key that is non-readable by external entities and *non-migrateable* (i.e. cannot be extracted) from the trusted hardware. Thus, the recipient (e.g. a verifier) of the evidence obtains assurance that the signed report came from a particular device with the specific trusted hardware [23, 41].

For VASPs and asset insurance providers, there are several types of *attestation evidence* information that can be obtained from a wallet regarding keys used to sign asset-related transactions. The type of attestation evidence is dependent on the specific type trusted hardware but generally consists of the following [22]:

- *Key creation evidence*: The trusted hardware used in a wallet must have the capability to provide evidence regarding the origin of cryptographic keys held by the hardware. More specifically, it must be able to attest as to whether it generated a private-public key-pair internally or whether the key-pair was imported (injected) from the outside.
- *Key-movability evidence*: The trusted hardware used in a wallet must have the capability to provide evidence as to whether a private-key is migrateable or non-migrateable [20]. This evidence permits the VASP to perform risk-evaluation regarding the possibility that the wallet holder (i.e. a customer) has exported a copy of its private-key to another wallet system.
- *Wallet system composition evidence*: The trusted hardware used in a wallet should have the capability to provide evidence of the software stack present in the wallet [23, 41].

A given VASP may demand that customers use only approved wallets based on suitable trusted hardware. The VASP may also demand customers to create and use new key-pairs in the trusted hardware for all transactions (i.e. from the time the user becomes a legal customer of the VASP). This strategy provides the VASP with a clear line of responsibility and accountability under the Travel Rule with regards to customer-originated transactions. The VASP has exculpatory evidence regarding the on-boarding of the new customer and the start of use of the new key-pair.

Virtual asset insurance providers (e.g. crypto-funds insurers) must have the ability to directly query wallets in order to obtain signed attestation evidence from the trusted hardware in the wallets. This gives funds-insurance providers with visibility regarding the robustness of the key management lifecycle employed by the VASPs for their regulated wallets, and provides them with tangible information upon which to make their risk-assessment.

6.2   On-Boarding and Off-Boarding Customers

There are a number of challenges related to the on-boarding of a customer already possessing a wallet. In the case that the customer wallet is regulated and previously known to another regulated VASP, then there are some practical considerations that the *acquiring* VASP needs to address. These include: (i) validating whether prior to on-boarding the wallet was regulated or private; (ii) validating that the keys present within the wallet corresponds to the customer's historical transactions (confirmed on the blockchain); (iii) verifying whether a backup/migration of the wallet has occurred in the past; (iv) determining whether the customer's assets should be moved to new keys, and if so, how the "old" keys will be treated; and so on.

The case of a customer leaving a VASP (i.e. off-boarding) also introduces a number of questions that may be relevant under the Travel Rule. The *releasing* VASP may need to address the following: (i) preparing evidence that the wallet was in a regulated state whilst the owner of the wallet was a customer of the VASP; (ii) whether the customer's assets should be moved to a temporary set of keys, denoting the end of the VASP's responsibilities for the customer under the Travel Rule; (iii) obtaining evidence from the wallet that the "old" keys (non-migrateable keys) have been erased from the wallet device, thereby rendering the keys unusable in the future by the customer; and so on.

7   Conclusions

The VASP information sharing network is a core component of the trust infrastructures needed if blockchain systems and virtual assets are to be the foundation of the future global digital economy. VASPs need to view this information sharing network as a foundational building block for other infrastructures to be developed.

VASPs also require a trusted identity infrastructure that allow VASPs to authenticate each other and to rapidly ascertain the business legal status of other VASPs. The use of extended-validation digital certificates offers a promising solution to this problem, based on well understood and widely deployed public key certificates management technologies.

Finally, other trust infrastructures will be needed in order to address use-cases related to customer wallets and device attestations from wallets. In particular, VASPs may need evidence that the customer's private-key truly resides within the wallet device. This provides a means for VASPs to prove that they are not the legal operator of the customer's private-public keys.

Acknowledgement. We thank the following for various inputs, discussions and comments: Sandy Pentland and Alexander Lipton (MIT); Ned Smith (Intel); Anne Wallwork (US Treasury); Dave Jevans, John Jefferies (CipherTrace); David Riegelnig (Bitcoin Suisse); Aanchal Malhotra (Ripple); Justin Newton (NetKi); Eve Maler (ForgeRock); Justin Richer (Bespoke Engineering); Nat Sakimura (OIF).

References

1. Apple Inc.: Apple Public CA Certification Practice Statement. Certificate practices statement Apple Inc., June 2019. https://images.apple.com/certificateauthority/pdf/Apple_Public_CA_CPS_v4.2.pdf
2. CAB-Forum: Guidelines For The Issuance And Management of Extended Validation Certificates. Specification version 1.7.2, CA Browser Forum, March 2020
3. CableLabs: Cablelabs New PKI Certificate Policy Version 2.1. Technical specifications, Cable Laboratories, January 2019. https://www.cablelabs.com/resources/digital-certificate-issuance-service
4. Canellis, D.: 76 percent of laundered cryptocurrency was washed with an exchange service. The Next Web, January 2019. https://thenextweb.com/hardfork/2019/01/29/cryptocurrency-laundering-chainalysis/
5. Cooper, D., Santesson, S., Farrell, S., Boeyen, S., Housley, R., Polk, W.: Internet X.509 public key infrastructure certificate and certificate revocation list (CRL) profile, May 2008. RFC5280. http://tools.ietf.org/rfc/rfc5280.txt
6. EEA: Off-Chain Trusted Compute Specification. Technical specification v1.1, Enterprise Ethereum Alliance, March 2020. https://entethalliance.github.io/trusted-computing/spec.html
7. Commission, E.: Regulation (EU) 2016/679 of the European Parliament and of the Council of 27 April 2016 on the protection of natural persons with regard to the processing of personal data and on the free movement of such data (General Data Protection Regulation). Off. J. Eur. Union **L119**, 1–88 (2016)
8. FATF: International Standards on Combating Money Laundering and the Financing of Terrorism and Proliferation. FATF Revision of Recommendation 15, Financial Action Task Force (FATF), October 2018. http://www.fatf-gafi.org/publications/fatfrecommendations/documents/fatf-recommendations.html
9. FATF: Guidance for a Risk-Based Approach to Virtual Assets and Virtual Asset Service Providers. FATF Guidance, Financial Action Task Force (FATF), June 2019. www.fatf-gafi.org/publications/fatfrecommendations/documents/Guidance-RBA-virtual-assets.html
10. FATF: 12-Month Review of Revised FATF Standards on Virtual Assets and Virtual Asset Service Provider. FATF report, Financial Action Task Force (FATF), July 2020. http://www.fatf-gafi.org/publications/fatfrecommendations/documents/12-month-review-virtual-assets-vasps.html
11. Finextra: Swift to introduce PKI security for FIN. Finextra News, October 2004. https://www.finextra.com/newsarticle/12620/swift-to-introduce-pki-security-for-fin
12. FINMA: FINMA Guidance: Payments on the blockchain. Finma guidance report, Swiss Financial Market Supervisory Authority (FINMA), August 2019. https://www.finma.ch/en/~/media/finma/dokumente/dokumentencenter/myfinma/4dokumentation/finma-aufsichtsmitteilungen/20190826-finma-aufsichtsmitteilung-02-2019.pdf

13. GLEIF: LEI in KYC: A New Future for Legal Entity Identification. Gleif research report? A new future for legal entity identification, Global Legal Entity Identifier Foundation (GLEIF), May 2018. https://www.gleif.org/en/lei-solutions/lei-in-kyc-a-new-future-for-legal-entity-identification
14. Goldwasser, S., Micali, S., Rackoff, C.: The knowledge complexity of interactive proof systems. SIAM J. Comput. **18**, 186–208 (1988). https://doi.org/10.1137/0218012
15. Haber, S., Stornetta, W.S.: How to time-stamp a digital document. In: Menezes, A.J., Vanstone, S.A. (eds.) CRYPTO 1990. LNCS, vol. 537, pp. 437–455. Springer, Heidelberg (1991). https://doi.org/10.1007/3-540-38424-3_32
16. Hardjono, T., Maler, E., Machulak, M., Catalano, D.: User-Managed Access (UMA) Profile of OAuth2.0 - Specification Version 1.0. Kantara published specification, Kantara Initiative, April 2015. https://docs.kantarainitiative.org/uma/rec-uma-core.html
17. Hardjono, T., Pentland, A.: Core identities for future transaction systems. In: Hardjono, T., Pentland, A., Shrier, D. (eds.) Trusted Data - A New Framework for Identity and Data Sharing, pp. 41–81. MIT Press, New York (2019)
18. Hardjono, T.: Compliant Solutions for VASPs, May 2019, presentation to the FATF Private Sector Consultative Forum (PSCF) 2019, Vienna, 6 May 2019
19. Hardjono, T.: Federated authorization over access to personal data for decentralized identity management. IEEE Commun. Stand. Mag. Dawn Internet Identity Layer Role Decent. Identit **3**(4), 32–38 (2019). https://doi.org/10.1109/MCOMSTD.001.1900019
20. Hardjono, T., Kazmierczak, G.: Overview of the TPM Key Management Standard (2008). http://www.trustedcomputinggroup.org/files/resource_files/
21. Hardjono, T., Lipton, A., Pentland, A.: Towards a public key management framework for virtual assets and virtual asset service providers. J. FinTech **1**(1), 2050001 (2020). https://doi.org/10.1142/S2705109920500017. https://arxiv.org/pdf/1909.08607
22. Hardjono, T., Lipton, A., Pentland, A.: Wallet Attestations for Virtual Asset Service Providers and Crypto-Assets Insurance, June 2020. https://arxiv.org/pdf/2005.14689.pdf
23. Hardjono, T., Smith, N.: TCG Core Integrity Schema. TCG Specification - Version 1.0.1 Revision 1.0, Trusted Computing Group, November 2006. https://trustedcomputinggroup.org/wp-content/uploads/IWG-Core-Integrity_Schema_Specification_v1.pdf
24. InterVASP: InterVASP Messaging Standards IVMS101. interVASP data model standard - Issue 1 - FINAL, Joint Working Group on interVASP Messaging Standards, May 2020
25. ISO: Information Technology - Open Systems Interconnection - The Directory - Part 8: Public-key and Attribute Certificate Frameworks. ISO/IEC 9594-8:2017, International Organization for Standardization, February 2017
26. Jevans, D., Hardjono, T., Vink, J., Steegmans, F., Jefferies, J., Malhotra, A.: Travel Rule Information Sharing Architecture for Virtual Asset Service Providers. Version 7, TRISA, June 2020. https://trisa.io/wp-content/uploads/2020/06/TRISAEnablingFATFTravelRuleWhitePaperV7.pdf
27. Kharif, O., Louis, B., Edde, J., Chiglinsky, K.: Interest in crypto insurance grows, despite high premiums, broad exclusions. Insur. J. (2018). https://www.insurancejournal.com/news/national/2018/07/23/495680.htm

28. Kuhn, D.R., Hu, V.C., Polk, W.T., Chang, S.J.: Introduction to Public Key Technology and the Federal PKI Infrastructure. NIST Special Publication 800–32, National Institute of Standards and Technology, February 2001. https://nvlpubs. nist.gov/nistpubs/Legacy/SP/nistspecialpublication800-32.pdf
29. Protocol Labs: Inter Planetary File System (IPFS) (2019). https://docs.ipfs.io. Accessed 23 Sept. 2019
30. Lizar, M., Turner, D.: Consent Receipt Specification Version 1.0 (March 2017). https://kantarainitiative.org/confluence/display/infosharing/Home
31. Maler, E., Machulak, M., Richer, J.: User-Managed Access (UMA) 2.0. Kantara published specification, Kantara Initiative, January 2017. https://docs. kantarainitiative.org/uma/ed/uma-core-2.0-10.html
32. Malhotra, A., King, A., Schwartz, D., Zochowski, M.: PayID Protocol. Technical whitepaper v1.0, PayID.org, June 2020. https://payid.org/whitepaper.pdf
33. NACHA: Operating Rules and Guidelines. Specification, National Automated Clearing House Association (NACHA) (2019). https://www.nacha.org
34. Nakamoto, S.: Bitcoin: A Peer-to-Peer Electronic Cash System (2008). https:// bitcoin.org/bitcoin.pdf
35. OASIS: Assertions and Protocols for the OASIS Security Assertion Markup Language (SAML) V2.0, March 2005. http://docs.oasisopen.org/security/saml/v2.0/ saml-core-2.0-os.pdf
36. Reddy, A.: Hackers stole $40 million of bitcoin from one of the world's largest crypto exchanges (BTC). Business Insider, May 2019. https://markets.businessinsider. com/currencies/news/btc-binance-suffers-40-million-hack-2019-5-1028182318
37. Reed, D., Sporny, M.: Decentralized Identifiers (DIDs) v0.11. Draft community group report 09 July 2018, W3C, July 2018. https://w3c-ccg.github.io/did-spec/
38. Rescorla, D.: The Transport Layer Security (TLS) Protocol Version 1.3, August 2018. https://tools.ietf.org/html/rfc8446, IETF Standard RFC8446
39. Riegelnig, D.: OpenVASP: An Open Protocol to Implement FATF's Travel Rule for Virtual Assets, November 2019. https://www.openvasp.org/wp-content/uploads/ 2019/11/OpenVasp_Whitepaper.pdf
40. Schoenberg, T., Robinson, M.: Bitcoin ATMs May Be Used to Launder Money. Bloomberg, December 2018. https://www.bloomberg.com/features/2018-bitcoin-atm-money-laundering/
41. Smith, N. (ed.): TCG Attestation Framework. TCG Draft Specification - Version 1.0, Trusted Computing Group, February 2020
42. Sporny, M., Longley, D., Chadwick, D.: Verifiable Credentials Data Model 1.0. W3C Recommendation, W3C, November 2019. https://www.w3.org/TR/ verifiable-claims-data-model
43. Su, J.: Hackers Stole Over 4 Billion From Crypto Crimes In 2019 So Far, Up From 1.7 Billion In All Of 2018. Forbes, August 2019. https://www.forbes.com/ sites/jeanbaptiste/2019/08/15/hackers-stole-over-4-billion-from-crypto-crimes-in-2019-so-far
44. Trusted Computing Group: TPM Main - Specification Version 1.2. TCG Published Specification, Trusted Computing Group, October 2003. http://www. trustedcomputinggroup.org/resources/tpm_main_specification

Risk Assessment of Sharing Cyber Threat Intelligence

Adham Albakri[1,2], Eerke Boiten[1(✉)], and Richard Smith[1]

[1] School of Computer Science and Informatics, De Montfort University, Leicester, UK
{adham.albakri,eerke.boiten,rgs}@dmu.ac.uk
[2] School of Computing, University of Kent, Canterbury, UK

Abstract. Sharing Cyber Threat Intelligence (CTI) is advocated to get better defence against new sophisticated cyber-attacks. CTI may contain critical information about the victim infrastructure, existing vulnerabilities and business processes so sharing CTI may carry a risk. However, evaluating the risk of sharing CTI datasets is challenging due to the nature of the CTI context which is associated with the evolution of the threat landscape and new cyber attacks that are difficult to evaluate. In this paper, we present a quantitative risk model to assess the risk of sharing CTI datasets enabled by sharing with different entities in various situations. The model enables the identification of the threats and evaluation of the impacts of disclosing this information. We present two use cases that help to determine the risk level of sharing a CTI dataset and consequently the mitigation techniques to enable responsible sharing. Risk identification and evaluation have been validated using experts' opinions.

Keywords: Cyber threat intelligence · Information sharing · Risk assessment

1 Introduction

Sharing CTI datasets increases due to the number of attacks, threat actors' motivations and capabilities. It helps organisations get better defence and increase the accuracy of threat detection [1]. However, sharing CTI datasets has specific consequences which makes organisations reluctant to share. The barriers can be: (1) the probability of undesirable information disclosure increases when sharing with organisations that do not have a high level of trust or when sharing with the public, (2) CTI datasets can contain various kinds of information such as personal, organizational, financial and cybersecurity information [2]. Thus, evaluating the risk of sharing CTI datasets containing critical information such as the existing vulnerabilities is a challenge especially with the evolving of the cyber threat landscape and sophisticated cyber-attacks for various business sectors. When considering the different sources of CTI information and the intention to share with various entities, a risk assessment model is needed. By evaluating the associated risk of sharing CTI datasets, organisations would know how critical their CTI datasets are before sharing [2] and use the right methods and processes to manage the risk to respect the organization's acceptable risk level. In addition, they need to

© Springer Nature Switzerland AG 2020
I. Boureanu et al. (Eds.): ESORICS 2020 Workshops, LNCS 12580, pp. 92–113, 2020.
https://doi.org/10.1007/978-3-030-66504-3_6

obtain legal compliance as the General Data Protection Regulation (GDPR) [3] mandates organisations to undertake risk assessments and fulfill security mitigation controls.

In this paper, we will propose a specific quantitative risk model for evaluating the risk of sharing CTI datasets. This builds on the identification and partial assessment of threats in cyber incident information sharing in our earlier work [2]. This model will help improve the decision of sharing CTI information with multiple entities. During the evaluation phases, we take into consideration the threats of sharing each attribute in the CTI dataset and the likelihood of such threats occurring and the level of trust in the receiving party. The remainder of this paper is organized as follows. Section 2 discusses related work. Section 3 describes the steps of the methodology to build the model. Section 4 gives several use cases of sharing CTI datasets to validate the model through involving cybersecurity experts. Section 5 gives threats to validity. Finally, Sect. 5 presents the conclusion and future research directions.

2 Related Work

In [4] the authors addressed the types of information that could be shared between SMEs while addressing the risk of disclosure cyber-attack scenarios. However, the study was limited to SMEs and a small size sample with specific security metrics which could be different in different business scenarios. In our work, we are evaluating the risk and proposing a more general model not related to specific business for calculating the risk of sharing CTI datasets. In [5] the authors proposed a cyber security risk model using a Bayesian network model for the nuclear reactor protection system (RPS) then applying the analytical result to an event tree model. In their model, they have only focused on four cyber threats and six mitigation measures according to the design specification of an RPS. This evaluation was only on the network layers not covering other types of possible threats. In [6] the authors proposed a quantitative asset and vulnerability centric cyber security risk assessment methodology for IT systems. They defined and extended metrics based on CVSS and presented a formula for computation and aggregation. The work focused only on the CVEs without considering other factors in the impact. Also, the calculation was based on the defined CVSS list without including zero-day attacks. The model did not consider the threat actor and the attack vector, and the focus was only on the individual asset and the vulnerabilities at the assets which satisfy the consideration of the assets and the system design. They proposed a base risk assessment model and an attack graph-based risk assessment model. However, these methods do not consider a quantitative approach for risk evaluation when sharing CTI datasets, such as the one presented in this paper. In this paper, we propose a new model to compute this risk by identifying threats, severity and probability of sharing CTI information.

3 Methodology

3.1 Risk Assessment Approach/Background

Risk is defined in the business world enterprise as "the extent to which the outcomes from the corporate strategy of a company may differ from those specified in its corporate objectives, or the extent to which they fail to meet these objectives" [7].

There are outstanding risk assessment methodologies including ISO/IEC 27005 [8] that provide guidelines for information risk management activities as an aspect of the business process in organisations. Also, NIST SP 800-30 [9] is a framework to help conduct risk assessments of critical infrastructure systems and organizations. This framework helps senior management to select the course of action for specific threats. Octave [10] focuses on identifying vulnerabilities that exist in the organization's structure and implements security strategies and plans. There are various ways to assess risk including quantitative, qualitative, or semi-quantitative. Quantitative risk assessment is based on using mathematical methods and rules. In this type, numbers represent information, for example, a numerical value of 1 is assigned to the high probability of a specific attack that could occur. Understanding the context and explaining the constraints helps in assigning the numbers in meaningful way; thus, the meaning of the quantitative results would be clearer. However, in some cases the results need additional justifications and clarifications to understand what the numerical results represent. For example, before sharing any CTI dataset, the owner may ask if the risk assessments results are reliable based on the assumptions used in the calculations. On the other hand, qualitative risk assessment is based on applying non-numerical methods according to levels such as low, medium and high. This type of assessment has a limited number of results which make it more comprehensible to decision makers. Each value should be defined clearly and categorised by a clear description and an example. Without a clear description, experts may rely on their experience and opinion which might provide different assessment results. Finally, semi-quantitative risk assessment combines rules and methods for evaluating the risk based on numeric values and levels. For example, the range between 1 and 10 can easily be converted into qualitative expressions that help risk communications for decision makers. The role of expert judgment in assigning values in the semi-quantitative risk is more palpable than in a purely quantitative approach. Moreover, if the scales or sets of levels provide sufficient granularity, relative prioritization among results is better supported than in a purely qualitative approach. In this type, all ranges and values need to be explained and defined by clear description and examples. Semi-quantitative assessments use various methods or rules for evaluating risk based on levels, scales or numeric values that are meaningful in the context. For example, a score of 90 for a CTI dataset can represent a very high risk. The role of experts' judgment still exists in this type and similar to the qualitative and quantitative models each numeric value and range needs to be defined and explained.

3.2 Associated Risk Model (ARM)

In this section, we present our associated risk model (ARM). The first step in our ARM procedure is to examine the dataset. In this step, we will be indicating the roles that the various attributes may play: they could contain sensitive information, or help to identify people and organisations. We then point out threats, using the ENISA threat taxonomy [11]. We compute the severity for each property in the dataset because if there is a disclosure of sensitive and critical information, there would be a risk that an associated threat could exploit the system. Then the organisation may face an unexpected cybersecurity attack, reputational damage and legal consequences. We have precisely identified the associated threat by analyzing each property in the STIX 1.2 incident model separately and mapping it to the ENISA threat taxonomy [11]. Then, for each property we have calculated the severity value that was assigned in our previous work [2]. After identifying the potential threats, we can derive the level of associated risk for this sharing by estimating the likelihood of the threats in case of property disclosure. Our goal is to reduce the risk value by selecting the appropriate privacy preserving techniques to improve the sharing between organisations. Figure 1 illustrates the flow chart of ARM which describes the risk assessment steps, including identification of risks through the disclosure of the shared dataset properties, their total risk value through the analysis of threats mapped based on the disclosed properties.

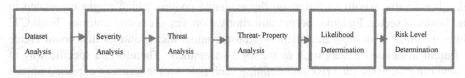

Fig. 1. ARM Steps

3.3 Dataset Analysis

First, we need to identify the associated risk of disclosing any property of the shared CTI dataset. Each property may have a different severity level in an organisation. In previous work [2], we have estimated the cybersecurity severity score for each property int the STIX 1.2 incident model [12]. The severity score range is [1, 8], where 1 is the lowest level of severity and 8 is the highest level of severity. Based on the severity score, severity assigned to four impact levels: negligible, limited, significant and maximum which can be represented as 10, 50, 75 and 100. Let each property be represented as a single bit in the property vector:

$$\vec{P} = \{P_i\} \in \{0, 1\} \forall i, \ i = 1, 2, \ldots n \tag{1}$$

Here, P_i represents an individual property. The value 1 indicates the existence of this property in the shared dataset, otherwise it is 0. Because disclosing any property in the shared dataset is a potential risk, we include all properties into our analysis. If we are fully sharing a dataset with 10 properties, we set n to 10 and $P_i = 1 \forall n$.

3.4 Threat Analysis

The second step in our model is to perform a threat analysis, which consists of identifying the potential threat action that may exploit the system or the organisation based on the CTI information disclosure. Information about threats can be collected from the organisation's CTI database and threat taxonomies which can define a list of potential threats to the organisation. Let each threat be represented as a single bit in the threat vector:

$$\vec{T} = \{T_j\} \in \{0, 1\} \forall j, j = 1, 2, \ldots m. \tag{2}$$

Here T_j represents an individual threat, the value 1 indicates the presence of this threat when sharing the CTI dataset and otherwise it is 0. Thereafter, based on the CTI dataset disclosure and the associated threats, we can match threats to the CTI property and estimate the likelihood of a threat occurring based on disclosure of CTI information. The likelihood values L_{ij} are based on how easy it is for a threat to be executed by a motivated and powerful adversary. This likelihood can adopt three values: low, medium, high represented as 0.1, 0.5 and 1. In case there is no risk, we assign value $L_{ij} = 0$. In the previous step, there will be a subjective factor - expert judgment- because of the diverse perception of associated threats for each property, what impact that would have on the organisation and likelihood of an event happening. The judgment of the likelihood value would be based on the available context which might be related to the business sector, location, perpetrator motivation, resources and abilities. Each CTI dataset comes from separate business sector, context and countries that could create different associated threats such as the legal assessment. Therefore, a specific way of calculating the associated risk and defining each risk level in terms of expected impact and expected techniques to share securely might be a mandatory pre-requirement for sharing CTI datasets. For example, the impact of gaining access over the ATM control system in order to withdraw money is different than the impact of gaining control over CCTV cameras in a critical infrastructure.

3.5 Total Associated Risk (TAR)

Total Associated Risk (TAR) is the sum of sub associated risks of disclosing CTI information and can be computed as follows:

$$TAR = \sum_{i=1}^{n} \sum_{j=1}^{m} L_{ij} * S_i * P_j * T_i \text{ where } TAR \in \mathbb{R}^+ \tag{3}$$

Where n represents the number of the properties, m represents the number of the threats, L_{ij} represents likelihood of the presence of the threat i when disclosing the property j and S_i represents the severity score. The likelihood values L_{ij} represent how easy it is for a powerful and motivated adversary to execute threat j knowing property i. Once TAR is computed, the organisation becomes aware of how this could provide the appropriate information to decision makers about how to make a clear decision about sharing this dataset and how to evaluate the associated risk.

4   Evaluation

To evaluate the ARM model, we have conducted an experiment on two case studies that were analyzed manually using our model by independent experts.

4.1 Expert Selection

In this study, we have developed two use cases aiming to validate our model. Two use cases were analyzed by independent experts with different levels of experience working on cybersecurity and privacy during a privacy workshop. Also, we have asked PhD students (third year) during a PhD summer school to fill a questionnaire, all PhD students are working in cyber security.

4.2 Case Studies

The presented ARM is here tested through three use case studies. Case study 1 discusses sharing a CTI dataset for correlation purposes while case study 2 discusses sharing a CTI dataset for aggregation purposes. In all case studies we consider sharing with trusted and untrusted entities.

4.2.1 Case Study 1: CTI Contains Malware Information & Personal Information - Sharing for Detections

This scenario consists of two cyber threat companies, CyberA and CyberB. CyberA has been attacked by specific malware. This malware was designed to steal encrypted files and was even able to recover files that had been deleted. CyberA wants to share this incident dataset with others in their sharing community. The purpose of this sharing is to let recipients check if they have spotted the same malware on their system. Table 1 shows the sample CTI dataset which contains the properties that might be shared.

Table 1. Use Case 1 (CTI Dataset)

Property	Value
TTP[a] Malware Type	Capture Stored Data, Remote Access Trojan
Indicator Name	File hash for malicious malware
Indicator Description	This file hash indicates that a sample of malware alpha is present.
Indicator Value	Hashes.'SHA-256' = 'ef537f25c895bfa7jfdhfjns73748hdfjkk5589fjfer8fjkdndkjn7yfb6c' Win-Reg-key: = "HKEY_LOCAL_MACHINE\\SYSTEM\\ControlSet01\\Services\\MSL3"
Vulnerability	CVE-2009-3129, CVE-2008-4250, CVE-2012-0158, CVE-2011-3544
Incident Title	Incident associated with CyberA campaign. Malware was designed to steal encrypted files - and was even able to recover files that had been deleted.
Date	2012-01-01T00:00:00
Reporter Name	Alex John
Reporter Email Address	alex@pro-it.com
Reporter Address	US - LA
Victim Name	CyberA/The CEO Device
Victim sector	Financial sector
Victim Device	IP address: 146.227.239.19

(continued)

Table 1. (*continued*)

Property	Value
Victim Email Address	cybera@cyber.com/ceo-cybera@cyber.com
Victim Address	CyberA Ltd, IT Department, LONDON, W5 5YZ
Affected Assets Type	Desktop, Mobile phone, Router, Server, Person
Affected Assets Property	Confidentiality (Classified, Internal, Credentials, Secrets, System) Integrity (Software installation, Modify configuration, Alter behaviour)
Incident Status	Not solved
Total loss	£ 65,000

[a]Tactics, Techniques and Procedures

Associated Risk Evaluation

To compute the associated risk of sharing this CTI dataset, we apply our model as follows. The first step is to identify and analyse the severity for each property in the dataset. Table 2 defines the threats associated with disclosing the CTI dataset as derived from Table 1. We have assigned the sets of potential threats for each property and evaluated those for severity in cyber security contexts.

Table 2. Severity value and Associated threats

Property	Property ID	Threat	Severity
Victim (Name, Sector, Address, Role)	P1	T1, T2, T3, T4, T10	10
Malware (Type, Description)	P2	T3, T6	10
IoC (Name, Description, Value)	P3	T2, T3, T4	10
Vulnerability	P4	T2, T3, T4	10
Affected Assets (Type, Property)	P5	T2, T4, T7, T9, T10	10
Status	P6	T2, T6	10
Total Loss	P7	T6, T11, T10	50
Impact Assessment	P8	T6, T11, T10	10
Reporter	P9	T1, T2	10

Table 3 represents the same relationship between the threats and the properties of the CTI dataset by focusing on the threats.

Based on the CTI dataset disclosure and the associated threats we estimate the likelihood of a threat occurring based on the property value and the context which varies depending on the organisations' requirements. Table 4 presents our estimates of the

Table 3. Threats and matched property

Threat	Threat ID	Matched Property
Identity theft (Identity Fraud/Account)	T1	P1, P9
Social engineering	T2	P1, P3, P4, P5, P6, P9
Unauthorized activities	T3	P1, P2, P3, P4
Targeted attacks (APTs etc.)	T4	P1, P3, P4, P6
Misuse of information/information systems	T5	P3, P4
Compromising confidential information (data breaches)	T6	P2, P3, P4, P7, P8
Unauthorized physical access	T7	P5
Violation of laws or regulations/Breach of legislation	T8	P5
Failure to meet contractual requirements	T9	P5
Loss of reputation	T10	P1, P2, P7, P8
Judiciary decisions/court orders.	T11	P7

likelihood L_{ij} of the threats and the total risk score TAR when sharing with public sharing communities. Table 5 presents the estimated likelihood of the threats and the total risk score value when sharing with trusted communities. Finally, we evaluated the risk in three different scenarios: sharing the CTI dataset with public communities, sharing when involving/considering a high level of trust with the receiver and finally, sharing after removing the unrelated information.

Table 4. Likelihood and total risk value (public sharing communities)

	P1	P2	P3	P4	P5	P6	P7	P8	P9	SUB-RISK
T1	0.1	0	0	0	0	0	0	0	0.1	2
T2	1	0	0.1	0.1	1	0.5	0	0	0.1	28
T3	0.5	1	0.5	0.5	0	0	0	0	0	25
T4	1	0	0.5	0.5	1	1	0	0	0	40
T5	0	0	0.1	0.1	0	0	0	0	0	2
T6	0	1	0.1	0.1	0	0	1	1	0	72
T7	0	0	0	0	0.5	0	0	0	0	5
T8	0	0	0	0	0.5	0	0	0	0	5
T9	0	0	0	0	0.5	0	0	0	0	5
T10	0.5	0.1	0	0	0	0	1	0.5	0	61
T11	0	0	0	0	0	0	0.1	0.1	0	6
TAR										**251**

Table 5. Likelihood and total risk value (trusted communities)

	P1	P2	P3	P4	P5	P6	P7	P8	P9	SUB-RISK
T1	0.1	0	0	0	0	0	0	0	0	1
T2	0.5	0	0.1	0.1	0.5	0.1	0	0	0.1	14
T3	0.1	0.5	0.5	0.5	0	0	0	0	0	16
T4	0.1	0	0.1	0.1	0.1	0.5	0	0	0	9
T5	0	0	0.1	0.1	0	0	0	0	0	2
T6	0	0.5	0.1	0.1	0	0	0.5	0.5	0	37
T7	0	0	0	0	0.1	0	0	0	0	1
T8	0	0	0	0	0.1	0	0	0	0	1
T9	0	0	0	0	0.1	0	0	0	0	1
T10	0.1	0.1	0	0	0	0	0.5	0.5	0	32
TAR										114

When sharing with public communities, the risk value is 251. On the other hand, sharing within trusted communities decreases the risk value to 114. In this scenario, the purpose of sharing is to check the existence of the same malware thus we need to know the type and description of the malware, in addition to the indicators of compromise such as hash file value and windows registry key. Therefore, the properties needed for sharing are P2 and P3. Therefore, the associated risk value if we only share these essential properties will be reduced to 34 as shown in Table 6. Reducing the risk value is important for encouraging CTI sharing, and to achieve that, the organisation filters out the sensitive information that is not relevant to the purpose of this sharing.

Table 6. Likelihood and total risk value for sub-dataset

Threat ID	P2	P3	SUB-RISK
T2	0	0.1	1
T3	1	0.5	15
T4	0	0.5	5
T5	0	0.1	1
T6	1	0.1	11
T10	0.1	0	1
T11	0	0	0
TAR			34

Our model allows for each risk assessment to be combined in different ways for different purposes. For instance, Fig. 2 demonstrates a risk assessment visualisation for the same CTI dataset. For each field in the CTI dataset, we displayed the sum of the risks posed by that property in case of disclosure. This visualisation shows which properties of CTI dataset are the greatest risk when sharing and might be used in the context of raising organisational awareness of the CTI dataset properties.

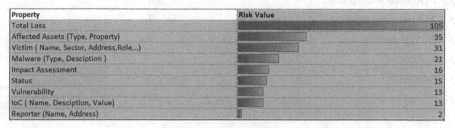

Property	Risk Value
Total Loss	105
Affected Assets (Type, Property)	35
Victim (Name, Sector, Address,Role,..)	31
Malware (Type, Desciption)	21
Impact Assessment	16
Status	15
Vulnerability	13
IoC (Name, Desciption, Value)	13
Reporter (Name, Address)	2

Fig. 2. A risk assessment visualisation showing risk value per type of information.

Evaluation - Data Collection and Analysis
This section presents the results of the data collection from a questionnaire[1] conducted within privacy and cybersecurity workshops with 15 experts in privacy and cybersecurity. The study provided anonymity to the participants. The questionnaire contains 3 parts. The first part focuses on identifying the threats associated with disclosing the CTI dataset. We proposed a list of threats and free text for extra suggestions. The second part focuses on the security controls that might be applied to preserve privacy of the dataset such as redaction/selection, anonymisation, aggregation, encryption and so on. Finally, the third part focuses on giving a risk value to the dataset in both cases, before and after applying the security controls. Fifteen experts filled out the questionnaire and a summary of the data collected is presented in Table 7 and discussed in more detail below. The question Q1 was answered by 15 experts for sharing the CTI dataset with public sharing communities and by 12 when sharing with trusted communities. Nine experts selected in detail the possible associated threats of disclosing this dataset. Table 8 presents the threats and how many experts have selected that threat as a possible threat in case of disclosing this CTI dataset. For example, six experts out of nine agreed that disclosing this dataset would be associated with "Compromising confidential information" and "Loss of reputation" threat. The remaining did not consider these as possible threats. The result indicates that the list we have proposed in Table 3 matches the experts' selections in Table 8.

Table 9 presents the number of experts who decided which threats might be associated with disclosing the CTI dataset when sharing with trusted entities. The possible threats have decreased due to the increase of trust level among the sharing organisations. However, the result still shows that the list we have proposed in Table 3 matches the experts' selections in Table 9.

---

[1] https://docs.google.com/document/d/1y0N18P-C34b93AVc2u-I44BX7uRLuobS0kkQyXud
XCw/edit?usp=sharing.

Table 7. UC1 summary: responses returned

Question	Part 1- Sharing with public (Number of responses)	Part2- sharing with trusted entities (Number of responses)
Q-1	15	12
Q-2	15	13
Q-3.1 (Redaction/Selection)	8	0
Q-3.2 (Anonymisation)	7	7
Q-3.3 (Aggregation)	6	7
Q-3.4 (Enc)	7	7
Q-3.5 (others)	3	3
Q4	14	14

Table 8. UC1-Part1-Threat Summary

Threat	Count	Threat	Count
Social engineering (Phishing, Spear phishing)	4	Loss of reputation	6
Failure to meet contractual requirements	3	Unauthorized physical access	0
Violation of laws or regulations	2	Failed business process	1
Compromising confidential information	6	Man-in-the-middle	0
Identity theft (Identity Fraud/Account)	4	Terrorists attack	0
Abuse of authorizations	0	Targeted attacks (APTs etc.)	2
Misuse of information/information systems	4	Unauthorized activities	4
Generation and use of rogue certificates	0	Manipulation of information	3

For question Q2, eight experts indicated that we cannot share this dataset. On the other hand, 7 indicated that we can share after mitigation. This result indicates that sharing this dataset without applying any security controls will be a high risk to CyberA.

For questions Q3.1 and Q3.2 experts selected values that should be anonymized or removed from the dataset before sharing, such as "Reporter Name", "Reporter Email", "Reporter Address", "Victim Name", "Victim Sector", "Victim Device", "Victim Email", "Victim Address" and "Total Loss".

Many experts agreed to remove any personal data, such as the victim information which will reduce possible threats such as "Violation of laws or regulations" and make the decision of sharing compliant with the regulation such as the GDPR [13]. In our

Table 9. UC1-Part2-Threat Summary

Threat	Count	Threat	Count
Social engineering (Phishing, Spear phishing)	1	Loss of reputation	6
Failure to meet contractual requirements	4	Unauthorized physical access	0
Violation of laws or regulations	1	Failed business process	2
Compromising confidential information	4	Man-in-the-middle	0
Identity theft (Identity Fraud/Account)	1	Terrorists attack	0
Abuse of authorizations	0	Targeted attacks (APTs etc.)	0
Misuse of information/information systems	1	Unauthorized activities	0
Generation and use of rogue certificates	0	Manipulation of information	0

model we looked at the properties that will be useful for the purpose of sharing and the analysis as it is presented in Table 6. These fields are (Malware, observed-data, Indicator). Therefore, the experts' selection is relevant to our model of risk value evaluation because the excluded properties will not be useful for the purpose of this sharing.

For question Q3.3, six experts gave an answer which included Address, Date and Affected Assets Type. This indicates that some information needs to be grouped and aggregated before sharing as part of reducing the risk of sharing individual information.

Also, sharing the full dataset would not be necessary to achieve the goal of this analysis, and it could reveal sensitive information which might be unimportant to other organisations and highly risky to share. Therefore, after evaluating the dataset we have extracted a sub-dataset which contains only the relevant information. For question Q3.4, seven experts indicated that some attributes should be encrypted, such as indicator of compromise values, email addresses and victim information. This decision will work properly when CyberA needs to share the sub-dataset with other organisations where the level of trust is low and to avoid any inferring of sensitive information, such as network infrastructure from the network traces [14]. We can apply one of the several techniques to protect privacy in correlation, such as salted hashes [15] and homomorphic encryption [16]. By applying these techniques, an analyst can ask for a correlation and analysis without revealing extra information about what they are looking for. For question Q3.5, three experts confirmed that specific fields such as IP addresses and email addresses should be generalized. For question Q4.1, experts were asked to evaluate overall risk on a 1–5 scale, with 5 being the worst. Nine experts indicated that the risks are between 4 and 5 which constitutes a high level of risk. On the other hand, after applying the suggested controls, five experts suggested that the risk value would be between 1 and 2 which constitutes a low risk level. However, when sharing the CTI dataset with trusted entities, the overall value changed from a medium risk level to a low risk level. Eight experts stated that the risk value is between 2 and 3, and after applying the security controls, eight stated it was between 1 and 2. As a result, the case study findings suggest that sharing this CTI dataset is possible after applying specific security controls, mainly by removing unrelated data and applying encryption. From the questionnaire results we find out that our model reached an acceptable match with respect to the cybersecurity and privacy experts. All the threats we identified were also identified by the experts. Experts identified different controls to reduce the risk of sharing and they agreed that sharing this dataset without applying these controls is high risk. Although some experts had different decisions, this difference was due to the different expertise levels and the experts' subjective view of how they define the granularity level of the risk. Also, threat and technical details such as network information can have different meaning between security experts. For example, five experts have not selected the encryption as a security control which should have been applied before sharing, and others focused mainly on the anonymization techniques as a security control. In our model the dataset admin is free to select the security control of choice, for example homomorphic encryption [16, 17] or Secure multi-party computation [18, 19].

4.2.2   Use Case 2: "CTI Contains Malware Information & Personal Information – Aggregation of Data"

This scenario consists of cyber threat companies, CyberA and other companies which share threat intelligence with one another. CyberA has been attacked by a specific threat actor and would like to know how many companies have been attacked by the same threat actor. Sharing the threat actor information is sensitive due to the possibility of identifying the techniques and procedures used in the attack, the victim information and the targeted sector such as oil business, health and diplomatic offices. The incentive of this sharing is to understand and analyse this threat actor. CyberA needs to determine how many companies have been targeted by the same threat actor. In this case study, we have used the STIX report about the "Red October" Campaign [20]. Before sharing the STIX report, we need to evaluate the associated risk of sharing this information within the CTI sharing communities. Table 10 shows the sample CTI dataset which contains the properties that might be shared.

Associated Risk Evaluation

Analogous to use case 1, we have evaluated the associated risk of sharing the CTI dataset, we are applying our model as follows. Table 11 defines the threats associated with disclosing the CTI dataset and identifies the cybersecurity severity for each property as derived from Table 10.

Then we have Table 12 which represents Table 11 in a different way by focusing on the threats.

We estimate the likelihood of a threat occurring based on the property value and the context. For example, targeting high profile victims such as embassies will increase the probability of the "Misuse of information" threat in case of disclosing victim and attack vector information. The total associated risk (TAR) is the sum of sub associated risks of disclosing CTI information. Table 13 presents the likelihood L_{ij} of the threats and the total associated risk score *TAR* when sharing with public sharing communities. Table 14

Table 10. UC3 dataset

Property	Value
TTP Malware Type	Command and Control, capture stored data, Scan network, Exploit vuln, Remote Access Trojan, Downloader, Export data, Spyware/Keylogger, Brute force
TTP Attack Patterns[a]	CAPEC-98
Vulnerability[b]	CVE-2009-3129, CVE-2010-3333, CVE-2012-0158, CVE-2011-3544
Title	Incident associated with Red October campaign. Phishing email with malware attachment leading to infection, C2, credential compromise, and lateral movement through network. Goal to steal classified info and secrets
External ID	4F797501-69F4-4414-BE75-B50EDCF93D6B
Incident Date	2012-01-01T00:00:00
Reporter	Alex John, W-baker org, alex@w-baker.org, (LE1 9BH, Leicester, UK)
Victim	Japan Fair Trade Commission – intnldiv@jftc.go.jp
Victim Address	International Affairs Division (16th floor), Japan Fair Trade Commission, 6-B building, Chuo Chosha, 1-1-1 Kasumigaseki, Chiyoda-ku Tokyo 100-8987
Affected Assets Type	Desktop, Mobile phone, Router or switch, Server, Person
Affected Assets Property	Confidentiality (Classified, Internal, Credentials, Secrets, System) Integrity (Software installation, Modify configuration, Alter behaviour)
Security Compromise	Yes
Discovery Method	Ext - suspicious traffic

(continued)

Table 10. (*continued*)

Property	Value
Threat Actor Title	Lone Wolf Threat Actor Group
Threat Actor Description	Notes: Basing on registration data of command and control servers and numerous artifacts left in executables of the malware, we strongly believe that the attackers have Russian-speaking origins. Current attackers and executables developed by them have been unknown until recently, they have never related to any other targeted cyberattacks
Threat Actor	The Lone Wolf/Gookee Organisation
Threat Actor/Country	Russia
Threat Actor/Area	Moscow
Threat Actor/Address Identifier	lone-wolf@stealthemail.com/facebook.com/theLonewolf
Threat Actor Language	Russian
Threat Actor Motivation	Espionage
Threat Actor Observed TTPs	"example:ttp-fcfe52c2-3060-448b-b828-3e09341485b1""/"example:ttp-2a884574-bf2b-4966-91ba-3e9ff6fea2e3""/"example:ttp-22290611-0125-4c62-abcc-ddd4b8d3fb5d"

[a]Common Attack Pattern Enumeration and Classification - https://capec.mitre.org/index.html
[b]Common Vulnerabilities and Exposures (CVE) https://cve.mitre.org/

Table 11. Associated threats and severity value

Property	Property ID	Threat ID	Severity
TTPs	P1	T1, T2, T3	50
Reporter	P2	T2, T4, T7	10
Victim	P3	T2, T3, T5, T6, T7	50
Affected Asset	P4	T2, T3, T7, T8	10
Threat Actors	P5	T1, T2, T3	50
Security Compromise	P6	T6	10
Discovery Method	P7	T6	10

Table 12. Threats and matched property

Threat	Threat ID	Matched property
Compromising confidential information	T1	P1, P5
Social engineering	T2	P1, P2, P3, P4, P5
Targeted attacks (APTs etc.)	T3	P1, P3, P4, P5
Identity theft (Identity Fraud/Account)	T4	P2, P3
Unauthorized activities	T5	P3
Loss of reputation	T6	P3, P6, P7
Violation of laws or regulations	T7	P2, P3, P4, P5
Failure to meet contractual requirements	T8	P4

presents the likelihood of the threats and the total risk score value when sharing with trusted communities.

When sharing with public communities, the risk value is 493. On the other hand, sharing within trusted communities decreases the risk value by 58% making the value 207. To reduce the risk of sharing and preserve the privacy in the shared information, minimization should be applied to exclude sensitive information that is not relevant to the analysis from the original dataset. The sanitized dataset would fulfil the purpose and usefulness of sharing. In this use case we keep two properties which are "TTPs" and "Threat_Actors". The total risk score of the sub dataset after removing unrelated properties will be reduced to 280 as explained in Table 15.

Table 13. Likelihood and total risk value (public sharing communities)

Threat ID	P1	P2	P3	P4	P5	P6	P7	SUB RISK
T1	1	0	0	0	1	0	0	100
T2	1	0.1	1	0.5	0.5	0	0	131
T3	0.5	0	0.5	0.5	0.5	0	0	80
T4	0	0.1	0.1	0	0	0	0	6
T5	0	0	0.1	0	0	0	0	5
T6	0	0	1	0	0	0.1	0.1	52
T7	0	0.1	0.1	0.1	0.1	0	0	12
T8	0	0	0	0.1	0	0	0	1
T9	0.5	0.1	1	0.5	0.5	0	0	106
TAR								**493**

Table 14. Likelihood and total risk value (trusted communities)

Threat ID	P1	P2	P3	P4	P5	P6	P7	SUB RISK
T1	0.5	0	0	0	0.5	0	0	50
T2	0.5	0.5	0.5	0.1	0.1	0	0	61
T3	0.5	0	0.5	0.1	0.1	0	0	56
T4	0	0.1	0	0	0	0	0	1
T6	0	0	0.5	0	0	0.1	0.1	27
T7	0	0	0	0	0.1	0	0	5
T9	0	0.1	0.1	0.1	0	0	0	7
TAR								**207**

Table 15. Likelihood and total risk value for sub-dataset

Threat	ID	P1	P5	SUB RISK
Compromising confidential information	T1	1	1	100
Social engineering	T2	1	0.5	75
Targeted attacks (APTs etc.)	T3	0.5	0.5	50
Violation of laws or regulations	T7	0	0.1	5
Misuse of information	T9	0.5	0.5	50
TAR				280

Evaluation - Data Collection and Analysis

This section presents the result of the data collection from a questionnaire[2]. Eleven experts filled the survey and a summary of the data collected is presented in Table 16 and discussed in more detail below.

Table 16. UC2 analysis summary: responses returned

Question	Part 1- Sharing with public	Part2- sharing with trusted entities
Q-1	11	10
Q-2	11	9
Q-3.1 (Redaction/Selection)	7	5
Q-3.2 (Anonymisation)	3	5
Q-3.3 (Aggregation)	3	1
Q-3.4 (Enc)	3	4
Q-3.5 (others)	0	0
Q4.1	9	9
Q4.2	6	6

The first question was answered by 11 experts for sharing the CTI dataset with public sharing communities and by 10 when sharing with trusted communities. Nine experts selected in detail the possible associated threats of disclosing this dataset. Table 17 presents the threats and how many experts selected that threat as a possible threat in case of disclosing this CTI dataset. For example, seven experts agreed that disclosing this dataset would be associated with "Compromising confidential information" and six experts agreed on "Social engineering" and "Loss of reputation" threat. The result indicates that the list we have proposed in Table 11 is very similar to the experts' selections in Table 17. For example, we have not considered the "Man-in-the-middle" (MITM) threat. MITM relies on weakness of the communication between two components and based on the report context and the dataset information, we found difficulty in executing this threat. Also, this threat was identified by only one expert.

Table 18 presents the number of experts who decided which threats might be associated with disclosing the CTI dataset when sharing with trusted entities. As shown in Table 18 the set of possible threats has been reduced due to the increase of trust level among the sharing organisations. However, the result still shows that the list we have proposed in Table 11 is very similar to the experts' selections in Table 18.

For question Q2, eleven experts indicate that we cannot share this dataset, or we can share after applying specific security controls. This result indicates that we need to apply security controls before sharing this dataset in order to reduce the risk of sharing.

For questions Q3.1 and Q3.2 experts select values that should be anonymized or removed from the dataset before sharing. Many of the experts propose that we need to

---

[2] https://docs.google.com/document/d/1y0N18P-C34b93AVc2u-I44BX7uRLuobS0kkQyXud
XCw/edit?usp=sharing.

Table 17. UC2-part1-threat summary

Threat	Count	Threat	Count
Social engineering	6	Loss of reputation	6
Failure to meet contractual requirements	2	Unauthorized physical access	0
Violation of laws or regulations	4	Failed business process	2
Compromising confidential information	7	Man-in-the-middle	1
Identity theft (Identity Fraud/Account)	3	Terrorist attack	3
Abuse of authorizations	2	Targeted attacks (APTs etc.)	5
Misuse of information	5	Unauthorized activities	3
Generation and use of rogue certificates	1	Manipulation of information	4

Table 18. UC2-Part2-threat summary

Threat	Count	Threat	Count
Social engineering	1	Loss of reputation	5
Failure to meet contractual requirements	3	Unauthorized physical access	0
Violation of laws or regulations	2	Failed business process	1
Compromising confidential information	3	Man-in-the-middle	0
Identity theft (Identity Fraud/Account)	1	Terrorists attack	1
Abuse of authorizations	0	Targeted attacks (APTs etc.)	1
Misuse of information	2	Unauthorized activities	1
Generation and use of rogue certificates	0	Manipulation of information	1

remove all personal information and victim information such as the organisations name. In this case the victim information is not related to the purpose of sharing which matches our model and evaluation. For question Q3.3, three experts gave answers which included Address, Date and Affected Assets. This indicates that some information needs to be grouped and aggregated before sharing as part of reducing the risk of sharing individual information. For question Q3.4, three experts indicate that some attributes should be encrypted, such as threat actor and TTPs information and we can use techniques that support operations on encrypted data such as homomorphic encryption and multiparty computation. Finally, for question Q4.1, nine experts indicate that the risks are between 5 and 4 which constitute a high level of risk. On the other hand, after applying the suggested controls, five experts suggest that the risk value would be between 1 and 2 which constitutes a low risk level. When sharing the CTI dataset with trusted entities, the overall value changed from a medium risk level to a low risk level. eight experts state that the risk value is between 2 and 4, and after applying the security controls, six state that it is between 1 and 2. Tables 17 and 18 show that the number of selected individual threats in this use case is higher than the first use case. In addition, Tables 13,

14 and 15 present that the total risk value of this use case is higher than the first use case risk value. This is rational due to the context of the second use case. The second use case is about an attack and threat actor targeting diplomatic institutions worldwide [21]. The threat actor developed their own malware for stealing sensitive information and used techniques such as valid accounts to get access to the victim network. From the questionnaire results we find that our model matches the experts' decisions. The risk value is high, so sharing this information publicly will put the organisation at a higher risk. Therefore, sharing this dataset with trusted communities or applying multiparty computation to get the analytics result will decrease the sharing risk.

5   Threats to Validity

In terms of the participants and sample size, 23 experts (3rd year PhD students, Academics and industrial practitioners all working in cybersecurity) participated in this study where their feedback and evaluation used to evaluate the model. The experts were introduced to the use cases they had in order to evaluate without a previous tutorial, so it is possible that the experts were not completely familiar with the cyber threat intelligence and cyber incident reports. We neither tracked the time of the evaluation nor created a controlled environment where experts are tracked more closely. Concerning maturation, we have started with four use cases to be validated by each expert, but we noticed that the participants became tired and did not complete the full use cases. Therefore, we just used fifteen experts to validate the two use cases. Finally, concerning the generalization, using academic and professional experts might help the generalization of the results to be used in the industrial context. On the other hand, we might need more use cases to be able to generalize to real-world cyber threat intelligence platforms.

6   Conclusion and Future Work

In this work, we present a new quantitative risk model for sharing CTI datasets. The main objective of this model is to develop a framework to support sharing decisions regarding which information to share, and with whom. We have extended our previous works, in [2] we performed a comprehensive analysis of incident reporting information through the STIX incident model to identify the threats of disclosing sensitive and identifying information and in [13] we addressed the legal risks associated with sharing datasets. Here we have identified the potential threats associated with sharing a CTI dataset, computed the severity for each property, and we propose an estimating of the likelihood of the threats in case of property disclosure. Finally, we have calculated the total risk score of sharing a CTI dataset, and we addressed all risks associated with the data which will be shared. Based on the risk value, the organisations can select appropriate privacy preserving techniques to reduce the risk of sharing. In order to evaluate the model, we have asked experts' opinions for risk identification and evaluation for three different use cases. As future work, we intend to consider the level of trust among the organisations which might be beneficial to implement the model to be included and integrated in existing cyber threat intelligence platform such as MISP [22]. Furthermore, the future work involves further assessment to confirm our risk assessment model practicality through applying it to more real-world scenarios.

References

1. Katti, S., Krishnamurthy, B., Katabi, D.: Collaborating against common enemies. In: Proceedings of the ACM SIGCOMM Internet Measurement Conference, IMC (2005)
2. Albakri, A., Boiten, E., De Lemos, R.: Risks of sharing cyber incident information. In: Proceedings of the 13th International Conference on Availability, Reliability and Security - ARES 2018, pp. 1–10 (2018)
3. European Union: Regulation 2016/679 of the European parliament and the Council of the European Union of 27 April 2016 on the protection of natural persons with regard to the processing of personal data and on the free movement of such data, and repealing Directive 95/46/. Official Journal of the European Communities, vol. 59, May. pp. 1–88 (2016)
4. Lewis, R., Louvieris, P., Abbott, P., Clewley, N., Jones, K.: Cybersecurity information sharing: a framework for information security management in UK SME supply chains. In: ECIS 2014 Proceedings - 22nd European Conference on Information Systems (2014)
5. Shin, J., Son, H., Heo, G.: Cyber security risk evaluation of a nuclear I&C using BN and ET. Nucl. Eng. Technol. **49**, 517–524 (2017)
6. Aksu, M.U., et al.: A quantitative CVSS-based cyber security risk assessment methodology for IT systems. In: Proceedings - International Carnahan Conference on Security Technology (2017)
7. Dickinson, G.: Enterprise risk management: its origins and conceptual foundation. Geneva Pap. Risk Insur. Issues Pract. **26**(3), 360–366 (2001)
8. ISO 27005: Information Technology- Security techniques-Information security risk management (2011)
9. NIST: Guide for Conducting Risk Assessments - Information Security (2012)
10. Alberts, C., Dorofee, A., Stevens, J., Woody, C.: Introduction to the OCTAVE approach. In: Pittsburgh, P.A., Carnegie Mellon University (2003)
11. ENISA: ENISA Threat Landscape Report 2016: 15 Top Cyber-Threats And Trends (2017). https://goo.gl/N3xP1F. Accessed 25 Apr 2018
12. MITRE: STIX Incident Model (2018). https://stixproject.github.io/data-model/1.2/incident/IncidentType/. Accessed 10 Dec 2019
13. Albakri, A., Boiten, E., De Lemos, R.: Sharing cyber threat intelligence under the general data protection regulation. In: Naldi, M., Italiano, G.F., Rannenberg, K., Medina, M., Bourka, A. (eds.) APF 2019. LNCS, vol. 11498, pp. 28–41. Springer, Cham (2019). https://doi.org/10.1007/978-3-030-21752-5_3
14. Coull, S.E., Wright, C.V., Monrose, F., Collins, M.P., Reiter, M.K., et al.: Playing devil's advocate: inferring sensitive information from anonymized network traces. In: NDSS (2007)
15. Kent, A.D., Liebrock, L.M.: Secure communication via shared knowledge and a salted hash in Ad-hoc environments. In: Proceedings - International Computer Software and Applications Conference (2011)
16. Gentry, C.: A fully homomorphic encryption scheme, Stanford University (2009)
17. Armknecht, F., et al.: A Guide to Fully Homomorphic Encryption, Cryptol. ePrint Arch. (2015)
18. Yao, A.C.: Protocols for secure computations. In: Annual Symposium on Foundations of Computer Science - Proceedings (1982)
19. Bogdanov, D., Talviste, R., Willemson, J.: Deploying secure multi-party computation for financial data analysis. In: Keromytis, A.D. (ed.) FC 2012. LNCS, vol. 7397, pp. 57–64. Springer, Heidelberg (2012). https://doi.org/10.1007/978-3-642-32946-3_5
20. MITRE: Red October. https://github.com/STIXProject/schemas-test/blob/master/veris/. Accessed 09 Dec 2019

21. Kaspersky: Attackers Created Unique, Highly-Flexible Malware to Steal Data and Geopolitical Intelligence from Target Victims' Computer Systems, Mobile Phones and Enterprise Network Equipment. https://www.kaspersky.com/about/press-releases/2013_kaspersky-lab-identifies-operation–red-october–an-advanced-cyber-espionage-campaign-targeting-diplomatic-and-government-institutions-worldwide. Accessed 25 Feb 2020
22. MISP-Project: MISP (2016). http://www.misp-project.org/. Accessed 12 Dec 2017

kUBI: A Framework for Privacy and Transparency in Sensor-Based Business Models for Consumers: A Pay-How-You-Drive Example

Christian Roth$^{(\boxtimes)}$ (iD), Mario Saur, and Dogan Kesdogan

University of Regensburg, Regensburg, Germany
{christian.roth,mario.saur,dogan.kesdogan}@ur.de

Abstract. Ubiquitous computing has fundamentally redefined many existing business models. The collected sensor data has great potential, which is being recognized by more and more industries, including car insurance companies with Usage-Based Insurance (UBI). However, most of these business models are very privacy-invasive and must be constructed with care. For a data processor, the integrity of the data is particularly important. With *kUBI* , we present a framework that takes into account the interests of the providers as well as the privacy of the users, using the example of Android. It is fully integrated into the Android system architecture. It uses hybrid data processing in both stakeholder domains. Protected enclaves, whose function can be transparently traced by a user at any time, protect company secrets in the hostile environment, i.e. a user's smartphone. The framework is theoretically outlined and its integration into Android is shown. An evaluation shows that the user in the exemplary use case UBI can be protected by *kUBI* .

Keywords: Privacy Enhancing Technology · Transparency Enhancing Technology · Sensor data · Smartphone · Privacy framework.

1 Introduction

Ubiquitous computing fundamentally changes our understanding of existing business models. Personal-agents such as smartphones are kept close to a user. They collect sensor data which are of great value for companies because they enable user-specific products. Benndorf & Normann found that the *readiness-to-share* this data is related to monetary aspects [5]. Threats to privacy are knowingly or unknowingly disregarded [13]. As a result, the majority of users are willing to disclose comprehensive information about their digital identity [14]. The loose nature of the data exchange may also be related to the *nothing-to-hide* mentality of the users; as long as no negative consequences are feared, the willingness to share data increases or unjustified data flows are accepted [21]. The consequences of data protection violations are often unclear from the outside,

© Springer Nature Switzerland AG 2020
I. Boureanu et al. (Eds.): ESORICS 2020 Workshops, LNCS 12580, pp. 114–132, 2020.
https://doi.org/10.1007/978-3-030-66504-3_7

so that this danger is sometimes disregarded. This can also be seen in the lack of awareness when dealing with (sensitive) data. Felt et al. [9] show that the majority of users accept Android permissions requested by applications without question. Permissions once granted are generally not revoked [14]. This can lead to a dangerous spiral, which is exacerbated by observing the results of Weydert et al. [24]: The willingness to share data continues to grow as users are given the opportunity to actively participate in and control the data process. Thus, a Transparency Enhancing Technology (TET) is essential for users to understand which data is shared with a foreign party and for what reason.

Another serious threat is the lack of awareness of privacy attack vectors in smartphones. This is serious, since smartphones have broad tracking capabilities and are part of the private sphere. It is known that sensors such as cameras, microphones or device memory are sensitive [18]. However, literature shows that even on the basis of so-called zero-permission sensors like accelerometers or gyroscopes, which belong to the Inertial Measurement Unit (IMU) family, attacks on privacy are possible. A IMU produces Floating Phone Data (FPD) which are mandatory for sensor-based business models. This motivates the need for a Privacy Enhancing Technology (PET) which is suitable to protect the data of the users.

Contribution. In this paper, we propose a PET/TET in form of a holistic framework for balancing privacy and integrity. It takes into account the diverse and conflicting interests of the stakeholders involved. In fact, we

- present threats related to sensor data in smartphones and place them in the context of (UBI),
- present our comprehensive framework *kUBI* that takes into account the various demands of the stakeholders,
- show how to embed *kUBI* into Android to enable privacy-friendly Pay-How-You-Drive (PHYD), and
- use an existing attack from previous work [20] to show that the proposed procedure can increase privacy and integrity in PHYD.

Structure. The remainder of this paper is organized as follows. In Sect. 2, we list related work and present some basics for this work. Afterwards, Sect. 4 presents the UBI scenario including the stakeholders. A short insight into the creation of sensor data using Android is given in Sect. 3. Subsequently, the framework *kUBI* is described in detail and integrity and privacy aspects are considered. An evaluation (c.f. Sect. 6) shows on the basis of an existing attack and real data that *kUBI* can protect privacy. We conclude the paper in Sect. 7.

2   Related Work

It is obvious that the current permission system in Android is not sufficient in certain cases [6]. Therefore, there is active research to foster understanding of sensor data usage (e.g. [4]) or to provide protection mechanisms (e.g. [3,7]). Many of the approaches either block sensor access altogether or introduce blurring elements into the collected data to prevent sensor misuse. In the context of many sensor-based business models, this is not a practicable way, because the data lose their meaningfulness. A correct evaluation is no longer possible. Policy-driven systems must support multiple stakeholders [6] to be applicable in the given context. However, a policy might contain sensitive information, which has to be protected. This is a dilemma, since the policy is issued by a business, but for reasons of privacy, it is to be enforced in the domain of the user, without the user knowing the contents.

Furthermore, the right conclusions have to be derived from the data for many business models to be usable. Therefore, Privacy Preserving Data Mining (PPDM) techniques have to be found. In their survey, Hong et al. [12] analyze multiple perturbation methods for time series, although not in the context of UBI. Roth et al. [20] motivated the need for a new privacy-enhanced framework to enable trust and privacy in sensor-based business models, because it was shown that existing PPDM techniques such as anatomization, permutation, and perturbation are insufficient in this area.

When focusing on the context of UBI, there is little work, although these kind of insurance models are on the rise. Troncoso et al. [22] already proposed a privacy-enhanced model for Pay-As-You-Drive (PAYD). However, PAYD is significantly different to PHYD, because here, it is often only the location that is problematic [10]. Thus, the need for privacy-enabled PHYD models still exists, since PHYD-enabled rates are common in the UBI business model.

3   Mobile Application Environment

This section gives a brief overview of sensor data processing.

3.1   Android Sensor Stack

Modern smartphones offer a broad range of sensors. Built-in sensors may measure motion, orientation, and environmental conditions. They are accompanied by virtual sensors which deliver preprocessed data. In the context of mobility, data from a smartphone is often called Floating Phone Data (FPD).

We present the sensor stack at the example of Android (Fig. 1; c.f. [2]). Application developers interact with the Android OS via the SDK which represents a high level view of the sensors. The Framework links multi-

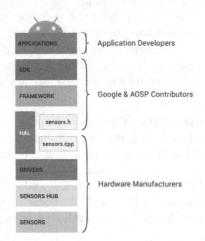

Fig. 1. Layers of the Android sensor stack [2].

ple applications to the Hardware Abstraction Layer (HAL). It introduces multiplexing, enabling multiple applications to access a sensor at the same time.

Virtual sensors are also created within this layer. The HAL is the link between Android and a hardware manufacturer's implementation for a concrete sensor. It follows a well defined interface (sensors.h). Lower layers are in the sole responsibility of hardware manufacturers and may be closed source. Android itself is unable to alter any sensor behavior unless defined in sensors.h. For security reasons, the stack is organized bottom-up, i.e. higher levels cannot send data to lower instances. Multiple applications reading data from the same sensor do not interfere. It is simple to register to sensor readings. First, an Android-wide SensorManager gives access to the SensorService which in turn can be used to access various sensors. Then, a SensorEventListener can be used to handle sensor updates. The following example queries the accelerometer and is updated everytime a new SensorEvent is acquired.

```
1   val sensorManager = getSystemService(Context.SENSOR_SERVICE) as SensorManager
2   val accelerometerSensor: Sensor? = ↩
        sensorManager.getDefaultSensor(Sensor.TYPE_ACCELEROMETER)
3   val sensorListener = object: SensorEventListener {
4       override fun onAccuracyChanged(sensor: Sensor, accuracy: Int) { }
5       override fun onSensorChanged(event: SensorEvent) {
6           val dT: Long = event.timestamp
7           val axisX: Float = event.values.get(0)
8           val axisY: Float = event.values.get(1)
9           val axisZ: Float = event.values.get(2)
10          // further process values
11      }
12
13  }
14  sensorManager.registerListener(sensorListener, accelerometerSensor, ↩
        SensorManager.SENSOR_DELAY_FASTEST)
```

3.2   Attacks on Sensor Data

Both prominent mobile operating systems, Android and iOS, protect specific sensors using a sophisticated permission system. These permissions control which app is allowed to use the information by a sensor. However, as of the current Android 11, some sensors are not protected by the user-controlled permission system, which indicates a threat for privacy. A corrupt application can read the sensor data for further processing without the user noticing and never asking for permission. It may be used to gather the needed sensor data. The privacy violation facing the user solely using sensor data from an IMU is extensive:

– **Identification attacks.** The first class of attacks wants to identify a driver from a set of drivers (e.g. [17]). In some cases, a learning phase is necessary so that the attack can name the entity afterwards. Typically, this is a closed-set problem. Furthermore, the device used can also be the target of an identification attack in which it is to be uniquely recognized (e.g. [25]).
– **Trajectory reconstruction.** In addition, in some cases it is of interest to trace the route taken by a user (e.g. [15]). The motivation can be versatile and ranges from hotspot identification (such as the place of work) to the derivation of movement patterns, as well as the conclusion of characteristics of the driver (e.g. hospital visits indicate an illness).

- **Reconstruct environment.** Furthermore, not only can route and driver be deduced from the sensor data, but also the surroundings and means of transport such as bus or train (e.g. [11]).
- **Spoken word reconstruction.** Another kind of attack is even more privacy-invasive since it tries to reconstruct words from the accelerometer and thus can gain additional information without the need to ask for microphone permission. The main motivation for this research is hot-word detection for personal assistants [26], but can also be used as an invasive technology.

Even though this is only a short list, it motivates the need for privacy-protection of frameworks. Deactivating a sensor, however, is not a feasible approach. In our scenario, everyone with access to the raw sensor values can act as an attacker executing one of the mentioned attacks.

4   Usage-Based Insurance

In the following section we clarify the given scenario of UBI [23]. In addition to the well-known payment model based on no-claims classes, the models PHYD [8] and the related but significantly different model PAYD [16] are used in the automotive insurance industry. Both are innovative pricing models in the category UBI. In contrast to PAYD, which places value on generally valid characteristics when calculating the premium, e.g. kilometers driven and the main area covered [23], PHYD takes into account the individual driving behavior of a driver. As with existing vehicle insurance policies, a vehicle is priced, and there is no individual allocation of costs to the respective drivers.

We use UBI as the running example for our framework, although it can be adapted to other sensor-based business models such as health insurance.

4.1   Stakeholders and Their Respective Interests

The UBI scenario introduces two stakeholders, first the policyholder and then the insurer. It is obvious that both parties have different priorities regarding the business model.

The policyholder wants to protect his own privacy. In the PHYD business model, data such as GPS or sensor data from the accelerometer or gyroscope are collected while driving to give multiple insights into a user's driving style. One can argue that this data are critical in terms of privacy. According to e.g. Pfitzmann [19], privacy is conveyed among other things by the fact that users can decide for themselves which data are passed on and to what extent. This is not the case for most PHYD models, since data are gathered solely as defined by the insurer. However, a user only receives a discount if he transmits the data. Thus, he too has an interest in ensuring the integrity of the data.

An insurer on the other side is primarily interested in correct information, i.e, sensor data with integrity. One can further differentiate between two integrity aspects. Firstly, an insurer is interested in correct data (data integrity), so he can derive the correct driver classification for a trip. Secondly, system integrity is important to guarantee a correct workflow according to the given business model.

4.2 Workflow

In Roth et al. [20], PHYD and PAYD products from different major insurance companies in Germany were analyzed. Typically, a vehicle in this context that is driven by several people is insured, one of whom is the policy holder. FPD are recorded using a smartphone or, in rare cases, with a black box. The transmitted raw sensor values denoted as S are usually not analyzed by the insurer itself, but by an external data processor. Aggregated statements are then made available to the insurer. Often certain events in the data are analyzed, so-called maneuvers m, which are patterns in the raw data S. These include, for example, braking or acceleration events. The exact process of information extraction is a protected company secret and is usually not communicated. We assume that the classification process uses a blackbox classification function $\mathcal{C}$ to assign each m to one of μ classes (e.g. aggressive, neutral, passive). The data processor often works for several insurance companies. After analysis of the trips of a certain period of time, a discount is given to the policy holder by the insurance company. The amount of the discount depends on the type of driving.

Interestingly, data are mostly processed by a third party agency. This is often motivated as a privacy foundation since the third party processor only receives the raw sensor data and an identifier independent of customer information. The insurance companies claim that personal data are thus separated from driving data. On that basis, privacy shall be provided, although, this seems like a poor approach to convince a user. Data processing through a third party requires an additional level of trust from the user, especially since some of the processors are not even located in Europe. At the moment, illegal use of the data should be prevented from an organizational and legal point of view by the General Data Protection Regulation (GDPR) in article 5. However, we motivate the need for a technological protection mechanism to, along with others, protect one from privacy attacks. This is underlined by the fact that at this time, there are no TETs or PETs, which make the evaluation of the driving data comprehensible.

In the interest of data economy and expediency, only data that actively allow pricing within the framework of a UBI rate should be collected by the insurer. If further information can be read out of the data, allowing an increase in knowledge, this should be viewed critically by the client in the sense of privacy. Consequently, the question arises whether an insurer will misuse data to derive further information. A PET should prevent such kinds of attacks.

5 *kUBI*

There is obvious need for a privacy-enhanced version to process sensor data. Our proposed pattern named *kUBI* is device agnostic, hence not bound to a specific implementation. Furthermore, it is flexible to enable multiple business models which rely on sensor data.

5.1   Potential Strategies

A holistic pattern for privacy-enhancing existing business models has to take into account the contradicting requirements of the stakeholders. We now discuss four different strategies which are possible in the given context.

1. **Processor-based.** All data are collected by a user using a (blackbox) device or smartphone application and submitted as raw data to the processor. The user can neither control nor is there technical evidence that the data is only used for a specific use case, resulting in a less trustful model. Hence, this model is a classical example of *undercover-agent trust*, where an insurer wants to protect his interests from the legitimate user of the device. This is the per-se standard model in the context of UBI.
2. **User-based.** Since a user always trusts his local device (called *personal agent trust*), it is desirable that a user collects and processes the data in his trusted domain. To enforce privacy, only results or aggregated partitions of data are transferred (after approval) to a processor. Integrity is harder to validate on the processor side.
3. **Balanced.** The processor defines the needed service quality via a policy. The user anonymizes data w.r.t service policy and only sends aggregated results. Furthermore, a user can ensure within his anonymization that his own private goals are reached. Hence, integrity can be controlled by the process while privacy is solely controlled by a user.
4. **Trustee-based.** Trust is moved from the processor to a trustee, however, this is a limited enhancement for the user compared to the processor-based approach since trustworthiness in a model is not increased.

5.2   Privacy Enhanced Model

According to the balanced strategy, we now present our pattern for privacy-enhanced business models relying on and processing sensor data from users. The pattern is designed w.r.t Pfitzmann et al. [19] and has two different zones. One is the local trust zone of a user (*User Domain*) and the other the domain of the processor (*Business Domain*). Nobody trusts the zone of his counterpart with one exception: the user's trust zone has an isolated environment called *Hostile Domain* (i.e. a Trusted Execution Environment (TEE)) which can execute hostile but authenticated code in a well defined manner. The user is unable to see or tamper with functions in this isolated environment. Even though we show our model's feasibility at the example of PHYD, it can be ported to other use cases as well.

kUBI protects users' privacy by establishing k-anonymity in a data set. Recall that in the PHYD model, a vehicle is insured, the rate of which is calculated by the classification of the trips made with this vehicle. The classification of a trip is done by the classification of maneuvers. The way the maneuvers are recognized in the sensor data stream is the same for all drivers, but each driver shows an individual behavior during a maneuver. This allows an unnecessary identification of the

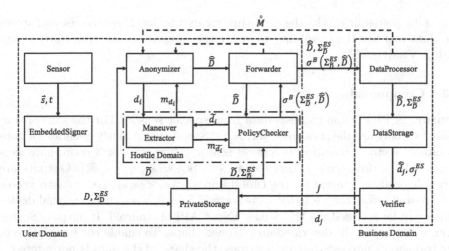

Fig. 2. Pattern for privacy enhanced business models relying and processing sensor data from users.

driver. *kUBI* first performs Complex Event Processing to identify these maneuvers in a continuous data stream. It then replaces the detected maneuvers in such a way that although the correct classification of the maneuvers (by the insurer) is still ensured, the entropy of the maneuvers is reduced to such an extent that no conclusions can be drawn about the driver. This is achieved by using reference maneuvers of the same class as drop-in replacements for recognized, driver-derived maneuvers. Performing the whole trip classification in the user domain and only forward that data to an insurer is not feasible since e.g. additional or historical knowledge is needed and computation resources are limited.

The proposed framework *kUBI* is organized in several modules, as illustrated in Fig. 2, which are either placed in the users domain (i.e. mobile phone) including the hostile environment, or the business domain (i.e. insurer). We consider *kUBI* being a PET because a user can actively decide what is sent and establish anonymity himself. We also consider it aTET because the user sees the data including evaluation, i.e. maneuvers, which are passed on.

Data are generated using a SENSOR $\mathcal{S}$ such as the accelerometer and then directly forwarded to an EMBEDDEDSIGNER unit $\mathcal{E}$ which aggregates multiple sensor values into a data block d. This unit signs each data block value to prevent changing sensor values in a block afterwards. The signature and the respective value is then forwarded to a persistent PRIVATESTORAGE $\mathcal{PS}$ and is forwarded from here in the form of a trip to two modules. The ANONYMIZER $\mathcal{A}$ is responsible for replacing driven maneuvers with a suitable reference maneuver. The maneuver identification is performed by a MANEUVEREXTRACTOR $\mathcal{M}$, which is initialized by the insurer and located in the Hostile Domain. A POLICYCHECKER $\mathcal{P}$ (also in the hostile domain) checks the correct functioning of $\mathcal{A}$. It confirms an integer anonymization by issuing a signature σ and passes it to the forwarder in the user's domain. According to Pfitzmann et al. [19], the forwarder decides whether the anonymized data blocks $\widetilde{\widehat{D}}$ will be forwarded to the data processor.

The data processor checks the signature created by the $\mathcal{P}$, processes and stores the data and has the possibility to verify the integrity of the transmitted data with a VERIFIER $\mathcal{V}$.

5.3   Components

Sensor. A PHYD app requests data from specific sensors. For the sake of simplicity we only use the accelerometer. A SENSOR $\mathcal{S}$ continuously generates a data stream of vectors consisting of several sensor values (say for 3 coordinate axes x, y, z) and a timestamp t, denoted as $s = [s_x, s_y, s_z, s_t]^T \in \mathbb{R}^4$. Outputs are chronologically organized by the timestamp $s_{i,t}$ ($s_i < s_{i+1}$, i.e. the i-th vector was created before the $i + 1$-th)[1]. As shown in Sect. 3, a sensor is a virtual device which can be accessed via the Sensor Event API of Android. It outputs Sensor Events (i.e. $\vec{s}s$) in the described and defined shape. To enable the integration of our framework into existing applications, the shape of the data is not altered.

EmbeddedSigner. An application registers at a Signed Sensor Event API to receive Signed Sensor Events. Signed Sensor Events are extended versions of the existing Sensor Events with additional information to provide integrity. A Signed Sensor Event is a concatenation of multiple s based on a timestamp δt_{SSE} (e.g. 1 s). We call such a Signed Sensor Event data block with i elements,

$$d_k = \{[s_1, \ldots, s_i], \sigma_k^{ES} \mid s_{l,t} \in (t_{Start}, t_{Start} + \delta t_{SSE}) \text{ for } l = 1, 2, \ldots, i\}$$

which starts at t_{Start} and includes all s generated up to Δt_{SSE}. Data blocks are non overlapping, i.e. the $k + 1$-th data block's first element is s_{i+1}. Each d_k also has, next to its payload, a signature $\sigma_{d_k}^{\mathcal{E}} = (\mathcal{H}_{\mathcal{E}}(\vec{s}_1 \| \ldots \| \vec{s}_i))^{d_{ES}}$ of that payload. The signature is created by using a secure and publicly known hash function $\mathcal{H}_{\mathcal{E}})$ to hash the concatenation of all Sensor Events in that data block and then signing the hash value using the EMBEDDEDSIGNER's private key $d_{\mathcal{E}}.$. Furthermore, let id be a function defined as $id(d_k) = \{0,1\}^3 2$ which deterministically creates a unique ID for a data block (independent of the payload).

The EMBEDDEDSIGNER and its Signed Sensor Event API should be used as a drop-in replacement for the current Sensor Event API and be provided by Android itself for wide and easy adoption. The Android Sensor Stack architecture enables the separation of data acquisition by means of the physical sensor and data processing in the application, hence compatibility of the proposal is ensured.

It is meaningful to place the EMBEDDEDSIGNER, which is provided by the OS, in a secure and tamper-proof enclave. For example, Trusty [1] can be used here. Trusty is an Android specific implementation of a TEE for various practical purposes and runs on the same processor of the end device, but according to the TEE definition independent of userland applications. With the Keystore API, Android already offers secure key management, used to create and verify signatures. It is thus suitable for the EMBEDDEDSIGNER. *kUBI* can use digital

---

[1] We use {} to denote such an ordered set and [] to specify an unordered list.

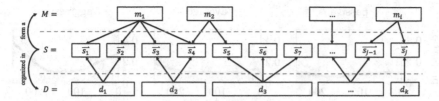

Fig. 3. Relationship of D, S and M. S form M and are organized in D.

certificates whose root CA is Google itself and whose device-specific private key $d_{\mathcal{E}}$ is deposited once by Google in the Keystore API of the respective device. The device's public certificate can be freely distributed, e.g. for a data processor to verify signatures.

PrivateStorage. The PRIVATESTORAGE is a persistent storage which holds all data blocks D of a device, including the set Σ^{ES} of all signatures $\sigma^{ES}_{d_1,\ldots,|D|}$. It also serves as a buffer, since a trip is only classified by the insurer's app after it has been completed. It concatenates multiple data blocks $d_i,\ldots,d_j$ to a trip $\widetilde{D} \subset D$ which is subject to classification and thus anonymization with the respective signature set $\Sigma^{ES}_{\widetilde{D}} = \{\sigma^{ES}_{d_i}\|\ldots\|\sigma^{ES}_{d_j}\}$ for that trip.

ManeuverExtractor. According to the setting (c.f. Sect. 4), maneuvers are interesting in terms of trip classification. For instance, many hard braking maneuvers occurring in a trip indicate aggressive or inattentive driving. Typically, all maneuvers M are derived by analyzing patterns in the sensor data stream and e.g. thresholds are not communicated by an insurer. *kUBI* takes this into account by placing a customizable MANEUVEREXTRACTOR into the hostile domain of the system. The MANEUVEREXTRACTOR works as-a-service by sticking to blackbox principles to protect the insurer's business case (*undercover-agent trust*). This provides secrecy, one important requirement from the stakeholder analysis. Hence, the MANEUVEREXTRACTOR extracts maneuvers from the data block stream using a confidential process. However, the user is able to control in and output to enhance trust: $\mathcal{M} : \{d_1,\ldots,d_i\} \longrightarrow \{m_{d_1},\ldots,m_{d_i}\} = \widetilde{M}$ with $\forall d \in \widetilde{D}$. The output is a list of maneuvers crafted by these data blocks including derivable start and end timestamps.

Figure 3 illustrates the relationship of maneuvers M, data blocks D and single sensor values S. The EMBEDDEDSIGNER concatenates multiple sensor values into data blocks which, in turn, can form maneuvers. However, a sensor value does not need to form a maneuver, e.g. if the driver is only going straight without accelerating or braking. $len_s(m)$ defines the number of sensor values that form a maneuver, while $len_d(m)$ counts the number of data blocks. It is likely that $\exists m_a, m_b \in M : len_s(m_a) \neq len_s(m_b)$ holds. Further, we define a transformation function $\mathcal{T}^z(x^*) = y^*$ where $x, y \in [s, m, d]$ and z is the destination type. All elements are time series, but are different subsets. $\mathcal{T}$ transforms units accordingly

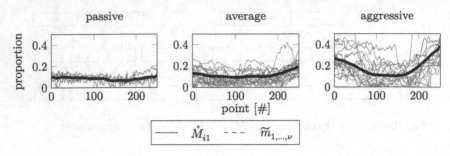

Fig. 4. Reference maneuvers $\mathring{M}_{i1}$ with $i = 1, \dots, \mu = 3$ are representative for a category. Shown are maneuvers of type *braking* for a single s (λ is set to 250).

to Fig. 3. For instance, $\mathcal{T}^s(m) = [s_1, s_2, \dots]$ transforms a maneuver to a list of sensor values that form that maneuver.

Anonymizer. Since maneuvers are used to categorize a trip, their integrity is important. However, at the same time, maneuvers help to identify a driver as shown in [20]. Furthermore, sending raw data to foreign domains is critical, thus the ANONYMIZER module is responsible for balancing the mentioned interests. *kUBI* achieves this by replacing identified $\widetilde{M}$ in a privacy-friendly, but comprehensible way with so-called reference maneuvers using a one-way function with similar properties like a hash function: $\mathcal{A} : \widetilde{D} \longrightarrow \widehat{\widetilde{D}}$. It is easy to replace a driven maneuver with a reference maneuver using $\mathcal{A}$.. However, it is very hard to reconstruct the original maneuver from a reference maneuver.

A reference maneuver is representative for a maneuver type of a class. *kUBI* assumes that a reference maneuver is created on the basis of real maneuvers by overlaying them (which is also common in speech recognition), e.g. using Soft-DTW barycenter, although it is basically independent of that because reference maneuvers $\mathring{M}$ are provided by the data processor (i.e. insurer). $\mathring{M}$ is a $\mu \times \nu$ matrix where μ is the number of classes an insurer uses to categorize a trip and ν is the number of reference maneuvers selectable for replacement of a maneuver class. We recall that in the given scenario, $\mu = 3$ classes exist. Figure 4 illustrates how reference maneuvers can be constructed from previous, globally recorded maneuvers of a category in the data-processor's domain using the weighted average.

The ANONYMIZER processes any maneuver $\widetilde{M}_{i=1,\dots,\mu;j=1,\dots,\nu}$ to select a suitable reference maneuver to replace m. One speaks in the following of the anonymous maneuver $\widehat{\widetilde{m}}$, once the original maneuver is replaced. In order to perform the selection, we use Dynamic Time Warping (DTW). DTW can compare two time series by finding the so-called optimal warping path, denoted as $dtw(m_1, m_2)$. The warping path can be interpreted as a similarity between two time series, i.e. two maneuvers m_1, m_2, although maneuvers are previously resampled to same length and normalized to enable comparison. Let $\mathcal{R} : \mathbb{R}^{*\times 4} \longrightarrow \mathbb{R}^{\lambda \times 4}$ be a resampling function $\mathcal{R}$ to transform any given maneuver $m \in M$ of arbitrary length so that $len_s(m) = \lambda$ holds afterwards. The (already normalized) $\mathring{M}_{ij}$ with the minimal warping path is selected for replacement, transformed to a data block and respective sensor values. The result of the ANONYMIZER is a set $\hat{\tilde{D}}$ which contains the trip but all maneuvers have been replaced (and thus anonymized to provide k-anonymity) with a corresponding reference maneuver. However, since the maneuver (and its corresponding data blocks resp. sensor values) has to be adjusted to fit into the data stream, we call it $\hat{\tilde{d}}$. Note that the characteristics of a trip, its maneuver class distribution and order have not been altered at all, allowing to draw the same conclusions by the data processor.

Forwarder. Trust in the system is established, among other things, by the fact that the data is not sent to the insurer through an app provided by the insurer, but is under the control of the user (personal-agent trust [19]). If a user decides to submit data to a data processor, he needs a valid signature $\sigma^B(\Sigma_{\hat{\tilde{D}}}^{ES}, \hat{\tilde{D}})$ to prove an anonymization process as it was agreed on with the data processor. Therefore, he forwards the anonymized trip $\hat{\tilde{D}}$ to a POLICYCHECKER to have its correctness confirmed.

PolicyChecker. By defining a policy Φ, the data processor can determine the extent to which the sensor values may deviate between the original and the resulting trip. By specifying a policy, the data quality of the trip is guaranteed despite the anonymization of the sensor data. It is an important building block to balance privacy and integrity. First, it verifies that the anonymized trip $\hat{\tilde{D}}$ was created on behalf of the real trip data $\tilde{D}$. This can be validated by executing a specific Φ. Recall that each $\vec{S} \subset \tilde{D}$ has a timestamp which cannot be altered due to the signature $\Sigma_{\tilde{D}}^{ES}$. Hence, this combination is used to prove integrity to a data processor and is transmitted to him via a signature from its POLICYCHECKER. Let $\mathcal{P}$ be a function that creates a valid signature if Φ holds: $\mathcal{P} : \hat{\tilde{D}}, \tilde{D}, \Sigma_{\tilde{D}}^{\mathcal{E}} \to \sigma^{\mathcal{P}}(\Sigma_{\tilde{D}}^{ES}, \mathcal{H}_{\mathcal{P}}(\hat{\tilde{D}}))$ where $\mathcal{H}_{\mathcal{P}}$ is a secure hash function. The signature is essential for further integrity checks within the framework as seen in DATA PROCESSOR/VERIFIER. For reasons of trust, POLICYCHECKER is implemented in the hostile domain within the user domain. A user can not alter or analyze the behavior of that blackbox. However, he controls the input and output parameters which is an important criterion for user acceptance. The box is unable to send any information using a side-channel to the data processor. The output is verifiable by a user and cannot contain any hidden information. Similar to the MANEUVEREXTRACTOR, Trusty can be used.

Since the POLICYCHECKER is flexible in terms of the applied policy, we give an example of a potential Φ. An anonymization may be correct if 1. The number of maneuvers in $\hat{\tilde{D}}$ equals $\tilde{D}$, 2. Input $\tilde{D}$ from the PrivateStorage can be used to verify if the distribution of maneuver types in the anonymized trip $\hat{\tilde{D}}$ equals $\tilde{D}$, and 3. Each $d \in \tilde{D}$ has a valid signature $\sigma^{ES}(d)$, i.e. no recorded trip is used to deceive the PHYD system (replay attack); datablocks contain s which in turn have a timestamp s_t signed into $\sigma^{ES}(d)$.

For privacy reasons and to clearly separate the domains, the POLICY-CHECKER does not have access to the ANONYMIZER, hence is unable to anonymize a given maneuver in $\tilde{D}$. Within this framework, the design of the policy is therefore deliberately limited.

DataProcessor/Verifier. Once the data processor receives data $\hat{\tilde{D}}$ from a user along with a corresponding signature $\sigma^{\mathcal{P}}\left(\Sigma_{\tilde{D}}^{\mathcal{E}}, \mathcal{H}_{\mathcal{P}}\left(\hat{\tilde{D}}\right)\right)$ crafted by the processor-controlled POLICYCHECKER, he needs to validate $\sigma^{\mathcal{P}}$ in the first place. This ensures that the data has not been modified and comes from an accepted domain. Therefore, once he has received the data, he checks that the signed and acknowledged hash $\mathcal{H}_{\mathcal{P}}(\hat{\tilde{D}})$ matches the data blocks that were transmitted.

Thus, a user must submit the anonymized data $\hat{\tilde{D}}$ that was checked by the POLICYCHECKER, otherwise the data processor can detect this. The signatures $\Sigma_{\tilde{D}}^{\mathcal{E}}$ as well as the trip $\hat{\tilde{D}}$ will be saved and evaluated. To further increase integrity or in case of suspicion of fraud by the user, the data processor has another tool at his disposal. Recall that the ANONYMIZER performed an anonymization operation $\tilde{D} \longrightarrow \hat{\tilde{D}}$, which is very hard to reverse. The VERIFIER is used to perform a knowledge proof, where the user must prove that he is the originator of the transmitted data, otherwise fraud is assumed. Therefore, the VERIFIER selects up to μ percent of random elements from the received trip $\hat{\tilde{D}}$ (denoted as prove-set $P \subset \hat{\tilde{D}}$) and requests raw data blocks from the prover, i.e. the user. μ is a security parameter to balance integrity and anonymity. Consequently, a trip is only considered valid if $\forall \hat{\tilde{d}}_i \in P : \exists d_i \left[\mathcal{PS} \leftarrow d_i \wedge id(d_i) = id\left(\hat{\tilde{d}}_i\right) \right]$ holds, i.e. a user can submit the raw data block for a given anonymized data block. Note that the ID of data block cannot be altered in the process since it is part of the data blocks signature thus lookup form PERSISTENTSTORAGE is done using id. In addition, the VERIFIER also needs to verify that the given maneuver was not manipulated in terms of any sensor readings or timestamp since the id is not bound to a data block's payload. $\Sigma_{\tilde{D}}^{\mathcal{E}}$ holds all signatures $\sigma_{d_{1,...,|\tilde{D}|}}^{\mathcal{E}}$ of the data blocks as processed by the EMBEDDEDSIGNER. Hence, he calculates—using $\mathcal{H}_{\mathcal{E}}$—the hash of every received d_i and verifies if that signature is part of $\Sigma_{\tilde{D}}^{\mathcal{E}}$. The proof is completed once the user can submit all needed requested data blocks and if each datablock is part of the trip which is verifiable thanks to the signatures.

5.4   Basic Design Decisions

kUBI was designed to balance integrity and privacy. These aspects are integrated at several points in the design.

Integrity. The pattern design implements three different proofs which are needed for a privacy-balanced business model. A user has also an interest in integrity because he only gets a discount once an insurer accepts the sent and anonymized data, thus fraudulent behavior is not beneficial.

P1 Data has not been tampered with: A trustworthy EmbeddedSigner unit processes each sensor value as soon as it is generated on a lower level of the Android Software Stack. Each s is then hashed and signed by this entity, using its private key $d_{\mathcal{E}}$. A user altering some values of a s cannot create a valid signature, eventually being detectable by the data processor's VERIFIER.

P2 Data has not been modified out of boundaries: A data processor rejects submitted items from a user unless a valid signature $\sigma^B \left(\Sigma_{\widetilde{D}}^{ES}, \mathcal{H}_{\mathcal{P}} \left(\widetilde{D}^* \right) \right)$ is shown. This in turn is generated by the POLICYCHECKER according to conditions of the data processor. This protected control unit allows the data processor to specify the Quality-of-Service (QoS).

P3 User has produced the data: A user has to prove knowledge of raw data blocks for any anonymized datablock on request by the VERIFIER. Although a user may use data generated by another device, this can easily be handled by using device-dependent credentials in the POLICYCHECKER to generate unique signatures σ^B.

Trust. Our pattern provides trust at four significant positions.

T1 Box only outputs user verifiable signature: There is no hidden information in the POLICYCHECKER's output since it is easily comprehensible by a user using $d^{\mathcal{P}}$ to verify the given signature, created using a known hash function $\mathcal{H}_{\mathcal{P}}$ and user controlled input data.

T2 Box is in a secure enclave and cannot be tampered with: Trustee guarantees that sensitive processes are carried out in the protected environment. A user cannot create a signature for the POLICYCHECKER because he does not have the cryptographic material, i.e. the secret key $d_{\mathcal{P}}$. Trustee makes sure that it cannot be read.

T3 User controls which data to forward: The paradigm of user personal-agent trust was chosen over undercover-agent trust. Each information is processed in the local domain of the user. Every data transmission is solely controlled by a user by relying on a forwarding engine.

T4 User can choose freely from policy defined values: A user can select any $\overset{\circ}{M}_{ij}$ to replace a maneuver from a trip $\widetilde{D}$. As long as the POLICYCHECKER verifies the integrity, the data processor accepts a value. It is comprehensible for a user if policy Φ does not hold.

5.5   Modified Android Implementation

Based on the presented model, the following is an exemplary implementation of the API for working with sensors as shown in Sect. 3. It is ensured that due to the interchangeability of the components, a fast adaptation to existing applications is possible.

```
1   val signedSensorManager = getSystemService(Context.SIGNED_SENSOR_SERVICE) as ↪
        SignedSensorManager
2   val accelerometerSensor: Sensor? = ↪
        sensorManager.getDefaultSensor(Sensor.TYPE_ACCELEROMETER)
3   val signedSensorListener = object: SignedSensorEventListener {
4       override fun onAccuracyChanged(sensor: Sensor, accuracy: Int) {
5       }
6       override fun onSensorChanged(event: SignedSensorEvent) {
7           val dT: Long = event.timestamp
8           val axisX: Float = event.values.get(0)
9           val axisY: Float = event.values.get(1)
10          val axisZ: Float = event.values.get(2)
11          val datablockId: UUID = event.datablockId
12          // use sensor values
13      }
14      override fun onDatablockComplete(id: UUID, signature: ByteArray) {
15      }
16  }
17  signedSensorManager.registerListener(signedSensorListener, accelerometerSensor, ↪
        SensorManager.SENSOR_DELAY_FASTEST)
```

One can see that all API calls are the same as in the Android reference implementation. However, every SignedSensorEvent also holds a data block ID. Each time a data block is completed, e.g. after 1 s, onDatablockComplete is called. A developer can then get the data block's ID to map all sensor values to it. Furthermore, he gets a signature of that data block (which is the output of $\mathcal{H}_{\mathcal{E}}$).). Applications that do not require the integrity protection features can discard the optional information accordingly. The separation of onSensorChanged and onDatablockComplete ensures that real-time processing is still possible when a new sensor value arrives.

6   Evaluation

Even if the framework is designed generically and the structure is also conceivable for other scenarios, it should nevertheless be shown in the evaluation that *kUBI* can increase the anonymity of individual drivers of a vehicle within its system boundaries, using the proposed idea of replacing maneuvers with reference maneuvers and the given PHYD scenario.

6.1   Identification Attack

The identification attack from Roth et al. [20] was used in this work to assess the quality of the proposed framework. We used the same setting, i.e. same data set and same parameter settings. In the context of that work it could already be shown that classical anonymization methods are not sufficient to protect drivers in the complex context of PHYD. The presented attack is based on supervised machine learning and assigns with the help of DTW and k-Nearest Neighbor a maneuver of the types braking, acceleration and cornering to a driver. It is very robust against noise and other environmental influences.

6.2   Anonymization

An example trip based on real-world data was anonymized using the proposed approach. A $\mathring{M}$ of shape 3×1 served the ANONYMIZER as a basis to replace the real maneuvers against reference maneuvers. From Fig. 5, one can see all speed recording of a trip. Maneuvers were extracted using the known approach and data blocks were recreated using sensor values from the respective reference maneuvers. We classified the trip before and after anonymization using the same classification pipeline. The class of each maneuver stayed the same as intended but the sensor readings are, as shown, much smoother removing any identifying behavior of a user while e.g. accelerating ultimately reducing entropy. At the same time, the needed classification can still be drawn from the data. Our framework will enable data processors to roll their own classification method using the adaptable MANEUVEREXTRACTOR and verify correct results using also a data processor controlled POLICYCHECKER.

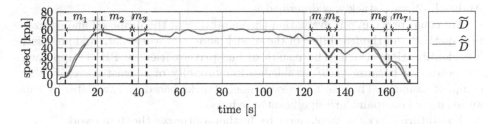

Fig. 5. Comparison of a trip from raw data and its anonymized version.

Table 1. Accuracy for prediction using the identification attack and data set from [20].

(a) Data set without anonymization

	A	B	C	D	E	F
A	0.58	0.06	0.08	0.20	0.05	0.10
B	0.02	0.75	0.03	0.11	0.04	0.05
C	0.02	0.13	0.59	0.10	0.15	0.01
D	0.09	0.04	0.02	0.71	0.05	0.09
E	0.06	0.08	0.03	0.08	0.73	0.03
F	0.05	0.03	0.05	0.10	0.03	0.74

Rows labelled "Actual", columns labelled "Predicted".

(b) Anonymized data set using *kUBI*

	A	B	C	D	E	F
A	0.44	0.05	0.05	0.09	0.11	0.26
B	0.17	0.29	0.27	0.10	0.08	0.10
C	0.16	0.13	0.30	0.02	0.11	0.28
D	0.27	0.15	0.09	0.29	0.09	0.10
E	0.13	0.21	0.14	0.14	0.30	0.09
F	0.27	0.06	0.16	0.04	0.07	0.39

Rows labelled "Actual", columns labelled "Predicted".

6.3   Privacy

Drivers are considered anonymous if the probability of a true prediction is less than or equal to the probability of a false prediction of his maneuvers for at least one other driver (k-anonymity). Section 1 illustrates the accuracy for prediction using the identification attack and data set from [20] a confusion matrix. Table 1a shows the results for the non-anonymized data set. It clearly states that the driver is almost in every case identifiable using the illustrated attack, as the other drives can be excluded with a very high probability. However, using our proposed PET *kUBI*, k-anonymity of at least 2 drivers can be ensured as Table 1b shows. Furthermore, results are very dense, thus the anonymity can be estimated even higher, since the prediction probability of many drivers is around 20%.

7   Conclusion

In this paper, it was first shown using the example of UBI that sensor-based business models can benefit from powerful user devices, but that this is accompanied by significant risks for privacy. An analysis of the stakeholders shows the different interests. Based on this, a holistic framework called *kUBI* was presented, which as PET allows to balance integrity and anonymity as primary protection goals. The framework was presented in detail and a potential extension in the Android software stack was described.

We could prove in our evaluation the suitability of the proposed anonymization method and the feasibility of the model using real-world data and an existing identification attack. The results of our privacy-friendly PHYD approach are promising because *kUBI* establishes k-anonymity of at least 2 even in this complex scenario. The risk for side-channel attacks based on raw data, by e.g. an insurance company, are significantly reduced.

For future work, it is planned to further optimize the framework. Thus, the integer swapping of data points can possibly compensate for other attacks described in this work. In addition, various fraud possibilities will not only be theoretically examined, as is the case here, but will also be implemented in practice as a distributed system. The generalization of the framework shall be advanced by means of further use cases.

References

1. Android: Trusty TEE — Android Open Source Project (2016). https://source.android.com/security/trusty
2. Android: Sensors — Android Open Source Project (2020). https://source.android.com/devices/sensors
3. Bai, X., Yin, J., Wang, Y.-P.: Sensor Guardian: prevent privacy inference on Android sensors. EURASIP J. Inf. Secur. **2017**(1), 1–17 (2017). https://doi.org/10.1186/s13635-017-0061-8
4. Bal, G., Rannenberg, K., Hong, J.I.: Styx: privacy risk communication for the Android smartphone platform based on apps' data-access behavior patterns. Comput. Secur. **53**, 187–202 (2015)
5. Benndorf, V., Normann, H.T.: The willingness to sell personal data. Scand. J. Econ. **120**, 1260–1278 (2018)
6. Bugiel, S., Heuser, S., Sadeghi, A.R.: Flexible and fine-grained mandatory access control on android for diverse security and privacy policies. In: Proceedings of the 22nd USENIX Security Symposium, pp. 131–146 (2013)

7. Chakraborty, S., Raghavan, K.R., Johnson, M.P., Srivastava, M.B.: A framework for context-aware privacy of sensor data on mobile systems. In: Proceedings of the 14th Workshop on Mobile Computing Systems and Applications - HotMobile '13, p. 1. ACM Press, New York (2013)

8. EY: Introducing 'Pay How You Drive' (PHYD) Insurance - Insurance that rewards safe driving (2016)

9. Felt, A.P., Ha, E., Egelman, S., Haney, A., Chin, E., Wagner, D.: Android permissions: user attention, comprehension, and behavior. In: SOUPS 2012 - Proceedings of the 8th Symposium on Usable Privacy and Security (2012)

10. Greaves, S., De Gruyter, C.: Profiling driving behaviour using passive global positioning system (GPS) technology. In: Outside the Square, Operations, Transport and Safety (2002)

11. Hemminki, S., Nurmi, P., Tarkoma, S.: Accelerometer-based transportation mode detection on smartphones. In: SenSys 2013 - Proceedings of the 11th ACM Conference on Embedded Networked Sensor Systems. Association for Computing Machinery (2013)

12. Hong, S.K., Gurjar, K., Kim, H.S., Moon, Y.S.: A survey on privacy preserving time-series data mining. In: 3rd International Conference on Intelligent Computational Systems (ICICS'2013) (2013)

13. Kang, R., Dabbish, L., Fruchter, N., Kiesler, S.: "My data just goes everywhere": user mental models of the internet and implications for privacy and security. Symp. Usable Priv. Secur. (SOUPS) **2015**, 39–52 (2015)

14. Kreuter, F., Haas, G.C., Keusch, F., Bähr, S., Trappmann, M.: Collecting survey and smartphone sensor data with an app: opportunities and challenges around privacy and informed Consent. Soc. Sci. Comput. Rev. **38**, 533–549 (2018)

15. Li, Z., Pei, Q., Markwood, I., Liu, Y., Pan, M., Li, H.: Location privacy violation via GPS-agnostic smart phone car tracking. IEEE Trans. Veh. Technol. **67**, 5042–5053 (2018)

16. Litman, T.A.: Pay-as-you-drive pricing for insurance affordability. Victoria Transp. Policy Inst. **10**(June), 19 (2011)

17. Martínez, M.V., Echanobe, J., Del Campo, I.: Driver identification and impostor detection based on driving behavior signals. In: IEEE Conference on Intelligent Transportation Systems, Proceedings, ITSC, pp. 372–378 (2016)

18. Mylonas, A., Theoharidou, M., Gritzalis, D.: Assessing privacy risks in android: a user-centric approach. In: Bauer, T., Großmann, J., Seehusen, F., Stølen, K., Wendland, M.-F. (eds.) RISK 2013. LNCS, vol. 8418, pp. 21–37. Springer, Cham (2014). https://doi.org/10.1007/978-3-319-07076-6_2

19. Pfitzmann, A., Pfitzmann, B., Schunter, M., Waidner, M.: Trusting mobile user devices and security modules. Computer **30**(2), 61–68 (1997)

20. Roth, C., Aringer, S., Petersen, J., Nitschke, M.: Are sensor-based business models a threat to privacy? the case of pay-how-you-drive insurance models. In: Gritzalis, S., Weippl, E.R., Kotsis, G., Tjoa, A.M., Khalil, I. (eds.) TrustBus 2020. LNCS, vol. 12395, pp. 75–85. Springer, Cham (2020). https://doi.org/10.1007/978-3-030-58986-8_6

21. Solove, D.J.: Nothing to Hide: The False Tradeoff Between Privacy and Security. Yale University Press, New Haven (2011)

22. Troncoso, C., Danezis, G., Kosta, E., Preneel, B.: PriPAYD: privacy friendly pay-as-you-drive insurance. In: WPES 2007 - Proceedings of the 2007 ACM Workshop on Privacy in Electronic Society, vol. 8, pp. 742–755 (2007)

23. Tselentis, D.I., Yannis, G., Vlahogianni, E.I.: Innovative insurance schemes: pay as/how you drive. Transp. Res. Procedia **14**, 362–371 (2016)

24. Weydert, V., Desmet, P., Lancelot-Miltgen, C.: Convincing consumers to share personal data: double-edged effect of offering money. J. Consum. Mark. **37**, 1–9 (2019)
25. Zhang, J., Beresford, A.R., Sheret, I.: SensorID: sensor calibration fingerprinting for smartphones. In: Proceedings of the 40th IEEE Symposium on Security and Privacy (SP). IEEE (2019)
26. Zhang, L., Pathak, P.H., Wu, M., Zhao, Y., Mohapatra, P.: AccelWord: energy efficient hotword detection through accelerometer. In: MobiSys 2015 - Proceedings of the 13th Annual International Conference on Mobile Systems, Applications, and Services, pp. 301–315. Association for Computing Machinery Inc, New York (May 2015)

Verifiable Contracting

A Use Case for Onboarding and Contract Offering in Financial Services with eIDAS and Verifiable Credentials

Sérgio Manuel Nóbrega Gonçalves[2] (iD), Alessandro Tomasi[1](✉) (iD),
Andrea Bisegna[1,3] (iD), Giulio Pellizzari[2] (iD), and Silvio Ranise[1,2] (iD)

[1] Security and Trust, FBK, Trento, Italy
{altomasi,a.bisegna,ranise}@fbk.eu
[2] University of Trento, Trento, Italy
{sm.nobregagoncalves,giulio.pellizzari}@studenti.unitn.it
[3] DIBRIS, University of Genoa, Genoa, Italy

Abstract. We investigate the combined use of eIDAS-based electronic identity and Verifiable Credentials for remote onboarding and contracting, and provide a proof-of-concept implementation based on SAML authentication. The main non-trivial value derived from this proposal is a higher degree of assurance in the contract offering phase for the Contracting Service Provider.

Keywords: Verifiable Credentials · Digital identity proofing · Digital contracting

1 Introduction

From the point of view of a Service Provider (SP), offering a contract to a remote applicant can be a risky proposition. Reliably establishing firstly that someone not physically present really is who they claim to be, and secondly that the details they have provided to enter into a legally binding agreement with the SP are correct, is no trivial task. There are long established procedures to address these problems when the person is physically present, usually involving a form of photographic ID and any number of proofs of other details, such as utility bills to prove current address and/or bank statements to prove account numbers. In the case of remote applicants, however, digital solutions for identity proofing and remote contracting are still a work in progress. In this paper, our contribution is a proof-of-concept to test the combination of two recent and emerging technologies: electronic identity cards and verifiable credentials.

We consider a Contracting Service Provider (CSP) wishing to enter a legally binding contract with an applicant before providing their services. Important examples include utilities and telecoms. In establishing a legally binding contract, CSPs commonly incur costs due to fraud and erroneously entered information. Concretely, a utility billing the wrong bank account, or having to enter a legal dispute over information entered by an applicant during a past contracting phase, will incur legal costs and delays. In this work we focus on the initial

© Springer Nature Switzerland AG 2020
I. Boureanu et al. (Eds.): ESORICS 2020 Workshops, LNCS 12580, pp. 133–144, 2020.
https://doi.org/10.1007/978-3-030-66504-3_8

offering phase, in which a CSP wishes to have a high degree of assurance that the information being entered in the contract is correct before offering it to the applicant; our goal is to determine whether the combination of two innovative technologies can assist in this process.

As a concrete minimal example, we consider the case of a utility CSP requiring (a) an applicant's personal information and (b) an applicant's bank account number (IBAN). The eIDAS [10] framework is designed to enable a public service infrastructure for secure and remote identity proofing[1], and the potential of eIDAS-based eID for strong customer authentication in the banking sector is well-known - see for instance [6]. The Verifiable Credentials W3C recommendation [26] is designed to enable the sharing of verifiable claims about subjects with cryptographic proofs of integrity and authenticity.

In this paper we examine how these two frameworks could be usefully combined in order to enable secure remote contracting. To the best of our knowledge, this is the first PoC combining the two technologies without recourse to Self-Sovereign Identity, e.g. as in the SSI eIDAS bridge [25]. The main non-trivial value derived from this proposal is a higher degree of assurance in the contract offering phase for the CSP. Considering the novelty particularly of the VC recommendation, our objective was first and foremost to test the practical feasibility of the idea; we leave a proper security assessment to future work.

In Sect. 2 we describe the use case and a scenario we propose to address it. In Sect. 3 we briefly summarize some of the relevant aspects of the technologies in our proposal. In Sect. 4 we describe our proof-of-concept implementation. Finally, in Sect. 6 we evaluate our findings.

2   Use Case: Contract Offering

We consider the case of a utility CSP requiring (a) an applicant's personal information and (b) an applicant's International Bank Account Number (IBAN) in order to offer them a contract for services. In the case of an unknown applicant, this information will be considered Claims by the applicant and which the CSP will have to either verify or accept at their own risk. In order to mitigate against fraud, the CSP would prefer a high level of assurance in these claims, and a means of verifying that: the claims are correct and valid, the applicant at the time of offering is the same as the claim subject, and the issuer is a trusted party.

2.1   Proposed Use Case Scenario

Concretely, our proposal is to consider the IBAN to be an attribute of a Subject, and to have the Account Servicing Payment Service Provider (ASPSP) issue a

---

[1] Identity proofing is the process of establishing that an unknown applicant really is who they claim to be, and is performed during customer onboarding (e.g. opening a new bank account); after onboarding, accounts are associated with an authenticator, and subsequently authentication is required for a remote claimant to access an enrolled identity's resources (e.g. online banking). See [18].

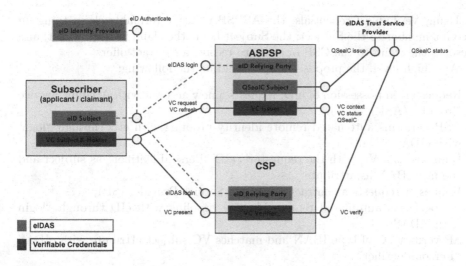

Fig. 1. Entities involved in the proposal and their roles under the two main trust frameworks - eIDAS and VC.

Verifiable Credential to that effect. A rough component diagram of our proposal is shown in Fig. 1.

From the perspective of identity management in the cybersecurity context of, e.g. SP 800-63B [18], the required information about the applicant can be considered as attributes of an identity, i.e. claims made about a Subject by an Issuer or Identity Provider (IDP) with some associated proofs of authenticity.

The Verifiable Credentials [26] W3C recommendation is designed specifically to enable the sharing of verifiable claims about subjects with cryptographic proofs of integrity and authenticity. In our use case, they can be viewed as a form of authorization certificates [19], for which it is critical for security purposes to map the authenticated identity to the certificate holder.

In order to accomplish this, Issuer (ASPSP) and Verifier (CSP) of the VC can identify the Subject by their eIDAS unique identifier (See Section eIDAS-based eID for identity proofing). The eIDAS framework is designed to enable a public service infrastructure for secure and remote identity proofing; the potential of eIDAS-based eID for strong customer authentication in the banking sector is well-known - see for instance [6]. For instance, one of the eIDAS-notified schemes is the Italian eID card, CIE 3.0, and its use as a means of identity proofing during remote onboarding is already explicitly permitted Italy Bankitalia AML regulations, which state that authentication through an eIDAS-compliant scheme is sufficient to perform due diligence for the specific step of identity proofing, even without the physical presence of the applicant ([2] part 2 Sect. 3 comma 2).

Using eIDAS, a citizen with an eID is the Subject of identity assertions by their national IDP. The Subject acting as a Subscriber first applies for an account at an Account Servicing Payment Service Provider (ASPSP, in the sense of PSD2), then receives a contracting offer from a Contracting Service Provider (e.g. utilities or telecoms).

Using Verifiable Credentials, the ASPSP issues a verifiable claim tying an account number to the Subject; the Subject holds the claim in their wallet, and presents the claim to the CSP in order to receive a contract offer.

At a high level, the proposed steps would be the following:

1. Requester, in possession of eID, requests a new account with Account Service Provider (ASP)
2. ASP performs automated remote identity proofing with eID through "login with eIDAS"
3. Bank issues a VC with the requester's eID "PersonIdentifier" as subject and the new IBAN as attribute
4. Requester requests a contract offer from Service Provider (SP)
5. SP performs automated remote identity proofing with eID through "login with eIDAS"
6. SP verifies VC of type IBAN and matches VC subject attribute with eIDAS "PersonIdentifier"

3   Background: eIDAS and SAML SSO

3.1   EIDAS-based eID

eIDAS allows Relying Parties (RP) to receive assertions on a core attribute set [12] of eID bearers from the eIDAS attribute profile. Between member state eIDAS nodes, the protocol chosen for such assertions is SAML v2 [24]. For natural persons, the core attributes are summarized in Table 1.

Table 1. eIDAS attributes for natural persons ([12]).

Mandatory	Optional
Current Family Name	First Names at Birth
Current First Names	Family Name at Birth
Date of Birth	Place of Birth
Unique Identifier	Current Address
	Gender

The Unique Identifier field can be leveraged by VC issuers to identify claim subjects. The assertion by the member state IDP on mandatory attributes can be leveraged by the CSP in the contracting phase. A list of notified eIDAS schemes is informally maintained by the eID User Community [9]. The eIDAS interoperability framework [11] enables each member state to notify one or more eID schemes based on different technology and processes, from national identity cards to mobile-based solutions. The eIDAS regulation [10] establishes a Level of Assurance (LoA) for each scheme - low, substantial, or high. Minimum requirements for each LoA set out in [7], and guidelines on how each scheme may concretely attain an LoA are published by the Cooperation Network [8]. Security considerations on eIDAS compliant eID schemes have also been published by ENISA [14].

The security of eIDAS schemes has been the subject of scrutiny in [13]. The security properties of each scheme depend on its technology and processes. Cooperation Network guidelines offer some clues as to the properties that can be expected from each LoA; for instance, a substantial LoA requires the means of authentication to be based on at least two factors and be demonstrably under the control of the subject to whom it belongs (e.g. one biometric and/or knowledge factor), whereas the high LoA requires additional protection against duplication, tampering, and use by others. By way of example, CIE 3.0 has been accorded a high LoA; it contains a chip with Common Criteria certification against duplication and tampering, and the private key in the chip is unlocked by PIN number, thereby providing factors of possession and knowledge during authentication. CIE 3.0 chip specifications [23] have more detail on compliance with PACE and EAC mechanisms for authentication, confidentiality, and integrity.

3.2 SAML SSO

In this paper we consider the SAML 2.0 Web Browser SSO Profile [24] (SAML SSO) since the concrete eID scheme we have in mind is based on a SAML 2.0 IDP [20], and the web browser profile fits our use case (Sect. 2) and our implementation (Sect. 4). Fully mobile and hybrid scenarios are also considered in the documentation but beyond the scope of the present proof of concept.

Three entities are involved: a Client (C), an Identity Provider (IDP), and a Service Provider (SP). C is a web browser with which a user interacts; the user's goal is to have access to a service or a resource provided by the SP. IDP authenticates C and issues authentication assertions that are trusted by SP - the SSO trust relationship is depicted with a handshake icon in Fig. 2. SP uses the assertions generated by the IDP to decide on C's entitlement to the requested service or resource.

Figure 2 shows a Message Sequence Chart (MSC)[2] of the main steps of the SAML SSO protocol, which we can briefly describe as follows:

S1 C asks SP to provide the resource at URI.

A1-2 SP sends C an HTTP redirect response (status code 302) for IDP, containing an authentication request AuthReq(ID,SP), where ID is a randomly generated string uniquely identifying the request (steps A1 and A2). A frequent implementation choice is to use the `RelayState` field to carry the original URI that C has requested (see [24]).

↔ IDP challenges C to provide valid credentials (dotted double arrows in the figure): this is not specified in the standard of the SAML SSO in order to accommodate any authentication process offered by IDP.

---

[2] Each vertical line in an MSC represents an entity, and horizontal arrows represent messages from one component to another. Identity management protocols are often expressed as MSC to identify any flaws.

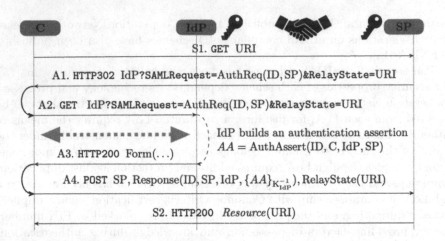

Fig. 2. Message Sequence Chart (MSC) of the SAML SSO protocol [1].

A3-4 If the authentication succeeds, IDP builds an authentication assertion as the tuple AA = AuthAssert(ID, C, IDP, SP) and embeds it in a response message Resp = Response(ID, SP, IDP, $\{AA\}_{K_{IDP}^{-1}}$) where $\{AA\}_{K_{IDP}^{-1}}$ is the assertion signed with IDP's private key (the key icon in Fig. 2). IDP places Resp and the value of RelayState received from SP into an HTML form and sends the result back to C in an HTTP response (step A3) together with some script that automatically posts the form to SP (step A4).

S2 Finally, the SP sends C an accepted HTTP response (status code 200) containing the requested resource.

3.3 EIDAS-compliant Certificates and PSD2

eIDAS-compliant Qualified Certificates conforming to ETSI TS 119 495 [15] are the standard for PSD2 API for both authentication (Qualified Website Authentication Certificates - QWAC) and non-repudiation / content commitment (Qualified Electronic Seal Certificates - QSealC).

The Berlin group access-to-account implementation guidelines [4] require mutual authentication of TPP and ASPSP using eIDAS- and RTS-compliant Qualified Certificates, which must include all the roles for which the TPP is authorized. Open Banking Europe[3] maintains a list of Qualified Trust Service Providers issuing PSD2-compliant Qualified Certificates.

4   Scenario and Implementation

The entities involved in the scenario and their roles are:

1. eID holder - Subject of an IDP-issued eIDAS-based eID document

---

[3] https://www.openbankingeurope.eu/qtsps-and-eidas/.

2. eID IDP
3. eID OCSP responder
4. ASPSP - Relying Party to IDP under eIDAS, QWAC and QSealC Subject under eIDAS, Issuer of VC
5. CSP - Relying Party to IDP under eIDAS, Verifier of VC

Our eID subjects are authenticated to SPs through an X.509 certificate, designed to resemble the basic elements of the Italian eID certificate specifications [23]. In particular, the Subject commonName field contains an unique identifier of the person independent of the individual certificate or document, the only allowed key usage is authentication (digital signature), and extended key usage is client authentication.

All the servers (entities 2–5) are developed using NodeJS, and their services have been configured to work over a secure communication channel (HTTPS) to protect them from man-in-the-middle attacks, in the protocol for the CIE 3.0 eID scheme as described in the manual for SPs [20]. Servers have two separate certificates, one for server authentication and one for non-repudiation. In general, these could be issued by any authorized CA; in our specific use case, we think it plausible that these would be Qualified Website Authentication (QWAC) and Qualified Seal Certificates (QSealC), respectively.

Our sample implementation is concerned mainly with the Service Provider part of the architecture supporting authentication and verifiable credential issuing and verification to support the use case. Our proof-of-concept implementation is available on github[4]. We give a high-level description here and refer the interested reader to the repository for implementation details.

4.1 SAML

The two SPs (entities 4,5) implement SAML through the passport-saml module. The IDP uses the saml-idp module.

After receiving the SAMLRequest from the SP, the IDP verifies if together with the authentication request the client has also provided the certificate. If that is the case, a verification process starts. The IDP checks if the client certificate has been signed by the Certification Authority (CA) it expects, whether it has expired, and finally whether it has been revoked. The latter operation is achieved by an API call to the OCSP service, which exposes an API that accepts as input a certificate, checks if its serial number belongs to the list of revoked ones and returns 'good', 'revoked', or 'unknown' accordingly.

If all these checks are successful and the user grants access to their data to the SP, the SAMLResponse is generated and sent back to the SP, which parses it and shows the contained attributes.

The SAML implementation has been designed with a view towards integration with our container-based identity management training environment, Micro-Id-Gym [5].

---

[4] https://github.com/stfbk/vc-saml-node.

4.2   Verifiable Credentials

Verifiable Credentials (VC) allow Issuers to issue Claims - signed statements about Subjects. Issuers are identified by a URI, Subjects may be identified by a URI or a set of attributes.

We highlight the following steps taken to adapt the VC data model [26] to our use case, and we note that the issuer has to provide information about itself and the credentials it has issued via specific endpoints, in a manner not unlike an identity provider. The endpoints are to be taken as following the issuer's domain, `https://<issuer_host>`[5]. An example of an issued VC is shown in Listing A (Sect. A).

Verification. The VC has an embedded proof property constructed as a digital signature with the issuer's non-repudiation private key, corresponding to their trust provider-issued non-repudiation certificate. The public key can be obtained from the controller document at the `/issuer` endpoint.

Credential type and context. We needed to introduce the subject attributes of eIDAS unique identifier and IBAN in the VC issued by the ASPSP. This was done by defining a custom context, which the issuer makes available through an `/credential/iban` endpoint.

Issuance, expiration, and status. Issuance and expiration dates are added, and a `/credential/status` endpoint can be called to check whether the VC has been revoked.

5   Related Work

An application of VCs to a financial use case (KYC) was shown in [21], based on the FIDO UAF protocol in an adaptation described by the same authors in [22]. The subject is assumed to have already been enrolled with attribute authorities, which issue VCs that can be used as part of the KYC process. Broadly speaking, this use of VCs is similar to the one here proposed. However, FIDO is strictly an authentication protocol, not covering identification. In [22], a new public-private key pair is created for each authenticator-service provider pair, so there is no such notion as a unique identifier for the subject; this is by design, for privacy reasons. The exclusive use of FIDO in this manner thus requires issuing a separate VC to the same subject for every new service provider, with an exponential increase in VCs to be managed, and seems counter-intuitive to the use case of contract signing.

In our proposal, the use of a unique identifier for the subject is one of the key features leveraged from eIDAS. The use of FIDO2 authenticators may then play an important role as part of eID schemes, for instance as proposed in a FIDO alliance white paper on the use of FIDO2 for eIDAS [17], either using the authenticator in lieu of the eID card itself, or to authenticate the subject to a QTSP remotely storing their Qualified Certificate and private key.

---

[5] In our simple nodejs-based proof-of-concept implementation, this is `localhost` followed by a port identifying the service provider.

6   Lessons Learned and Conclusion

Added Value. The main non-trivial value derived from this proposal is a higher degree of assurance in the contract offering phase for the Contracting Service Provider. While there are some costs and technical know-how required in becoming a Service Provider under eIDAS, these are predictable costs and expected to be quite small, as opposed to costs incurred as a consequence of fraud, litigation against repudiation, and plain errors due to manually entered data.

The ability to perform identity proofing remotely is of course highly valuable, but on its own it is enabled by eIDAS as an explicit design goal, and is not new or specific to this proposal. At the same time, for a financial use case it is extremely plausible to use an eIDAS login as a starting point since it strongly contributes to an ASPSP's AML compliance. The addition of Verifiable Credentials based on eIDAS is a synergy expected to enable an ecosystem of high-assurance contracting services.

ASPSP as VC Issuers. The solutions adopted by financial services providers often form the gold standard for identity proofing and authentication, and in some cases banks act as identity providers themselves (e.g. BankID [3]). It is not unreasonable to assume that financial institutions would be willing to offer VC issuing services; the set-up involved is in some ways less onerous, in the sense that they do not require federation between Issuer and Verifier, and the Subject is responsible for their sharing.

With reference to the API commonly proposed to comply with PSD2, VCs also appear more adequate for sharing long-term information that may be considered an attribute of the subject, as opposed to live information about their ASPSP-managed account, such as availability of funds and initiation of payments etc. In our proposal, a contracting SP does not have to take the subject's identity attributes and request information about a related IBAN through a PISP; the SP can immediately match the subject's authentication to the subject of the VC and only has to verify the validity of the VC itself.

Contract Signing. We note that an important piece we have not covered in this proposal is how to close the contracting phase with an electronic signature carrying adequate legal weight (advanced or qualified) depending on CSP requirements. Just as legal persons can apply for a QSealC, natural persons can also be issued Qualified Certificates. eIDAS does allow remote electronic signatures, in which the qualified signature certificate is stored by the trust service provider, to which the subject authenticates. In any case, the signature process would require a careful study of client-side issues such as the informed consent by the signer, and their exclusive and secure control over the signing device and the keys within. Other factors such as cost and user experience would undoubtedly play a role. Since our focus here is the server-side logic and proof-of-concept for the back-end, we have not considered these issues for the moment.

Other Remarks. We have assumed that the Service Providers have a constant, resolvable online presence that adequately guarantees a resolvable address for all relevant endpoints, such as eSeal certificate, VC context, refresh, and revocation status endpoints. This seems to us a fair assumption where ASPSP are concerned.

We expect that for authentication purposes the overall scheme here described can inherit the security properties of the base eID scheme. Specific use case requirements may be met for instance by requiring a minimum eIDAS LoA, following e.g. Cooperation Network guidelines [8]. The VC data model does not specify strict validation procedures; while our proposal is closely modeled on PKI standard practices for issuance, verification, and revocation of claims, we have not performed a thorough security analysis at this stage.

Lastly, in the same way that Financial API are undergoing a standardization process, such as the one being carried out by the FAPI working group [16], VCs would benefit from a reference API without regard of the underlying service infrastructure.

Acknowledgments. The authors would like to thank Istituto Poligrafico e Zecca dello Stato (IPZS) for the collaboration on the development of the authentication solution based on the CIE 3.0 carried out in the context of the joint laboratory DigimatLab between FBK and IPZS.

The research has been partly supported by CherryChain S.r.l. in the context of a research and innovation project funded by Autonomous Province of Trento non-refundable contribution under PAT - APIAE agency resolution n. 333 of 18/12/2019.

This work has been partly developed in the context of the Integrated Framework for Predictive and Collaborative Security of Financial Infrastructures (FINSEC) project, which receives funding from the European Union's Horizon 2020 Research and Innovation Programme under Grant agreement 786727.

A   Listings

Listing 1.1. Example of a Verifiable Credential for the use case described in Sect. 2.

```
1  {
2    "@context": [
3      "https://www.w3.org/2018/credentials/v1",
4      "https://<issuer_hostname>/credential/iban"
5    ],
6    "id": "https://<issuer_hostname>/credential/<
          serialNumber>",
7    "type": ["VerifiableCredential", "ibanCredential"],
8    "issuer": "https://<issuer_hostname>/issuer",
9    "credentialSubject": {
10     "eIDASuniqueIdentifier": <eIDAS unique identifier>,
11     "iban": <iban>
12   },
13   "issuanceDate": <datetime>,
14   "expirationDate": <datetime>,
```

```
15    "credentialStatus": {
16        "id": "https://<issuer_hostname>/credential/status
              /<credentialSerialNumber>",
17        "type": "OCSP-like"
18    },
19    "proof": {
20  "type": <signatureType>,
21  "created": <datetime>,
22          "jws": <jws>,
23          "proofPurpose": "assertionMethod",
24          "verificationMethod": "https://<issuer_hostname
                >/issuer#nonRepudiationKey"
25    }
26  }
```

References

1. Armando, A., Carbone, R., Compagna, L., Cuéllar, J., Pellegrino, G., Sorniotti, A.: An authentication flaw in browser-based single sign-on protocols: impact and remediations. Comput. Secur. **33**, 41–58 (2013). https://doi.org/10.1016/j.cose.2012.08.007
2. Banca d'Italia: Disposizioni in materia di adeguata verifica della clientela per il contrasto del riciclaggio e del finanziamento del terrorismo, July 2019. https://www.bancaditalia.it/compiti/vigilanza/normativa/archivio-norme/disposizioni/20190730-dispo/index.html. (in Italian)
3. BankID. https://www.bankid.com/en/
4. Berlin Group: NextGenPSD2 Access to Account Interoperability Framework - Implementation Guidelines, July 2019. https://www.berlin-group.org/nextgenpsd2-downloads
5. Bisegna, A., Carbone, R., Martini, I., Odorizzi, V., Pellizzari, G., Ranise, S.: Micro-Id-Gym: identity management workouts with container-based microservices. Int. J. Inf. Secur. Cybercrime **8**(1), 45–50 (2019). https://doi.org/10.19107/IJISC.2019.01.06
6. Deloitte: Value proposition of eIDAS-based eID - banking sector, July 2018. https://ec.europa.eu/cefdigital/wiki/display/EIDCOMMUNITY/Study+on+the+opportunities+and+challenges+of+eID+for+Banking
7. Commission implementing regulation (EU) 2015/1502 of 8 September 2015 on setting out minimum technical specifications and procedures for assurance levels for electronic identification means pursuant to Article 8(3) of Regulation (EU) no 910/2014 of the European Parliament and of the Council on electronic identification and trust services for electronic transactions in the internal market (text with EEA relevance). http://data.europa.eu/eli/reg_impl/2015/1502/oj
8. eIDAS guidance documents on Level of Assurance and Notification. https://ec.europa.eu/cefdigital/wiki/display/EIDCOMMUNITY/Guidance+documents
9. Overview of pre-notified and notified eID schemes under eIDAS. https://ec.europa.eu/cefdigital/wiki/display/EIDCOMMUNITY/Overview+of+pre-notified+and+notified+eID+schemes+under+eIDAS

10. Regulation 910/2014 of the European Parliament and of the Council of 23 July 2014 on electronic identification and trust services for electronic transactions in the internal market and repealing Directive 1999/93/EC. http://data.europa.eu/eli/reg/2014/910/oj
11. eIDAS interoperability architecture v1.2, September 2019. https://ec.europa.eu/cefdigital/wiki/download/attachments/82773108/eIDAS%20Interoperability%20Architecture%20v.1.2%20Final.pdf
12. eIDAS eID Technical Subgroup: eIDAS SAML Attribute Profile, July 2014. https://ec.europa.eu/cefdigital/wiki/display/CEFDIGITAL/eIDAS+eID+Profile
13. Engelbertz, N., Erinola, N., Herring, D., Somorovsky, J., Mladenov, V., Schwenk, J.: Security analysis of eIDAS – the cross-country authentication scheme in Europe. In: 12th USENIX Workshop on Offensive Technologies (WOOT). USENIX Association, August 2018. https://www.usenix.org/conference/woot18/presentation/engelbertz
14. ENISA: eIDAS compliant eID solutions, March 2020. https://www.enisa.europa.eu/publications/eidas-compliant-eid-solutions
15. ETSI: Electronic Signatures and Infrastructures (ESI); Sector Specific Requirements; Qualified Certificate Profiles and TSP Policy Requirements under the payment services Directive (EU) 2015/2366, November 2019. https://www.etsi.org/standards-search#page=1&search=TS119495
16. Financial-grade api (FAPI) working group. https://openid.net/wg/fapi/
17. White paper: Using FIDO with eIDAS services, April 2020. https://fidoalliance.org/white-paper-using-fido-with-eidas-services/
18. Grassi, P.A., et al.: Digital Identity Guidelines: Authentication and Lifecycle Management. NIST, June 2017. https://doi.org/10.6028/NIST.SP.800-63b, https://csrc.nist.gov/publications/detail/sp/800-63b/final
19. IETF RFC 5755: An Internet Attribute Certificate Profile for Authorization, January 2010. https://tools.ietf.org/html/rfc5755
20. IPZS: Accesso ai servizi in rete mediante la CIE 3.0 - Manuale operativo per gli erogatori di servizi, April 2020. https://www.cartaidentita.interno.gov.it/identificazione-digitale/entra-con-cie/. (in Italian)
21. Laborde, R., et al.: Know your customer: opening a new bank account online using UAAF. IEEE, January 2020. https://doi.org/10.1109/CCNC46108.2020.9045148
22. Laborde, R., et al.: A user-centric identity management framework based on the W3C verifiable credentials and the FIDO universal authentication framework. IEEE, January 2020. https://doi.org/10.1109/CCNC46108.2020.9045440
23. Ministero dell'Interno: Carta d'Identità Elettronica CIE 3.0 - Specifiche Chip, November 2015. https://www.cartaidentita.interno.gov.it/wp-content/uploads/2016/07/cie_3.0_-_specifiche_chip.pdf. (in Italian)
24. OASIS: SAML V2.0 Tech. Overview, March 2008. http://www.oasis-open.org/committees/download.php/27819/sstc-saml-tech-overview-2.0-cd-02.pdf
25. SSI eIDAS bridge. https://joinup.ec.europa.eu/collection/ssi-eidas-bridge
26. W3C: Verifiable Credentials Data Model, November 2019. https://www.w3.org/TR/vc-data-model/

DeSECSyS 2020

ICITPM: Integrity Validation of Software in Iterative Continuous Integration Through the Use of Trusted Platform Module (TPM)

Antonio Muñoz[1]([✉]), Aristeidis Farao[2], Jordy Ryan Casas Correia[1], and Christos Xenakis[3]

[1] Computer Science Department, University of Malaga Campus de Teatinos s/n, 29071 Malaga, Spain
amunoz@lcc.uma.es, ryan@uma.es
[2] Neurosoft S.A., Athens, Greece
a.farao@neurosoft.gr
[3] Department of Digital Systems, University of Piraeus, Piraeus, Greece
xenakis@unipi.gr

Abstract. Software development has passed from being rigid and not very flexible, to be automated with constant changes. This happens due to the creation of continuous integration and delivery environments. Nevertheless, developers often rely on such environments due to the large number of amenities they offer. They focus on authentication only, without taking into consideration other aspects of security such as the integrity of the source code and of the compiled binaries. The source code of a software project must not be maliciously modified. Notwithstanding, there is no safe method to verify that its integrity has not been violated. Trusted computing technology, in particular, the Trusted Platform Module (TPM) can be used to implement that secure method.

Keywords: CI/CD pipeline · Code integrity · Trusted computing · TPM

1 Introduction

We are witness to the increasing adoption of development tools. These building tools are the Agile, the Development and Operations (DevOps) and the Continuous integration/continuous delivery (CI/CD). Automation is a key aspect in both of them to build, deliver, and test high-frequent increments of features [11,20,36].

We share the perspective of DevOps practices intended for optimizing times between change commitment to the system and change implemented in normal production code. While Agile practice focuses on eliminating processes. Thus, today CI/CD pipeline is considered among the best practices for delivering code

© Springer Nature Switzerland AG 2020
I. Boureanu et al. (Eds.): ESORICS 2020 Workshops, LNCS 12580, pp. 147–165, 2020.
https://doi.org/10.1007/978-3-030-66504-3_9

changes more frequently and reliably in code implementation. Continuous integration (CI) and continuous delivery (CD) embody a culture, set of operating principles, and collection of practices that enable application development teams to deliver code changes more frequently and reliably.

CI/CD is one of the best practices for DevOps teams due to CI/CD automated enabling software developers to dedicate themselves to collection accurate requirements, security, and improved codes. The major challenges, which specifically concern security in a CI/CD pipeline are the following:

- *Automation* is frequently used, withal the most times is not integrated with security tools; lack of these tools is an event that leads to malicious behaviors requiring alerts.
- *Accountability* in CI/CD pipelines is a vital dependency that ensures transparency among developers' actions, e.g., Man-In-The-Middle, [21].
- *Low performance of security tools* leads to delay the process of automation; developer's daily commitments demand real-time interactions and results.
- *Deploying virtual machines* leads to a single-point-of-failure, enabling adversaries to execute attacks without any trace if they get control over the Hypervisor, e.g., "hyperjacking" [33].

Notwithstanding, the CI/CD technique entails the next future consequences resulting in information leakage in a big corporation DataBase. Based on the above challenges, this paper presents a solution for an identified gap to grant integrity in the CI/CD process. We proposed a mechanism for integrity validation of software in iterative continuous integration based on secure hardware elements. Our solution uses the Trusted Computing technology, in particular, we have designed the proposed solution using the Infineon Trusted Platform Module (TPM) 2.0 version [9]. A gap in the whole process to grant software integrity in CI/CD process has identified. Particularly between Assembly and Testing Server communications as we further describe.

It emphasizes in on-demand deployments cases on developer premises. We have developed a tool that from TPM functionalities assists in the CI/CD process to bridge the identified gap granting integrity in the whole process. This tool enables alerts about any change in the software from the final development to deployment versions. For this purpose, we provide a review of agile methodologies and the importance of security in automation. Then, a description of security risks in assembly and test server is provided, including current security threats identified, implementation of a scenario as a proof of concept with some threats, and our approach as a solution to the considered problem. TPM functionalities are used to grant software and platform integrity as seal-bind key, remote attestation, and signing functions.

The rest of the paper is organized as follows. In Sect. 2, we present the background and give a high-level description of the utilized agile methodologies and their security role in automation. Next, Sect. 3 presents the related work. Next, Sect. 4 describes the security role in automation. Section 5 presents a proof-of-concept on a vulnerable Jenkins server. Section 6 is dedicated to describe the code integrity challenge in the CI/CD pipeline we have afforded. Section 7 presents our proposal the Trusted Integrity Platform (TIP), while Sect. 8 demonstrates the implementation setup, the tested scenario, and the results. Finally, Sect. 9 summarizes the paper and presents future work.

2 Background

CI can be understood as those guided practices that enable continuous surveillance in code repositories allowing development teams to implement changes in code and their check in. While they require mechanisms for the integration and validation of code changes derived from multi-platform features from contemporary applications. Technically, we can define CI's main goal as a set of tools to build, package and test applications in an automated and consistent way. This consistency implies teams increase the frequency in code changes commitments triggering improved team collaborations and increased quality in software.

CD technique binds at the end of CI performing an automation in application delivery to particular infrastructures. It is widely extended the use of different environments (i.e. production, development and testing) with code changes submission between them. CD provides an automated way to actually perform those changes, keeping stored packaging parameters bound to every delivery. We aimed to be an automated process since any service calls to databases, web servers, and any other services to be resumed, restarted, stopped or followed to deploy the application must be automatically performed.

We have previously mentioned that the objective is delivering quality code and applications to users, for this reason CI/CD demands constant testing, which is generally offered as performance, regression and other set of tests done within CI/CD pipeline. Developers submit their code to commit into the version control repository. Also it is usual to establish a minimal rate of daily committing code per team to facilitate tasks in identifying defects and bugs on smaller delta pieces of code rather than large developments. Also, working on smaller commit cycles reduces parallel working on the same code in multiple developer teams. Many teams that implement continuous integration often start with version control configuration and practice definitions. Even though checking in code is done frequently, features and fixes are implemented on both short and longer time frames.

Different techniques are used to control and filter code for production in CI. Among the most applied practices is to require developers run regression tests in their own environments, which implies that only code that passed regression tests were committed. We notice that it is common that development teams have at least one development and testing environment. This environment allows reviewing and testing application changes. A CI/CD tool such as Jenkins[1], CircleCI[2], AWS CodeBuild[3], Azure DevOps[4], Atlassian Bamboo[5], or Travis CI[6] is used to automate the steps and provide reporting.

---

[1] https://jenkins.io/.
[2] https://circleci.com/.
[3] https://aws.amazon.com/es/codebuild/.
[4] https://docs.microsoft.com/en-us/azure/devops/?view=azure-devops.
[5] https://www.atlassian.com/software/bamboo.
[6] https://travis-ci.com/.

A typical CD pipeline [20] includes the following stages: (i) built; (ii) test and (iii) deploy. Nonetheless, improved pipelines include also the following stages:

- Picking code from version control and executing a build.
- Allowing any automated action such as restarting or shutting down both cloud infrastructure, services or service endpoints.
- Moving code to the target computing environment.
- Setting up and managing environment variables.
- Enabling services as API services, database services or web servers to be pushed to application components.
- Allowing rollback environments and the execution of continuous tests.
- Alerting on delivery state and data log are provided.

Jenkins provides files to manage records about building, testing and deploying stages that describe their pipelines. Those files define keys, certificates, environment variables, and other parameters. The CI/CD technique provides mechanisms to the misalignment between developers with operations. We notice that developers push frequent changes in their codes and operations while they expect stable applications after changes. However, they can push these changes with automated procedures to achieve stability in their operations. With standardized environment configurations, rollback procedures are automated and provide continuous testing in delivery, and separation of environment variables from applications.

Additionally, there are mechanisms to measure the impact of implementing the CI/CD pipeline, like as a key performance indicator (KPI). Nevertheless, we have to consider that KPIs can change the lead time, and the mean time to recovery (MTTR) from an incident when CI/CD with the implementation of continuous testing [22]. We have identified a gap of security in the CI/CD pipeline. In particular, as it is next briefly described, a threat in the code integrity. Also we have proposed an approach for that based on Trusted Computing advanced security features.

3   Related Work

Most of tools used in CD pipeline are web-based applications as Jenkins. Several approaches have focused on detecting vulnerabilities. Deepa et al. [15] provide approaches for Securing web applications from injection and logic vulnerabilities. Other solutions [19] follow approaches based on static analysis and runtime Protection and mitigation of vulnerability impact based on security testing techniques [24].

OWASP [29]proposes threat modeling focused on detecting threats and vulnerabilities as early as possible. The most widely used threat modeling method is known as STRIDE [18]. Secure DevOps [28, 30] is a set of tools designed to help organizations implant secure coding in the CD process. Lipke [25] studied threats in CD pipeline using STRIDE methodology. This work implements a proof of concept based on Docker. Some approaches follow detection of vulnerabilities in CD pipeline applications as Bird [13]. Schneider [34] proposes a four-staged dynamic security scanning methodology (pre-authentication scanning, post-authentication scanning, backend scanning and scanning workflows specific to the targeted application). Also, this author introduces the SecDevOps Maturity Model(SDOMM). This can be considered as instrunctions for automatically achieve particular security aspects in CI pipeline. Kuusela proposes different testing techniques [23]. There are techniques based on improve the security of CD pipelines as Bass et al. [10] approach that proposes an engineering process within trusted components embedded in parts of the pipeline, which is intimately related to our approach although no trusted hardware is mentioned. In [37] have applied different tactics of security between CD components communications with encouraging results. Rimba et al. [31] present an approach based on the use of composing patterns to address security issues in CD pipeline.

Regarding the security tools the OWASP Zed Attack Proxy (ZAP) [12] is an open source security test initially designed as a security application and as a professional tool for penetration testing. Behaviour Driven Development Security [38] is a security framework for self-verifying testing by your own security specifications using a natural language in terms of "given that", "when", "then", etc. to describe security requirements in "stories" (specifications) also considered as executable tests. JFrog [3] is a set of DevOps tools following the approach to accelerate the delivery of binaries, securely through delivery pipeline, enabling end-to-end DevOps automation pipeline. Security Monkey [5] is an OpenSource project from Netflix that enables monitor Amazon EC2 (AWS), OpenStack, Google Cloud Platform (GCP) and GitHub instances changes for assets. Black Duck software toolbox [1] provides automatic means to track your code, providing solutions to mitigate security risks. Finally, Snyk [7] provides tools for monitoring vulnerabilities and fix them for npm, Maven, NuGet, RubyGems, PyPI among others. Notwithstanding, all of these methodologies and tools do not provide a solution to grant source code integrity avoiding a malicious modification of the code in CI/CD pipeline.

4   Security Role in Automation

A CI/CD environment consists of (i) the *Source Code Control Server* which is responsible to manage changes to project's documents (ii) the *Assembly Server* which receives the changes and assembles them; (iii) the *Testing Server and Deployment Server* that validates that the project work and then publishes the latest version. Conceptually every server is located on different premises. Many developers integrate CI/CD procedures only to Assembly and Testing Servers. This fact is a consequence of the drastic change in today's software delivery way, Source Code Control Server repositories and product development (mostly manually) are not innovations of CI/CD. Henceforth, our solution uses CI/CD for Assembly and Testing Servers.

Prior development environments and project deployments were performed only on trust premises without presuming the security of the platform but trusting on software robustness. This case used to occur because security measures implemented on software to operate against a various number of adversary models. Nowadays, dockerization and virtualization are getting used to protect against unexpected events. Nevertheless, currently deployed software is not considered trustworthy. It occurs because, on most occasions, software security measures are not carefully considered. It tends to isolate deployment in host machines, restricting privileges and hardware access at maximum, but only these measures are questionable. The underlying software that controls these virtual machines acting as an intermediary layer among every virtual machine and hardware is the *Hypervisor*. Being dedicated to handling virtual machines, this leads it to a single-point-of-failure. If an attacker gets control over it, then she will be able to handle every virtual machine without tracking of the source of this attack. This technique is known as "hyperjacking" [33], and its most common implementation is to insert a malicious *Hypervisor* to forge the original one.

Figure 1 depicts how this attack can be implemented in four steps:

1. Developer implements a new feature and this is uploaded to Source Code Control Server (Git based server in most cases).
2. Changes finished in Source Code Control Server are sent to Assembly and Tests Server.
3. Assembly and Tests Server assembles a new software version and conducts unitary test and linkage prepared for this software.
4. Once recommended tests are passed, a new version of the software is made public (deployment).

Under the assumption that every communication between every point described is secure, we have identified several weak points. For this reason, we have considered the next cases: If developers' computers are infected, then it is plausible malicious code modifies the Source Code Control Server could be infected, but it is even harder to implement uncontrolled changes due to the incremental control version at the file level, which identifies quickly an undesired change. We consider that the most important vulnerability is identified in Assembly and Testing Server. By default this is considered as trusted because its interaction is restricted to insert source code. Notwithstanding, we have identified a gap in this process described in next example.

We assume that a malicious agent granted access to *Assembly and Testing Server*. This pretends to insert a piece of code for detecting every time source code is generated and files modified. Then that routing replaces some key source code file opening a backdoor. This case is not trivial to detect as previously described since source code is assumed that has been checked and then it is valid.

4.1   Security Risks in Assembly and Testing Servers

DigitalOcean [21] published that the proper way to ensure a CI/CD environment for a company devoted to virtual server deployment under premises is the isolation from external access. Since the CI/CD system has granted access to your repository and credentials to deploy in different environments, it is essential to keep in a safeguard your credentials to guarantee the final product integrity. However, a CI/CD server protection is not trivial, several alternatives exist as secure shell (SSH), private key APIs connecting through services as GitHub[7] or GitLab[8] to our CI/CD environment. It is recommended to have a proper password and implement 2-factor authentication. Despite this fact Milka [27] revealed that less than 10% of Google users make use of 2-factor authentication. A fail in securing those keys could lead into source code filtering or code modifications by impersonation attacks. Using an intermediate interface, some CI/CD solutions provide an interface to manage Assembly and testing server (i.e. Jenkins or GitLab) through a web interface. In the case of Jenkins, it is enabled as credential based access. Thus, the security of access interface is another issue to consider. We notice that many providers ignore recommendations about CI/CD server isolation. Indeed, in "Who is Using Jenkins"[9] there are projects as KDE[10], Apache[11], AngularJS[12] and Ubuntu[13] that are publicly accessible. We have used Apache Software Foundations from Jenkins public access.

A huge number of software projects are based on open source tools to streamline its development. Among others, the capability to observe, modify and publicly discuss any part of source code provide considerable advantages. Whichever from all identified risks could take place, especially avoiding recommendations. An example of this is found in 2003, attacking Linux kernel [17] inserting a backdoor in a CVS repository as mirror of the main repository. A digital interruption was performed in the server and then the change was inserted. It is detailed "that change was never approved and it is not present in the main repository". Detected change was the next in wait function 1.1. Although this threat could seem harmless, it assigns users under execution identifier **0**. This fact grants all privileges over the computer.

```
1    if ((options == (__WCLONE|__WALL)) && (current->uid =
     0))
2 retval = -EINVAL;
```
Listing 1.1. Wait function

In [21] authors present "Failures in a CI/CD pipeline are immediately visible and halt the advancement of the affected release to later stages of the cycle. This is a gatekeeping mechanism that safeguards the more important environments from untrusted code". They physically separate Testing Server and Assembly Server producing a fake perception of security since the integrity of source code is not granted. The mere fact of using a CI/CD environment does not prevent severe security breaches.

---

[7] https://github.com/.
[8] https://about.gitlab.com/.
[9] https://wiki.jenkins.io/pages/viewpage.action?pageId=58001258.
[10] https://kde.org/.
[11] https://www.apache.org/.
[12] https://angularjs.org/.
[13] https://ubuntu.com/.

We have to consider the potential facts of an attacker with administrative access granted to the server. The computer hosting Assembly and Testing Server is a precious target for external attackers. In some cases, the use of underlying hardware for particular benefits in these servers is powerful (able to compile and execute several proofs quickly to reduce development and deployment possible delays). In most cases, CI/CD solutions offer the possibility to multimode execution simultaneously. For instance, for bitcoin mining, in [8] is described a campaign of crypto-jacking in China with more that 50000 infected servers. Other possibilities as malicious emails, executing DDoS coordinated using botnets as occurred in 2017 with Mirai [6], or economic data rescue with a ransomware, are lower probable since data used in this kind of server should be sited in a different computer just to manage source code. There are cases of ethical hacking and vandalism, harms to development computer and intellectual property stored and damages to final user data.

5   A Proof-of-Concept: Vulnerable Server Launching Jenkins

Let us introduce an example to show the identified breach in the security of the CI/CD process. We make use of a simple application with a form for initializing sessions. This application provides service to dog owners, a gadget bound to the collar enabling owners to know the precise location of their pets in an emergency. Such as a case is when users login to the portal to see these data.

The application that evidences the identified weakness is developed using *Nuxt.js* and *Vue.js* for the front-ent and *PHP* for the back-end. Its functionality is presented in Fig. 2 through a UML flow diagram. Deployment is done through a *PHP internal server*, and *Nuxt.js* interface is compiled using Web Package.

On the one hand, GitLab was chosen as the *Source Code Control Server* for the project and is categorized as private. GitLab allows login sessions to its platform username/password and supports single sign on through social networks. Also, 2-factor authentication mechanisms are available. On the other hand, Jenkins is chosen as the *Assembly and Testing server*. This is an open source automation server enabling developers to reliably build, test, and deploy their software. The connection between Jenkins and GitLab is done with a mere configuration, to automate the generation of a new version to test for each new change in the repository. We can consider this is a comprehensive and mature CI/CD solution.

Let us assume that the *Assembly Server* violates the administrator's privileges after the access granted. The code has been developed in C# simulating a malware to install in a violated server. This code detects when project files are written when cloning from GitLab and replaces their contents and is executed in the background to be unnoticed.

To perpetrate the attack, the *dog pictures* utilized by the application are replaced by cat pictures and form text is manipulated during the login session. Moreover, changes produced by replying to the repository are not undone.

The workflow is presented below:

- GitLab is properly contacted using the SSH key that is provided
- Folder is updated with changes uploaded to GitLab as initially configured. Dependencies are downloaded then it audits its correctness.
- Deploy the package.
- A "success message" indicates that CI/CD pipeline was properly completed.

Internal php server is used to deploy the project, we pay attention to everything while assembly is correct, but indeed deployment was not as initially expected.

This case as a real use-case of CI/CD environment presenting that only by passing Jenkins tests the project is ready to be published, keeping malicious modifications without any additional control measures. Inspecting the remote repository in GitLab, it is not possible to realize any change. It happens due to the fact that all files are just as uploaded files, even though the change was done by an authorized developer and it is empty. We facilitate to inject malware code to open backdoors or tasks. While we fill in the login session form, we perpetrate a man-in-the-middle attack exposing final client credentials hardly perceptible in CI/CD pipeline. This process includes source code inspection just after uploading changes to the Source Code Control Server repository, but the result after the package assembling is not carefully inspected since it is produced by a "trustworthy server" *Assembly and Testing server.*

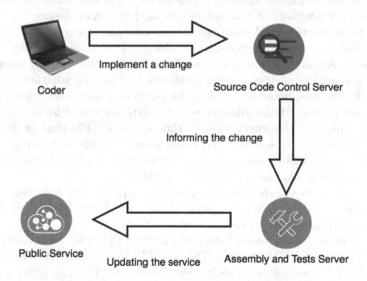

Fig. 1. Identified risk in continuous integration process

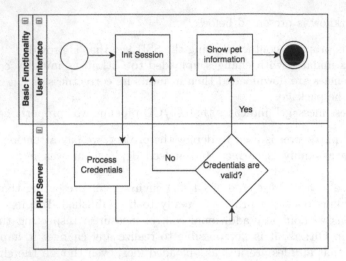

Fig. 2. UML Flow diagram describing basic functionality of our code

6 Code Integrity in the CI/DP Pipeline

Our challenge is to establish a secure and trustworthy integrity code control when an assembly code computer is not trusted. This solution is based on TPM. We have decided to include it, since it provides a set of functionalities related to software integrity with trust guarantees provided by device design.

TPM is an international standard for a secure crypto-processor (ISO/IEC 11889). TPM is a secure microcontroller designed to issue integrated cryptographic keys. Among its features it is affordable (around €20[14]), indeed it is included in a large number of current platforms (not adding additional costs). It is widely documented allowing its usage for particular users and work purposes. Also, it is accepted as a trust solution as a cornerstone element for secure booting in modern computers, file encryption (BitLocker [26]). TPM enables device and user trust identification, key and certificate issuing, secure key storage, detecting not authorized modification, secure encryption with several algorithms and producing cryptographic hash values among others.

Our target is to ensure software integrity deployed on premises, such as developed code and final code remains unchanged. For this purpose, we propose TPM's utilization to provide a secure platform.

We have named the Trusted Integrity Platform (TIP) to our solution as is a new component in CI/CD pipeline. This is a TPM provided server with a trust software stack for testing software project integrity. TPM provides guarantees to build a TIP server with a controlled software stack so we can assure that no malicious code can alter the project code. This is the anchor for integrity

---

[14] https://www.amazon.com/914-4136-105-Module-Infineon-Chip-9665/dp/
B075FBGTG9/ref=sr_1_2?dchild=1&keywords=TPM+Chip+infineon&
qid=1592740968&sr=8-2.

validation comparisons. TPM public key is used to control TIP server integrity because TIP server trusted boot is bound to TPM sealed key.

Git provides data integrity in the sense that those repositories that store source code have integrity measures, in [14] "this functionality is implemented in lower stages in Git as part of its philosophy". A list with all hash values from every project file is created and an ensemble hash for every commit record change (using git commit).

Each commit is bound to an associated hash issued from file tree data. When a commit is requested, as a file change, this change is propagated by hashes in the tree and commit. This enables Git repository to detect any change produced. We assume that information from a Git server is trusted and therefore data integrity is achieved. Next step describes security measures for a TIP server as an element dedicated to integrity verification. TIP containing the TPM conducts integrity verification.

Given that software under execution in a TIP server is predictable, this allows implementing secure booting protocol as a TPM functionality to check and verify that software stack remains unchanged. This is useful for securing TIP server using TPM functionalities. We consider that 3-factor integrity proof [16, 32] is needed in the whole CI/CD pipeline. This is the cornerstone contribution of this approach, it is based on checking source code integrity from three different sources for detecting a possible code manipulation:

- The *first integrity proof measure:* is taken before installing all dependencies required for the project; this guarantees that source code from the assembly and testing server is identical to Source Code Control Server.
- The *second integrity proof measure:* it guarantees that source code under assembly remains unchanged from external agents in assembly and testing servers.
- The *third integrity proof measure:* it guarantees that the whole process was successfully completed without undesired modifications after the project was assembled.

Every integrity proof measure is taken following particular steps we have categorized in three phases:

- **Suspicious code reception:** Assembly and testing server forwards to TIP server a compress file with source code, this is considered as "suspicious.zip". If the *uncompressing* phase is not successful, this file is discarded and integrity proof given as invalid.
- **Trust code reception:** TIP server retrieves source code from Git repository considered as trusted.
- **BigHashes proofs:** TIP server verifies, using TPM functionalities, that "suspicious.zip" content and source code from repository are identical. This is conducted consulting every hash file from Git server. These Git registered metadata are linked as a unique chain named bigHash and TPM hash functionalities are used to verify bigHash values. Therefore, when both bigHash values (project bigHash and suspicious.zip bigHash) are identical, integrity proof is considered successful.

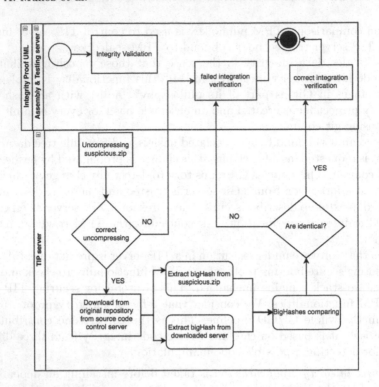

Fig. 3. Integrity proof verification UML flow diagram

Figure 4 shows a sequence diagram with TIP process communications in CI/CD pipeline. This shows the 3-factor verification described as well as the point of check of every integrity proof checking. Retrieving source code by TIP server is conducted in every integrity check, but it has been simplified in the diagram (likewise assembly and testing commands from every project).

7   Our Proposal: Trusted Integrity Platform

We have presented a solution based on three integrity proofs. The first one is taken before installing and guarantees integrity between code instances from the assembly and testing server and Source Code Control Server. The second integrity validation compares code from an external agent and assembly and testing server remain unchanged. And the third validation checks that the whole process was successfully completed and code in unchanged after the assembling (Fig. 3).

This section describes a TIP server implementation for testing its feasibility and as a proof of concept. We have implement a solution based on Windows 10 1809. We have implemented a component written in C# that relies on TPM functionality to access code. The *TIP* server has been implemented with PowerShell scripts and receives PHP script as input. The internal PHP server may

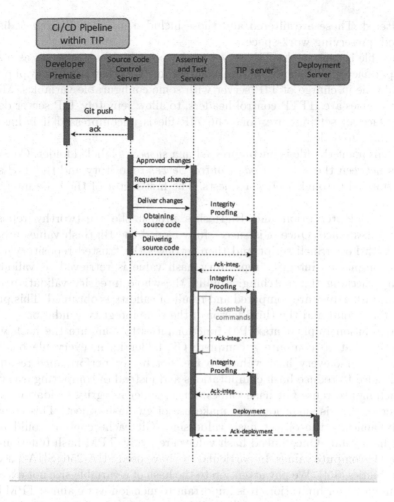

Fig. 4. Sequence diagram CI/CD pipeline within TIP server

attend requests from both *Assembly and Testing Servers* for this implementation. The algorithm that enables communication with the TIP server actually implements project integrity validation. This script is based on PowerShell and it is tested on Jenkins. The procedure script is included as part of CI/CD pipeline testing batches. Also, we have included the TIP server script communication from Jenkins in PowerShell. A comprehensive description of the full procedure is following described.

Suspicious code reception: Firstly, setting uploading parameters are required. Hence, a temporal folder within the TIP Server is created to contain every Jenkins work-space file. Next, all files from Jenkins work-space are compressed into a file. Once the compression step is completed files from selected folder are taken and filtered. These are filtered and those included in label *ToExclude* list are removed, preserving work-space.

Once file is sent to the TIP server we have a variable $tipServer as a script input parameter. TIP server is implemented in PHP, then a gateway.php file is the main file in charge of TIP server with some configurable variables. Most of those variables are HTTP control headers, to allow remotely TIP server deployment. Once all settings are done the ZIP file is uncompressed if it has been successfully uploaded.

At this point the file is uncompressed in a *suspect*'s labeled folder. Communications between the *Source Code Control Server* repository and the *TIP* server are performed through *POST* requests. The first factor of the code integrity is fulfilled.

Trust code reception and BigHashes proofs: the trustworthy repository cloning takes place. Once it is successfully cloned the BigHash values are computed with PowerShell script and then retrieves the trusted repository's TPM hashes. Suspicious integrity repository hash value is retrieved to validate its integrity checking the matching. Finally, the whole integrity validation procedure bigHash values are compared and result of validity is obtained. This process fulfills the second and the third factor of the code integrity validation.

Our solution implements TPM functionalities to compute the hash values. We notice that to compute a complete Git folder hash, every file has to be accessed to link every hash values to file. For better performance results, we have decided to reduce hash computations and instead of computing every hash (for each file) to reuse Git hash values. Once, folder integrity validation is done whether content is suspicious, we make use of git hash-object. This command gets dynamically the object hash value since Git cache content could not be object hash value. Once linked hash values are ready, TPM hash functionalities are used to compute values. In particular, we have used SHA-256 (SHA-1 security vulnerabilities [35]). We pay attention to the hash of a variable size not exceeding TPM input buffer limitation. It is important to mention as we aimed TPM buffer is limited to 32 bytes [2], therefore addition manual control is required.

7.1   Utilization of TPM Public Keys in TIP Server

We have proposed an additional security measure on the TIP server that represented the third integrity code validation. TPM equipped computers can use TPM functionalities for key generation and encryption with the particularity that decryption can only be performed by the TPM (binding key) protecting created key from disclosure. TPM works with a particular key hierarchy that starts with endorsement root key that is unique for each TPM chipset and is assigned while manufacturing. We highlight that endorsement key private part will not be exposed as we have used in TIP server.

This step consists of each change submitted to Git server carrying a complete copy of the project is signed using the Developer private key considered as trusted. TIP server stores the project copy accessed when an integrity proof is required, that is decrypted using Developer public key (previously loaded).

Therefore, three copies are taken as input (Developer version, Git stored version and suspicious from Assembly and testing server version) integration proofs are computed, then three versions should be identical (Fig. 5).

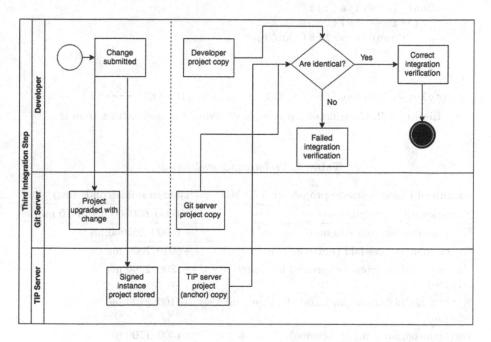

Fig. 5. Third integration verification step - developer verification

Creating a private key inside TPM is a trivial process, while extracting this key to a hard disk is not. Indeed, until 2016 a Microsoft functionality to extract public keys in XML format was used, but this was deprecated.

```
1  var rsaParams = (RsaParms)keyPublic.parameters;
2  var exponent = rsaParams.exponent != 0
3      ? Globs.HostToNet(rsaParams.exponent)
4      : RsaParms.DefaultExponent;
5
6  var modulus = (keyPublic.unique as Tpm2bPublicKeyRsa).
       buffer;
7  // RFC 4716
8  var pemKey = Combine(
9      new byte[] {0x00, 0x00, 0x00, 0x07},
10     new byte[] {0x73, 0x73, 0x68, 0x2d, 0x72, 0x73, 0x61},
11     new byte[] {0x00, 0x00, 0x00, 0x03},
12     exponent,
13     new byte[] {0x00, 0x00, 0x00, 0x80},
14     modulus
15 );
```

```
16
17 Console.WriteLine("---- BEGIN SSH2 PUBLIC KEY ----");
18 uint i = 0;
19 foreach(char c in System.Convert.ToBase64String(pemKey)){
20     Console.Write(c);
21     if(++i == 72){
22         Console.Write("\n");
23         i = 0;
24     }
25 }
26 Console.WriteLine("---- END SSH2 PUBLIC KEY ----");
```

Listing 1.2. Creation of a private key inside TPM and extract from it

Table 1. Performance evaluation

Examined Phase Software project with 50 MB	Time in milliseconds (ms)
Traditional CI/CD pipeline	360000–600000 ms (6–10 min)
Un-compress file (our scheme)	+16000–165000 ms
Check un-compress fold (our scheme)	+6000–7000 ms
Extract bigHask from compressed file (our scheme)	+1300–2200 ms
Extract bigHash from downloaded server (our scheme)	+1100–2100 ms
bigHash comparison (our scheme)	+1300–1700 ms
Integrity Proof Verification (our scheme)	+31000–38400 ms

We pretended a replica of deprecated functionality computing RSA public key using its module and index data following RFC 4716 [4] standard specification, as it is shown in algorithm 1.2. The computation of this code gives us as results the public key. Hopefully we made use of TPM2 TSS Engine library that implements functionalities for OpenSSL for TPM 2.0. This library facilitates all tasks using the tpm2-tss software stack following TCG Specifications.

8   Performance Evaluation

We analyze the computational cost of our approach measuring each new added process: (i) Extract the compressed file; (ii) Check the correction of the extracted file; (iii) Extract bigHash from compressed file; (iv) Extract bigHash from downloaded server; (v) bigHash comparison and (vi) Total Integrity Proof Verification. We use Windows 10 1809 with an Intel Core i5-7200K CPU at 2.5 GHz, 16 GB RAM. We measure execution time of each stage with a software project with 50 MB on a TPM simulator to present and extrapolate real results on a physical chipset. Results are shown in Table 1. From the comparisons we can notice that our proposed implementation adds maximum 44900ms as delay against the traditional process without integrity check. This minor delay is worthy of acceptance from developers since this leads to a safer CI/CD pipeline. Moreover, check of code's integrity provides high security levels to the delivered software project.

9   Conclusions and Future Work

The paper presented an identified security gap in the CI/CD pipeline in terms of integrity validation. To confront this gap we proposed a solution and delivered a proof-of-concept implementation of it. The proposed solution achieves i) to prove code integrity validation in CI/CD pipelines; ii) to develop a lightweight implementation for secure automation and iii) to deliver a solution in which the additional cost is much less than the benefit gained by its adoption by developers. We believe that this solution may contribute to open the way for a secure CI/CD pipeline ecosystem. As future work, multi-threaded tasks in the TIP server will be considered. Since tasks are parallelizable such as getting Trusted Git repository while suspicious.zip received file is uncompressed and retrieving bigHashes values in parallel can improve the current sequential version performance. Moreover, we aim to use hard-links (Junctions in Windows) instead of a mere copy of temporal work-space saving disk-space and time.

Acknowledgment. This research has been funded by the Marie Skłodowska-Curie ScaledGRID grant agreement No. 777996 and the H2020-SC1-FA-DTS-2018-1 CUREX under grant agreement No. 826404.

References

1. Black duck. https://www.blackducksoftware.com/. Accessed 3 July 2020
2. IBM's TPM 2.0 TSS. https://sourceforge.net/projects/ibmtpm20tss/. Accessed 19 June 2020
3. Jfrog. https://jfrog.com/. Accessed 3 July 2020
4. The secure shell (SSH) public key file format. https://tools.ietf.org/html/rfc4716
5. Security monkey. https://securitymonkey.readthedocs.io/en/latest/quickstart.html/. Accessed 3 July 2020
6. Servico Antibotnet. https://www.osi.es/es/servicio-antibotnet/info/mirai. Accessed 19 June 2020
7. Snyk. https://snyk.io/. Accessed 3 July 2020
8. Harpaz, O., Goldberg, D.: The Nanshou Campaign - Hackers Arsenal Grows Stronger (2013). https://www.guardicore.com/2019/05/nansh0u-campaign-hackers-arsenal-grows-stronger/. Accessed 19 June 2020
9. Arthur, W., Challener, D., Goldman, K.: Platform security technologies that use TPM 2.0. A Practical Guide to TPM 2.0, pp. 331–348. Apress, Berkeley, CA (2015). https://doi.org/10.1007/978-1-4302-6584-9_22
10. Bass, L., Holz, R., Rimba, P., Tran, A.B., Zhu, L.: Securing a deployment pipeline. In: 2015 IEEE/ACM 3rd International Workshop on Release Engineering, pp. 4–7. IEEE (2015)

11. Bass, L., Weber, I., Zhu, L.: DevOps: a software architect's perspective. sei series in software engineering. Addison-Wesley, New York (2015). http://my. safaribooksonline.com/9780134049847
12. Bennetts, S.: Owasp zed attack proxy. AppSec USA (2013)
13. Bird, J.: DevOpsSec: Securing Software Through Continuous Delivery. O'Reilly Media, Sebastopol (2016)
14. Chacon, S., Straub, B.: Pro Git. Springer Nature, Switzerland (2014)
15. Deepa, G., Thilagam, P.S.: Securing web applications from injection and logic vulnerabilities: approaches and challenges. Inf. Softw. Technol. **74**, 160–180 (2016)
16. Dheerendra, M., Sourav, M., Saru, K., Khurram, K.M., Ankita, C.: Security enhancement of a biometric based authentication scheme for telecare medicine information systems with nonce. J. Med. Syst. **38**(5), 41 (2014)
17. Felten, E: The Linux Backdoor Attempt of 2003. https://freedom-to-tinker.com/ 2013/10/09/the-linux-backdoor-attempt-of-2003/
18. Guan, H., Chen, W.R., Li, H., Wang, J.: Stride-based risk assessment for web application. In: Applied Mechanics and Materials, vol. 58, pp. 1323–1328. Trans Tech Publ (2011)
19. Huang, Y.W., Yu, F., Hang, C., Tsai, C.H., Lee, D.T., Kuo, S.Y.: Securing web application code by static analysis and runtime protection. In: Proceedings of the 13th International Conference on World Wide Web, pp. 40–52 (2004)
20. Humble, J., Farley, D.G.: Continuous Delivery: Reliable Software Releases through Build, Test, and Deployment Automation. Addison-Wesley, Upper Saddle River (2010). http://my.safaribooksonline.com/9780321601919
21. Ellingwood, J.: An Introduction to CI/CD Best Practices (2013). https://www. digitalocean.com/community/tutorials/an-introduction-to-ci-cd-best-practices. Accessed 19 June 2020
22. Krusche, S., Lichter, H., Riehle, D., Steffens, A.: Report of the 2nd workshop on continuous software engineering. In: CSE@ SE, pp. 1–6 (2017)
23. Kuusela, J., et al.: Security testing in continuous integration processes (2017)
24. Lee, T., Won, G., Cho, S., Park, N., Won, D.: Detection and mitigation of web application vulnerabilities based on security testing. In: Park, J.J., Zomaya, A., Yeo, S.-S., Sahni, S. (eds.) NPC 2012. LNCS, vol. 7513, pp. 138–144. Springer, Heidelberg (2012). https://doi.org/10.1007/978-3-642-35606-3_16
25. Lipke, S.: Building a secure software supply chain (2017)
26. Microsoft: BitLocker most frequently asked questions. https://docs.microsoft.com/ es-es/windows/security/information-protection/bitlocker/bitlocker-overview-and-requirements-faq. Accessed 19 June 2020
27. Milka, G.: Anatomy of account takeover. In: Enigma 2018 (Enigma 2018) (2018)
28. Mohan, V., Othmane, L.B.: Secdevops: is it a marketing buzzword?-mapping research on security in devops. In: 2016 11th International Conference on Availability, Reliability and Security (ARES), pp. 542–547. IEEE (2016)
29. OWASP: pen web application security project (OWASP) howpublished = https:// www.owasp.org/. Accessed 2 July 2020
30. Rahman, A.A.U., Williams, L.: Software security in devops: synthesizing practitioners' perceptions and practices. In: 2016 IEEE/ACM International Workshop on Continuous Software Evolution and Delivery (CSED), pp. 70–76. IEEE (2016)
31. Rimba, P., Zhu, L., Bass, L., Kuz, I., Reeves, S.: Composing patterns to construct secure systems. In: 2015 11th European Dependable Computing Conference (EDCC), pp. 213–224. IEEE (2015)

32. Kumari, S., Das, A.K., Li, X., Wu, F., Khan, M.K., Jiang, Q., Hafizul Islam, S.K.: A provably secure biometrics-based authenticated key agreement scheme for multi-server environments. Multimed. Tools Appl. **77**(2), 2359–2389 (2017). https://doi.org/10.1007/s11042-017-4390-x
33. Sathyanarayanan, N., Nanda, M.N.: Two layer cloud security set architecture on hypervisor. In: 2018 Second International Conference on Advances in Electronics, Computers and Communications (ICAECC), pp. 1–5. IEEE (2018)
34. Schneider, C.: Security devops-staying secure in agile projects. OWASP AppSec Europe (2015)
35. Stevens, M., Bursztein, E., Karpman, P., Albertini, A., Markov, Y.: The first collision for full SHA-1. In: Katz, J., Shacham, H. (eds.) CRYPTO 2017. LNCS, vol. 10401, pp. 570–596. Springer, Cham (2017). https://doi.org/10.1007/978-3-319-63688-7_19
36. Tichy, M., Goedicke, M., Bosch, J., Fitzgerald, B.: Rapid continuous software engineering. J. Syst. Softw. **133**, 159 (2017)
37. Ullah, F., Raft, A.J., Shahin, M., Zahedi, M., Babar, M.A.: Security support in continuous deployment pipeline. arXiv preprint arXiv:1703.04277 (2017)
38. XebiaLabs: Behaviour driven development security. https://xebialabs.com/technology/bdd-security/. Accessed 3 July 2020

Making Picnic Feasible for Embedded Devices

Johannes Winkler[1,2](✉) , Andreas Wallner[1](✉), and Christian Steger[2](✉)

[1] Infineon Technologies Austria AG, Graz, Austria
{johannes.winkler,andreas.wallner}@infineon.com
[2] Graz University of Technology, Graz, Austria
steger@tugraz.at

Abstract. Picnic is a post-quantum digital signature scheme, where the security is based on the difficulty of inverting a symmetric block cipher and zero-knowledge proofs. Picnic is one of the alternate candidates of the third round of the standardization process. Hence, it could be standardized in case of any weakness found in the round three candidates. Based on our paper at the 23rd Euromicro Conference ([6]), we found an optimization, which reduces memory usage to make it usable on IoT devices. This paper focusses on approaches for the implementation of this optimization. As a proof-of-concept, we implemented our implementation of Picnic on a ST Nucleo-L476RG and measured the cycles of the implementation.

1 Introduction

Post-quantum cryptography is a special field of cryptography, which has the goal to be resistant against attacks from quantum computers as far as we know. In 1994 Peter Shor published an algorithm [5], which can solve the integer factorization problem (and the discrete logarithm problem) in polynomial time. Therefore, a sufficient strong quantum computer can break RSA, ElGamal and Diffie-Hellman algorithms. The main target of post-quantum cryptography is to replace classical asymmetric cryptography by post-quantum resistant algorithms.

In 2017 *National Institute of Standards and Technology* (NIST) started a post-quantum cryptography standardization process. At the end of 2017, 82 cryptographic algorithms were submitted, 69 of them were accepted for the first round. On January 30, 2019, 26 of these candidates were accepted for the second round. Most of the accepted algorithms are based on lattices or error-correcting codes. If there is a structural weakness found in lattices or codes, many schemes can be broken. Picnic is the only algorithm based on zero-knowledge proofs (see [3]). Thus, Picnic is a valuable alternative to lattice and code-based post-quantum cryptography.

Supported by Infineon Technologies Austria AG.

I. Boureanu et al. (Eds.): ESORICS 2020 Workshops, LNCS 12580, pp. 166–180, 2020.
https://doi.org/10.1007/978-3-030-66504-3_10

As an advantage over lattice- and code-based schemes, Picnic has smaller key sizes (max. 256 bit for the secret key) depending on the security strength category. The levels of security are defined by NIST [4]. However, Picnic signatures are very large compared to other post-quantum algorithms, e.g., for security strength category 5 the maximum size of a signature is 132,856 bytes. Consequently, current Picnic implementations are not suited for memory-limited devices, such as IoT nodes or smartcards. In [6], we provided an optimization, which reduces the memory consumption of the implementation. In this paper, we focus on the implementation of Picnic on a microcontroller.

2 Preliminaries

Picnic signature scheme was first published in 2017 [2]. The security of the scheme relies on the hardness of inverting the LowMC [1] block cipher. Given the public key (C, p), the signer generates a Fiat-Shamir transcription proving the knowledge of y with $\text{LowMC}(p, y) = C$. For generating the Fiat-Shamir transcript the to-be-signed message is included to the hashed value for the challenge. Hence, the transcript is connected to the public key and the message and can be verified by any user knowing the public key and the message.

2.1 Picnic

There are various variants of Picnic. On our optimization, we focus on the Fiat-Shamir version of the Picnic algorithm. We do not cover Unruh transformation or Picnic 2. This section describes the parameters used to instantiate Picnic with respect to the security strength categories L1, L3, and L5.

Table 1. Picnic parameters by security strength category [3]

Security level	S	r	T	ℓ	XOF
L1	128	20	219	256	SHAKE128
L3	192	30	329	384	SHAKE256
L5	256	38	438	512	SHAKE256

Table 1 shows the parameters of the algorithm depending on the security strength category. S is the length of the state (i.e. the length of the input, output, and key of the LowMC cipher) in bits. Furthermore, all generated seeds also have this length. The number r represents the number of rounds needed to compute the result of one LowMC encryption. The number of repetitions of the *Multi Party Computation* (MPC) protocol is denoted as T. All commitments have the length ℓ. An *Extendable Output Function* (XOF) is a hash function with variable output length. It is used for commitments and for generating pseudorandom bit strings, such as the challenge or the seeds.

2.2 Picnic Structure

The structure of the Picnic algorithm consists of four steps. Figure 1 shows the main structure of the signature generation and visualizes the steps.

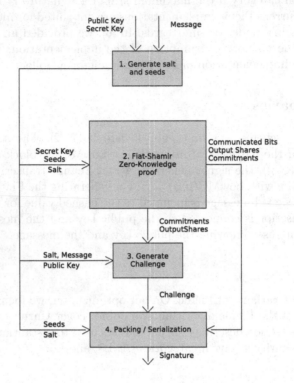

Fig. 1. Picnic algorithm data flow. In the original Version the four steps are processed sequentially.

Generate Salt and Seeds. The seeds and the salt are generated by SHAKE-128 or SHAKE-256 and have to be kept in memory during the whole execution of Picnic. In total one salt and $3 \cdot T$ seeds are generated, 3 for each MPC repetition. As defined in [3], the output of the XOF is defined as the concatenated seeds followed by the salt. Therefore, in order to generate the salt the XOF has to generate all the seeds at first.

However, according to [3], the generation of seeds and salts can be changed, without breaking the compatibility to the verification function of the reference implementation. For security reasons, the generation of seeds and salt has to be collision-free and unpredictable.

Running the MPC Repetitions. This step consists of T repetitions of the MPC protocol. One repetiton consists of the generation of three tapes and the input shares using the secret key, the execution of the evaluation of LowMC using the MPC protocol, and finally the computation of the commitments for this run of the protocol.

The tapes and the first two input shares are pseudorandomly generated from the seed. The third input share is chosen such that the XOR-sum of all shares yields the secret key.

The MPC protocol computes the output shares from the input shares and the tapes and the inter-party-communication (here denoted as *communicated bits*). The length of the communicated bits per party is $30 \cdot r$ bits, where r is the number of repetitions of the LowMC computation. For further computations, the bit string is filled with zeros up to a full byte, namely a size of 75, 113, and 143 bytes for each security strength category respectively.

The commitments are hash values of communicated bits, input, and output shares. One commitment has $S/4$ bits.

Generate Challenge. When all runs of the MPC protocol are finished the challenge is computed by an XOF. The inputs for the XOF is all output shares, followed by all commitments, the salt, the public key and finally the message itself.

The challenge consists of values $\{0, 1, 2\}$ where each element is represented via 2 bits of the XOF output. In case of two consecutive ones i.e. 0b11 = 3 these bits are skipped to achieve uniform distributed challenges. The binary representation of the challenge is filled to a full byte with zeros at the end. Thus, the size of the challenge string is 55, 83, and 110 bytes respectively.

Packing and Serialization. The signature is the concatenation of the challenge and the salt. For each round depending on the challenge $e \in \{0, 1, 2\}$ a commitment for party $e + 2$ and the inter-party communication for party $e + 1$ is appended. Additionally, if $e \neq 0$ the share of the third party is also appended.

Based on Fig. 1 our optimizations target on reusing data and withdraw it as soon as possible. In the original version, the seeds have to stay in RAM for the whole execution. There is a similar situation for the commitments and the output shares. As step 2 (Fiat Shamir Zero-Knowledge proof) is run 219, 329 or 438 times depending on the security strength category, all intermediate results have to be stored until the generation of the challenge in step 3. Our basic idea is to run steps 1, 2 and 3 simultaneously in a way that all results can be reused and then withdrawn immediately.

3 Our Optimizations

We provide three optimizations. The first one is for generating the seeds and the salt. In contrast to the reference implementation, we use AES instead of SHAKE128/SHAKE256. We justify this step with two reasons. Firstly, we need random access to the seeds and the salt. Secondly, as far as we know, most IoT devices or smartcards, are equipped with an accelerator for AES. Furthermore, for hardware implementations of Picnic, this optimization allows parallelizing the MPC rounds. As our paper is focussed on memory consumption, we will not go deeper into this topic. According to the specification, the generation of seeds and salt does not affect the verification function. Therefore, signatures generated with this optimization are fully compatible with the verification function of the reference implementation.

The second optimization is the way how the challenge is generated. By reordering the input values of the hash function, we can avoid caching the commitments of all MPC rounds. By the definition of a appropriately secure cryptographic hash function, the order of the input values does not affect security. However, as the challenge also has to be generated for the verification, this optimization breaks backward compatibility.

As a third modification, we suggest transferring parts of the signature from the IoT device to the host system. The signature itself is assembled by the host. This increases the amount of data which is transferred between the host and IoT device. On the other hand, the transferred data does not have to be stored at the IoT device. This optimization depends on the context of the IoT device.

3.1 Generation of Seeds and Salt

According to the specification of Picnic [3] the seeds are generated by an XOF such as SHAKE128 (for security strength category L1) or SHAKE256 (for higher security). By definition, the input of the XOF is

    XOF(sk||M||pk||S)

where pk and sk are public and secret key, M is the message to be signed and S is the size of a seed in bit, encoded as 16 bit little endian integer. In total the XOF outputs $3 \cdot T$ seeds, each of them of size $S/8$ followed by the 32 byte salt. The output of the SHAKE function follows the pattern

    seed[0][0] || seed[0][1] || seed[0][2] ||
    seed[1][0] || seed[1][1] || seed[1][2] ||
    ...
    seed[T-1][0] || seed[T-1][1] ||
    seed[T-1][2] || salt

As it can be seen due to the properties of SHAKE-functions the seeds can only be generated sequentially. Additionally, the salt is obtained at last after all seeds have been generated. This prevents on-the-fly-computation in each repetition. As an optimization we recommend to change the order, i.e. generating the salt at first, and then generating the seeds. Algorithms 1 and 2 describe an independent seed and salt generation based on AES counter mode. As it is also stated in the Picnic specification, the generation of seed and salt does not affect the interoperability of the Picnic scheme. Therefore, signatures generated by our optimized version can be verified by the official reference implementation.

With this modification, we do not have to store $3 \cdot T$ (one for each of the three parties and for T rounds) seeds, where each seed has S bits. Depending on the security strength category the amount of reduced space is

$$3 \cdot 219 \cdot 16 = 10,512 \text{ bytes for L1,}$$
$$3 \cdot 329 \cdot 24 = 23,688 \text{ bytes for L3,}$$
$$3 \cdot 438 \cdot 32 = 42,048 \text{ bytes for L5.}$$

Figure 2 shows the optimized version. If operated on a device with a multi-core processor, the operation can be parallelized.

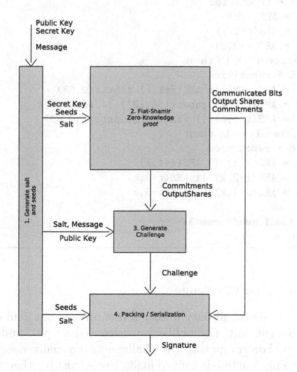

Fig. 2. Picnic algorithm data flow with modified seed/salt generation.

Algorithm 1. Picnic's salt generation

```
1: procedure GENERATESALT(sk, M, pk, S)
2:     g = sk||M||pk||S
3:     r = SHAKE-256(SHA3-256(g), 128)
4:     k = SHAKE-256(g, S)
5:     return salt = AES(r,k) || AES(r+1,k)
6: end procedure
```

Algorithm 2. Picnic's seed generation

```
1: procedure GENERATESEED(sk, M, pk, S, seclevel, repetition)
2:     g = sk||M||pk||S
3:     r = SHAKE-256(SHA3-256(g), 128)
4:     k = SHAKE-256(g, S)
5:     r += 2
6:     if seclevel == L1 then
7:         k += 3 * repetition
8:         seed1 = AES(r,k)
9:         seed2 = AES(r+1,k)
10:        seed3 = AES(r+2,k)
11:    else if seclevel == L3 then
12:        k += 5 * repetition
13:        seed1 = AES(r,k) || AES(r+1,k).substr(0,63)
14:        seed2 = AES(r+1,k).substr(64,127) || AES(r+2,k)
15:        seed3 = AES(r+3,k) || AES(r+4,k).substr(0,63)
16:    else if seclevel == L5 then
17:        k += 6 * repetition
18:        seed1 = AES(r,k) || AES(r+1,k)
19:        seed2 = AES(r+2,k) || AES(r+3,k)
20:        seed3 = AES(r+4,k) || AES(r+5,k)
21:    end if
22:    return (seed1,seed2,seed3)
23: end procedure
```

3.2 Computation of Challenge

The challenge depends on all output shares (denoted as out), all commitments (denoted as com), the salt, the public key (denoted as pk), and the message (denoted as msg). For computing the challenge a specially designed H3 hash function is used. This function is defined in [3]. In contrast to other hash functions H3 maps on $\{0, 1, 2\}^T$, which represents a list of challenge for each repetition. The order of the input data as specified in [3] is

```
e = H3(
out[0][0] || out[0][1] || out[0][2]
out[1][0] || out[1][1] || out[1][2]
...
out[T-1][0] || out[T-1][1] || out[T-1][2]
com[0][0] || com[0][1] || com[0][2]
com[1][0] || com[1][1] || com[1][2]
...
com[T-1][0] || com[T-1][1] || com[T-1][2]
salt, pk, msg).
```

As a way of saving memory, the output shares obtained in one particular MPC repetition can be hashed immediately after the repetition and then be discarded. However, the commitments have to be stored in memory until all output shares are hashed. Our approach is to hash three output shares and three commitments per repetition.

```
e = H3(
out[0][0] || out[0][1] || out[0][2]
com[0][0] || com[0][1] || com[0][2]
out[1][0] || out[1][1] || out[1][2]
com[1][0] || com[1][1] || com[1][2]
...
out[T-1][0] || out[T-1][1] || out[T-1][2]
com[T-1][0] || com[T-1][1] || com[T-1][2]
salt, pk, M)
```

It follows that we do not need to keep commitments or output shares in memory during the signing operation.

With this modification, we do not need to store $3 \cdot T$ commitments, where each seed has ℓ bits. Depending on the security strength category the amount of reduced space is

$$3 \cdot 219 \cdot 32 = 21,024 \text{ bytes for L1,}$$
$$3 \cdot 329 \cdot 48 = 47,376 \text{ bytes for L3,}$$
$$3 \cdot 438 \cdot 64 = 84,096 \text{ bytes for L5.}$$

Figure 3 shows the first two optimizations. It can be seen that step 1 and step 3 of Picnic can be parallelized.

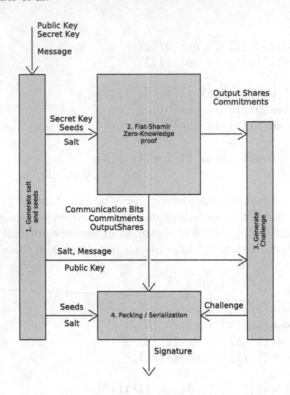

Fig. 3. Picnic algorithm data flow with modified seed/salt/challenge generation.

3.3   Stream Encrypted Temporary Results

Due to the limited memory of IoT devices, some intermediate results have to be transferred to the host system. However, deciding which information can be sent outside is a non-trivial task from a security perspective.

Encryption. As an encryption method, we suggest AES-128, AES-192, or AES-256 depending on the security strength category. The security of these algorithms exactly matches to the NIST security strength categories 1, 3, and 5. In order to avoid generating a random initialization vector, we use *Electronic Codebook* (ECB) mode. We do not expect any problems with ECB mode, as our data is pseudorandom and has a fixed length.

We suggest to derive the encryption keys from the seeds. Therefore, we are not required to generate keys randomly and store them. As a result, we do not have to transfer the key from the device to the host.

Seeds. Transferring the seeds could be critical, as the seed of the first two parties also generates the input share. For any challenge $e \neq 0$, the input share of the last party is given. By construction, XORing all input shares gives the secret key. Therefore, the IoT device must not send all three seeds to the host.

As the seeds are withdrawn in each repetition, they have to be generated again. According to our proposal, the generation of the seeds is AES-based and, therefore, it is faster than the generation by SHAKE XOF and the seeds can be randomly accessed.

Commitments. As the commitments are needed for the final signature, we suggest transfering all three commitments to the host in each repetition. As only one of three commitment per repetition is necessary for the signature, we increase the amount of data which is transferred between the IoT device and the host system. However, as the commitments can be transferred by the end of each repetition, no speed losses occur. From the security perspective, the commitments can be computed by anyone knowing the signature and the public key, and therefore our approach does not affect the security of the scheme.

Input Share of 3rd Party. The input share of the 3rd party has to be included in the signature if, and only if, the challenge is not 0. On the other hand, it must not be included for any other challenge. Our approach is to derive the encryption key from the seed of the 3rd party. It can be easily seen, that the seed for encryption is only known, if the challenge is 1 or 2.

In comparison to the classical Picnic, the third (encrypted) input share is sent for each repetition of the MPC protocol and, therefore, also increases the size of the communication.

As a consequence, the communication stream between host and IoT device has a fixed length.

Communication Bits. The communication bits are the result of the AND gates of a party. As there are $30 \cdot r$ AND gates per repetition, there are 75 bytes, 113 bytes, and 143 bytes for each party at a security strength categories L1, L3, and L5 respectively. For one repetition with challenge e, only the communcation bits of party $e + 1$ are needed. As the challenge is unknown while running the MPC protocol, all communications bits have to be transferred to the host system. As the communication bits can leak information about the secret key, they have to be encrpyted. The key for decryption is derived from seed $e + 1$.

Serialization of the Signature. To parallelize computation and communication, parts of the signature are sent to host. Therefore, the host has to convert all parts of the signature to a valid format according to the specification. A valid Picnic signature has to start with the challenge followed by the salt. For each repetition of the MPC protocol, following values have to be included to the signature: commitment for party $e + 2$, communication for party $e + 1$ (decrypted by the host), seeds for party e and $e + 1$. The serialization of the signature will be executed on the host system. The result of this procedure is a valid signature according to [3] (except the changes of optimization 2).

This modification avoids storing $3 \cdot T$ communication bits with the length of $\{75, 113, 143\}$ bytes depending on the security strength categories. Furthermore, it avoids storing the share of the third party, which has S bits. For the security strength categories L1, L3 and L5, the reduced amount of space is

$$219 \cdot (3 \cdot 75 + 16) = 52,779 \text{ bytes,}$$
$$329 \cdot (3 \cdot 113 + 24) = 119,427 \text{ bytes,}$$
$$438 \cdot (3 \cdot 143 + 32) = 201,918 \text{ bytes,}$$

respectively.

Algorithm 3 is the code of the algorithm which generates the signature from the data which is transferred from the IoT device (Fig. 4).

Algorithm 3. Packing and Serialization (Host system)

```
 1: procedure    SERIALIZATION(challenge,   salt,   commitments,   seeds,
        communication, ishare3)
 2:     sig = challenge || salt
 3:     for k = 0 to T do
 4:         e = challenge.getBit(k)
 5:         key1 = deriveKey(seeds[0])
 6:         key2 = deriveKey(seeds[1])
 7:         sig.append(commitments[k][e + 2])
 8:         sig.append(decrypt(communication[k][e + 1], key2))
 9:         sig.append(seeds[0])                          ▷ only 2 seeds incl.
10:         sig.append(seeds[1])
11:         if e = 1 then
12:             sig.append(decrypt(ishare3[k]), key2)
13:         else if e = 2 then
14:             sig.append(decrypt(ishare3[k]), key1)
15:         end if
16:     end for
17: end procedure
```

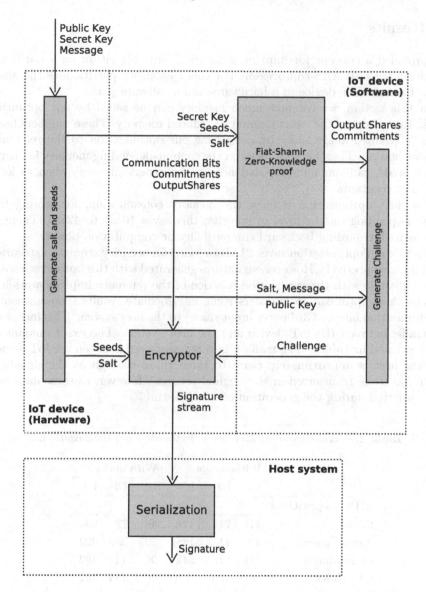

Fig. 4. Picnic algorithm on IoT device partitioned in a hardware and a software part. The algorithm for serialization is on the host system and, therefore, does not have to be optimized.

4 Results

We provided a concept for implementing the Picnic algorithm on a hardware plattform with an AES-coprocessor. For this reason, we partitionate the algorithm from the IoT device to a hardware- and a software part.

In this section, we list how much memory can be saved by our optimizations. Table 2 shows the exact amount of reduced memory. These numbers have been determined analytically by comparing our optimization to the reference implementation. Therefore, we focus on the content-depending memory i.e. keys, states, seeds, random numbers and not on the generic memory such as loop indices or constants.

The first optimization reduces the memory consumption, for storing the seeds. Depending on the level of security, this saves 10 kB to 42 kB. There is no drawback regarding backward compatibility or computation power.

The second optimization saves 21 kB to 84 kB for security strength categories L1 and L5, respectively. However, signatures generated with this optimization are not compatible with the verification function of the reference implementation.

The third optimization transfers some intermediate results (commitments, communication bits and 3rd party input share) to the host system. This increases the traffic between the IoT device and the host system. The exact amount of traffic is listed in Table 3. The traffic which is transferred between the IoT device and the host is approximately twice to three times as high as the signature which has to be transferred in the original version. However, as some data can be transferred during the generation of the signature.

Table 2. Secret-depending memory in bytes after our optimization.

	Without opt.			With opt.		
	L1	L3	L5	L1	L3	L5
MPC repetition:						
Seeds	11k	24k	42k	48	72	96
Tapes/comm	49k	112k	188k	225	339	429
Commitments	21k	47k	84k	96	144	192
I/O shares	≈ 0	≈ 0	≈ 0	96	144	192
3rd party share	3k	8k	14k	–	–	–
Total per rep.	–	–	–	**465**	**699**	**909**
Total for all rep.	**84k**	**191k**	**328k**	–	–	–
Salt	32	32	32	32	32	32
Challenge	55	83	110	55	83	110
Total	**84k**	**191k**	**328k**	**552**	**814**	**1.051**

Table 3. Picnic signature size by security strength category compared to traffic size of our third optimization

Security strength category	Min in bytes	Max in bytes	Transferred data in bytes
L1	30,528	34,032	80,898
L3	68,876	76,772	182,710
L5	118,840	132,856	314,188

5 Implementation

We provide the benchmarked embedded implementation in [...] and a PC reference implementation in [...].

The computation of the LowMC cipher requires predefined constants, which are hardcoded in our implementations.

Currently, our implementations run on a STM32L476RG. As this processor does not have an AES accelerator, we use an AES software implementation for the third optimization. In our implementation, we do not use AES for the seed and salt generation (Table 4).

Table 4. Picnic cycles on ST Nucleo-L476RG

Security strength category	Cycles	Cycles for one AES encryption	AES calls
L1	$1.0 \cdot 10^9$	12,793	3,504
L3	$3.1 \cdot 10^9$	16,059	7,567
L5	$6.7 \cdot 10^9$	17,593	12,702

Related Work

In [6] we presented three optimizations for reducing the space consumption of the Picnic algorithm.

1. Generating seeds and salt on demand, which saves up to 42 kB RAM.
2. Modified generation of the challenge to avoid caching the commitments. This saves up to 84 kB.
3. Streaming parts of the signature to client while generating. This saves memory for communication bits and input shares. This can save memory up to 200 kB.

Our optimizations focus on the generation of the signature, specifically on the secret-key depending part. The verification does not use the secret key and, therefore, it does not have to be done on a hardware-secured device, such as an IoT device or a smartcard.

Future Work

The message is needed for the generation of seeds, salt, and challenge. However, for the functionality of Picnic it is only necessary to include the message in the generation of the challenge. Therefore, the seeds and the salt can be generated independently from the message. However, the output of the random number generator has to be unpredictable and the seeds have to be collision-free.

Another aspect is the implementation on a system with a contactless interface. Due to our optimizations the traffic increases by the factor ≈ 2.5. This leads to a delay and to higher power consumption. This topic highly depends on the use-case. For a given use-case the tradeoff between space consumption and traffic has to be discussed individually.

We expect our optimization to be as secure as the original Picnic. However, we do not provide a proof of the security of our modifications. The security of Picnic is proven in [2].

Acknowledgment. This work was supported by the FutureTPM project of Horizon H2020 Framework Programme of the European Union, under GA number 779391.

References

1. Albrecht, M., Rechberger, C., Schneider, T., Tiessen, T., Zohner, M.: Ciphers for MPC and FHE. Cryptology ePrint Archive, Report 2016/687 (2016). https://eprint.iacr.org/2016/687
2. Chase, M., et al.: Post-quantum zero-knowledge and signatures from symmetric-key primitives. Cryptology ePrint Archive, Report 2017/279 (2017). https://eprint.iacr.org/2017/279
3. Chase, M., et al.: The picnic signature algorithm: Specification version 2.1, 2019. 20 Aug 2019
4. National Institute of Standards and Technology. Submission requirements and evaluation criteria for the post-quantum cryptography standardization process (2016). https://csrc.nist.gov/CSRC/media/Projects/Post-Quantum-Cryptography/documents/call-for-proposals-final-dec-2016.pdf
5. Shor, P.: Algorithms for quantum computation: discrete logarithms and factoring. In: Proceedings 35th Annual Symposium on Foundations of Computer Science (1994). https://doi.org/10.1109/SFCS.1994.365700
6. Winkler, J., Höller, A., Steger, C.: Optimizing picnic for limited memory resources. In: 23rd Euromicro Conference on Digital System Design (DSD) (2020)
7. Dinur, I., Kales, D., Promitzer, A., Ramacher, S., Rechberger, C.: Linear equivalence of block ciphers with partial non-linear layers: application to LowMC. Cryptology ePrint Archive, Report 2018/772 (2018). https://eprint.iacr.org/2018/772
8. Kales, D., Perrin, L., Promitzer, A., Ramacher, S., Rechberger, C.: Improvements to the linear operations of LowMC: a faster Picnic. Cryptology ePrint Archive, Report 2017/1148 (2017). https://eprint.iacr.org/2017/1148

Sandboxing the Cyberspace for Cybersecurity Education and Learning

Stylianos Karagiannis[1]($\boxtimes$) (ID), Emmanouil Magkos[1] (ID), Christoforos Ntantogian[1] (ID), and Luís L. Ribeiro[2]

[1] Department of Informatics, Ionian University, Plateia Tsirigoti 7, 49100 Corfu, Greece
{skaragiannis,emagos,dadoyan}@ionio.gr
[2] PDM&FC, R. Fradesso da Silveira, 4-1B, 1300-609 Lisbon, Portugal
luis.ribeiro@pdmfc.com

Abstract. Deploying the appropriate digital environment for conducting cyberse-curity exercises can be challenging and typically requires a lot of effort and system resources. Usually, for deploying vulnerable webservices and setting up labs for hands-on cybersecurity exercises to take place, more configuration is required along with technical expertise. Containerization techniques and solutions provide less overhead and can be used instead of virtualization techniques to revise the existing approaches. Furthermore, it is important to sandbox or replicate existing systems or services for the cybersecurity exercises to be realistic. To address such challenges, we conducted a performance evaluation of some of the existing deployment techniques to analyze their benefits and drawbacks. We tested techniques relevant to containerization or MicroVMs that include less overhead instead of the regular virtualization techniques to provide meaningful and comparable results from the deployment of scalable solutions, demonstrating their benefits and drawbacks. Towards this direction, we present a use case for deploying cybersecurity exercises that requires less effort and moderate system resources. By using the deployed components, we provide a baseline proposal for monitoring the progress of the participants using a host-based intrusion system.

Keywords: Cybersecurity · Docker · Sandbox · Security labs · Cyber range

1 Introduction

Designing and deploying effective cybersecurity labs requires a combination of various technologies which usually include a lot of effort for the deployment of effective cyberse-curity exercises. For computer security students to benefit from hands-on experiences, a large variety of security tools must be used, making difficult and time-consuming the task of properly designing and deploying the exercises [1–3]. Creating authentic computer security scenarios has been identified in the past as a very demanding and challenging task, requiring much effort from the instructor and the lab personnel. Virtualization tech-nologies provide beneficial ways for hosting multiple machines within one single system, decreasing the required deployment effort and system resources, enhancing the instruc-tor's ability to deploy complex scenarios for education purposes [4]. Our purpose is to

© Springer Nature Switzerland AG 2020
I. Boureanu et al. (Eds.): ESORICS 2020 Workshops, LNCS 12580, pp. 181–196, 2020.
https://doi.org/10.1007/978-3-030-66504-3_11

create a flexible and portable solution without requiring any existing deployed infrastructure and to deploy multiple systems for conduct security testing that includes complex processes such as adversary emulations and incident response. Existing cybersecurity exercises are usually deployed using virtualization and restrict the learning processes without maintaining significant interactions between the deployed services (e.g. interactions between Intrusion detection systems, adversaries, and the usage of Elastic Search). Not only this but virtual machines include a lot of overhead and a high demand in system resources for deploying relevant services that are required by the exercises. On the other hand, containers have several advantages [5–8]. The performance that containers have, comes with the cost of providing less isolation than virtual machines. Restrictions also apply in terms of compatibility for deploying kernelless operating systems using containerization.

A main difficulty that persists is to match the security scenarios and the required infrastructure to specific knowledge areas and technical topics. In order to identify the knowledge areas that are relevant during the exercises, it is considered important to establish well-defined taxonomies that address the acquired knowledge and skills [9]. For example, Security Operations Center (SOC) teams are meant to offer high quality IT-security services using tools that actively detect potential threats and attacks and respond accordingly [10]. In such cases, not only the deployment effort is big, but for each participant it is best to have an individual cyberspace as the environment that includes the deployed systems and services. Therefore, scalability issues derive from the fact that it is required to replicate each cyberspace for each participant. Usually, the tools required for conducting such tasks are complex and their deployment is time-consuming [11]. Finally, the learning outcomes of using hands-on practices need to follow curriculum guidelines or frameworks, which address the collaborative activities that are required in cybersecurity within the industry, government and academic organizations [2, 12, 13].

Modern technologies for deploying services or operating systems, include docker[1] containers, Linux Containers (LXC), MicroVMs[2], RancherVM[3] and other options for deploying and running Kernel-based Virtual Machine (KVM) or docker containers inside a docker. Current operating systems and especially Linux distributions enhance the ability for portable and flexible deployments. Therefore, the existing exercises and tools can be easier deployed and managed accordingly.

There are specific benefits and drawbacks from using the existing technologies for deploying systems and services. This research aspires to analyze the state-of-the-art approaches for deploying cyber security exercises, considering the portability, flexibility and capability of featuring easy-deployment and to reduce the total overhead. Our intention is to deploy, evaluate and investigate the best practices for using such technologies to maintain cybersecurity exercises and hands-on labs, while requiring less deployment effort. Therefore, the main research questions that this work attempts to answer are reflected below:

---

[1] https://docker.com/.

[2] https://github.com/firecracker-microvm/firecracker/.

[3] https://github.com/rancher/vm/.

RQ1: What are the features, challenges and drawbacks that the different virtualization or containerization technologies include for designing and deploying cybersecurity exercises?

RQ2: Which are the best practices for deploying complex cybersecurity exercises while maintaining the least overhead in terms of resources and having increased compatibility?

RQ1 and RQ2 intend to evaluate the current deployment options using sandboxing for maintaining cybersecurity exercises and to discover the current possibilities of containerization and virtualization technologies. Towards this direction, we conducted an in-depth analysis and a performance evaluation of the most common technologies, while we also deployed example exercises accordingly for discovering the benefits and drawbacks for each approach. The research paper is organized as follows: In section the related work is provided, while in Sect. 3 common virtualization technologies and containerization approaches are analyzed, presenting the capability for using a sandbox as the main learning environment. In Sect. 4 the potential a solution of using a sandbox for maintaining complex Cyber Ranges is discussed, concluding with Sect. 5 by discussing future action points.

2   Related Work

The idea of using LXC or docker containers instead of virtual machines has been under research during the last years [14, 15]. For example, Irvine et al. introduced a framework for parameterizing cybersecurity labs using containers [2]. The key benefits from using containers instead of virtual machines include the higher performance that containers score, which allows to deploy a high number of systems and services more easily, requiring less resources. For example, AlSalamah et al. [13], analyze how containerization techniques could open new possibilities, highlighting the difference between virtual machines and containers. They assess the benefits that containers provide regarding configuration, networking and performance, as well as their flexibility for deploying large number of services. Likewise, research has been conducted in terms of the design of architectures and toolsets for providing learning cyberspaces related to network security and for creating hands-on lab exercises [16]. In their research the significant benefits of using dockers instead of virtualization technologies are also highlighted.

Significant work has been done in the past in providing security education hands-on labs including practical cybersecurity exercises. For example, SEED labs[4] provided prebuilt virtual machine images including about 30 exercises and featuring a wide range of cybersecurity topics [17]. Similarly, the ENISA's Computer Security and Incident Response Team (CSIRT)[5], since 2008, released and introduced training material that is constantly updated by new exercise scenarios containing toolsets and virtual images to support hands-on training sessions.

Other similar approaches include reinforced learning approaches that include simulation and emulation processes derived from complex deployments. Such approaches

---

[4] https://seedsecuritylabs.org/.

[5] https://enisa.europa.eu/topics/trainings-for-cybersecurity-specialists/online-training-material/.

include important elements that enterprise networks have such as workstations, fire-walls and servers, among others for creating a high-fidelity training environment [18–20]. Instead, deployment options that include more complex infrastructures and network topologies are not very frequently found in CTF (Capture The Flag) exercises and are usually related to cyber ranges, where more complex topologies are presented [21, 22]. As a result, the deployment options for cybersecurity exercises are currently revised for using containerization technologies along with virtualization technologies to extend and provide more interactive cybersecurity learning environments.

3   Virtualization Technologies and Sandboxing

Virtualization technologies are frequently used for creating and deploying vulnerable virtual systems for testing purposes. Popular approaches include HackTheBox[6], TryHackMe[7] and the vulnerable images published on VulnHub[8], an open repository providing hands-on lab cybersecurity exercises.

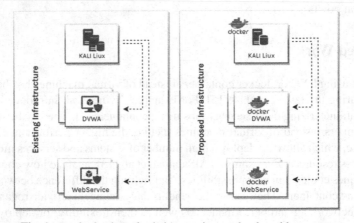

Fig. 1. Dockerization of existing services and vulnerable systems

Similarly, SEED labs and ENISA CSIRT introduced training material containing cybersecurity exercise scenarios in the form of Virtual Images to support hands-on training sessions. The benefits of using virtualization techniques are many, however, the total performance and size overhead could be difficult to manage. Therefore, specific cybersecurity scenarios can be revised to reduce the total overhead accordingly. For example, existing services are possible to be revised and deployed as docker containers (Fig. 1). Even services provided from Linux distributions such as Kali Linux[9] are possible to be deployed in a docker container for the participants to use instead of a virtual

---

[6] https://hackthebox.eu/.

[7] https://tryhackme.com/.

[8] https://vulnhub.com/.

[9] https://kali.org/.

machine. Towards this direction, some of the existing cybersecurity exercises that include DVWA[10] or Webgoat[11] have been released as docker containers. The main idea of our approach is that docker containers can be used for deploying multiple service instances for the participants to have their own cyberspace environment to practice with (Fig. 2).

Fig. 2. Webgoat instances running as different docker containers

Despite their benefits, containers include a few security issues, mainly deriving from the fact that they share access to a single host, meaning that any potential malicious code could get full access and take over the host system. Such incidents of escalating the privileges from a docker container are not addressed in the content of this research paper.

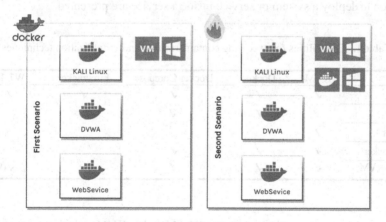

Fig. 3. Dockers and Ignite Firecracker

On the other hand, containers are easier to manage than virtual machines making it possible to create a network topology that includes more software components to properly initiate the exercises, requiring less deployment and integration effort. Despite the security concerns, new containerization solutions are on the process of mitigating such threats. For example, Firecracker and more particularly Ignite Firecracker[12], is

---

[10] https://hub.docker.com/r/vulnerables/web-dvwa/.

[11] https://hub.docker.com/r/webgoat/webgoat-8.0/.

[12] https://github.com/weaveworks/ignite/.

an existing solution providing kernel isolation running Kernel-based Virtual Machine (KVM), while including less overhead.

As shown in Fig. 3, docker containers are possible to be deployed as nested containers using a specific flag for running the docker image (–privileged). Another option we investigate is the case where dockers inside a docker are deployed using the same or different docker daemon when required. Such options come with the risk of triggering inconsistencies on the processed data or creating unstable environments. Therefore, the solution of using Firecracker is more applicable providing strong isolation. Taking the above into consideration, it is important to conduct a performance evaluation and deploy test cases to understand and discover any potential security or performance issues. Using either the Dockers inside a Docker or MicroVMs with Firecracker, it is possible to deploy multiple instances for the participants to exercise, giving them the opportunity to interact with their own isolated cyberspace. The isolation capabilities along with the performance evaluation, benefits and drawbacks of each approach are presented in detail in the next section.

3.1 Evaluation of Popular Virtualization and Containerization Techniques

The purpose of this evaluation was to discover the performance capabilities and measure the total overhead of each of the existing techniques and to deploy various approaches for analyzing the benefits and drawbacks. In Table 1 the compatibility capabilities and the option to deploy a system or service inside a service are presented.

Table 1. Capabilities for executing containerization and virtualization techniques

	KVM	Docker	Docker Compose	Firecracker	W7-10
KVM	✓	✓	✓	✓	✓
DinD	✓	✓	✓		
Docker	✓				
Firecracker	✓	✓	✓		
RancherVM	✓	✓	✓		✓(W7)

For example, it is possible to execute a KVM inside a KVM, a docker inside a KVM, the ability to run microservices using Docker containers inside a KVM or Firecracker inside a KVM and to test deployment options for Windows services. The above cases investigate the current deployment possibilities in response to RQ1 mentioned in Sect. 1 and the benefits as well as the challenges and drawbacks are described further below (Table 1, Table 2). In our tests, we discovered quite a few compatibility issues regarding Windows hosts, and we also included RancherVM in our tests as another solution for creating virtual images with less overhead and successfully run Windows 7 machines using KVM. Our efforts for creating a Windows 10 machine for using in RancherVM was not successful and might require more effort to proceed with this approach. The approach of using RancherVM is included in Table 2, however we excluded the results from the evaluation considering the deployment issues we had for executing properly the evaluation tests for RancherVM (we could not deploy Windows10 hosts). An approximately summary of the performed tests is presented in terms of the total overhead, compatibility, performance, isolation capabilities and scalability per approach (Table 2) derived from the extracted metrics described below. The main benefits are in terms of scalability from using docker containers or firecracker and the color highlights and describes the benefits and drawbacks for each of the selected approaches. For conducting the evaluation tests, a native Linux system was used (Fedora Workstation 32) and a computer system that contained an i7-9750H CPU with 24 GB DDR4 RAM memory and 1 TB NVME-SSD hard disk.

Table 2. Summary matrix for benefits and drawbacks for each of the approaches

Benefits	KVM	Docker	Firecracker	Rancer.VM	Indices	
Less Overhead					0-20%	
Compatibility					20-40%	
Performance					40-60%	
Isolation					60-80%	
Scalability					80-100%	

In all our tests we ensured that all the other applications were closed, and no additional overhead was added except for the main system services. For the evaluation tests of the Linux hosts/services we used Sysbench[13] for the memory tests and Stress-ng[14] for testing the Control Process Unit (CPU) and collecting disk cache input/output (I/O) benchmarks. For the Windows system hosts we used Novabench[15]. The details of the system tests are presented in Fig. 4 considering the following benchmarks:

1. **CPU:** CPU performance tests using the Stress-ng for each different technology. Rating is considered as the number of iterations of the CPU stressor during the run for 20 s.
2. **I/O – Hard disk:** Performance test using Stress-ng related to the disk's cache measuring the input/output operations per second. Rating is considered as the number of iterations of the disk cache stressor during the run for 20 s.
3. **RAM memory:** Effective RAM performance by calculating the writing speed (Mega/Giga Bytes per second).

The evaluation metrics of course depend on the main system resources and our purpose was to compare the difference between the used technologies. The results from the performance evaluation and benchmarks are presented in Fig. 4. Taken the above into

---

[13] https://github.com/akopytov/sysbench/.
[14] https://wiki.ubuntu.com/Kernel/Reference/stress-ng/.
[15] https://novabench.com/.

consideration the results from the performance evaluation present that docker containers maintain low overhead, mainly in terms of I/O – disk cache writing and reading speeds (Fig. 4) in response to RQ2 (Sect. 1). Furthermore, we have also investigated the total overhead in terms of both the used hard disk space and memory size for deploying the vulnerable systems or services.

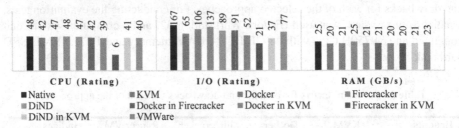

Fig. 4. Performance evaluation for the selected approaches

Results from the performance evaluation for WebGoat (a popular vulnerable web application for using in cybersecurity exercises), running in a Docker container instead of a KVM, are presented in Fig. 5. It is important to mention that the I/O hard disk latency can significantly affect the total performance.

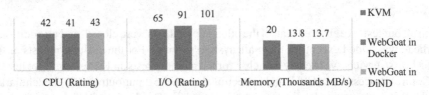

Fig. 5. Performance evaluation for WebGoat

After deploying 10 different docker containers of WebGoat, it was concluded that only 931 MB of the system's memory was used (398 MB for deploying all the containers) instead of 12 GB system memory that WebGoat required running as a virtual machine. The total disk space that WebGoat required was 1.2 GB, while the disk space required for deploying it as a docker was 533 MB for the docker image and 398 MB for each container. The deployed containers required no additional disk space after deploying the first container unless further changes to the container files are applied. Therefore, the total disk space required for deploying the services is significantly reduced. Furthermore, every docker container has a separate IP and therefore each participant is able to conduct an isolated and independent assessment to the potential vulnerable service or system.

In Fig. 6 the results from the performance evaluation for Windows hosts are presented, using KVM and also the deployment of a windows hosts running on KVM in a docker container.

As presented in Fig. 7 each one of the deployed containers are managing KVM and include 3 already deployed virtual machines.

Fig. 6. Performance evaluation of Windows Hosts

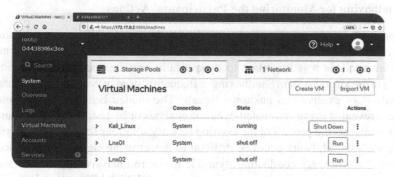

Fig. 7. KVM running in two different docker containers

The drawbacks from the deployments using containerization include various security risks that could allow the participants to take over the host Windows hosts currently cannot be deployed using containers, but only using KVM or similar virtualization technologies. Therefore, the total overhead in terms of disk space, RAM and CPU is difficult to be reduced when it is required to deploy a large number of windows hosts (Fig. 8).

```
root@sphinx-virtual-machine:~
        root@sphinx-virtual-machine:~                    root@sphinx-virtual-machine:~
root@sphinx-virtual-machine:~# docker ps
CONTAINER ID    IMAGE                  PORTS                    NAMES
94ba526eb708    webgoat/webgoat-7.1    0.0.0.0:8088->8080/tcp   sharp_mayer
035584ca5e60    webgoat/webgoat-8.0    0.0.0.0:8085->8080/tcp   eager_buck
da2e8b88afc5    webgoat/webgoat-8.0    0.0.0.0:8084->8080/tcp   stoic_meitner
38b105fe13df    webgoat/webgoat-8.0    0.0.0.0:8083->8080/tcp   elated_wright
05daf73f6465    webgoat/webgoat-8.0    0.0.0.0:8082->8080/tcp   zealous_williams
610a6f562c86    webgoat/webgoat-8.0    0.0.0.0:8081->8080/tcp   lucid_elbakyan
eb3102cbe45e    webgoat/webgoat-8.0    0.0.0.0:8080->8080/tcp   nifty_fermi
```

Fig. 8. The running docker container that include KVM and docker in a docker capabilities

The overhead for the docker container that runs the KVM service is affordable in comparison with the direct KVM deployment. A solution for the compatibility issues of Windows hosts is to use Image2Docker[16] a way to containerize workloads of Windows applications and services. However, such approaches are not presented in this research

---

[16] https://github.com/docker-archive/communitytools-image2docker-win.

paper. In summary and responding to RQ1, RQ2 it seems that both virtualization tech-nologies and containerization technologies hold both benefits and drawback as presented in this section. However, scalability capabilities which docker containers have makes the choice for our deployment more appropriate. However, the usage of KVM is not excluded but we decided to include KVM inside a docker container for creating unique cyberspaces which are running on different containers that include KVM mostly for running Windows hosts.

3.2 Sandboxing for Monitoring the Participants' Actions

A sandbox, in general terms, is a testing environment which allows the validation of code, services, or software components before migrating to the production environment. In malware analysis it is important to dynamically execute auditing and monitoring processes in the virtual system Sandboxing is frequently used in cybersecurity to perform deep analysis of evasive and unknown threats. The hidden behavior of the potential malware is revealed using automated dynamic analysis or by testing the code manually. Figure 9 represents the process of the existing security solutions for conducting dynamic malware analysis. Malware could be difficult to detect using signature-based security solutions. Therefore, for conducting dynamic malware analysis, approaches such as Cuckoo sandbox and virtualization techniques such as KVM, VMWare[17] or Virtualbox[18] are used [21, 22].

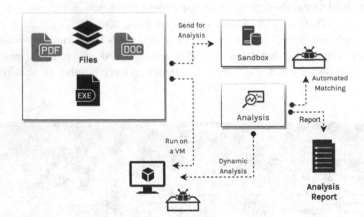

Fig. 9. Existing sandbox approaches

The process includes files that are sent for malware analysis to a sandbox which initi-ates a virtual machine for executing the file. After the execution of the file from the sand-box, screenshots are generated accordingly, and the system shuts down in case of malware infection. While the procedure is dynamic, the results and reports are static, solely focus-ing on the potential infected file. Therefore, such approaches do not include vulnerability

---

[17] https://vmware.com/.
[18] https://virtualbox.org/.

assessments in cases where a vulnerable service is deployed that might not be malicious, however the deployed service could intentionally open specific vulnerabilities in the system (e.g. deploying an outdated apache server).

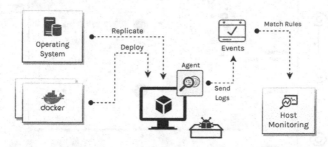

Fig. 10. Dynamic and continuous system auditing using sandboxing

Figure 10 presents the possibility of conducting security auditing in systems not only for malware analysis but for overall monitoring the behavior of sandboxed systems. In our case we used Wazuh[19], a host-based intrusion detection system (HIDS) for combining anomaly and signature-based technologies to detect intrusions, potential threats and behavioral anomalies triggered by the security events generated from the participants of the cybersecurity exercise. Our intention was to further extend the potential of dynamic analysis, using sandboxing to conduct security and auditing tests including procedures such as file integrity monitoring, vulnerability detection, regulatory compliance, among others.

4   Towards a New Model for Cyber Range Deployment

Containers, as discussed above, present a lot of benefits and new technologies such as Firecracker extend the possibilities for deploying systems or services requiring less effort and inducing less overhead. The performance evaluation presented in this paper supports this fact; however, the tests were not conducted in a stressful or overloaded network environment to provide more accurate metrics regarding the system responses. Security aspects and isolation capabilities should be tested as well to better define the security posture of the proposed deployments. RancherVM was not completely tested since some deployment issues were present which would result in having additional overhead and thus it was excluded from the evaluation metrics. However, admittedly, the existing approaches could be revised to include more options and capabilities during hands-on practices. Not only the performance issues and deployment options are mature enough, but the cybersecurity exercises could extend further to more reactive security scenarios that include incident response and blue teaming. Furthermore, it is easier to deploy existing infrastructures and network topologies using both virtualization and containerization.

---

[19] https://wazuh.com/.

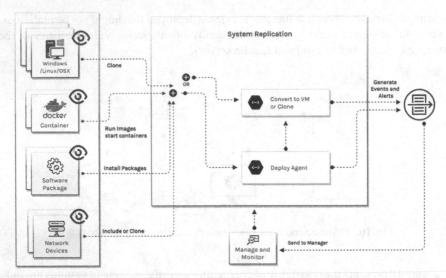

Fig. 11. A Cyber Range deployment for educational purposes

The benefits and drawbacks for each approach were presented in Sect. 3 and educators could use the options that fit better to their preferences. For example, the option to use Dockers inside a Docker could be easy deployed requiring less effort as it requires no further configurations and could be easily deployed in seconds. Not only this but the required hard disk size is reduced, and the facilitator could easier deploy more than one services or operating systems running in a docker container. A significant benefit from using containers instead of a virtual machine is the low overhead induced for the RAM size since virtual machines require a different kernel which requires a significant amount of memory (about 1 GB for a modern Ubuntu distribution). Indeed, there are solutions which might reduce the total overhead even more, but currently the easier approach for mitigating such issues is using containerization.

An approach towards this direction is presented in Fig. 11, presenting the possibility to replicate or sandbox entire systems deployed for educational and learning purposes. The potential systems are imported for security testing, while we enable host-based agents on each of them for monitoring the related security events. Using the above topology, the participants is possible to conduct red/blue assessments and apply for a specific role. Using the proposed technologies, it is easier to deploy or replicate the above environment and therefore the deployment of attack and defense scenarios are easier to implement. Another important factor is that we intend to enable a scoreboard which will retrieve metrics automatically from the security events, transforming the current approaches of static flag submissions.

An important aspect of such approaches is that multiple complex systems and services could interact each other, which is an important attribute for the cyber ranges. Therefore, we present the case where the systems are interacting with each other and participants are invited to conduct security tests or red team assessments on a cyberspace instance that includes multiple components. The network topology is automatically deployed along with the used ports providing easier deployment. The agents are already deployed as presented in Fig. 12, reducing the required effort for the total deployment. Finally, as mentioned in Sect. 3.2 the monitoring process is used for collecting the progress from each participant. As a result, the standard approaches for using CTF challenges as an assessment tool could be extended since we are able to actually monitor the participants' actions and trigger events related to security rulesets, policies or to create custom rules that matches to the offensive actions.

Fig. 12. Monitored virtual systems and docker containers

Being able to monitor the deployed assets the exercises could include more interactive elements, enabling attack and defense scenarios extending exercises focused also on blue teaming and incident response.

The monitored assets could include docker containers, services or virtual systems (Fig. 12, Fig. 13). Therefore, the total required effort decreases providing us the opportunity to deploy more complex security scenarios for conducting cybersecurity exercises. In this research paper we tested the capabilities to host and deploy the proposed approach and we successfully deployed the manager for monitoring, Webgoat and DVWA for having a hands-on lab ready for replication. The Dockerfile retrieves and deploy all the required images for the cybersecurity exercises. The APIs for executing the security scenarios and to enhance automation for deploying labs according to specific learning goals is still under research.

Docker listener

Monitor and collect the activity from Docker containers such as creation, running, starting, stopping or pausing events.

Alerts summary

Container	Action	Date
jrei/systemd-ubuntu	pull	Jun 7, 2020 @ 17:16:57.524
systemd-ubuntu	start	Jun 7, 2020 @ 17:16:59.546
systemd-ubuntu	create	Jun 7, 2020 @ 17:16:59.188
dazzling_engelbart	die	Jun 7, 2020 @ 17:23:14.434
dazzling_engelbart	destroy	Jun 7, 2020 @ 17:23:14.598
confident_villani	start	Jun 7, 2020 @ 17:23:25.100
confident_villani	create	Jun 7, 2020 @ 17:23:24.412

Fig. 13. Capability to monitor specific docker containers

5 Conclusions and Future Work

This paper discusses the potential benefits of using containerization instead of virtualization technologies to deploy cyberspaces for maintaining cybersecurity exercises. In response to our research questions mentioned in Sect. 1, we discovered the various features that containerization and MicroVMs provide, in contrary to virtualization technologies (RQ1). More specifically, docker containers include a lot of benefits and more specifically the reduced overhead and of the required system resources, however specific security issues apply. In response to RQ2, we concluded that by using containerization techniques or MicroVMs, the overall overhead is reduced in comparison with the traditional virtualization technologies. More specifically, a significant reduction in terms of the used memory and amount of disk was observed, among other performance benefits. Towards this direction, we created a docker image that contained multiple docker containers for the facilitators or educators to deploy Cyber Ranges. The results confirm that the total overhead is decreased, and that the total management is easier for creating and deploying cybersecurity hands-on labs.

Future work includes the creation or alignment of the rulesets that will apply for monitoring the participants' progress by collecting security events that triggered from their offensive tasks. Furthermore, specific cybersecurity exercises need to be deployed for further testing the appropriateness of our proposal. Extended research will be carried on deploying specific Common Vulnerabilities and Exposures (CVEs) using docker containers. Finally, the connection to the National Initiative for Cybersecurity Education (NICE) from NIST is in scope of our future research as well as the revision of the existing cybersecurity exercises to align with our approach. Towards this direction we intend to further investigate the existing taxonomies that might help identifying the learning impact during the exercises.

Acknowledgments. This work is performed as part of the SPHINX project that has received funding from the European Union's Horizon 2020 research and innovation program under grant agreement No. 826183 on Digital Society, Trust & Cyber Security E-Health, Well-being, and Ageing. The funding body have not participated in the elaboration of this research paper.

References

1. Childers, N., et al.: Organizing large scale hacking competitions. In: Kreibich, C., Jahnke, M. (eds.) DIMVA 2010. LNCS, vol. 6201, pp. 132–152. Springer, Heidelberg (2010). https://doi.org/10.1007/978-3-642-14215-4_8
2. Irvine, C.E., Michael, F., Khosalim, J.: Labtainers: a framework for parameterized cybersecurity labs using containers(2017)
3. Schreuders, Z.C., Shaw, T., Shan-A-Khuda, M., Ravichandran, G., Keighley, J., Or-dean, M.: Security scenario generator (SecGen): a framework for generating randomly vulnerable rich-scenario VMs for learning computer security and hosting CTF events. In: ASE 2017 (2017)
4. Hay, B., Dodge, R., Nance, K.: Using virtualization to create and deploy computer security lab exercises. In: Jajodia, S., Samarati, P., Cimato, S. (eds.) SEC 2008. ITIFIP, vol. 278, pp. 621–635. Springer, Boston, MA (2008). https://doi.org/10.1007/978-0-387-09699-5_40
5. Tsiakas, K., Abujelala, M., Rajavenkatanarayanan, A., Makedon, F.: User skill assessment using informative interfaces for personalized robot-assisted training. In: Zaphiris, P., Ioannou, A. (eds.) LCT 2018. LNCS, vol. 10925, pp. 88–98. Springer, Cham (2018). https://doi.org/10.1007/978-3-319-91152-6_7
6. Furnell, S., Fischer, P., Finch, A.: Can't get the staff? The growing need for cyber-security skills. Comput. Fraud Secur. **2017**, 5–10 (2017)
7. Burley, D.L.: Special section: Cybersecurity education, Part 2. ACM Inroads. **6**, 58–59 (2015)
8. Baldassarre, M.T., Barletta, V.S., Caivano, D., Raguseo, D., Scalera, M.: Teaching cyber security: the hack-space integrated model. In: CEUR Workshop Proceedings, vol. 2315 (2019)
9. Zimmerman, C.: Cybersecurity Operations Center (2014)
10. Debatty, T., Mees, W.: Building a cyber range for training CyberDefense situation awareness. In: 2019 International Conference on Military Communications and Information Systems, ICMCIS 2019, pp. 1–6 (2019)
11. Beltran, M., Calvo, M., Gonzalez, S.: Experiences using capture the flag competitions to introduce gamification in undergraduate computer security labs. In: Proceedings - 2018 International Conference on Computational Science and Computational Intelligence, CSCI 2018, pp. 574–579 (2018)
12. Thompson, M.F., Irvine, C.E.: Individualizing cybersecurity lab exercises with labtainers. IEEE Secur. Priv. **16**, 91–95 (2018)
13. AlSalamah, A.K., Cámara, J.M.S., Kelly, S.: Applying virtualization and containerization techniques in cybersecurity education. In: Proceedings of the 34th Information Systems Education Conference, ISECON 2018, pp. 1–14 (2018)
14. Perrone, G., Romano, S.P.: The docker security playground: a hands-on approach to the study of network security. In: 2017 Principles, Systems and Applications of IP Tele-communications, IPTComm 2017, September 2017, pp. 1–8 (2017)
15. Yin, Y., Shao, Y., Wang, X., Su, Q.: A flexible cyber security experimentation plat-form architecture based on docker. In: Proceedings - Companion of the 19th IEEE Inter-national Conference on Software Quality, Reliability and Security, QRS-C 2019, pp. 413–420 (2019)
16. Du, W.: SEED: hands-on lab exercises for computer security education. IEEE Secur. Priv. **9**, 70–73 (2011)
17. Baillie, C., Standen, M., Schwartz, J., Docking, M., Bowman, D., Kim, J.: CybORG: an autonomous cyber operations research gym (2020)
18. Costa, G., Russo, E., Armando, A.: Automating the generation of cyber range virtual scenarios with VSDL (2020)
19. Chaskos, E.C.: Cyber-security training: a comparative analysis of cyber- ranges and emerging trends, 78 (2019)

20. Vykopal, J., Vizvary, M., Oslejsek, R., Celeda, P., Tovarnak, D.: Lessons learned from complex hands-on defence exercises in a cyber range. In: Proceedings - Frontiers in Education Conference, FIE, October 2017, pp. 1–8 (2017)

21. Jamalpur, S., Navya, Y.S., Raja, P., Tagore, G., Rao, G.R.K.: Dynamic malware analysis using cuckoo sandbox. In: Proceedings of the International Conference on Inventive Communication and Computational Technologies, ICICCT 2018, pp. 1056–1060 (2018)

22. Keahey, K., Doering, K., Foster, I.: From sandbox to playground: dynamic virtual environments in the grid. In: Proceedings - IEEE/ACM International Workshop on Grid Computing, vol. 3, pp. 34–42 (2004)

CloudVaults: Integrating Trust Extensions into System Integrity Verification for Cloud-Based Environments

Benjamin Larsen[✉], Heini Bergsson Debes, and Thanassis Giannetsos

Cyber Security, Department of Applied Mathematics and Computer Science,
Technical University of Denmark, 2800 Kgs. Lyngby, Denmark
{benlar,heib,atgi}@dtu.dk

Abstract. While the rapid evolution of container-based virtualization technologies, emerging as an integral part of cloud-based environments, brings forth several new opportunities for enabling the provision of distributed, mixed-criticality services, it also raises significant concerns for their security, resilience, and configuration correctness. In this paper, we present CloudVaults for coping with these challenges: a multi-level security verification framework that supports trust aware service graph chains with verifiable evidence on the integrity assurance and correctness of the comprised containers. It is a first step towards a new frontier of security mechanisms to enable the provision of Configuration Integrity Verification (CIV), during both load- and run-time, by providing fine-grained measurements in supporting container trust decisions, thus, allowing for a much more effective verification towards building a global picture of the entire service graph integrity. We additionally provide and benchmark an open-source implementation of the enhanced attestation schemes.

Keywords: Cloud-based environments · Container-based microservices · Configuration integrity verification · Privacy-oriented attestation

1 Introduction

The vision of cloud-based Smart Connectivity Networks (SCNs), comprising multiple edge and fog computing node deployments, is seen today as a key enabler for evolving sectors like automotive, smart factories, smart grids, or healthcare [8,25]. Simultaneously, their number is expected to increase significantly with the advent of new mixed-criticality services. To this end, the cloud community is already embracing recent well-known technologies, like Network Functions Virtualization (NFV) and Mobile Edge Computing (MEC) [21] intelligent orchestration. These frameworks are based on the unrestrainable "softwarization" process, which will transform physical infrastructures into distributed data

I. Boureanu et al. (Eds.): ESORICS 2020 Workshops, LNCS 12580, pp. 197–220, 2020.
https://doi.org/10.1007/978-3-030-66504-3_12

centers with advanced virtualization and software-driven capabilities. They are considered the two key enablers for intelligent edge computing and the cloud to operate in tandem; Virtual Functions ($\mathcal{V}$Fs) allow for flexibly customizing cloud-based networks to the needs and peculiarities of mixed-criticality applications and expose them as Service Graph Chains (SGCs) and network slices.

Furthermore, with the advent of the Internet of Things (IoT), we have just begun reaping the benefits of this evolution that, however, also brings several new challenges (or rather makes old unsolved challenges urgent to be tackled with); with *security*, *resilience* and *configuration correctness* being some of the major concerns at both logical extremes of a network. While virtualization offers some security advantages (such as isolation and sandboxing), it has issues such as insecure production system configuration, vulnerabilities inside the images, and vulnerabilities directly linked to various container-based technologies (e.g., Docker, LXC, rkt) [7]. The primary existing mechanisms to alleviate such issues leverage the concept of trusted computing [4,5,7,18,23], which addresses the need for verifiable evidence about a system and the integrity of its trusted computing base and, to this end, related specifications provide the foundational concepts such as *measured boot* and *remote attestation*. A key component in building such trusted computing systems is a highly secure anchor (either software- or hardware-based) that serves as a Root-of-Trust (RoT) towards providing cryptographic functions, measuring, and reporting the behavior of running software, and storing data securely. Prominent examples include Trusted Execution Environments (TEEs, e.g., TrustZone) [22] and Trusted Platform Modules (TPMs) [13].

Despite recent intensive research efforts towards trust aware containers [7,18], none of the existing mechanisms are sufficient to deal with the security challenges of container-based $\mathcal{V}$Fs. Firstly, there is the perceived aspect of the incompleteness of integrity measurements or guarantees, due to the traditional focus of trusted computing on the system boot time or, at most, the load-time of applications, without covering system integrity beyond these stages, during system execution, which is especially crucial for high-availability cloud-based environments. After a $\mathcal{V}$F is deployed, the integrity of its loaded components is ignored. Indeed, while a containerized $\mathcal{V}$F should work correctly (as constructed by the orchestrator) just after it has been deployed, it could start behaving unexpectedly (e.g., modify data in an unauthorized way) if it receives a malformed input from a corrupted module acting on the $\mathcal{V}$F. The assurance that a $\mathcal{V}$F works correctly after loading is known as *load-time integrity*, while *run-time integrity* refers to the whole process life-cycle. Secondly, it is imperative to ensure the privacy of the $\mathcal{V}$F (and the underlying host) configuration. One overarching theme of building trust for containers is to leverage IBM's Integrity Measurement Architecture (IMA) [23] that measures the integrity of a designated platform. Since IMA measures all components and records them into a single log, each verifier ($\mathcal{V}$rf) with access to this log (when validating the integrity of a $\mathcal{V}$F) will also get all configuration information of the prover ($\mathcal{P}$rv). Adversaries benefit from such artifacts and are capable of stealing the information of other users' containers.

Compounding these issues sets the challenge ahead: *Can we identify sufficient Configuration Integrity Verification (CIV) schemes that can capture the chains-of-trust, needed for the correct execution of a VF during both load- and run-time, and that allow for inter- and intra-VF attestation without disclosing any information that can infer identifiable characteristics about individual VF configurations?* Solutions will, in turn, enable the provision of adequate trust models for assessing the trustworthiness and soundness of the overall SGC.

Contributions: In this paper, we design and implement CloudVaults, a security verification framework for supporting privacy- and trust-aware SGCs, in lightweight cloud-based environments, with verifiable evidence of the integrity and correctness of the VFs. The solution can be either applied separately to each deployed VF, equipped with a virtual TPM (vTPM) security anchor, or the entire SGC, and it enables CIV of the constructed container(s). Key features provided that extend the state-of-the-art include the: (i) possibility to distinguish which container is compromised, (ii) the possibility for low-level fine-grained tracing capability (Attestation by Quote), and (iii) Secure Zero Touch Provisioning (S-ZTP) capability which allows for inter- and intra-VF attestation without disclosing any VF configuration information (Attestation by Proof). Our proposed solution is scalable, (partially) decentralized, and capable of withstanding even a prolonged siege by a pre-determined attacker as the system can dynamically adapt to its security and trust state. We make an open-source reference implementation of all CloudVaults schemes and protocols and benchmark their performance for VFs that are equipped with either a software- or hardware-TPM[1]. The implementation can be used to develop enhanced attestation schemes further using TPM 2.0 and comparative benchmarking. It should also lower entry barriers for other researchers who want to explore TPM-based Configuration Integrity Verification solutions. Overall, our approach is viable for remedying limitations of existing attestation techniques; nonetheless, there is still a need to overcome other open issues towards a holistic end-to-end security approach.

2 Towards Trust-Aware Service Graph Chains (SGCs)

Leveraging cryptographic techniques and Trusted Components ($\mathcal{T}$Cs) towards protecting and proving the authenticity and integrity of computing platforms has been extensively researched. Both *integrity* and *authenticity* are two indispensable enablers of trust. Whereas integrity provides evidence about correctness, authenticity provides evidence of provenance. There are two possible avenues towards achieving configuration integrity: either make the configurations themselves immutable or make the hashes of the configurations immutable. The latter approach follows the Trusted Computing Group's (TCG) open integrity standards [24], which recommends the utilization of hardware TPMs for storing an accumulated hash over its Platform Configuration Registers (PCRs). TPMs also inherently provide indisputable evidence of authenticity in the form of signatures over data using securely stored keys (Sect. 2.1).

---

[1] The CloudVaults C reference implementation is available at [16].

As aforementioned, IMA accumulates measurements in a TPM. It extends the principle of measured boot, where components are measured in the order in which they are loaded into the Operating System (OS) using Linux OS kernel functionality. By default, IMA measures the load-time integrity of user-space applications and files read by the root user during runtime. It is based on the Binary-Based Attestation (BBA) scheme proposed by TCG, where measurements and attestation consider hashes of binaries. However, even the smallest change in a binary dramatically changes its hash, making IMA measurements susceptible to grow unwieldy as the number of measured objects increases. Furthermore, the temporal order in which files are accessed or applications are loaded can be highly unpredictable, making it difficult to verify the accumulated measurements. The inherent disadvantage of BBA paradigms is the disclosure of the platform's software and hardware configuration, which is a legitimate privacy concern since an intermediate adversary $\mathcal{A}dv$ (or a malicious $\mathcal{V}rf$) can use this information to infer identifiable characteristics about the platform.

Further, the variety and mutability of software and their configurations make it difficult to evaluate the platform's configuration integrity [4] during runtime. Several architectures extend upon the IMA-BBA paradigm [7,18] to provide integrity verification. DIVE [7] and Container-IMA [18] both incorporate IMA for virtualized Docker containers to enable orchestrators (remotely) determine the runtime integrity of containers in cloud-based environments. DIVE distills the measurements to only present configuration information related to containers of interest, while Container-IMA proposes *xor-ing* measurements belonging to distinct containers with container secrets to preserve their privacy. Irrespectively, both solutions necessitate the exchange of some identifiable information.

In the same line of research, Property-Based Attestation (PBA) [4,5] schemes map the platform configurations to attestable properties in order to avoid the disclosure of the host configurations altogether. Attesting properties has the advantage that different platforms with different components may have different configurations but still yield the same fulfillment of properties. In particular, PBA gives more flexibility for handling system patches and updates [5], but with the deficiency of detail. [26] presents a PBA-BBA hybrid to the cloud environment where an attestation proxy mediates attestation requests between the prover ($\mathcal{P}rv$) platform and $\mathcal{V}rf$, such that only the proxy can be aware of the correct configurations of a $\mathcal{P}rv$. It then presents to $\mathcal{V}rf$ only the security property of $\mathcal{P}rv$ as the attestation proof, thus, preventing exposure of platform configuration information. The inherent limitation of PBA, however, is that it is only applicable to specific properties (which require accurate identification) and is not directly transferable to reflect changes of mutable configurations.

2.1   Solidifying the $\mathcal{V}$Fs: Inter-trustability of Service Function Slices

A combination of these concepts is of great interest to the secure composability of SGCs, encompassing a broad array of mixed-criticality services and applications. In particular, CloudVaults strives to enable orchestration of heterogeneous $\mathcal{V}$Fs containing mutable configurations by leveraging the profoundness of BBA while retaining the privacy-centered approach of PBA. In what follows, we elaborate on the inherent functionalities of a TPM that are leveraged by CloudVaults.

Monotonic Counters for Trusted Measurements. Internally, each TPM has several PCRs that can be used for recording irreversible measurements through accumulation, e.g., extending PCR slot i with measurement m, the TPM accumulates: $PCR_i = hash(PCR_i\|m)$. This is an indispensable property towards the creation of strong and transitive CoT. For instance, to enforce and regulate trustworthiness of the system boot sequence we can require that all components measure and verify their successors by the following recurrence construct [22]: $I_0 = true; I_{i+1} = I_i \wedge V_i(L_{i+1})$, where $i \leq n \wedge n \in \mathbb{N}^*$, I_i denotes the integrity of layer i and V_i is the corresponding verification function which compares the hash of its successor with a trusted reference value. For example, as in [6], let us assume that we require the boot sequence: $seq\langle sinit, BL(m), OS(m), VS(m), VM(m), APP(m)\rangle$, where $sinit$ is the value that the PCR is reset to. If we know that the sequence will yield PCR extensions with the values $v_1, \ldots, v_n$, and all components extend PCR j, then we will trust the chain *if and only if (iff)* $PCR_j = hash(\ldots(hash(sinit\|hash(v_1))\|hash(v_2))\ldots\|hash(v_n))$.

Attestation & Policy-Based Sealing/Binding. Attestation can be either *local* or *remote*. Local attestation is based on Attestation Keys (AKs), which are asymmetric key pairs $AK = \{AK_{pub}, AK_{priv}\}$. To perform local attestation, we enforce usage restrictions (authorization policies) onto AK_{priv}, such as requiring that PCRs must be in a certain state to permit signing operations, e.g., PCR_j (from the example above) actually reflects the accumulation of $v_1, \ldots, v_n$. Thus, using AK_{priv} to sign a nonce chosen by $\mathcal{V}$rf provides indisputable evidence that the machine state is correct. Remote attestation is delegating the verification of PCR_j to $\mathcal{V}$rf, through TPM quotes comprising a signed data structure of the nonce and the contents of a specified choice of PCRs, which $\mathcal{V}$rf verifies against trusted reference values. Regardless of the attestation method, $\mathcal{P}$rv must also prove authenticity to $\mathcal{V}$rf. The TPM contains several key hierarchies, but authenticity is founded specifically in the *endorsement hierarchy*. The root endorsement seed, from which Endorsement Keys (EKs) are generated, passes irrefutable evidence to the EK in a transitive manner. The credibility of the seed, and hence loaded EKs, is usually based on the trustworthiness of the Original Equipment Provider (OEP), which during manufacturing signs, loads, and later vouches that the seed corresponds to a valid TPM [25].

3   System and ($\mathcal{A}$dv)ersarial Model

System Model. The considered system (Fig. 1) is composed of a virtualized network infrastructure in which the application orchestrator ($\mathcal{O}$rc) spawns and governs a set of heterogeneous $\mathcal{V}$F instances as part of dedicated service graph chains. Each graph is composed of the ordered set of $\mathcal{V}$Fs that the service runs to manage better the correct execution of the onboarded (safety-critical) application workloads and guarantee its offered attributes (e.g., reliability, availability, performance). As aforementioned, state-of-the-art software engineering trends are based on the $\mathcal{V}$F microservice concept for achieving high scalability and adequate agility levels [14]. In our model, we assume the integration of lightweight virtualization techniques, namely *containerization* [2], where applications are decomposed into a mesh of cloud-native containerized $\mathcal{V}$Fs, each one with specific and "small-scope"-stateless processing objectives, packaged on independent virtual execution environments equipped with highly secure anchors (i.e., vTPMs) that serve as our RoTs. Each deployed $\mathcal{V}$F contains workload configurations, such as its software image, platform configuration information, and other binaries (see Definition 1), which are measured and securely accumulated into the PCRs of the loaded vTPM.

Table 1. Notation used

Symbol	Description
$\mathcal{V}$F	A Virtual Function $\mathcal{V}$F
$\mathcal{A}$dv	An adversary resident in a $\mathcal{V}$F
$\mathcal{T}$C	Trusted component
EK	Endorsement Key containing a public and private part (EK_{pub} and EK_{priv}) and a protected symmetric key used for encrypting child keys (EK_{priv}^{sk})
AK	Attestation Key
σ	Cryptographic signature
KH	Key handle to a loaded key in the $\mathcal{T}$C
$\mathcal{I}$	Selection of PCR identifiers
n	Randomly generated nonce
S	Internal session digest in $\mathcal{T}$C
A_{tmp}	Key template
$h_{Conf}{}^{\dagger}$	Expected configuration (PCR hash)
h_{Pol}	Policy digest based on h_{Conf}
h_{Create}	Key creation hash, w. $\mathcal{T}$C state and parent key
$T^{\dagger}$	Creation ticket proving origin of creation hash
A_{cert}	Key creation certificate
Q_{Cert}	Quote Certificate
$h_{\beta}{}^{\dagger}$	Hash of a binary

†We further use a prime to denote a reference, e.g., h'_{Conf} is a calculated reference to the actual hash of the PCR contents.

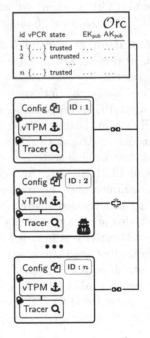

Fig. 1. Orchestration of segregated $\mathcal{V}$Fs

Definition 1 (Configurations). *The configuration set of a* $\mathcal{V}$F *encompasses all objects (blobs of binary data) accessible through unique file identifiers.*

More formally, the $\mathcal{O}$rc maintains a Service Forwarding Graph ($\mathcal{SG}$), of function chains, defined as $\mathcal{SG} = \{s_1, s_2, \ldots, s_n\}$, where $n \in \mathbb{N}^*$. Each service chain comprises a set of deployed $\mathcal{V}$Fs, $s_i = \{vf_1, vf_2, \ldots, vf_m\}$, where $m \in \mathbb{N}^*$ and $s_i \in \mathcal{SG}$, deployed over the substrate virtualized network. The ownership of the physical resources, over which the secure deployment and placement of these SGs take place, is not of interest. Each $vf_i \in \left\{ \bigcup_{j=1}^{n} \mathcal{SG}_j \right\}$ is defined as a tuple of the initial form: $vf_i = (id, vPCR, state, EK_{pub}, AK_{pub})$, where id is the unique $\mathcal{V}$F identifier, $vPCR$ refers to an artificial set of PCRs that reflect the obligatory policy (measurements) that must be enforced in the actual PCRs of the target $\mathcal{V}$F, *state* denotes whether the $\mathcal{V}$F is considered trusted or not (policy-conformant), EK_{pub} and AK_{pub} are the public parts of the EK and AK of the vTPM that is uniquely associated with vf_i.

In addition, each $\mathcal{V}$F is equipped with a Runtime Tracer ($\mathcal{T}$rce) for recording the current state of the loaded software binary data (during both boot-up time and system execution) to be then securely accumulated into the PCRs of the hosted vTPM. Tracing techniques are used to collect statistical information, performance analysis, dynamic kernel or application debug information, and general system audits. In dynamic tracing, this can take place without the need for recompilation or reboot. In the context of CloudVaults, a detailed dynamic tracing of the kernel shared libraries, low-level code, etc., and an in-depth investigation of the $\mathcal{V}$F's configuration is performed to detect any cheating attempts or integrity violations. Such a $\mathcal{T}$rce can be realized either as: (i) a static binary analyzer for extracting hashed binary data measurements (i.e., digests) [1], or (ii) a general, lightweight tracer with kernel-based code monitoring capabilities based on the use of "execution hooks" (e.g., extended Berkeley Filters) [15].

This process builds on top of the IMA feature [23] and records measurements of the $\mathcal{V}$F's software binary images of interest (as specified in the deployed security/attestation policy) that reflect its state/integrity: these can span from *hardware-related properties* related to the BIOS/UEFI and kernel information, to *dynamic properties* such as executable code, structured data and temporary application data (e.g., configuration files, file accesses, kernel module loading). When a measurement is extracted (Sect. 5.2), a register of the TPM accumulates the digest of the captured event data to protect the integrity and constitutes the basis of the subsequent verification of a $\mathcal{V}$F's trusted state: The trust state is the result of the remote attestation functionalities of CloudVaults (Sect. 5.2), in which the measurements of the software loaded on a $\mathcal{V}$F is verified either locally (Attestation by Proof) or by the $\mathcal{O}$rc (Attestation by Quote) against reference values that characterize known (and, thus, trusted) software configurations.

Definition 2 (Tracer, $\mathcal{T}$rce). *Given an object identifier (see Definition 1), the* $\mathcal{T}$rce *utility returns (in a secure way) the corresponding object's binary data.*

*(**Adv**)ersarial Model.* Our in-scope threats include both external attackers who exploit existing vulnerabilities in the $\mathcal{V}$F stack, and insiders such as cloud

users and tenant administrators who cause security breaches either by mistake or with malicious intentions. Like most security verification solutions, we trust the $\mathcal{O}$rc responsible for the provision, management, and deployment of the $\mathcal{V}$F Forwarding Graphs. The focus is on detecting threats that can lead to the violation of the specified integrity properties, and attacks by those adversaries who can remove or tamper with dynamic data (e.g., configuration files, logged events, etc.) as these can also be inferred from our integrity analysis: the only cause, a verifier would be aware of, whereby an application can get compromised at run-time is the reading of a malformed datum previously written by a malicious process. Unlike existing schemes, our solution can also cope with adversaries that try to manipulate such dynamic, unstructured data which, together with regular configuration files and network sockets, represent the majority of processes interfaces and, thus, can allow a verifier to determine the integrity and trusted state of a $\mathcal{V}$F with a high degree of confidence.

We assume an $\mathcal{A}$dv that has unrestricted virtual access to the user space of a $\mathcal{V}$F, including oracle access to its attached vTPM. Similar to other attestation architectures, we do not consider availability threats, such as Denial of Service (DoS). Further, the computational capabilities of $\mathcal{A}$dv are restricted to the Dolev-Yao model [9], where $\mathcal{A}$dv cannot break cryptographic primitives (e.g., forging signatures without possessing the correct credentials), but can, nonetheless, perform protocol-level attacks. Note also, that we do not consider a sophisticated $\mathcal{A}$dv that can perform stateless attacks that target a program's control flow [11,20] where the measurement of a binary can remain unchanged even though the software's behavior has been altered. In particular, a residential $\mathcal{A}$dv has the following Capabilities:

C-1 Unrestricted *passive* and *active* oracle access to the attached vTPM: (passive) $\mathcal{A}$dv can monitor the exchange of commands and responses between the TSS and the vTPM; (active) $\mathcal{A}$dv can unilaterally craft and exchange illicit commands to the vTPM trying to manipulate the CIV process. However, as with any oracle, $\mathcal{A}$dv cannot access the underpinnings and secure structures (e.g., PCRs) of the vTPM.

C-2 Unrestricted ability to Create, Read, Update, and Delete (CRUD) $\mathcal{V}$F software binary configurations (by Definition 1). Note that we do not consider attestation of memory contents (objects without a unique system identifier); thus, we do not audit direct accesses to the disks and the memory.

4   High-Level Security Properties of CIV

In this section, we provide an intuitive description of the security properties our CIV scheme is designed to provide and extract the corresponding axioms (Table 5 in Appendix C) representing the trust properties that must be satisfied by the various components (i.e., $\mathcal{V}$F, vTPM, $\mathcal{O}$rc) involved in the creation and management of SGCs. Such end-to-end definitions for $\mathcal{V}$F soundness and security are then analyzed in Sect. 6, where we prove how CloudVault's design satisfies them in their entirety. Recall that the focus is on trust-aware SGCs with verifiable evidence on the integrity assurance and correctness of the comprised $\mathcal{V}$Fs. Verification of the host Virtual Machine (VM), its kernel, and the entire virtualization infrastructure (NFVI) [17] is beyond the scope of this paper.

Trust is evaluated by (securely) measuring the state (and configuration behavior) of a $\mathcal{V}$F at any given point in time, and then comparing the measured state with the reference (expected) state. Note that the vTPM component of a $\mathcal{V}$F is the trusted element that generates the signatures, certified attestation keys, and quoted PCR values in conjunction with the (potentially untrusted) host. Thus, the **Properties** that must be achieved are:

P-1 $\mathcal{V}$F Configuration Correctness. Both load-time and run-time configurations of a $\mathcal{V}$F (by Definition 1) must adhere to the attestation policies issued by $\mathcal{O}$rc (thus, ensuring *load-time* and *run-time $\mathcal{V}$F integrity*).

P-2 SGC Trustworthiness. It must, at all times, be possible for the $\mathcal{O}$rc to determine the trustworthiness of the entire SGC. An SGC is trusted if all $\mathcal{V}$Fs are attested correctly and have shown verifiable evidence that their configurations comply with the enforced attestation policies. This transfers and extends the sound statements on the configuration security properties of single $\mathcal{V}$Fs (by **P-1**) to statements on the security properties of hierarchical compositions of $\mathcal{V}$Fs and SGCs.

P-3 Attestation Key Protection. To retain trust in a $\mathcal{V}$F, despite mutable configurations, it must be possible to deploy, during run-time, new (certified) AKs that reflect updates to the configuration policies deployed (i.e., an updated set of vPCRs about the $\mathcal{V}$F's expected configuration). The $\mathcal{V}$F, by leveraging the vTPM, must securely create AKs such that AK_{priv} is *never* leaked to an $\mathcal{A}$dv so that she cannot forge valid CIV messages (thus, ensuring *unforgeability*), and must present verifiable evidence that the created AK is "bound" to the newly deployed attestation/configuration policies.

P-4 Immutability. The measurement process must be immutable, such that $\mathcal{T}$rce (by Definition 1) always returns the correct (actual) measurements.

P-5 Liveness & Controlled Invocation. It is assumed that attestation inquiries reach the local $\mathcal{V}$F attestation agent and that the agent responds with an attestation response within a specified time limit. If a $\mathcal{V}$F fails to respond within the specified time limit, this can be considered as evidence of compromise and, thus, the $\mathcal{V}$F is deemed as untrusted.

Besides the aforementioned core security properties, in some settings, $\mathcal{P}$rv might need to authenticate $\mathcal{V}$rf's integrity verification requests in order to mitigate potential DoS attacks; e.g., an $\mathcal{A}$dv impersonating the $\mathcal{O}$rc might send a "bogus" configuration policy to a $\mathcal{V}$F representing an incorrect (reference) state. This functionality can be easily provided (and verified) by CloudVaults: In a case where the $\mathcal{O}$rc acts as the $\mathcal{V}$rf, the respective request (reflecting either a new policy digest or an update measurements request - Sect. 5), can be signed with its (trusted) certificate so that the target $\mathcal{V}$F can verify its authenticity (note that $\mathcal{V}$Fs are employed with $\mathcal{O}$rc's certificate when constructed and deployed over the substrate network). On the other hand, for achieving inter-trusted $\mathcal{V}$F communication, where a $\mathcal{V}$F (acting as the $\mathcal{V}$rf) tries to attest the correctness of another $\mathcal{V}$F, handling a potential forged request will not have any impact on the state measured by the $\mathcal{P}$rv since this cannot result in the update of the configuration policy (can only be initiated by the $\mathcal{O}$rc). Such a malevolent act will impose some additional performance overhead due to the verification process that will be performed. However, this is negligible as will be seen in Sect. 7.

Our work provides the missing fine-grained details of the already standardized IMA [23] and fills the perceived gaps of *dynamic* and *runtime* remote attestation and configuration integrity verification in a complex software stack as the one met in emerging virtualized environments; from the trusted launch and configuration to the runtime attestation of low-level configuration properties about a $\mathcal{V}$F's integrity and correctness. In Sect. 6, we provide game-based models for our enhanced CIV scheme satisfying all the above properties.

5 An Architectural Blueprint Towards Unified CIV

5.1 High-Level Overview

Our schema provides two specific functionalities, *Attestation by Proof* and *Attestation by Quote* (see Fig. 2), for enabling the automatic and secure establishment of trust between deployed $\mathcal{V}$Fs of a service graph. The attached vTPM authenticates the evidence of the integrity state of the service binary images running inside such containers. Key features provided include the: (i) possibility to distinguish which container is compromised, (ii) the possibility for low-level fine-grained tracing capability (Attestation by Quote), and (iii) S-ZTP capability for privacy-preserving attestation (Attestation by Proof). The former is a significant feature because, once a $\mathcal{V}$F is compromised, it can be immediately retracted and replaced by the $\mathcal{O}$rc without affecting the entire SGC, thus, catering to efficient

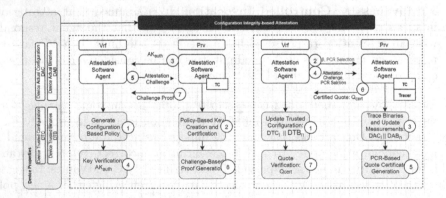

Fig. 2. CloudVaults work flow of $\mathcal{V}$F configuration integrity verification: attestation by Proof (**Left**) and attestation by quote (**Right**).

SGC management and flexible slicing [3] making CloudVaults viable for practical cloud-based applications. The latter enables the integrity verification of a designated $\mathcal{V}$F without conveying other $\mathcal{V}$F's information (or unnecessary information of the underlying host) to a remote $\mathcal{V}$F (acting as the $\mathcal{V}$rf), in case of a malicious $\mathcal{V}$rf being aware of which components the underlying host and other containers have. This is of paramount importance in emerging smart connectivity networks, leveraging cloud-based capabilities to support safety-critical services with strict security, trust, and privacy requirements [10].

The offered CIV allows to assess and preserve the integrity of the deployed $\mathcal{V}$F's Trusted Computing Base (TCB), at load and during system execution, by leveraging the capabilities of vTPMs while ensuring predictability of the internal vTPM PCR values regardless of the order of loading of applications/processes (inside the $\mathcal{V}$F) and reducing performance impact by minimizing the necessary interactions with the host trusted component. It supports complete, configurable attestation that acquires binary signature chains from different unique registers, enabling advanced tracing capabilities to localize areas of compromise. Both schemes rely on the $\mathcal{V}$F to access a $\mathcal{T}C$ (e.g., vTPM) with irreversible PCRs. The privacy-enhanced feature builds on the use of an AK within the $\mathcal{T}C$ that can only execute a cryptographic operation if a set of PCRs is in a particular (trusted) state, inferring the correctness of the component. Integration of our *Enhanced RA* protocols in cloud-based environments, comprising dispersed $\mathcal{V}$Fs, is convenient since the exchange of messages can piggyback conventional TLS protocols. CloudVaults also introduces the concept of *digest lists* to limit the reporting of measured software only to the case of unknown software (not added to the digest list deployed by the $\mathcal{O}$rc). This approach ensures predictable PCR values and reduces the usage of the $\mathcal{T}C$, therefore also the performance impact.

Following a similar workflow to the most prominent IMA-based architectures, Fig. 2 presents the information flow of CloudVaults between a $\mathcal{P}$rv and a $\mathcal{V}$rf: In a nutshell, CloudVaults detects offline and online attacks on mutable files by verifying their hashed digest with a trusted reference measurement extracted from a corresponding virtual PCR on the $\mathcal{O}$rc. Attestation reports produced by CloudVaults can include as much information as required based on the already defined attestation policies (including the configuration properties to be traced).

Attestation policies must be expressive and enforceable and can be dynamically updated by the $\mathcal{O}$rc. After defining proper policies, the $\mathcal{O}$rc can proceed to periodically (or on-demand) attest to the modeled configuration properties representing the current state of the target $\mathcal{V}$F. A $\mathcal{V}$F is trusted if its state (at that time) matches the (already measured) reference state. As each $\mathcal{V}$F is a software component, its hashed digest defines its state. By comparing the hashed digest (at any given time) to the reference (expected) hashed digest of the $\mathcal{V}$F, provided by the $\mathcal{O}$rc, we can determine the $\mathcal{V}$F trustworthiness.

5.2 CloudVaults Building Blocks

The core of our schemes (Fig. 2) is the manageability of mutable configurations throughout the lifespan of a $\mathcal{V}$F and is accomplished by having the $\mathcal{O}$rc mediating any security-critical updates towards the deployed $\mathcal{V}$Fs. Whenever the $\mathcal{O}$rc invokes a periodical or scheduled update, either to determine the trustworthiness of a $\mathcal{V}$F or due to changes in configurations, it proactively determines the update's expected implication by accumulating the artificial vPCR construct of the corresponding $\mathcal{V}$F (**Step 1R**). The $\mathcal{O}$rc then requests the $\mathcal{V}$F to similarly accumulate its PCRs to reflect potential changes (**Steps 2R-3R**). This update request contains only the PCR index i that must be updated and a configuration file identifier, β_{ID}, to measure. Upon receiving such update requests, the $\mathcal{V}$F then invokes the $\mathcal{T}$rce to measure the requested file(s) and subsequently invokes $\mathcal{T}$C to extend PCR i with the new measurement. The simple update protocol is depicted in Fig. 7 (see Appendix A). Recall that an $\mathcal{A}$dv must not be able to tamper with the measurement process, or the trustworthiness of the entire process will be compromised (Sect. 3).

Furthermore, as mentioned in Sect. 2.1, the privacy-preserving attestation (i.e., local attestation) requires the use of specialized signing keys, called attestation keys (AKs), which can be bound to specific PCR contents, hence making an AK operable *iff* the PCRs reflect the particular PCR state in which the AK is bound to. However, to retain the viability and correctness of such an attestation (despite mutable PCRs), we must create and bind a new attestation key whenever a $\mathcal{V}$F is updated. Since the key creation process is best achieved locally, the $\mathcal{O}$rc requests a $\mathcal{V}$F to create a new attestation key based on the trusted measurements that were artificially accumulated before requesting the $\mathcal{V}$F to update its PCRs. First, the $\mathcal{O}$rc computes an Extended Authorization (EA) policy digest based on the trusted measurements (**Step 1L**), denoted h_{Pol}, which reflects the trusted state in which the AK must be bound to. The policy digest is then deployed together with a subset of PCRs, $\mathcal{I}$, to which the policy applies. Upon receiving such a request, the $\mathcal{V}$F is responsible for creating the attestation key on the $\mathcal{T}$C (**Step 2L**). To trust that the policy is enforced and that the state of the $\mathcal{V}$F is conformant to the policy, the $\mathcal{V}$F must present indisputable evidence towards the: (i) creation of AK happened inside the $\mathcal{T}$C, (ii) provided policy digest governs the key, and (iii) proof originates from a distinct $\mathcal{T}$C.

Figure 3 presents the underpinnings of the protocol for AK creation, where a $\mathcal{V}$F initiates the process by constructing a "key template" based on the received policy digest. This template dictates the key's fundamental properties, i.e., whether it is a signing key, decryption key, or both, and whether it is restricted (operates *solely* on TPM-generated objects). The template is passed to $\mathcal{T}$C, which creates an AK as a child key of EK. This process outputs a creation hash h_{Create} and a ticket T, where T is computed with the inclusion of a secret value (Proof) known only by $\mathcal{T}$C, which proves that $\mathcal{T}$C created the AK (**Step 2L**). The ticket is subsequently passed as an argument to the *certifyCreation* functionality of the $\mathcal{T}$C, together with AK, to enable AK's certification using EK, which, due to being restricted, requires such indisputable evidence about the provenance of an object. The certificate and its signature are then sent to the $\mathcal{O}$rc for verification (**Step 3L-4L**). The generated AK is trusted *iff* the signature over the certificate is verified to be authentic, based on the $\mathcal{V}$F's EK_{pub}.

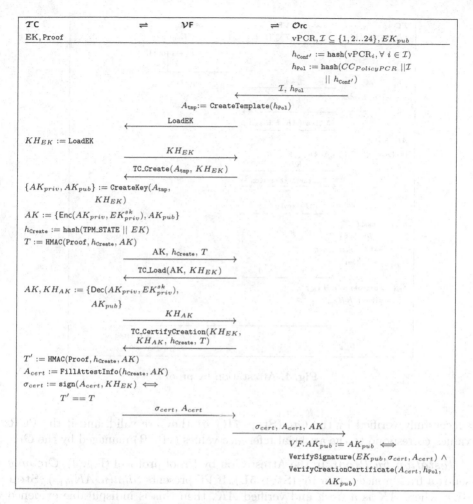

Fig. 3. Create new Attestation Key

The certificate reflects that the AK was created to require the correct attestation policy to be used for signing operations and that the certificate includes a (public) value called the "magic header" whose presence proves that the signed object was created internally on $\mathcal{TC}$.

Attestation by Quote. The protocol for remote attestation using the TPM quote structure is presented in Fig. 8 (Appendix A). In this protocol, the $\mathcal{O}$rc sends a nonce n (to enforce freshness and prevent replay attacks) and a selection of PCRs to attest, $\mathcal{I}$ (**Step 4R**). The $\mathcal{VF}$ subsequently passes these arguments to $\mathcal{TC}$ which constructs a quote structure comprising the current values of the chosen PCRs, and signs it with its EK (**Step 5R**), which as with AK creation, proves that the quote structure is internal to the $\mathcal{TC}$. The quote certificate and signature are then sent to the $\mathcal{O}$rc (**Step 6R**). The quote and its signature are

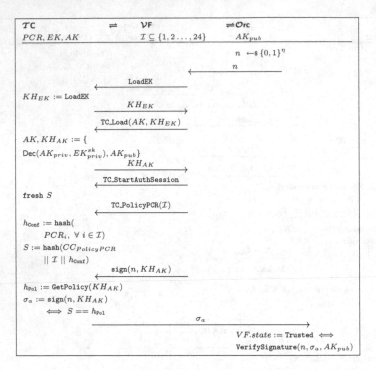

Fig. 4. Attestation by proof

successfully verified by the $\mathcal{O}$rc (**Step 7R**) *iff* they are valid, and if the PCR values correspond to the artificial reference values (vPCR) managed by the $\mathcal{O}$rc.

Attestation by Proof. In the Attestation by Proof protocol (Fig. 4), $\mathcal{O}$rc *only* sends a fresh nonce n to a $\mathcal{V}$F (**Step 5L**). If $\mathcal{V}$F presents $Sign(n, AK_{priv})$ (**Step 6L**), where AK is a fresh and verified AK, then this is indisputable evidence that $\mathcal{V}$F is in a trusted state (**Step 7L**). Note, that both the Attestation by Proof and Quote can *only* attest to the last known measurement. Thus, both attestation schemes are tightly coupled to run in conjunction with the update of measurements protocol for achieving run-time $\mathcal{V}$F integrity.

6   Security Analysis

We define four core security games where an $\mathcal{A}$dv (defined in Sect. 3) tries to manipulate the protocol's building blocks in order to diminish the provided security guarantees on a $\mathcal{V}$F's soundness and integrity. Our models aim to correctly detect alterations made to configurations (see Definition 1) by intermittently attesting their adherence to the reference values (vPCRs) in $\mathcal{O}$rc. We describe the circumstances and constraints required for $\mathcal{A}$dv to win and show why this, in some cases, is impossible under the current set of assumptions (Fig. 6).

Game 1 (Update Measurements).	Game 2 (Create new Attestation Key).
Notation: – β_{ID} is a non-empty set of unique file identifiers (see Definition 1) provided by $\mathcal{O}rc$ – h_β denotes the $\mathcal{O}rc$-conformant hash of β_{ID} – h'_β denotes the actual hash of β_{ID}, i.e., $h_\beta =$ hash($\mathcal{T}rce(\beta_{\mathrm{ID}})$) – i denotes the PCR that must be accumulated with the new measurement(s) – ϕ denotes the $\mathcal{O}rc$-conformant value of PCR$_i$ after remeasuring β_{ID}; $\phi =$ hash(PCR$_i\|h_\beta$) **The Game:** 1. **Goal:** $\mathcal{A}dv$ conceals non-conformant configurations by deceiving the remeasurement process. 2. **Setup:** $\mathcal{A}dv$ in $\mathcal{V}$F with **C-1** and **C-2**. 3. **Challenge:** An update request, $\mathrm{Req}^{\mathcal{O}rc}_{\mathrm{upd}}$, containing the pair $\{\beta_{\mathrm{ID}}, i\}$ is received from $\mathcal{O}rc$ and is accessible by $\mathcal{A}dv$, where β_{ID} identifies a file object blemished by $\mathcal{A}dv$. 4. **Response:** N/A. 5. **Win condition:** $\mathcal{A}dv$ wins the game *iff* PCR$_i$ = ϕ, although $h'_\beta \neq h_\beta$.	**Notation:** – $\mathcal{I}$ identifies a set of PCRs – h_{Pol} denotes the policy for using the key – A_{cert} denotes the creation certificate – σ_{cert} denotes the signature over A_{cert} – AK is public part of the key created – EK_{priv} denotes the secret endorsement key **The Game:** 1. **Goal:** $\mathcal{A}dv$ returns a verifiable key that $\mathcal{A}dv$ can use at own discretion. 2. **Setup:** $\mathcal{A}dv$ in $\mathcal{V}$F with **C-1** and **C-2**. 3. **Challenge:** $\mathcal{O}rc$ provides $\mathcal{A}dv$ with PCR Selection $\mathcal{I}$ and a policy digest h_{Pol}. 4. **Response:** $\mathcal{A}dv$ responds with creation certificate A_{cert}, signature σ_{cert}, and the certified public key AK, constructed by $\mathcal{A}dv$ or $\mathcal{T}$C. 5. **Win condition:** $\mathcal{A}dv$ wins the game *iff* the key created inside the $\mathcal{T}$C contains a different policy digest than provided, while simultaneously providing a valid and verifiable certificate, public key, and signature from the restricted signing key EK_{priv}.

Fig. 5. $\mathcal{A}dv$ present during updates (Game 1) and AK creation (Game 2).

When the $\mathcal{O}rc$ requests a $\mathcal{V}$F to remeasure specific configurations (Game 1 in Fig. 5), an $\mathcal{A}dv$ must deceive the $\mathcal{O}rc$ about non-conformant configurations to hide her presence. Such misleading, requires the $\mathcal{A}dv$ to manipulate the local measuring process to extend the $\mathcal{T}$C PCRs with expected (bogus) *"good"* measurements instead of the actual configurations. Obviously, if $\mathcal{T}rce$ is compromised, or the PCR extension of the (correct) measurement (conducted by $\mathcal{T}rce$) is disrupted and never reaches $\mathcal{T}$C but $\mathcal{A}dv$ instead manages to feed $\mathcal{T}$C with hashes that reflect "bogus" measurements, then $\mathcal{A}dv$ wins Game 1. However, if this were to be possible, then we could never trust the measurements in $\mathcal{T}$C. The enforcement of **P-4** and **P-5** on a $\mathcal{V}$F overcomes such attacks. **P-4** ensures that $\mathcal{A}dv$ cannot tamper with the execution of $\mathcal{T}rce$, and can in practice be achieved using more complicated (and resource-heavy) attestation methods, such as Control Flow Attestation (CFA) [15]. The latter, **P-5**, requires that a $\mathcal{V}$F always enforces the LTL invariant given in Eq. (1). This invariant states that when a $\mathcal{V}$F receives a measurement update request, $\mathrm{Req}^{\mathcal{O}rc}_{\mathrm{upd}}$, then the $\mathcal{V}$F must not process further requests that create new attestation keys, $\mathrm{Req}^{\mathcal{O}rc}_{\mathrm{createAK}}$, since they rely on the correctness of the PCRs. Only when $\mathrm{Req}^{\mathcal{O}rc}_{\mathrm{upd}}$ has been properly processed and the PCRs have been extended with the new measurements as requested by $\mathrm{Req}^{\mathcal{O}rc}_{\mathrm{upd}}$, then a $\mathcal{V}$F may proceed to process $\mathrm{Req}^{\mathcal{O}rc}_{\mathrm{createAK}}$ requests. Together, these properties guarantees prohibit $\mathcal{A}dv$ from ever winning Game 1.

$$\mathbf{G}: \left\{ \left[received\left(\mathrm{Req}^{\mathcal{O}rc}_{\mathrm{upd}}\right) \wedge process\left(\mathrm{Req}^{\mathcal{O}rc}_{\mathrm{upd}}\right) \right] \rightarrow \left[\left(\neg process\left(\mathrm{Req}^{\mathcal{O}rc}_{\mathrm{createAK}}\right)\right) \right.\right.$$

$$\left.\left. \mathbf{U}\;(PCR_i = \mathrm{hash}\left(PCR_i, \mathrm{hash}\left(\mathcal{T}rce(\beta_{\mathrm{ID}})\right)\right)) \right] \right\}, \text{where } i,\, \beta_{\mathrm{ID}} \in \mathrm{Req}^{\mathcal{O}rc}_{\mathrm{upd}} \tag{1}$$

In Game 2, an Adv tries to exploit the AK creation and certification process in such a way that Orc believes that the created key can only be used when the PCR values reflect the correct attestation policy, but Adv can use it at her discretion. This win condition is inherently difficult for Adv to achieve since the Orc requires a fresh and verifiable certificate and a signature over this certificate (Fig. 3). The signature cannot be forged by the Adv since it originates from the TC's secret EK. Furthermore, as described in Sect. 5.2, the certificate object must be generated by the TC in order to be signable by the restricted EK, evident through the inclusion of the magic header in the certificate. The only option for the Adv is to alter the policy digest during key creation, which will inevitably be discovered by the Orc, either through the actual policy digest in the returned key or if the hash of the key is not the certified name in the certificate. Since the policy digest is unique and strongly linked to the PCR contents, the magic header, and the fact that the EK is secret and restricted, Adv cannot win this game (under current assumptions).

Game 3 (Attestation by Quote).
Notation:
- σ_a denotes the signature over the certificate
- Q_{Cert} denotes the quote certificate
- n denotes the challenge (random number)
- EK_{priv} is the secret endorsement key
- $\mathcal{I}$ identifies a set of PCRs.

The Game:
1. **Goal:** Adv presents valid signature and certificate with PCR values that hide Adv presence.
2. **Setup:** Adv in VF with C-1 and C-2.
3. **Challenge:** Orc challenges Adv with n and PCR Selection $\mathcal{I}$.
4. **Response:** Adv responds with certificate Q_{Cert} and signature σ_a, constructed by Adv or TC.
5. **Win condition:** Adv wins *iff* Orc can verify σ_a over Q_{Cert} (containing n) signed by EK_{priv} and the accumulated digest in Q_{Cert} matches Orc's accumulated digest from vPCR.

Game 4 (Attestation by Proof).
Notation:
- σ_a denotes the challenge signature
- n denotes the challenge (random number)
- AK_{priv} is the private attestation key

The Game:
1. **Goal:** Adv provides verifiable signature over challenge, despite of modified binaries.
2. **Setup:** Adv in VF with C-1 and C-2 (see Section 3), and AK has been deployed.
3. **Challenge:** Orc (or secondary VF) challenges Adv with n.
4. **Response:** Adv responds with σ_a, either constructed by Adv or TC.
5. **Win condition:** Adv wins the game *iff* Orc (or secondary VF) can verify σ_a being a signature over n signed by AK_{priv}.

Fig. 6. Adv present during Attestation by Quote (Game 3) and Proof (Game 4).

In Game 3, an Adv tries to falsely convince the Orc that binaries have not been manipulated by exploiting either the quoting process or building a fraudulent certificate. The certificate comprises the current PCR values and the nonce from Orc. Assuming the accumulated PCRs reflect the Adv's presence, she can try to tamper with the certificate creation process to reflect a forged PCR digest. Unfortunately for the Adv, TC will be reluctant to sign the forged certificate since it did not create it.

Note that the PCRs will only reflect malicious alterations to configurations if an update of the measurements is requested and executed *after* the Adv has tampered with the configurations. We denote the time of an update as t_{up}, time of compromise as t_{Adv} and time of attestation as t_{att}. Our assumption (that PCRs reflect Adv's presence) holds (and Adv loses) if $t_{att} > t_{up} > t_{Adv}$. If Adv can precisely time the manipulation of binaries such that $t_{up} < t_{Adv} < t_{att}$, then the PCRs will not reflect her presence, and Adv will win the game (although will be detected in the next measurements update). This attack is called a Time-of-check to Time-of-use (TOCTOU) [19], which is a disadvantage in the proposed protocol and is discussed in more detail in Appendix B. However, as $t_{up}(n) - t_{up}(n+1) \rightsquigarrow 0$ (approaches 0), the disadvantage becomes insignificant since Adv's time window for malevolent behavior becomes very small, but will have an impact on the overall resource consumption of the system.

Game 4 shows how an Adv can try to exploit the signing process in order to provide a valid signature over the challenge n using the issued attestation key while having modified binaries. The overall goal is to convince the verifier that no manipulation of binaries has happened. Recall that usage of the key is bound to certain contents of the PCRs. The PCRs reflect the binary states; hence the Adv cannot execute the cryptographic signing operation while having modified the binaries, assuming the registers indeed reflect such modifications. This, of course, is also affected by the TOCTOU attack mentioned earlier, and in this case, with a more severe impact. After every update, a new attestation key has to be deployed, and local reference values have to be updated, taking essential resources from the primary operations of the system. We provide a more thorough analysis of this issue in Appendix B.

7   Experimental Performance Evaluation

Experimental Setup. Our testbed is deployed on a computer equipped with an Intel(R) Core(TM) i7-8665U CPU @ 1.90–2.11 GHz running the Windows 10 OS. The main goal of this setup is to evaluate the potential overhead of using a TC that will, in turn, allow us to assess the overall protocol scalability towards providing verifiable VF integrity evidence. Therefore, we have opted out of creating a true scale test environment with separate entities but consider a single binary file containing all components. To evaluate the performance of Cloud-Vaults, we constructed the protocols and tested them against IBM's software TPM V1628 using the IBM TSS [12] V1.5.0. Each experiment (protocol) is performed 1,000 times. Note that since we rely on a software TPM as the RoT, of a VF, we chose to create an attestation primary-key as an alternative to the EK for key storage, which adds a small overhead each time the AK is used. Also, we chose to use an ECC key as the EK instead of an RSA-based EK.

Performance Results. Our experiments (Table 2) highlight the efficiency of our protocols. The entire process of creating an AK takes no more than ≈ 17 ms (on average), while including the update of binary measurements still requires less than 20 ms (see Appendix B for more details and a comparison to an HW-based TPM implementation). The enhanced attestation schemes are also efficient (<12 ms); however, without considering any possible network delay that may be present when communicating the attestation data between the Prv and Vrf. With both supporting routines and attestation schemes being extremely lightweight, we can achieve low-cost, rapid attestation capabilities and provide advanced

Table 2. Timings of CloudVault's protocols (time in ms). Note that the hashing is done without any secure hashing schemes and might be slower in practice.

Command	Activity	Mean	95% (low)	95% (high)	Description
CreateAK	Prepare	0.01	<0.01	0.01	Compute expected vPCR
	Create	15.92	15.80	16.05	Create AK in $\mathcal{TC}$
	Verify	1.03	1.01	1.05	Verify certificate and key
	Total	16.96	16.81	17.11	
Update	Prepare	<0.01	<0.01	<0.01	Extend vPCR
	Hash/Extend	1.42	1.35	1.49	Hash file(s) and extend PCR
	Total	1.42	1.35	1.49	
Quote	Prepare	0.02	0.01	0.03	Create a nonce
	Quote	8.67	8.56	8.78	Sign PCRs with EK
	Verify	0.83	0.80	0.85	Verify quote and certificate
	Total	9.51	9.37	9.65	
Proof	Prepare	0.01	<0.01	0.02	Create a nonce
	Sign	10.83	10.76	10.89	Sign nonce
	Verify	0.84	0.79	0.88	Verify signature
	Total	11.67	11.56	11.79	

trust assurance services without consuming many computational resources. Such capabilities ensure trust from the perspective of the $\mathcal{O}$rc and further facilitate bilateral trust assurance (even) between service graphs. As described in Sect. 6, higher levels of trustworthiness result in the need for more resources. That is why it is imperative for the attestation protocols to be lightweight enough without, however, impeding on their accuracy and correctness. To better demonstrate the achieved effectiveness, we use Eq. (2) (Appendix B) to determine how fast we can detect binary manipulation. In the worst-case scenario, where an $\mathcal{A}$dv tampers with a binary just after an update, she will remain undetected for *at most* 293.40 ms, if we utilize as little as 20% of the CPU time.

The ease of operating CloudVault's protocols, including their efficiency, makes the framework highly applicable to be integrated into large-scale networks. While we did not take processing- or network-delay into consideration and only use the AK once, the experiments show that the time of detection is in the order of seconds. In Fig. 10 (Appendix B), we further see that even with 10% utilization, we can still detect a change after $\approx$1 s, making it extremely difficult for an $\mathcal{A}$dv to manipulate CloudVaults.

8 Conclusions

In this paper, we proposed CloudVaults, a multi-level security verification framework for supporting trust aware SGCs with verifiable evidence on the integrity assurance and correctness of the comprised containers: from the trusted launch and configuration to the run-time attestation of low-level configuration properties. Based on our analysis, we described how a $\mathcal{VF}$ achieves privacy-preserving integrity correctness and how to utilize vPCRs for binary data integrity with a virtual-based RoT. Our prototype and the evaluation results demonstrate that our architecture can satisfy the privacy, security, and efficiency requirements. Furthermore, by considering the salient characteristics of remote attestation, we identified several open research challenges. We believe that if these challenges are tackled now while container-based CIV is still at an early stage, this emerging security mechanism can reach its full potential.

Acknowledgment. This work was supported by the European Commission, under the ASTRID, RAINBOW, and FutureTPM projects; Grant Agreements no. 786922, 871403, and 779391.

A   Appendices

A Configuration Integrity Verification Sub-Protocols (Extended)

In this section, we present the remaining protocols, *Update Measurements* (Fig. 7) and *Attestation by Quote* (Fig. 8). To initiate the re-measurement process of a $\mathcal{V}$F, the $\mathcal{O}$rc sends an *Update Measurements* request detailing which file object should be re-measured (using $\mathcal{T}$rce) and into which PCR registers it should be registered. Note that the $\mathcal{O}$rc knows what the correct PCR values should be since it also accumulates the artificial PCR registers (vPCRs), as part of the attestation policy, corresponding to the target $\mathcal{V}$F. To perform a verifiable assessment of the current state of a $\mathcal{V}$F's PCRs, the $\mathcal{O}$rc sends an *Attestation by Quote* request detailing which PCR registers should be included in the quote, denoted $\mathcal{I}$, and a nonce n to enforce freshness and prevent replay attacks. After the $\mathcal{V}$F has securely instructed its $\mathcal{T}$C to construct the necessary quote certificate and signature (over the certificate), it forwards them to the $\mathcal{O}$rc. If the signature over the quote is deemed correct (signed by the $\mathcal{V}$F's EK_{priv}), the certificate can the be verified for determining whether it contains the "magic header" (proving that it was generated inside the $\mathcal{T}$C, as detailed in Sect. 5.2) and whether the PCR values correspond to the trusted PCR values (vPCR) that were artificially accumulated on the $\mathcal{O}$rc when the $\mathcal{V}$F was last updated.

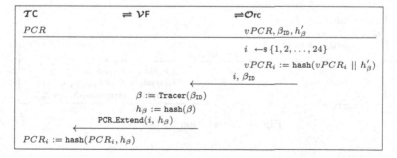

Fig. 7. Update PCR measurements

B   Timings and Benchmarks

Based on our adversarial model (Sect. 3), we do not consider $\mathcal{A}$dv that can perform transient attacks whereby alterations to binaries are only detectable for a short time. Thus, any alterations to binaries by an $\mathcal{A}$dv will be detected when the $\mathcal{V}$F is re-measured and attested, as shown in Fig. 9. The *advantage* of an $\mathcal{A}$dv is defined as the time that she can remain undetected. If, for instance, the *Update of Measurements* and *Attestation by Quote* protocols are executed immediately after the attack, then we will be able to detect any incompliant configurations from the quote structure. However, *Attestation by Proof* will inevitably take longer to complete since the creation of a new AK must occur in-between the *Update of Measurements* and *Attestation by Proof* protocols. Let t_d denote the time of detection (hence, a large t_d is desirable to $\mathcal{A}$dv), u the time to execute the update routine, c the time to execute the creation of a new AK, a the time to execute the attestation routine, and n the number of $\mathcal{V}$rf's that, in consecutive order, conduct *Attestation by Proof* on a specific $\mathcal{V}$F using a shared and verified AK_{pub} of that $\mathcal{V}$F, respectively. We further use the variable t_{CPU} to specify the amount of CPU resources allocated to execute these routines, e.g., for 20% utilization we have $t_{CPU} = 0.20$. Using Eq. (2) we calculate the time until the $\mathcal{A}$dv is detected (t_d) (Fig. 10). As we can see, the detection time (t_d) increases linearly with n (a) but decreases as we allocate more resources, t_{cpu} (b).

$$t_d = \frac{2c + a(1+n) + u}{t_{CPU}} \tag{2}$$

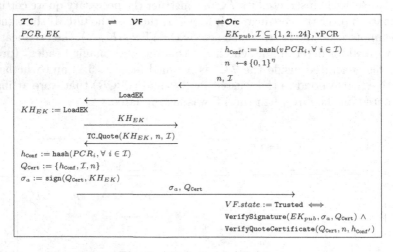

Fig. 8. Attestation by Quote

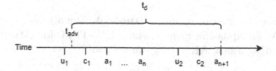

Fig. 9. Visual representation of how long an $\mathcal{A}dv$ can go undetected.

Implementation Note. Writing protocols in terms of TPM calls requires reading and understanding the TPM 2.0 specification and this makes TPM development challenging and causes a high-barrier of entry. While the TPM 2.0 specification was designed to be easily maintainable, it is nevertheless challenging to read mainly due to its sheer size. It consists of over 1400 pages split into four parts which not only cover the core specifications, but also numerous errata covering the continuous development of the TPM specification. Therefore, a particular TPM will be based on the core specification and all of the relevant errata which it implements.

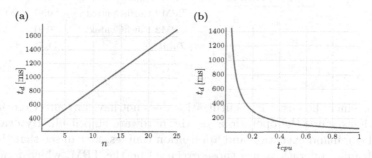

Fig. 10. (a) Changing the number of attestations each key has to do and its impact on the time of detection (20% utilization) and (b) shows how different utilization of resources impact the time of detection with one AK use.

HW-Based TPM Timings. The timings for executing the individual TPM commands of the CIV protocols are presented in Tables 3 and 4, and are performed using IBM's software (SW) TPM V1628 and the Infineon (HW) TPM 2.0 chip. The mean time is calculated from repeating all experiments 1,000 times for the SW-TPM and 100 times for the HW-TPM. The values reflect the time between executing a command in the IBM TSS [12] V1.5.0 and until receiving a response. The SW-TPM timings are much faster than those when using the HW-TPM. Even though a hardware TPM has some degree of hardware accelerated cryptography, it still cannot measure itself with a modern CPU, and is not designed to do so. Applying Eq. (2) on the HW-TPM yields a time of detection as $t_d = (2 \cdot 734.89 \text{ ms} + 417.49 \text{ ms}\,(1+1) + 6.09 \text{ ms})/0.20 = 11.5$ s, which is indeed larger than that for the SW-TPM. However, these values are somewhat

Table 3. Mean time (in ms) of using SW- and HW-TPM for updating measurements and creating a new AK.

Command	SW	HW
Update		
TPM2_PCR_Extend	0.44	6.09
Total	0.44	6.09
Create		
TPM2_CreatePrimary	0.92	238.35
TPM2_Create	0.98	243.75
TPM2_Load	0.44	58.04
TPM2_Load	0.33	59.83
TPM2_CertifyCreation	5.18	123.13
TPM2_FlushContext	1.64	4.10
TPM2_FlushContext	1.60	3.69
TPM2_FlushContext	2.21	4.00
Total	13.3	734.89

Table 4. Mean time (in ms) of using SW- and HW-TPM for Attestation by Quote and Proof.

Command	SW	HW
Quote		
TPM2_CreatePrimary	3.36	244.96
TPM2_Load	1.57	51.69
TPM2_Quote	2.16	112.71
TPM2_FlushContext	0.93	3.71
TPM2_FlushContext	0.89	3.77
Total	8.91	416.84
Proof		
TPM2_CreatePrimary	3.33	241.38
TPM2_Load	1.70	54.17
TPM2_StartAuthSession	1.38	6.72
TPM2_PolicyPCR	0.37	10.71
TPM2_Sign	3.06	95.36
TPM2_FlushContext	0.97	4.12
TPM2_FlushContext	0.91	4.98
Total	11.72	417.44

misleading since the host CPU's utilization does not have any effect on the HW-TPM as it executes the operations on the hardware chip itself. By evaluating the TPM command execution and application timings, we can see that the most time-consuming operations are those executed on the TPM, which is why the impact of the CPU utilization using an HW-TPM is significantly lower. Removing this constraint from Eq. (2) gives us $t_d = 2.310$ s (excluding the host times, such as verification, nonce generation, etc.). Additionally, the "create primary key" function is extremely time-consuming, which is why it might be useful to load this AK from NV storage.

C   CloudVaults Formal Trust Models

Table 5 presents the axioms (with descriptions) that must be satisfied by the various components (i.e., $\mathcal{VF}$, vTPM, $\mathcal{O}$rc) involved in the creation and management of SGCs to ensure the CIV security properties (Sect. 4).

Table 5. Formalized enablers (axioms) to achieve the CIV security properties.

$\boxed{\text{Ax}_1}$ $\left[\forall vf \in \left\{\sigma \mid \sigma \in \bigcup\limits_{j=1}^{n} S\mathcal{G}_j\right\}\right]$ $\left[\exists! \, vtpm\right] : Trusted_{VTPM}(vtpm) \wedge Bound(vtpm, vf) \wedge$

$HasInv(vtpm, vf.EK_{pub}) \wedge Signed(vtpm.pcr[idx], vtpm.EK_{priv}) \wedge Equals(vtpm.pcr[idx],$
$vf.vpcr[idx]) \equiv Conformant_{config}(vf.vpcr), \forall idx \in indices(vf.vpcr)$

(Ax$_1$ for P-1): Any $\mathcal{V}$F, with a unique and proper vTPM, has conformant configurations *iff* it proves through signing its PCRs with EK_{priv} that its PCRs are conformant to the policy (vPCR) issued by $\mathcal{O}$rc, where $EK_{priv} = \mathcal{V}F.EK_{pub}^{-1}$ and EK_{pub} is trusted by $\mathcal{O}$rc.

$\boxed{\text{Ax}_2}$ $\left[\nexists vf \in \left\{\sigma \mid \sigma \in \bigcup\limits_{j=1}^{n} S\mathcal{G}_j\right\}\right] : \neg Conformant_{config}(vf.vpcr) \equiv Trusted_{SGC}(S\mathcal{G})$

(Ax$_2$ for P-2): The entire SGC ($S\mathcal{G}$) is considered trusted *iff* all of its $\mathcal{V}$Fs are attested correctly, such that all configurations are conformant to their respective attestation policies.

$\boxed{\text{Ax}_3}$ $\left[\forall vf, vtpm, pol\right] : Trusted_{VTPM}(vtpm) \wedge Bound(vtpm, vf) \wedge Created_{AK}(vtpm.ak, pol) \wedge$

$Signed(vtpm.ak, vtpm.EK_{priv}) \wedge Has_{policy}(vtpm.ak, pol) \equiv Trusted_{AK}(vtpm.ak)$

(Ax$_3$ for P-3): An attestation key *ak* is trusted *iff* it is created on a trusted vTPM and contains the appropriate policy *pol*, which reflects the appropriate attestation policy (vPCR).

References

1. Abera, T., et al.: C-FLAT: control-flow attestation for embedded systems software. In: Proceedings of the 2016 ACM SIGSAC CCS Conference, pp. 743–754 (2016)
2. Bailey, K.A., Smith, S.W.: Trusted virtual containers on demand. In: 5th ACM Workshop on Scalable Trusted Computing, STC 2010, pp. 63–72 (2010)
3. Beck, M.T., Botero, J.F.: Scalable and coordinated allocation of service function chains. Comput. Commun. **102**, 78–88 (2017)
4. Chen, L., et al.: A protocol for property-based attestation. In: 1st ACM workshop on Scalable Trusted Computing (2006)
5. Chen, L., Löhr, H., Manulis, M., Sadeghi, A.-R.: Property-Based Attestation without a Trusted Third Party. In: Wu, T.-C., Lei, C.-L., Rijmen, V., Lee, D.-T. (eds.) ISC 2008. LNCS, vol. 5222, pp. 31–46. Springer, Heidelberg (2008). https://doi.org/10.1007/978-3-540-85886-7_3
6. Datta, A., et al.: A logic of secure systems and its application to trusted computing. In: 30th IEEE Symposium on S&P, pp. 221–236. IEEE (2009)
7. De Benedictis, M., Lioy, A.: Integrity verification of Docker containers for a lightweight cloud environment. Future Gener. Comput. Syst. **97**, 236–246 (2019)
8. Dimitriou, T., Giannetsos, T., Chen, L.: REWARDS: privacy-preserving rewarding and incentive schemes for the smart electricity grid and other loyalty systems. Comput. Commun. **137**, 1–14 (2019)

9. Dolev, D., Yao, A.: On the security of public key protocols. IEEE Trans. Inf. Theory **29**(2), 198–208 (1983)

10. Giannetsos, T., Krontiris, I.: Securing V2X communications for the future: can PKI systems offer the answer? In: 14th International ARES Conference (2019)

11. Giannetsos, T., et al.: Arbitrary code injection through self-propagating worms in Von Neumann architecture devices. Comput. J. **53**(10), 1576–1593 (2010)

12. Goldman, K.: IBM's Software TPM 2.0 and TSS. https://sourceforge.net/projects/ibmswtpm2/. https://sourceforge.net/projects/ibmtpm20tss

13. Ibrahim, F.A., Hemayed, E.E.: Trusted cloud computing architectures for infrastructure as a service: Survey and systematic literature review. Comput. Secur. **82**, 196–226 (2019)

14. Jamshidi, P., Pahl, C., Mendonça, N.C., Lewis, J., Tilkov, S.: Microservices: the journey so far and challenges ahead. IEEE Softw. **35**(3), 24–35 (2018)

15. Koutroumpouchos, N., et al.: Secure edge computing with lightweight control-flow property-based attestation. In: 2019 IEEE Conference on Network Softwarization (2019)

16. Larsen, B., Debes, H.B., Giannetsos, T.: Cloudvaults C implementation (2020). https://github.com/astrid-project/Configuration-Integrity-Verification

17. Lauer, H., et al.: Bootstrapping trust in a "trusted" virtualized platform. In: 1st ACM Workshop on Workshop on Cyber-Security Arms Race (2019)

18. Luo, W., Shen, Q., Xia, Y., Wu, Z.: Container-IMA: a privacy-preserving integrity measurement architecture for containers. In: 22nd International Symposium on Research in Attacks, Intrusions and Defenses (*RAID* 2019), pp. 487–500 (2019)

19. Nunes, I.D.O., Jakkamsetti, S., Rattanavipanon, N., Tsudik, G.: On the TOCTOU problem in remote attestation. arXiv preprint arXiv:2005.03873 (2020)

20. Roemer, R., et al.: Return-oriented programming: systems, languages, and applications. ACM Trans. Inf. Syst. Secur. **15**(1), 2:1–2:34 (2012)

21. Sabella, D., et al.: Mobile-edge computing architecture: the role of MEC in the Internet of Things. IEEE Electron. Mag. **5**, 84–91 (2016)

22. Sabt, M., Achemlal, M., Bouabdallah, A.: Trusted execution environment: what it is, and what it is not. In: 2015 IEEE Trustcom, pp. 57–64. IEEE (2015)

23. Sailer, R., et al.: Design and implementation of a TCG-based integrity measurement architecture. In: USENIX Security Symposium, pp. 223–238 (2004)

24. TCG: TCG Guidance for Securing Network Equipment Using TCG Technology Version 1.0 Revision 29, January 2018. https://trustedcomputinggroup.org/wp-content/uploads/TCG_Guidance_for_Securing_NetEq_1_0r29.pdf

25. Whitefield, J., et al.: Privacy-enhanced capabilities for VANETs using direct anonymous attestation. In: IEEE Vehicular Networking Conference (2017)

26. Xin, S., Zhao, Y., Li, Y.: Property-based remote attestation oriented to cloud computing. In: IEEE Conference on Computational International and Security (2011)

MPS 2020

Twizzle - A Multi-purpose Benchmarking Framework for Semantic Comparisons of Multimedia Object Pairs

Stephan Escher[✉], Patrick Teufert, Robin Herrmann, and Thorsten Strufe

TU Dresden, Dresden, Germany
{stephan.escher,patrick.teufert,robin.herrmann,
thorsten.strufe}@tu-dresden.de

Abstract. This paper describes Twizzle Benchmarking, a framework originally developed for evaluating and comparing the performance of perceptual image hashing algorithms. There are numerous perceptual hashing approaches with different characteristics in terms of robustness and sensitivity, which also use different techniques for feature extraction and distance measurements, making comparison difficult. For this reason, we have developed Twizzle Benchmarking, which enables comparison and evaluation regardless of the algorithm, distance calculation, data set or type of data. Furthermore, Twizzle is not limited to perceptual hashing approaches, but can be used for a variety of purposes and classification problems, such as multimedia forensics, face recognition or biometric authentication.

Keywords: Benchmarking · Perceptual hashing · Multimedia forensics · Face recognition

1 Introduction

The progressive digitalization of all areas of life and the associated accumulation of large amounts of data require tools that make such amounts of data efficiently and quickly searchable, comparable and analyzable. In the multimedia area, such tools extract certain features from a multimedia object that can be used to describe the object or its content. This feature extraction is used to reduce the sheer size of multimedia objects, to prevent redundancy and noise, as well as to be stable against changes such an object undergoes during its lifetime. Working with extracted features instead of the multimedia object itself allows a faster and more efficient processing of large amounts of data. However, by reducing the information to features, the decision whether a multimedia object resembles another or if it is the content to be identified is no longer unambiguous but depends on probabilities or thresholds. Thus, the quality of these tools is measured on the one hand by the robustness of the extracted features to changes of the multimedia object and on the other hand by their sensitivity to different multimedia objects.

© Springer Nature Switzerland AG 2020
I. Boureanu et al. (Eds.): ESORICS 2020 Workshops, LNCS 12580, pp. 223–230, 2020.
https://doi.org/10.1007/978-3-030-66504-3_13

An example to illustrate could be perceptual image hashing (PIH), an umbrella term for hash functions which produces a short and fix-sized finger-print out of an image file, based on the perceptible content, e.g. the structure of the scene. The goal of these PIH algorithms is to find image duplicates while being robust to perceptual preserving transformations (PPT), like rotation, com-pression or brightness adjustments, as well as sensitive to similar images.

The workflow of a PIH algorithm usually starts with preprocessing, like scal-ing [14], ring partition [11] or segmentation [8]. Subsequently, perceptual fea-tures are extracted from the preprocessed image. Examples are methods based on Wavelet coefficients [12], Fourier-Mellin coefficients [9] or Local Binary Pat-terns [2]. Finally the extracted features are often quantized and represented as a vector of fixed length. In order to examine two images for perceptible similarity, their generated hashes are subjected to a distance comparison. Fields of appli-cation range from reverse image search, image authentication [10] and digital forensics [8] up to phishing website detection [4].

So far, there are many different PIH approaches. Each of these algorithms allows different PPTs, but often solve only one aspect such as an affine transfor-mation with high performance. The evaluation of these algorithms vary widely, usually considers only a partial area of robustness and are only compared with algorithms of similar design. In addition, combinations of transformations and the sensitivity characteristics are rarely taken into account. Existing Benchmark-ing solutions which try to solve these issues are PHabs [16] and Rihamark [15]. However, for Phabs today neither code nor an exact description of the struc-ture can be found and is therefore outdated. The developers of Rihamark have already critically noted this and hence presented their own framework. Rihamark provides a plugin system and comes with predefined PPTs and PIH algorithms as well as support for sensitivity evaluation. Nevertheless Rihamark is limited to PIH algorithms that generate a binary hash and compare them with ham-ming distances, which means that algorithms with a different structure cannot be compared. Furthermore its dependent on the data set (only images), difficult to extend, difficult to apply to large data sets and to deploy on servers with higher resources.

For those reasons we propose our modern and modular benchmarking frame-work Twizzle, with which existing and new PIH algorithms can be easily evalu-ated and compared, by remedying the weaknesses of existing benchmarks. Due to the modular design and the independence of feature extraction, decision mak-ing and the data set, twizzle is not limited to PIH approaches, but can be used for a variety of similar applications.

2   Twizzle Benchmarking

Facing that every PIH algorithm has its own way of hash representation and distance calculation we realized that we have to abstract the task to the following Question: Are two objects (in this case images) the same or not? Therefore we have designed a benchmarking pipeline in which the algorithms to be compared have to solve this task independently of their feature extraction and decision making. The resulting framework is written in python 3 and freely available[1] under GPLv3. The whole workflow of the benchmarking pipeline could be seen in Fig. 1.

Overall, Twizzle consists of a "Challenge creator", the algorithm tests and the "Analyser", where the algorithm tests can be further separated into "Wrapping" the algorithms to be evaluated and the "Test runner". Each of these parts can be independently reused in several different pipelines for different algorithms and different problem cases.

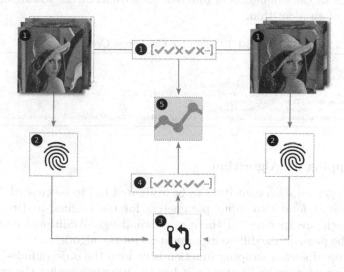

Fig. 1. General workflow of Twizzle. (1) Input: challenge - objects to compare and ground truth (2) feature extraction (3) decision making (4) Output: list of decisions (5) Analysis: decisions vs. ground truth

2.1   Challenge Creation

The first step of the benchmarking pipeline represents the creation of a specific challenge an algorithm has to solve (see Fig. 1 step 1). Twizzle originally was designed for challenges which have the form of a pairwise comparison of multimedia objects. I.e. the algorithm has to decide whether the objects or the content within the objects are the same or not. Thus a data set with comparison pairs, each consisting of an original object paired with a comparative object, has to be created. For each pair the expected decision (ground truth) needs to be specified. I.e. if a pair consists of the same objects the decision should be "True" ("These are the same objects.") otherwise "False".

For PIH-Challenges, object pairs could for example consist of similar but not same images for a sensitivity challenge, of same but modified images for a robustness challenge or of both as a practical use case challenge (see Listing 1.1).

---

[1] github.com/dfd-tud/twizzle.

From a practical point of view, the first step is to initiate a new instance of Twizzle where a name for the database, in which challenges and results will be saved, needs to be specified. Furthermore, a list of paths to original objects, a list of corresponding comparative objects and a Boolean list of ground truth decisions for each original-comparative pair has to be created. Dimensions of the lists of original objects, corresponding objects and ground truth decisions need to be the same. Optionally, additional metadata can be passed as python dictionary, for example to describe the specific challenge. Finally the created challenge is added to the database. Thus the challenge is prepared for any number of tests, such as the evaluation of different algorithms or the testing of different parameters of an algorithm.

Listing 1.1. Example Challenge Creation

```
DBPath = "test.db"
tw = Twizzle(DBPath)
sChallengeName = "pih_challenge"
aOriginals = ["img1.png", "img1.jpg", "img2.png"]
aComparatives = ["img1_r10.png", "img1_r20.png", "img1.png"]
aTargetDecisions = [True, True, False]
dicMetadata = { "transform": "rotation" }
tw.add_challenge(sChallengeName, aOriginals, aComparatives, aTargetDecisions, dicMetadata)
```

2.2 Wrapping an Algorithm

Next a wrapper for each algorithm to be evaluated has to be created. Wrappers need to have at least two input parameters for the original and comparative objects, which are specified in the created challenge. Additional named arguments can be passed, like different parameters for the algorithm to be evaluated. The first step of such a wrapper function is to load the objects linked to in the two lists. Then, for each object pair, it has to evaluate whether the two objects are the same or not, which is done via the user-defined algorithm.

An exemplary structure of a wrapper for a user-defined PIH-algorithm could consist of iterating over each image pair, extracting the features and generating the perceptual hash for each image (see Fig. 1 step 2). With the user-defined decision making algorithm, e.g. based on a normalized hamming distance of the two hashes and a threshold, it is decided if both hashes represent the same image or not (see Fig. 1 step 3). Finally, the wrapper must return the list of algorithm decisions for all object pairs (see Fig. 1 step 4) and if desired additional arbitrary metadata.

Listing 1.2. Example Wrapper

```
def wrapper(aOriginalImages, aComparativeImages, param1, ...)
    for i, sOriginalImage in enumerate(aOriginalImages):
        sComparativeImage = aComparativeImages[i]
        hashOriginal = algorithm(sOriginalImage, param1)
        hashComparative = algorithm(sComparativeImage, param1)
        deviation = distance(hashOriginal, hashComparative)
        if(deviation <= threshold): bDecision = true
        aDecisions.append(bDecision)
    return(aDecisions, dictMetadata)
```

2.3 Test Runs

Tests for Twizzle are black box tests. This means, that the internal workings of an algorithm are not known to Twizzle. All Twizzle expects from the user-defined algorithm is that it can handle a set of original objects and corresponding comparative objects and return some kind of decision values, which is done through the wrapper.

"Test runs" specifies which algorithm has to solve which challenge and provide any additional parameters for "Test wrappers". All decisions made during a test execution are returned to the Twizzle framework, where it compares the algorithm decisions with the ground truth decisions specified during "Challenge creation" and calculates the TPR, TNR, FPR, FNR, accuracy, precision and F1 score (see Fig. 1 step 5). Additional also user-defined metadata can be returned by each test, for example the used algorithm parameters. Based on this outputs an algorithm can be easily compared to others. Tests defined in Twizzle are executed in parallel with a user-defined number of threads and can therefore also be set up on a cluster.

Listing 1.3. Example Test Run

```
oRunner.run_test_async("pih_challenge", wrapper, {"param1":param1})
```

2.4 Analyse Results

Twizzle also provides an Analysis component, which will collect and merge all tests and the corresponding challenges and returns a pandas dataframe [6]. This dataframe contains the test results, evaluation metrics per test and all metadata added during "Challenge creation" and running the actual test. Comparing tested algorithms can be easily done due to Twizzle abstracting the binary classification task and generating typical classification evaluation metrics. The evaluation metrics provided by Twizzle include custom metrics, challenge name as well as the metrics mentioned above.

2.5 Twizzle Features

Overall Twizzle accepts any user-defined feature extraction and decision making algorithms, independent of their type and functionality and enables the comparison of them. Further, Twizzle enables the creation of user-defined Challenges, consisting of user-defined data sets independent of their data type, with which the algorithms can be evaluated. Although Twizzle was developed for image comparisons, it can therefore be used for any pairwise comparison task, e.g. of text documents. Thereby Tests and Challenges are independent of each other, i.e. each created Challenge can be used for other Tests, as well as each created algorithm wrapper can be tested for any challenge. Twizzle represents the test data and evaluation metrics for analysis of each test and simplifies the comparison of the results. Further tests and analysis can be extended with user-defined meta data. Finally test runs could be executed easily in parallel.

3   Use Cases

Twizzle's scope is not limited to perceptual hashing approaches, but can be used for a variety of purposes. This section contains some examples that describe the applicability of Twizzle to different use cases. Other use cases which are not mentioned here could be for example object detection or biometric authentication.

3.1   Multimedia Forensics

From a forensic point of view it is important to be able to determine the source device (e.g. a printer) of an unknown multimedia file (e.g. print-out) or at least to compare multimedia data with respect to their source device, e.g. for the analysis of blackmail letters. Forensic methods try to solve this problem by extracting so-called intrinsic signatures out of the multimedia data. These are artifacts caused by the source device during the creation of the multimedia file. Depending on the stability and distinguishability of the intrinsic signature, it can then be used as a fingerprint for the corresponding source device, device model or type.

In printer forensics for example intrinsic signatures like geometrical distortions of text [13] and image [1] elements, the texture and structure of printed characters [3] or the halftoning structure [5] could be used to identify the source printer model. All of these fingerprints have different properties regarding robustness (influences such as type of paper) and sensitivity (discriminating a bunch of printers). Furthermore their exist a lot of various algorithms which try to extract these signatures in different ways and even decide with different decision making algorithms (e.g. classification, euclidian distance or correlation with a reference pattern). Just like the perceptual hashing approaches, all of this methods use their own curtailed evaluations concerning sensitivity, robustness and data sets. However such different signatures, extraction algorithms, their settings as well as the combination of such methods could easily be evaluated and compared with Twizzle.

For the challenge of comparing two print-outs based on their signature similarity, the benchmarking pipeline looks exactly like for a PIH approach. Therefore the data set could consists of scanned print-outs from same and different printer devices with different robustness parameters (like different fonts, print settings or paper types), like (Table 1):

Table 1. Example challenge for a printer forensic algorithm

Original	["printer1_font2.png", "printer2.jpg"]
Comparative	["printer1_font1.jpg", "printer1.png"]
Ground truth	[True, False]

After extracting the fingerprint of original and comparative print-out, the decision algorithm used decides whether they are from the same source device or not. After the test runs, decisions and ground truth are compared whereby tested algorithms can be compared and evaluated, independent of used signatures, extraction algorithm or decision making. For a source printer classification challenge, Twizzle could also be used while be prepared as described in the next use case.

3.2 Face Recognition

Another use case could be face recognition. Face recognition is the task of identifying the person depicted in an image. Various biometric features (facial features) are extracted from the images, which often vary for different algorithms. These face features should ideally be robust to changes in image characteristics (brightness, contrast, resolution, aspect ratio etc.) and physical changes (beard, glasses, pose, hairstyle, scars, etc.) [7,17]. At the same time they should be sensitive, i.e. characteristics of different persons should be distinguishable in any case. We want to give an overview of how Twizzle can be used for the classification problem "Two pictures are given, is the same person shown?".

Challenge Creation. For a data set with face images and corresponding personal labels, the creation of challenges can be done as follows. A "Challenge creation" for a classification problem, e.g. using machine learning, would be done by splitting the data set into train and test data and then training the machine learning model on the train data. The test data can then be used to generate original-comparison object pairs, and the specification of the ground truth using already labeled images can be done simply by comparing the generated image pairs and the corresponding labels. If for a pair of images both images have the same label, the algorithm to be tested should return true, otherwise false. The generated pairs and the corresponding ground truths are stored for this challenge.

Test Wrapper. The test wrapping for our scenario can be done by generating labels for each image pair and comparing these labels. For each image in a pair, the label is predicted using the trained model. The decision is made by comparing the predicted image labels and adding the decision to the total decisions made, which the test returns at the end.

Test Run. The test runner itself simply specifies which "Test Wrapper" is used and in a machine learning scenario provides the test with the trained model as additional parameter, since in this case the model is needed by the algorithm to be tested.

Analysis. The analysis is individually necessary and is determined by the self-defined requirements for a "good" algorithm. When developing a face verification system for security, a "good" algorithm may need to have a very low false positive rate, while a higher false negative rate is acceptable. On the other hand, an image retrieval task could be the opposite case, where a "good" algorithm finds all images for a person and delivers false positive results rather than missing an image.

4   Conclusion

We have developed Twizzle, a multi-purpose benchmarking framework for various comparison tasks, originally designed to compare algorithms that determine whether multimedia objects are the same or not. Twizzle provides an easily extensible architecture to run and analyze many tests in parallel and for different problem scenarios. Twizzle users are provided with many important evaluation metrics for each test, making it easy to compare different algorithms for the same task and optimize algorithms for specific score metrics. Due to the high reusability of the Twizzle components, the algorithms can be quickly evaluated on multiple data sets by changing only the underlying challenge without having to develop a completely new pipelining and testing process.

References

1. Bulan, O., Mao, J., Sharma, G.: Geometric distortion signatures for printer identification (2009)
2. Davarzani, R., Mozaffari, S., Yaghmaie, K.: Perceptual image hashing using center-symmetric local binary patterns. Multimed. Tools Appl. **75**(8), 4639–4667 (2015). https://doi.org/10.1007/s11042-015-2496-6
3. Ferreira, A., Navarro, L.C., Pinheiro, G., Santos, J.A.D., Rocha, A.: Laser printer attribution: exploring new features and beyond. Forensic Sci. Int. **247**, 105–125 (2015)
4. Joshua S.W., Jeanna N.M., John L.S.: A method for the automated detection phishing websites through both site characteristics and image analysis (2012)
5. Kim, D.G., Lee, H.K.: Colour laser printer identification using halftone texture fingerprint. Electron. Lett. **51**(13), 981–983 (2015)
6. McKinney, W.: Data structures for statistical computing in python (2010)
7. Sharif, M., Naz, F., Yasmin, M., Shahid, M.A., Rehman, A.: Face recognition: a survey. J. Eng. Sci. Technol. Rev. **10**(2), 166–177 (2017)
8. Steinebach, M., Liu, H., Yannikos, Y.: Efficient cropping-resistant robust image hashing (2014)
9. Swaminathan, A., Mao, Y., Wu, M.: Robust and secure image hashing. IEEE Trans. Inf. Forensics Secur. **1**(2), 215–230 (2006)
10. Tabatabaei, S.A.H., Ur-Rehman, O., Zivic, N., Ruland, C.: Secure and robust two-phase image authentication. IEEE Trans. Multimedia **17**(7), 945–956 (2015)
11. Tang, Z., Zhang, X., Li, X., Zhang, S.: Robust image hashing with ring partition and invariant vector distance. IEEE Trans. Inf. Forensics Secur. **11**(1), 200–214 (2016)
12. Venkatesan, R., Koon, S.M., Jakubowski, M.H., Moulin, P.: Robust image hashing (2000)
13. Wu, Y., Kong, X., You, X., Guo, Y.: Printer forensics based on page document's geometric distortion (2009)
14. Yang, B., Gu, F., Niu, X.: Block mean value based image perceptual hashing (2006)
15. Zauner, C., Steinebach, M., Hermann, E.: Rihamark: perceptual image hash benchmarking (2011)
16. Zhang, H., Schmucker, M., Niu, X.: The design and application of PHABS: a novel benchmark platform for perceptual hashing algorithms (2007)
17. Zhao, W., Chellappa, R., Phillips, P.J., Rosenfeld, A.: Face recognition: a literature survey. ACM Comput. Surv. (CSUR) **35**(4), 399–458 (2003)

You've Got Nothing on Me!
Privacy Friendly Face Recognition
Reloaded

Stephan Escher$^{(\boxtimes)}$, Patrick Teufert, Lukas Hain, and Thorsten Strufe

TU Dresden, Dresden, Germany
{stephan.escher,patrick.teufert,lukas.hain,thorsten.strufe}@tu-dresden.de

Abstract. Nowadays, almost anyone can take pictures at any time. Simultaneously, services such as social networks make it easy to share and redistribute these images. Users who do not want pictures of them to be recorded and distributed can hardly defend themselves against this. With the introduction of the GDPR in the European Union, users can now at least demand the deletion of such unsolicited uploaded data from web platforms. To find such images, however, the user must first upload comparative images to such a web service so that this service can compare them with its database to show the user whether unwanted images exist or not. This means that the user must involuntarily pass on his biometric data to a web service where he does not actually want his data to be saved. Thus, in this paper, we present our privacy-friendly face recognition approach based on Local Binary Patterns and Error Correction Codes, that allows users to query web services for the presence of unwanted images without revealing biometric information. We evaluated each step of our approach with the "FERET database of facial images" and the "Yale Face Database".

Keywords: Privacy · Face recognition · Biometric data

1 Introduction

Nowadays, it is possible for anyone to take high-quality snapshots at any time thanks to a wide range of high-quality and affordable image capture devices. In addition, various Internet services enable the sharing, publishing and storage of these recordings for a global audience. However, the constant presence of visual recording devices such as smartphones, compact cameras or AR-glasses, also affects the privacy of users, who have no possibility to prevent unwanted capturing. Further, the unwanted upload of video and image material to platforms such as YouTube or Facebook can not be controlled by the user.

On Friday 25th May, 2018 the GDPR became active in the European Union [1], which enables users to request the deletion of their digital data on web platforms. However, even though the user now has the right to have these unauthorized uploaded data deleted, he must first find it.

© Springer Nature Switzerland AG 2020
I. Boureanu et al. (Eds.): ESORICS 2020 Workshops, LNCS 12580, pp. 231–242, 2020.
https://doi.org/10.1007/978-3-030-66504-3_14

In this paper we consider a scenario where a user wants to know if a particular web service contains images that depict him. To do this, currently, he must either browse this service manually or he has to upload comparative images of himself so that the service can process and compare them with images in its database. The latter means that in order to find and delete unwanted images, the user must first of all offer his own images to this service. Overall, this process could result in restrictions regarding privacy, esp. if the service does not have any data of the user.

An example could be the "Non-Consensual Intimate Image Pilot" by Facebook. This is a program that prevents individuals from uploading intimate pictures of others to the Facebook platform without their consent. This requires individuals "to establish which image is of concern by sending the image to themselves on Messenger". Then a "specially trained representative reviews and hashes the image". The hash is saved and the photo is finally deleted from the messenger and Facebook's servers [2]. It's easy to imagine that individuals might have concerns about uploading intimate photos of themselves on Facebook in the first place.

In general, users may not want to share private pictures with a platform provider they do not trust. Thus, in this paper, we propose our approach for privacy-friendly comparisons of facial images and thus for privacy-friendly requests to web services without leaking biometric data. We focus on an approach that is easy to implement, so that even smaller medium-sized companies can offer this solution.

2   Related Work

Erkin et al. [6] tried to solve this scenario with "Homomorphic Encryption" and the use of "Eigenfaces" for face recognition. They achieve good results in facial recognition and the protection of privacy, but the use of "Homomorphic Encryption" is computationally intensive and also has a high communication complexity between server and user. A desirable feature of "Homomorphic Encryption" is that neither the user needs to share private images nor does the server provider need to share its database or recognition model. A comparable approach is that of Sadeghi et al. [13], where they also use "Homomorphic Encryption" and build on that to achieve faster computation and less complexity.

Another approach was attempted by Chanyaswad et al. [5] using "Eigenfaces" to retrieve vectors representing facial images and Discriminant Component Analysis (DCA) to reduce the dimensions of such a vector in order to protect the privacy of users. Chanyaswad et al. analyzed a problem scenario where training data (image vectors) are uploaded into the cloud by the user to classify the training data, while the cloud provider is malicious and tries to reconstruct the original images from the training vectors received from the users. They achieved facial recognition results above 90% recognition rate and also that the images cannot be recovered by the provider. One disadvantage of this approach is that a training phase is required, which can be difficult for providers of small image databases as well as for users.

3   Towards Privacy Friendly Face Recognition

Our approach is based on a traditional Face Recognition algorithm using local binary pattern histograms (LBPH). The advantage of the usage of LBPH lies in its easy calculability as well as in its good ability to differentiate. In addition, a feature representation can be generated directly from an image and compared to others, without the need of training data or a training process. After quantizing the LBPH results to a binary representation we use the fuzzy commitment scheme for privacy friendly distance calculation. Furthermore we consider the possibility to apply error correction directly to the quantized LBPH representation to get a unique value for each person, instead of comparing the distance between two representations. The pipeline of our approach could be seen in Fig. 1.

Fig. 1. Pipeline of the privacy preserving face recognition approach

We assume a face detection algorithm, which can detect embedded faces in images of the user and the service [14]. By applying the pipeline to detected faces, facial features of the user can be compared privacy-friendly with all available ones of the web service.

3.1   Preprocessing

First of all the images are *aligned*, based on the eye coordinates given in the data sets. Therefore the image is rotated clockwise until the left and right eyes are on the same horizontal line parallel to the x-axis. Then the image is *cropped* so that the image consists only of the person's face. This is done in relation to the eye-center, calculated by the given eye coordinates. Next the aligned and cropped image is enhanced via *histogram equalization*, which was mentioned by [3]. Finally the images are resized to a fix size (depending on the LBPH settings). The whole preprocessing pipeline can be seen in Fig. 2.

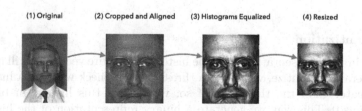

Fig. 2. Preprocessing steps

3.2   Local Binary Pattern Histograms

LBP is a type of visual descriptor, which describes the texture and local characteristics of an image. Therefore the original image is first divided into equal-sized
blocks. A histogram is generated per block, which describes the relationship of
the pixels to their neighbours. For this the grey value of each pixel in a block
is compared with its P neighbours which lie in the radius R. Usually $P = 8$
and $R = 1$ which represents the eight direct neighbours of a pixel. If the grey
value is higher then the neighbour value it returns 1 otherwise 0. This is done
clockwise for each P neighbours, resulting in a binary pattern of length P for
each pixel (see Fig. 3). The frequency of all patterns obtained are transferred
in a histogram with 2^P bins. Finally the LBPH feature vector for the image is
received by concatenating the histograms of each block.

One way to reduce the number of bins per histogram is to use uniform LBP,
an extension of LBP. There the histogram only includes binary patterns where
all 1 and all 0 are adjacent. These patterns can be interpreted as corners, edges
or areas. All other combinations are summarized as 'non-uniform'.

In our setting we used two different LBPH approaches for face recognition.
The first one is the original approach from Ahonen et al. [3]. They resized the
original images to (130, 150) pixels. Afterwards they divided each image into
blocks of size (11, 13) and get the best results with the extraction of uniform
patterns with a neighbourhood of eight and a radius of two ($P = 8, R = 2$).

The second one is an improvement of the LBPH face recognition approach by
Girish et al. [10]. They use multi-block LBP, which is similar to LBP but instead
of individual pixel values, summed blocks are used to generate the patterns. They
resized each image to a size of (92, 112) and divided it into blocks of the size
(23, 28). See also Fig. 4 right.

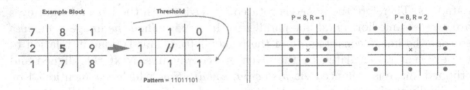

Fig. 3. Left: example binary pattern creation. Right: example impact of P and R value.

3.3   Quantization

To get a binary representation from the histogram feature vector we will quantize
it. In general to quantize, we create a threshold and check whether a histogram
bin is greater than the threshold. If so, we rewrite this histogram bin as 1,
otherwise as 0. This way we generate a binary representation of the histogram
values. For the threshold we use the mean of the histograms, the global and local
(for each histogram of a block) median as well as the relation between histogram
values (see Fig. 4 left). Further we used a double bit quantization (DBQ) [9].

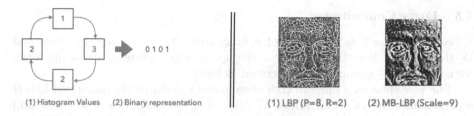

(1) Histogram Values   (2) Binary representation   (1) LBP (P=8, R=2)   (2) MB-LBP (Scale=9)

Fig. 4. Left: example of relation quantization. Right: example of LBP representations (1) uniform LBP $(P = 8, R = 2)$ (2) MB-LBP (Scale = 9)

3.4   Usage of Error Correction Codes

The first approach we took into consideration was the direct use of an Error Correction Code (ECC) on the binary representation of a facial image, so that each face is mapped to a unique value [8].

An error correction code described by the parameters (n, l, d_{min}) encodes information words of length l and adds $k = n - l$ redundant bits to the code words of length n. Binary codes can detect $f_e = d_{min} - 1$ errors in a distorted word $b = a \oplus e$ where e is the error word and a the information word. A distorted word can only be reconstructed if the error word e has a weight of $f_k = \lfloor (d_{min} - 1)/2 \rfloor$.

Assuming that the quantized LBPH representation of a facial image x is a distorted code word, we propose the utilization of a decoding $dec()$ function to correct the errors and to map the representation to a unique value. The f_k parameter of an error correction code is defined according to d_{min} and the error correction code aims to map a noisy channel code word to a *valid* one. However, in our setting we aim to map two noisy channel code words to a single valid one.

We are able to map both noisy channel code words to the same valid channel code word as long as the sum of the hamming distance between a noisy channel code word and a valid channel code word and the hamming distance between the two noisy channel code words is smaller than f_k. Furthermore, if the number of bit errors is greater than f_k for each true negative, the decoded values with length $\lfloor \frac{length(x)}{n} \rfloor \cdot l$ might be used to identify a person in a set of images. If we find a matching ECC we can use this setting for a privacy-friendly Face Recognition approach.

In our setting, the client calculates the LBPH pattern of their image to compare, quantizes it (x), corrects the errors and decodes the binary representation with the decoding function of the error correction code into the unique information word $(dec(x))$. This value is sent to the server after hashing it with a cryptographic hash function $y = h(dec(x))$. The server processes all facial images in its database in the same manner, computing $y' = h(dec(x'))$. Upon receiving y, the server determines whether or not y is part of its database $(y \overset{?}{=} y')$ and consequently presents all corresponding images.

3.5 Fuzzy Commitment

A second approach is the usage of a fuzzy commitment scheme by Juels and Wattenberg [7]. For the usage for a privacy-friendly face recognition approach we use the fuzzy commitment described as follows.

The user chooses a random code word c and calculates the quantized LBPH representation of an facial image x. After that he calculates $d = c \oplus x$ and computes a hash of the random code word c with a cryptographic hash function $h(c)$. To figure out if unwanted images of the user are uploaded to a specific web service, he sends $(h(c), d)$ to the aforementioned server. Note that this value does not include facial information about the user.

The server calculates for all his images x': $y = d \oplus x' = x \oplus x' \oplus c$. If x' is the binary LBPH representation of the same person as x, y only contains the errors caused by the LBPH algorithm and c. After that a decoding function of an Error Correction Code $dec()$ could correct these errors which should map back to c: $c' = dec(y) = dec(x \oplus x' \oplus c)$. For all $h(c) = h(c')$ the server is able to present the corresponding images, because they contain the same person the user was looking for.

4 Experimental Analysis

4.1 Experiment Setup

For the evaluation part we have used the Feret[1] [11,12] and the Yale data set [4]. For Feret we selected all images of a person from the "fa" and "fb" part of the data set. We created pairs for each person between each image of that person in "fa" and the images in "fb", in a way so that each image is only compared ones. In addition, we randomly selected images of different people and created a pair of images from their pictures.[2]

We used a different test setting for the Yale data set, as it contains fewer people, but each person is photographed in more poses. We randomly selected a picture of each person and created pairs with every other picture of that person. In addition, the randomly selected image of one person is compared with every image of the other persons in the same pose.[3]

The comparison for an image pair is performed using a distance metric. To evaluate the different steps, we use different distance metrics for the LBPH and binary representations of facial images. For LBP representations we use the "Histogram Intersection" [3] and for binary representations after quantization we use the "Hamming distance".

The calculated distances are used to decide whether a particular pair of images shows the same person or different people. This is done by evaluating

---

[1] "Portions of the research in this paper use the FERET database of facial images collected under the FERET program, sponsored by the DOD Counterdrug Technology Development Program Office".

[2] Resulting in an evenly distributed baseline of 50% true cases and 50% false cases.

[3] Resulting in a baseline of $\approx 61.11\%$ true cases and $\approx 38.89\%$ false cases.

whether the calculated distance is smaller than the threshold value. A threshold was found for each algorithm by performing various tests and selecting the threshold resulting in the best face recognition performance. In our scenario, a threshold is necessary because we are not trying to identify the person in one picture, but to find all pictures of a person.

4.2 Face Recognition with Local Binary Patterns

We used the configuration of the original LBPH approaches [3,10] (see Sect. 3.2) as baseline LBP variants for our privacy friendly face recognition approach.

In a first step we analyzed this LBPH baseline regarding their recognition rate. The results are shown in Table 1. We found that the approach by [10] outperformed the one from Ahonen et al. [3] overall slightly. In general the results show that both approaches could well used to distinguish people through frontal facial images and to correctly match two face images if they depict the same person.

Table 1. Results of the original LBPH approaches, showing the average results for the Yale and Feret data sets.

Variant	Accuracy	Precision	F1-score	AUC
LBP [3]	0.8363	0.8235	0.8685	0.9318
MB-LBP [10]	0.8732	0.8667	0.8947	0.9462

4.3 The Impact of Quantization on Recognition Performance

We found that the application of quantization to the LBP representations has a higher negative impact on the MB-LBP variant [10] than on the original LBP approach. Table 2 shows the results for the local median quantization for both approaches. The approach of Ahonen et al. [3] is even more powerful when considering the "Accuracy", "Precision" and "F1-score", while only the "AUC value" decreases by less than one percent. This was unexpected, since by quantizing the LBP representation we essentially lose information about certain patterns and abstract the occurrence of patterns to a simple binary number.

A possible explanation would be that the original LBPH vectors contain unnecessary and redundant information which is reduced by the quantization and thus improved the recognition rate. Otherwise the MB-LBP patterns already averaged the feature information in their approach, resulting in worse results after a further simplification through quantization.

Due to the original LBP variant being more robust to quantization we use this approach for further steps.

Table 2. Local median quantized LBP variants. The results represent the average results for the Yale and Feret data set.

Variant	Accuracy	Precision	Recall	F1-score	AUC
LBP [3]	**0.8759**	**0.9145**	**0.8629**	**0.8873**	**0.9298**
MB-LBP [10]	0.7787	0.8426	0.7490	0.7919	0.8522

4.4 Quantization Variants

The results for the different quantization methods used for the original LBP approach by [3] can be seen in Table 3.

The best results were obtained with the "Double-bit Quantization" [9], with the local median quantization taking second place for almost all metrics.

Although DBQ offers the best performance, it also uses twice the amount of binary values for a representation. The reason for this is that DBQ encodes each value with two bits during quantization, which, due to the much larger binary representation, results in higher computing power demands and problems when using "fuzzy commitment" [7] and other error correction codes. For this reason, and because of the only slight improvement over the "Local Histogram Median", we continue using the local median as quantization approach.

Table 3. Comparison of quantization approaches used for the configuration by [3]. The results represent the average results for the Yale and Feret data set.

Quantization	Accuracy	Precision	Recall	F1-score	AUC	Bit-Length
DBQ	**0.8883**	0.9215	**0.8793**	**0.8997**	**0.9340**	14278
Relation	0.8740	**0.9263**	0.8477	0.8853	0.9251	7139
Mean over Histogram	0.8522	0.8815	0.8575	0.8691	0.9158	7139
Global Histogram Median	0.8700	0.9141	0.8506	0.8808	0.9294	7139
Local Histogram Median	*0.8759*	*0.9145*	*0.8629*	*0.8873*	*0.9298*	7139

4.5 Usage of Error Correction

Before we can apply a decoding function of an ECC to the quantized LBPH representations we first analyse the error rate and shape of the representations. The error rate is analysed regarding representations of facial images which contain the same person. Therefore, we aim to choose an ECC that meets the requirements such that different binary representations of the same person are decoded into the same information word.

The results (see Table 4) show that the differences between binary representations of the same person are quite high and the distribution of the binary values is not balanced, which is not a good starting point considering the application of an ECC. The higher error rate for the Yale data set is based on the fact that the facial images show more different poses of the persons than in Feret.

Table 4. Analysis of the binary representations with local median quantization.

Data set	Avg. Hamming Dist.[a]	Std.[b]
Feret	0.1233	0.4898
Yale	0.1778	0.4747

[a] Average Hamming Distance means the average distance between all binary representations for the images of a person.
[b] The standard deviation shows the distribution of ones and zeros in the binary representation. A std. of 0.5 means that the distribution is equally divided.

We choose the $BCH(255, 9, 127)$ code as it has a low code rate of $\frac{l}{n} = 0.035$ and therefore a high error correction capability. The chosen BCH code maps 255 bits to a 9 bit information word and is capable of correcting $f_k = 63$ errors $(24, 706\%)$. This setting allows at least for the Feret data set a twice as high error correction capability than the average error between two images of the same person. This might enable a mapping of two noisy channel code words to a single valid one. The binary representation of each image is split into 255 bit blocks, remaining bits are discarded. After the aforementioned processing steps, the decoding function is applied to each block and the computed source code words are concatenated, resulting in a 243 bit information word. The results of the ECC approach applied to the Yale Dataset are depicted in Table 5.

Table 5. Results with BCH(255, 9, 127) applied to local median quantized LBPH pattern with the configuration of [3].

TPR	TNR	FPR	FNR	Accuracy	Precision
0.1152	1.0000	0.0000	0.8848	0.4593	1.0000

The results show that using a decoding process with a BCH(255, 9, 127) and our face recognition pipeline cannot recognize facial images in a desirable way. The accuracy is below the baseline and shows that almost every image pair is marked as not coming from the same person, as indicated by the false negative rate (FNR). On the positive side, there are also no false positive results (FPR), while there are still some true positive results (TPR). This means that some images of the same face in different poses have been decoded into the same information word.

By analysing the error rate for each block of a binary representation we can determine the reason for the result. Overall we recognize an average of 45 errors in each block between two noisy channel code words (binary representations) of the same person. On average, approximately 25% (7) of these blocks have more errors than can be corrected ($f_k = 63$). Additionally, not only the errors between two noisy representations must be corrected but also the errors between a noisy channel code word and the nearest valid one. As a result, the decoding process is not able to generate the same value for two images of the same person. However, in the best case, at the moment, we decoded three binary representations of the same person to the same value.

Better pre-processing, quantization or extended LBPH variants could improve the error rate of binary representations of the same person and with the choice of an appropriate ECC the approach could nevertheless be feasible, which should be evaluated in the future.

4.6   The Fuzzy Commitment Approach

To evaluate the "Fuzzy Commitment" approach we used the python implementation by Burkert[4]. Using this implementation we obtain a decision whether two binary LBPH representations are equal by subjecting an image of an image pair to the "Fuzzy Commitment" scheme, which results in a commitment. We then use this commitment and the comparative image to obtain a decision (see Listing 1.1).

Listing 1.1. Example usage of "Fuzzy Commitment"

```
tolerance = threshold * length
cs = FCS[list](length, tolerance, polynomial=32771)
commitment = cs.commit(original_binary_representation)
decision = cs.verify(commitment, comparative_binary_representation)
```

For the ECC we used a BCH Code using the polynomial 32771_{10}. The tolerance parameter describes the error correction capabilities of the BCH Code. In our case, we use the optimal threshold of the local median quantized LPB variant received via the hamming distance metric in previous tests to calculate the optimal tolerance of the ECC. The threshold indicates whether two images depict the same person or not.

The results are shown in Table 6. As it can be observed, with this setup, the use of "Fuzzy Commitment" achieves the same results as the quantized LBPH approach.

This demonstrates the possibility of using "Fuzzy Commitment" for a privacy-friendly face recognition approach that compares binary representations of images.

---

[4] https://github.com/cburkert/fuzzy-commitment.

Table 6. Fuzzy Commitment vs. LBP (local median quantization, Hamming distance)

Variant	Accuracy	Precision	Recall	F1-score
LBP [3]	0.8759	0.9145	0.8629	0.8873
"Fuzzy Commitment"	0.8759	0.9145	0.8629	0.8873

5 Conclusion

In this paper we presented an approach to allow users to query a web service for unwanted uploaded images without having to reveal their own image data. Thus we proposed a privacy friendly face recognition approach based on Local Binary Pattern Histograms (LBPH) and Error Correction Codes (ECC).

We have described our pre-processing pipeline, which was applied to two different data sets (Feret and Yale). After comparing two traditional LBPH face recognition approaches we quantized the results to obtain a binary representation of the facial features. We analyzed different quantization methods and showed that a local median quantization over histogram values shows the best results for our use case. Additionally we have shown that the use of quantization can preserve the results of LBP variants and does not diminish the results. In order to evaluate the possibility of a privacy friendly face recognition, we used the "Fuzzy Commitment Scheme" and showed that our quantized LBP representations can be used for "Fuzzy Commitment" without disturbing the face recognition results. This means that this approach can be used for a privacy friendly comparison of facial images and thus for a privacy friendly request to web services without leaking own biometric data. In addition, we propose to use ECC directly and analysed the use of a $BCH(255, 9, 127)$ code. We show that it is generally possible to decode image hashes from one person to the same hash. However, not yet practically applicable with our quantized LBPH features.

An important improvement in the future would be to reduce the average Hamming distance in the binary representations of quantized LBP representations, which would lead to easier use of error correction codes. In addition, other LBP variants may be able to improve the information displayed in a single image window by using more sophisticated algorithms, which could reduce the overall hash size. Quantization methods should be further analyzed to develop such quantizations that the histograms are binarized in a way that leads to good facial recognition results, a balanced binary distribution and a lower error rate between binary representations of two images of the same person.

References

1. EUR-Lex - 32016R0679 - EN. https://eur-lex.europa.eu/eli/reg/2016/679/oj. Library Catalog: eur-lex.europa.eu
2. The Facts: Non-Consensual Intimate Image Pilot. https://about.fb.com/news/h/non-consensual-intimate-image-pilot-the-facts/. Library Catalog: about.fb.com

3. Ahonen, T., Hadid, A., Pietikäinen, M.: Face recognition with local binary patterns. In: Pajdla, T., Matas, J. (eds.) ECCV 2004. LNCS, vol. 3021, pp. 469–481. Springer, Heidelberg (2004). https://doi.org/10.1007/978-3-540-24670-1_36

4. Belhumeur, P., Hespanha, J., Kriegman, D.: Eigenfaces vs. fisherfaces: recognition using class specific linear projection. IEEE Trans. Pattern Anal. Mach. Intell. 19(7), 711–720 (1997)

5. Chanyaswad, T., Chang, J.M., Mittal, P., Kung, S.Y.: Discriminant-component eigenfaces for privacy-preserving face recognition. In: 26th International Workshop on Machine Learning for Signal Processing (MLSP) (2016)

6. Erkin, Z., Franz, M., Guajardo, J., Katzenbeisser, S., Lagendijk, I., Toft, T.: Privacy-preserving face recognition. In: Goldberg, I., Atallah, M.J. (eds.) PETS 2009. LNCS, vol. 5672, pp. 235–253. Springer, Heidelberg (2009). https://doi.org/10.1007/978-3-642-03168-7_14

7. Juels, A., Wattenberg, M.: A fuzzy commitment scheme. In: Proceedings of the 6th Conference on Computer and Communications Security - CCS (1999)

8. Kerschbaum, F., Beck, M., Schönfeld, D.: Inference control for privacy-preserving genome matching. arXiv:1405.0205 (2014)

9. Kong, W., Li, W.J.: Double-bit quantization for hashing. In: Proceedings of the Twenty-Sixth AAAI Conference on Artificial Intelligence (2012)

10. Girish, G.N., Shrinivasa Naika, C.L., Das, P.K.: Face recognition using MB-LBP and PCA: a comparative study. In: International Conference on Computer Communication and Informatics (2014)

11. Phillips, P.J., Wechsler, H., Huang, J., Rauss, P.J.: The FERET database and evaluation procedure for face-recognition algorithms. Image Vis. Comput. 16(5), 295–306 (1998)

12. Phillips, P., Moon, H., Rizvi, S., Rauss, P.: The FERET evaluation methodology for face-recognition algorithms. IEEE Trans. Pattern Anal. Mach. Intell. 22(10), 1090–1104 (2000)

13. Sadeghi, A.-R., Schneider, T., Wehrenberg, I.: Efficient privacy-preserving face recognition. In: Lee, D., Hong, S. (eds.) ICISC 2009. LNCS, vol. 5984, pp. 229–244. Springer, Heidelberg (2010). https://doi.org/10.1007/978-3-642-14423-3_16

14. Zafeiriou, S., Zhang, C., Zhang, Z.: A survey on face detection in the wild: past, present and future. Comput. Vis. Image Underst. 138, 1–24 (2015)

OR-Benchmark: An Open and Reconfigurable Digital Watermarking Benchmarking Framework

Hui Wang[1]([✉]) [iD], Anthony T. S. Ho[2,3,4] [iD], and Shujun Li[4,5] [iD]

[1] Hangzhou Dianzi University, Hangzhou, China
h.wang@hdu.edu.cn
[2] Tianjin University of Science and Technology, Tianjin, China
[3] Wuhan University of Technology, Wuhan, China
[4] University of Surrey, Guildford, UK
a.ho@surrey.ac.uk
[5] University of Kent, Canterbury, UK
http://www.hooklee.com/

Abstract. Benchmarking digital watermarking algorithms is not an easy task because different applications of digital watermarking often have very different sets of requirements and trade-offs between conflicting requirements. While there have been some general-purpose digital watermarking benchmarking systems available, they normally do not support complicated benchmarking tasks and cannot be easily reconfigured to work with different watermarking algorithms and testing conditions. In this paper, we propose OR-Benchmark, an open and highly reconfigurable general-purpose digital watermarking benchmarking framework, which has the following two key features: 1) all the interfaces are public and general enough to support all watermarking applications and benchmarking tasks we can think of; 2) end users can easily extend the functionalities and freely configure what watermarking algorithms are tested, what system components are used, how the benchmarking process runs, and what results should be produced. We implemented a prototype of this framework as a MATLAB software package and demonstrate how it can be used in three typical use cases. The first two use cases show how easily we can define benchmarking profiles for some robust image watermarking algorithms. The third use case shows how OR-Benchmark can be configured to benchmark some image watermarking algorithms for content authentication and self-restoration, which cannot be easily supported by other digital watermarking benchmarking systems.

Keywords: Digital watermarking · Benchmarking · Performance evaluation · Reconfiguration · Content authentication · Self-restoration

---

A prototype of OR-Benchmark as a MATLAB software package is implemented and the source code will be released soon under an open source license.

© Springer Nature Switzerland AG 2020
I. Boureanu et al. (Eds.): ESORICS 2020 Workshops, LNCS 12580, pp. 243–260, 2020.
https://doi.org/10.1007/978-3-030-66504-3_15

1   Introduction

Digital watermarking, a branch of information hiding, involves research on the process of embedding digital information (watermark) within a cover signal to achieve different (often security-related) functionalities related to the cover signal and/or its consumption by end users [1]. Since the late 1980s a large number of digital watermarking algorithms have been proposed for many applications with different system requirements mostly for protecting different types of multimedia data such as still images, audio, video, 3-D models [5,11,24,27,31]. In copyright protection applications, robust watermarking schemes [11,13,32] are desired to embed copyright information as a watermark in the digital media that can be hard to remove. In some multimedia content authentication applications, fragile watermarking schemes [3,4] and semi-fragile watermarking schemes [16,18] are desired because of the need to capture the content changes. Besides, other applications of digital watermarking include transaction tracking, usage control, self-restoration, broadcast monitoring, *etc.*

There are a number of properties associated with a digital watermarking algorithm depending on different application requirements. It is well accepted that imperceptibility and robustness are the two most important but normally conflicting requirements. Besides, embedding capacity/efficiency, security (*i.e.*, the ability to resist malicious attacks) and computational complexity are also important properties for most digital watermarking systems. However, the importance of each property is different in different applications. Some properties also overlap with each other.

As in many other multimedia systems, a general-purpose, flexible and fair benchmarking environment with appropriate test criteria is of particular importance for performance evaluation and comparison of digital watermarking algorithms. With a properly-designed benchmarking system, end users and researchers can conduct performance evaluation of a given algorithm and compare performance of multiple algorithms more easily and fairly to know more about pros and cons of different algorithms and to draw more insights about how to further improve existing algorithms. Since the 1990s, a number of digital watermarking benchmarking systems have been proposed [15,19,22,23,25,28].

Generally speaking, benchmarking performance of digital watermarking algorithms is not an easy task because different digital watermarking applications often have very different sets of requirements and trade-offs among conflicting requirements. When multiple digital watermarking algorithms with changeable parameters have to be evaluated against each other, the benchmarking task becomes more complicated. Furthermore, for systems involving more than one type of watermarks, *e.g.*, content authentication watermarking with the capability of self-restoration, the complexity of the benchmarking task becomes even higher. While there have been some general-purpose digital watermarking benchmarking systems available, most of them can be applied to only certain digital watermarking systems for a limited range of applications. In addition, existing benchmarking systems normally do not support complicated benchmarking tasks and cannot be easily reconfigured to work with different algorithms and testing conditions. It is thus still a challenge to design an efficient and general-purpose benchmarking system that can be used to benchmark different digital watermarking algorithms.

In this paper, we propose OR-Benchmark, an open and highly reconfigurable general-purpose framework for benchmarking digital watermarking algorithms, which is designed to meet the needs of different digital watermarking algorithms and various benchmarking tasks. Its main features include:

- The framework has *open* interfaces for (re)configuring different parts of the benchmarking system and addition of new modules. The framework itself is implementation-independent, but we implemented a prototype in MATLAB (to be released once the paper is published).
- The framework defines a unified procedure of benchmarking different digital watermarking algorithms against different attacks and using different performance indicators to make the comparison more systematic.
- The framework is designed to be independent of the media type, so it can be applied to digital watermarking algorithms for different media types although in this paper we will only demonstrate it for image watermarking.

The rest of the paper is organized as follows. In Sect. 2, related work on digital watermarking benchmarking is introduced. Section 3 gives a detailed description of our proposed benchmarking framework, including our abstract modeling of digital watermarking systems, important evaluation criteria, the proposed OR-Benchmark framework, and comparison with other existing digital watermarking benchmarking systems. Next, in Sect. 4, we describe how we implemented a first prototype of OR-Benchmark in MATLAB with three use cases for different application scenarios. The paper is concluded by Sect. 5 with future work.

2 Related Work

While there have been a substantial number of digital watermarking algorithms proposed for different applications and usage scenarios, there are relatively less research on digital watermarking benchmarking especially general-purpose frameworks capable of handling multiple applications with different sets of requirements. Most existing digital watermarking benchmarking systems focus on some well-defined sub-areas among which image watermarking received the most attention. In this section, we briefly overview some representative work.

2.1 StirMark

StirMark, one of the earliest and the most well-known digital watermarking benchmarking systems, was firstly proposed by Petitcolas *et al.* in 1998 [23] as a generic tool for benchmarking digital image watermarking algorithms against various attacks, which was later contributed by more researchers in 2001 [20] to become a more general framework for benchmarking digital watermarking algorithms. Subsequently, several enhanced versions of StirMark were developed to include more attacks and cover audio watermarking [9,26]. The main aim of Stir-Mark is to develop a fully automated evaluation service, which could encapsulate different performance evaluation indicators and allow continuous development of new attacks to be integrated into the whole system. Since StirMark is among the most widely-used benchmarking systems by the digital watermarking community, we discuss it in greater detail below.

Interfaces. To use StirMark for benchmarking a digital watermarking algorithm, the user is required to supply three functions, *Embed* and *Extract* functions, and one *GetSchemeInfo* function which provides meta-information about the algorithm such as the name, version, author(s), the maximum byte-length of the embedded message, the maximum bite-length of the stego-key, *etc.*

Evaluation Criteria. The main performance indicators of a digital watermarking algorithm StirMark can evaluate include imperceptibility, capacity, robustness to attacks, false alarm rate and execution speed.

Benchmarking Framework. StirMark as a framework contains six main components including the marking scheme library, test library, evaluation profile library, quality metrics library, multimedia database and results database. According to different application requirements, there are different evaluation profiles, each of which is composed by a list of tests or attacks to be applied and a list of multimedia signals required for the test. The end user is required to add the watermarking algorithm under testing (in the form of three C++ functions including *GetSchemeInfo*, *Embed* and *Extract*) to the marking scheme library. The end users also selects evaluation profiles written as INI files with limited static structure. And it is not available to extend the structure of the evaluation profiles without StirMark source code changing. According to the information provided by the end user, StirMark runs the defined benchmarking process automatically by using its multimedia database, the tests (attacks) library and the quality metrics library. The results are stored in a database (an SQL server as stated in [20] and simple files as in actual implementations).

Implementation. StirMark was originally developed by Kuhn in 1997 [7] as a generic software tool for simple robustness testing of image watermarking algorithms. It simulates many common attacks to image watermarking algorithms including random bilinear geometric distortions to de-synchronize watermarking algorithms. Subsequently, StirMark was extended by Petitcolas and other researchers to support more tests and attacks [8,23]. Later on some more development work took place, including a set of tests for audio watermarking developed by Steinebach *et al.* [26] and by Lang and Dittmann [9]. There were also efforts of making StirMark a public automated web-based evaluation service made by Petitcolas *et al.* [20] which led to the 4.0 version of StirMark [21].

Limitations. Although StirMark has been widely used as a tool for robustness and security evaluation of digital watermarking algorithms, we feel it has the following limitations.

StirMark is reconfigurable but the level is limited. Reconfiguring StirMark for a digital watermarking algorithm can be done by defining the input and output arguments according to one of the six pre-defined types of algorithms. However, the modeling and interface do not cover all digital watermarking algorithms, and adding new parameters and extending existing parameter settings will require changing the source code of the StirMark implementation (in C++). Although StirMark allows adding new tests, attacks and PQA metrics, the unclear boundaries among components make it hard to do so without making changes to the source code of the StirMark implementation. Adding some new test, attack and quality metric may require a re-design of the framework, *e.g.*, if a non-PSNR PQA metric is introduced the *strength* parameter will need re-defining and many existing components need adapting to the new PQA metric.

The StirMark framework defined in [20] does not follow a clear data flow, *e.g.*, the test library does not really flow into the evaluation profile but reads data from the latter and the multimedia database.

In [20] StirMark is described to work with an SQL server to store all the evaluation results which can then be converted into web pages for reporting. However, the SQL-based web service has not been actually implemented. Instead, the latest C++ implementation of StirMark [21] produces a plain data sheet to store the evaluation results which cannot be easily converted into other formats or used to do further analysis.

2.2   Other Benchmarking Systems

Checkmark was developed by Pereira *et al.* [19] and downloadable from http://cvml.unige.ch/ResearchProjects/Watermarking/Checkmark/ (now discontinued). Checkmark was based on StirMark with the following main changes. First of all, a number of new attacks, which take statistical properties of images and watermarks into account, are incorporated into Checkmark. Secondly, weighted PSNR and Watson's metric are used as new metrics for evaluating image quality instead of just PSNR. Thirdly, evaluation results are represented in a flexible XML format and can be automatically converted into HTML web pages. Despite the changes to StirMark, the reconfigurability of Checkmark remains relatively low so normally users have to make changes to Checkmark's source code.

Optimark [25] is a benchmarking software package for image watermarking algorithms downloadable at http://poseidon.csd.auth.gr/optimark/, providing a graphical user interface (GUI) developed using C/C++. To use Optimark for benchmarking a digital watermarking algorithm, the user can choose a set of test images, define different watermark embedding keys and watermark messages for multiple trials of the watermarking detector and decoder, and select a set of attacks among 14 types of attacks and attack combinations. It allows evaluation of several statistical characteristics of an image watermarking algorithm, including Receiver Operating Characteristic (ROC) curves as watermark detection performance metrics.

Certimark is the outcome of a EU-funded research project (http://www.certimark.org/, lasting from 2000 to 2002). The objectives of Certimark are to design a benchmarking suite which permits users to assess the appropriateness and to set application scenarios for their needs, and to set up a standard certification process, for watermarking technologies [28]. Although the reconfigurability level of Certimark is higher than earlier systems, Certimark seems to have been discontinued and there is no source code publicly available.

Watermark Evaluation Testbed (WET) [2,6] is a web-based system developed by researchers from the Purdue University to evaluate the performance of image watermarking algorithms. WET consists of three major components: front end, algorithm modules, and image database. To achieve the goal of extensibility, the GNU Image Processing Program (GIMP) is used because it support plug-ins and extensions. Some watermarking algorithms, StirMark 4.0 and some evaluation metrics were implemented as GIMP plug-ins to be part of WET's algorithm modules. The end users can select some images, one or more watermarking algorithms, attacks, and specify needed parameters via a web interface of the front end. The evaluation results can be shown as ROC curves. Similar to other systems, WET has a limited reconfigurability. In addition, its source code is not publicly available.

OpenWatermark [14,17] is a web-based system for benchmarking digital watermarking algorithms. It is composed of three parts: 1) a web server and a remote method invocation (RMI) client for users to submit their benchmarking requests with specifications of the benchmarked algorithms, 2) a cluster of RMI benchmark servers automating the benchmarking process, and 3) a SQL database sorting all data used in the benchmarking process and results produced by the benchmark servers. OpenWatermark allows benchmarked algorithms to be submitted as Windows/Linux executables or MATLAB/Python scripts and all its components were developed in Java, so it has some reconfigurability. However, to support more features such as benchmarking profiles and other media types its source code has to be modified. OpenWatermark implementation was available to registered members at its website http://www.openwatermark.org/ which is currently unavailable.

Mesh Benchmark [30] was proposed for 3D mesh watermarking. It contains three different components: a data set, a software tool and two evaluation protocols. As a benchmarking system focusing on 3D mesh watermarking only, it considers only the payload, distortion and robustness for performance evaluation. Besides, the evaluation protocols are defined with fixed steps and thresholds so the reconfigurability of the mesh benchmark is low. The source code and datasets of the benchmarking system is available at http://liris.cnrs.fr/meshbenchmark/.

3   Proposed OR-Benchmark Framework

In this section, our proposed framework OR-Benchmark will be introduced in details. Firstly, we discuss general modeling of digital watermarking systems used in Sect. 3.1. Then the evaluation criteria considered are discussed in Sect. 3.2. After that, the architecture of the OR-benchmark framework and the open interfaces for end users are explained in details in Sects. 3.3 and 3.4, respectively.

3.1   Modeling of Watermarking Systems

Following the community's common understanding, OR-benchmark models a digital watermarking system as two separate processes: the *Sender* which embeds one or more watermarks into a given cover work to generate a watermarked work; the *Receiver* which extracts and/or detects one or more watermarks that may have been embedded in a received test work. Compared with StirMark, the modeling of watermarking systems in OR-benchmark aims to be suitable for any kinds of watermarking schemes in different application scenarios including some unsupported by StirMark such as self-restoration watermarking. We define the sender and the receiver to take at least one input (the cover and test work, respectively) and to produce one or more outputs. There are more optional inputs and outputs (some are system parameters and some are user-defined ones). Therefore, the users can easily reconfigure the sender/receiver's input/output setting according to the watermarking application scenario benchmarked.

The general models of the watermark embedding and extraction/detection processes are shown in Fig. 1. As shown in Fig. 1(a), the *Sender* will always have the cover work as the input and the watermarked work as the output. There are three groups of optional inputs including the watermark(s) to be embedded, the embedding key, and other optional parameters controlling the embedding process. Note that the watermark(s) in the embedding process can be either an input (if supplied by the user) or an output (if generated by the *Sender* automatically), which can be further used for performance evaluation purposes. As shown in Fig. 1(b), the *Receiver* takes at least one input (a test work) and possibly some other inputs and parameters to produce one or more outputs including one or more extracted watermarks, one or more binary decisions (if some given watermark(s) is/are detected), a restored work (if the watermarking algorithm supports self-restoration), and other outputs, *e.g.*, the confidence level and error rates. We model the inputs and outputs of the *Sender* and the *Receiver* this way to cover the full range of digital watermarking algorithms and applications.

3.2   Performance Evaluation Criteria

In OR-benchmark performance evaluation criteria (*i.e.*, indicators) are organized into two categories: 1) built-in indicators that can be selected by users directly; 2) user-defined indicators that are supported indirectly by generating a comprehensive set of raw results for users to further processing. In this section, the commonly required performance indicators are further discussed.

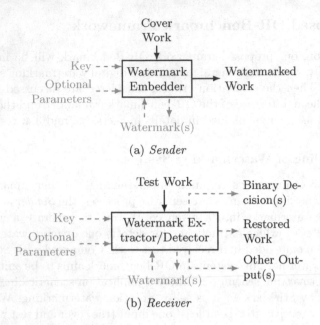

Fig. 1. Modeling of the *Sender* and the *Receiver* in OR-Benchmark. Dashed lines denote optional input/output.

Similar to StirMark, properties that designers and users of digital watermarking algorithms may wish to evaluate include imperceptibility or perceptual quality of the watermarked work (which is one aspect of security), embedding capacity, robustness to benign processing and attacks, resistance to malicious processing and attacks (which is another aspect of security), false positive/negative rates, and the speed of execution of both the sender and the receiver. Since these common criteria have been well studied in related work, here we focus on two other important properties for content authentication and self-restoration watermarking algorithms.

Authentication Accuracy. For content authentication watermarking, there are two basic metrics to measure the authentication accuracy of the detection process: the false positive (FP) rate indicating the level of errors for areas reported as "tampered", and the false negative (FN) rate indicating the level of errors for areas reported as "untampered". Many other performance metrics can be derived from the FP and FN rates, *e.g.*, the average authentication rate and the area under the ROC curve. OR-Benchmark supports the two main metrics and also provides needed raw data in the benchmarking results to allow users to define more metrics that cannot be derived directly from the FP and FN rates.

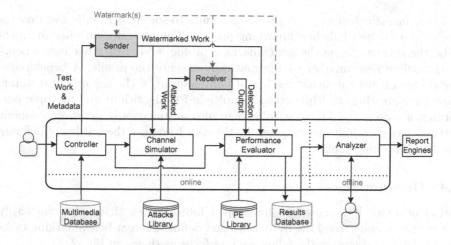

Fig. 2. The architecture of the OR-Benchmark framework.

Perceptual Quality of Recovered Work. For self-restoration watermarking algorithms (which require the use of content authentication watermarks as a prerequisite), a key performance indicator is the perceptual quality of the recovered work. In OR-Benchmark, some commonly used image quality assessment (IQA) metrics such as PSNR and SSIM are incorporated but users can add their own metrics (for any media formats not limited to digital images) easily via the open interface discussed in Sect. 3.4.

3.3 Our Benchmarking Framework

In this subsection, we introduce the overall architecture of OR-Benchmark in details. Figure 2 gives a schematic overview of the framework, which can be split into two parts: an *Online Benchmarker* takes input from the user and automates the benchmarking process to generate results for further analysis, and an *Offline Analyzer* allowing the user to conduct user-specific tasks (*e.g.*, statistics and visualization) based on the (raw) results produced by the *Online Benchmarker*. The *Offline Analyzer* can be equipped by one or more *Report Engines* to produce more user-friendly reports of benchmarking tasks. The *Report Engines* may also access the results from the *Online Benchmarker* without passing the *Offline Analyzer* (in that case the *Offline Analyzer* can be seen as a simple data forwarder).

The *Online Benchmarker* contains three groups of components: 1) the user-provided components – the *Sender* and the *Receiver* provided by the user as the subject of benchmarking, 2) a *Multimedia Database* holding the test media, an *Attacks Library* and a *PE (Performance Evaluation) library* providing attacks and performance evaluation algorithms, respectively, and 3) the core benchmarker composed of a central *Controller*, a *Channel Simulator* enabling incorporation of different types of attacks and processing on a watermark work, and a

Performance Evaluator which produces results to sore in a *Results Database* as the output of the whole benchmarking process. The central *Controller* interacts with the user to define the benchmarking profile, and with other components of the online benchmarker to automatically execute the profile. A benchmarking profile allows automatic testing of parameter(s) of the same digital watermarking algorithm, multiple attacks, multiple PE algorithms and multiple performance indicators. The *Controller* can also automatically determine default settings based on information given by the user to reduce the burden of defining the benchmarking profile.

3.4   Open Interfaces

OR-Benchmark is designed to have open interfaces so that users can easily (re)configure and extend the framework and define different benchmarking tasks easily. There are mainly the following interfaces as shown in Fig. 2.

The interfaces between the Sender/Receiver and the core benchmarker allow users to define digital watermarking algorithms for benchmarking. Following the general models of the *Sender* and the *Receiver* discussed in Sect. 3.1, the interfaces are materialized as the input and output interfaces of two functional units: `Sender`: (Original Cover Work, [Watermark(s)], [Key], [...]) → (Watermarked Work, [Watermark(s)]); `Receiver`: (Test Work, [Watermark(s)], [Key], [...]) → ([Watermark(s)], [Decision], [Restored Work], [...]), where arguments in the square brackets are optional and "..." denotes more optional (user-defined) arguments. A proper mechanism is required to inform the *Controller* about valid values each input argument can take and other meta information (*e.g.*, the display name of each argument), in order to create benchmarking profiles for enumerating all values of interest for any input argument. Such mechanisms can include a graphical user interface (GUI) and a machine-readable textual specification (*e.g.*, an XML schema) for defining a set of sample values for any given argument.

The interface between the Multimedia Database and the core benchmarker allows users to reconfigure and extend the *Multimedia Database*. This can be achieved by an agreed structure of the *Multimedia Database* such as a hierarchy structure of folders and files or using a human-readable configuration file (such as XML) to allow the system and end users to find test multimedia works. Note that OR-Benchmark can support any media types so the *Multimedia Database* can be a mixture of different types of media files.

The interface between the Attacks Library and the core benchmarker allows users to reconfigure and extend the *Attacks Library* used by the *Channel Simulator*. As discussed in Sect. 3.1, an attack in the *Attacks Library* is a simple functional unit as follows: `Attack`: (Input Work, [...]) → (Output Work). Again, a mechanism is needed to convey meta information about any optional input arguments. Compared with StirMark, where one attack test can only contain a single one with relevant values of parameter setting, the configuration of the combined attacks for once test with the values setting for more than one arguments of the combined attacks' functions is allowed by the interface of our benchmarking system.

The interface between the PE Library and the core benchmarker allows users to reconfigure and extend the *PE Library* used by the *Performance Evaluator.* There are different types of PE algorithms depending on the performance indicators used, so there are different input and output interfaces. An important class of PE algorithms are perceptual quality assessment (PQA) algorithms which can be defined as follows: PQA: (Work1, Work2, [...]) → (Metric), where the output is a numeric rating of the perceptual quality. Again, optional input arguments are used to define parameters of some PQA algorithms. While PQA algorithms are generally objective ones based on automated computer programs, OR-Benchmark's interface allows a visual quality assessment (VQA) algorithm to interact with human raters (*e.g.*, those recruited from crowdsourcing websites) to return subjective quality ratings since the user interface can be wrapped inside the PQA function thus transparent to end users of OR-Benchmark.

System search paths can be set up for all the above interfaces so that the *Controller* and other components of the core benchmarker can automatically discover candidate algorithms and test multimedia works. Each path can be a local file path or a URL representing a web address.

The interface between the core benchmarker and the Results Database allows users to reconfigure and extend the format of the results used by the *Offline Analyzer* and *Report Engines.* This is achieved by a machine-readable configuration file indicating the format of the results.

The interface between the user and the Controller allows creation of benchmarking profiles. Core elements of a benchmarking profile include digital watermarking algorithm(s) tested and candidate values of input parameters, test multimedia works, selected attacks, selected PE algorithms, and format of the results. This can be implemented as a graphical user interface (GUI) and/or a human-readable configurable file.

The user interfaces of the Offline Analyzer and Report Engines allow users to investigate the raw results recorded in the *Results Database* in an interactive way and to produce more user-friendly reports. The interface for the *Offline Analyzer* can be implemented as a GUI, but the *Report Engines* could be standalone tools which can be invoked from the *Offline Analyzer*'s GUI. The format of the produced reports can be defined using a human-readable configurable file and be represented in a more user-friendly way, *e.g.*, as a web page.

4   Case Studies

In this section, we demonstrate how our implemented OR-Benchmark prototype (in MATLAB) was used for three case studies. The first two cases are about two main applications of robust watermarking. For the two cases we explain how OR-Benchmark was used to benchmark for a given robust watermarking scheme without giving experimental results since the configurations and expected results are straightforward. The third case is about digital watermarking algorithms for content authentication and self-restoration. Such algorithms are among the most complicated ones with two types of watermarks per block of the cover work and are not supported by other benchmarking systems. For this case we will give details on how we used OR-Benchmark to conduct a full benchmarking task involving three different watermarking algorithms.

4.1   Case 1: Copyright Protection

In this case study, we report a benchmarking task on a blind robust digital watermarking scheme used for copyright protection purposes, which needs a given copyright declaration as the watermark for the *Sender* but not for the *Receiver*. For this case the benchmarking task was set up in the OR-Benchmark prototype as follows:

- Set system paths for the target digital watermarking algorithms, the *Multimedia Database*, the *Attacks Library*, the *PE Library* and the *Result Database*.
- For the test images, we collected 100 8-bit gray-scale images of size 256×256, 384×256 and 512×512, which were added to a sub-folder of the folder holding the *Multimedia Database*.
- The *Sender* and *Receiver* functions were implemented as MATLAB functions with the following interface:
  Sender: (Cover Work, Watermark, Key) → (Watermarked Work)
  Receiver: (Test Work, Key) → (Watermark)
  Both functions were added to the folder holding target digital watermarking algorithms. The benchmarking profile was set to select a number of predefined copyright claims and random keys as input parameters of *Sender* (and the keys for *Receiver* as well).
- A list of attacks was defined for the *Channel Simulator* to create watermarked images, including both malicious attacks for watermark removal and some benign image processing operations. All the attacks were implemented as separate MATLAB functions and were added to the folder holding the *Attacks Library*.
- A list of PE algorithms was created, which includes the imperceptibility property (*i.e.*, visual quality of watermarked images) in terms of PSNR and SSIM, the watermark detection accuracy in terms of correlation coefficient (CC) and bit error rate (BER), and the run-time performance in term of the processing times of the *Sender* and the *Receiver* functions. Each performance indicator was implemented as one MATLAB function which was added to the folder holding the *PE Library*.

After setting up the benchmarking profile and preparing all files needed, the online benchmarker was run to execute the profile automatically. All the benchmarking results were recorded in a MAT file and saved into the *Result Database*. A simple *Offline Analyzer* was produced to visualise results.

4.2   Case 2: Content Integrity Verification

In this case study, we report a benchmarking task on an informed watermarking scheme used to detect content integrity of digital images, which needs a given watermark at both the *Sender* and *Receiver* sides. The benchmarking profile of this case was configured and executed in a similar way as Case 1 but with the following changes:

- The *Receiver* function was implemented as a MATLAB function with the following interface:
  Receiver: (Test Work, Watermark, Key) → (Decision)
- A hypothesis test based adaptive attack is added as a new attack, which assign the Test Work to the Watermarked Work or Original Cover Work according to the result of a binary hypothesis test.
- In the list of PE algorithms, the metric for watermark detection accuracy was changed to false negative and false positive rates.

4.3   Case 3: Tamper Localization and Self-restoration

In this case study we report a benchmarking task on three content authentication and self-restoration watermarking algorithms used for detecting (localizing) and restoring tampered regions in an image: Lin and Chang's scheme [12] (M1), Li *et al.*'s scheme [10] (M2) and Wang *et al.*'s scheme [29] (M3). All watermarking algorithms use two different types of watermarks for each 8×8 block of the cover image, one for tamper localization and the other for self-restoration. Such algorithms are among the most complicated watermarking algorithms and are not (well) supported by other benchmarking systems.

Benchmarking Profile. We used the *Controller*'s GUI to set up the benchmarking task as follows (setup of system paths is omitted):

- The *Multimedia Database* was set up to include 100 test images representing a broad range of image types, *e.g.*, outdoor or indoor scenes images, portraits, photos of natural or man-made objects, and texture images.
- The *Sender* and *Receiver* functions were implemented as MATLAB functions with the following interface:
  Sender: (Cover Work, Key) → (Watermarked Work)
  Receiver: (Test Work, Key) →
                    (Detected Tampered Regions, Recovered Work)
  Here, the Detected Tampered Regions is a matrix storing the binary decision of tamper detection for each block.
- To ensure a fair comparison of the three watermarking schemes, we tuned their parameters so that the average visual quality of the 100 watermarked images is roughly aligned. This was achieved by conducting three separate smaller benchmarking tasks where each watermarking scheme was benchmarked with a number of parameters to produce a set of PSNR and SSIM values, and then the parameters were determined so that all three schemes have similar average PSNR and SSIM values.

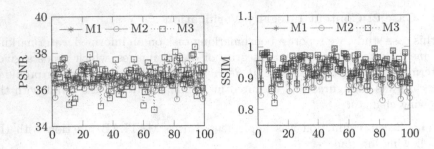

Fig. 3. The quality comparison of watermarked images produced by the three different watermarking schemes. The x-axis is the image index and the y-axis is the PSNR/SSIM value.

- For attacks, we chose simple "copy and paste attack", JPEG compression, additive and multiplicative Gaussian white noises as four separate attacking algorithms each of which is injected into the *Channel Simulator* to create attacked watermarked images sent to the *Receiver*. In addition to the simple "copy and paste attack" alone, we also considered combinations of the "copy and paste attack" with one of other attacks.
- For performance indicators, we used the following: PSNR and SSIM for visual quality of watermarked and recovered images, FP and FN rates for tamper detection accuracy, and processing times of the *Sender* and the *Receiver* functions for run-time performance.

The above benchmarking task was stored as a benchmarking profile which was then executed by the *Controller* to generate the results. The machine running the benchmarking task is a PC with an Intel Core 2 Duo CPU (3.16 GHz) and 2 GB RAM. The concurrency support of the dual-core CPU was disabled to get a more accurate estimate of the processing times.

After the results were produced by the core benchmarker, the *Offline Analyzer* was used to generate some 2-D plots for a better understanding of the performance of the three benchmarked image watermarking schemes. From the benchmarking results produced by OR-Benchmark, we were able to conclude that M3 has the best performance, followed by M1 and then M2. In the following, we show some selected benchmarking results we obtained.

Visual Quality of Watermarked Image. Figure 3 shows the PSNR and SSIM values of all the 100 test images after going through each of the three digital watermark embedding processes. As mentioned above, we selected parameters of the three schemes properly so that they produce roughly equal PSNR and SSIM values for all 100 images.

Tamper Detection Accuracy. To evaluate tamper detection accuracy of an image authentication watermarking scheme, attacks manipulating contents of

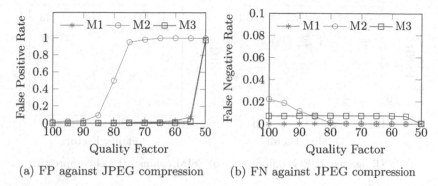

(a) FP against JPEG compression   (b) FN against JPEG compression

Fig. 4. Average FP and FN rates of M1, M2 and M3 w.r.t. different parameter values of JPEG compression.

watermarked images should be used at the *Receiver*. As mentioned above, we used a simple "copy and paste attack" as an example attack to manipulate 10% random-selected part of each test image after it is watermarked. The FP and FN rates are then calculated per image based on how many non-manipulated 8 × 8 blocks are reported as "manipulated" (false positives) and how many manipulated blocks are not detected (false negatives). The FP rates of M1 and M3 are nearly 0, and that of M2 is 1.36%. The FN rate of M1 remains close to 0, but those of M2 and M3 are 3.02% and 1.59%, respectively. It is thus clear that M1 is the best and M2 is the worst.

Visual Quality of Recovered Image. Similar to the case of tamper detection accuracy, for visual quality of recovered images we also focused on the condition where the 10% "copy and paste attack" is applied without other attacks. The mean PSNR values of 100 images recovered by M1, M2 and M3 are 27.8, 28.0 and 32.3 dB, respectively, and the mean SSIM values are 0.925, 0.927 and 0.951, respectively. The results show that M3 is the best scheme with a significant margin (more than 4.4 dB in PSNR and 0.023 in SSIM).

Robustness. For benchmarking robustness, we combined the 10% "copy and paste attack" with one additional attack (JPEG compression, additive or multiplicative Gaussian white noises) to gauge the robustness of each digital watermarking scheme against each additional attack. The results of combining with JPEG compression are shown in Figs. 4 and 5.

Here we average the performance indicators cross all 100 images to get the average values which are then shown against the QF as parameter value of each compression to see how the strength of the attack influences the performance of each digital watermarking scheme. We can observe that M3 outperforms M2 significantly with similar or lower FP and FN rates, and higher PSNR and SSIM values of recovered images. Between M1 and M3, we can also observe that M3 performs significantly better in terms of PSNR although just slightly for SSIM.

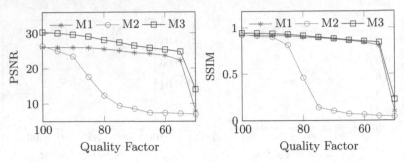

(a) PSNR against JPEG compression (b) SSIM against JPEG compression

Fig. 5. Average perceptual quality of images recovered by M1, M2 and M3 w.r.t. different parameter values of JPEG compression.

Processing Time. Except the embedding process of M1 which took around 2.6 s in average, all other processes of the three digital watermarking schemes consumed less than 1 s. Considering MATLAB is much less effective than other compiled programming languages, the results suggest that all the three schemes are practical for real-world applications.

5   Conclusion and Future Work

In this paper, we present OR-Benchmark, an open and highly reconfigurable general-purpose benchmarking framework, to meet the needs of benchmarking different digital watermarking schemes. To the best of our knowledge, this is the first and the only benchmarking framework supporting all known types of digital watermarking schemes including complicated ones involving multiple types of watermarks. We implemented the framework in MATLAB, and discussed three use cases including one on authentication and self-recovery watermarking to showcase the usefulness of OR-Benchmark as a convenient and flexible tool.

Although OR-Benchmark as a general framework can easily support any media type, attacks, test multimedia datasets, and PE algorithms, our current implementation has mainly built-in functional units for digital images. The *Offline Analyzer* is also tailored towards our own needs for benchmarking some special types of digital watermarking schemes. In future we plan to add more functional units to the prototype so that users can use it without adding too many user-defined algorithms but focus on the digital watermarking schemes themselves. We also plan to release our MATLAB prototype under an open source license and call for contributions from the whole digital watermarking community to further extend the current implementation and to create implementations based on other languages. A dedicated website will be set up to host related documents and source code of our MATLAB implementation.

References

1. Cox, I., Miller, M., Bloom, J., Fridrich, J., Kalker, T.: Digital Watermarking and Steganography. Morgan Kaufmann Publishers, Burlington (2007)
2. Guitart, O., Kim, H.C., III, E.J.D.: Watermark evaluation testbed. J. Electron. Imaging 041106 (2006). https://doi.org/10.1117/1.2400067
3. He, H., Chen, F., Tai, H.M., Kalker, T., Zhang, J.: Performance analysis of a block-neighborhood based self-recovery fragile watermarking scheme. IEEE Trans. Inf. Forensics Secur. **7**(1), 185–196 (2012). https://doi.org/10.1109/TIFS.2011.2162950
4. Ho, A.T.S., Zhu, X., Shen, J., Marziliano, P.: Fragile watermarking based on encoding of the zeroes of the z-transform. IEEE Trans. Inf. Forensics Secur. **3**(3), 567–569 (2008). https://doi.org/10.1109/TIFS.2008.926994
5. Houmansadr, A., Kiyavash, N., Borisov, N.: Non-blind watermarking of network flows. IEEE/ACM Trans. Networking **22**(4), 1232–1244 (2014). https://doi.org/10.1109/TNET.2013.2272740
6. Kim, H.C., Lin, E.T., Guitart, O., Delp III, E.J.: Further progress in watermark evaluation testbed (WET). In: Security, Steganography, and Watermarking of Multimedia Contents VII. Proceedings of SPIE, vol. 5681, pp. 241–251 (2005). https://doi.org/10.1117/12.593803
7. Kuhn, M.: StirMark - image-watermarking robustness test. http://www.cl.cam.ac.uk/~mgk25/stirmark.html
8. Kutter, M., Petitcolas, F.A.P.: A fair benchmark for image watermarking systems. In: Security and Watermarking of Multimedia Contents. Proceedings of SPIE, vol. 3657, pp. 226–239 (1999). https://doi.org/10.1117/12.344672
9. Lang, A.: StirMark Benchmark for Audio - SMBA. http://omen.cs.uni-magdeburg.de/alang/smba.php
10. Li, G., Pei, S., Chen, G., Cao, W., Wu, B.: A self-embedded watermarking scheme based on relationship function of corresponding inter-blocks DCT coefficient. In: Proceedings of CSCWD 2009, pp. 107–112. https://doi.org/10.1109/CSCWD.2009.4968043
11. Li, W., Xue, X., Lu, P.: Localized audio watermarking technique robust against time-scale modification. IEEE Trans. Multimedia **8**(1), 60–69 (2006). https://doi.org/10.1109/TMM.2005.861291
12. Lin, C.Y., Chang, S.F.: Semi-fragile watermarking for authenticating JPEG visual content. In: Security and Watermarking of Multimedia Contents II. Processings of SPIE, vol. 3971, pp. 140–151 (2000). https://doi.org/10.1117/12.384968
13. Lin, C.Y., Wu, M., Bloom, J.A., Cox, I.J., Miller, M.L., Lui, Y.M.: Rotation, scale, and translation resilient watermarking for images. IEEE Trans. Image Process. **10**(5), 767–782 (2001). https://doi.org/10.1109/83.918569
14. Lugan, S., Macq, B.: Thread-based benchmarking deployment. In: Security, Steganography and Watermarking of Multimedia Contents VI. Proceedings of SPIE, vol. 5306, pp. 248–255 (2004). https://doi.org/10.1117/12.538692
15. Macq, B., Dittmann, J., Delp, E.J.: Benchmarking of image watermarking algorithms for digital rights management. Proc. IEEE **92**, 971–984 (2004). https://doi.org/10.1109/JPROC.2004.827361
16. Maeno, K., Sun, Q., Chang, S.F., Suto, M.: New semi-fragile image authentication watermarking techniques using random bias and nonuniform quantization. IEEE Trans. Multimedia **8**(1), 32–45 (2006). https://doi.org/10.1109/TMM.2005.861293
17. Michiels, B., Macq, B.: Benchmarking image watermarking algorithms with Open-watermark. In: Proceedings of EUSIPCO 2006 (2006)

18. Ni, Z., Shi, Y.Q., Ansari, N., Su, W., Sun, Q., Lin, X.: Robust lossless image data hiding designed for semi-fragile image authentication. IEEE Trans. Circuits Syst. Video Technol. **18**(4), 497–509 (2008). https://doi.org/10.1109/TCSVT. 2008.918761

19. Pereira, S., Voloshynovskiy, S., Madueno, M., Marchand-Maillet, S., Pun, T.: Second generation benchmarking and application oriented evaluation. In: Moskowitz, I.S. (ed.) IH 2001. LNCS, vol. 2137, pp. 340–353. Springer, Heidelberg (2001). https://doi.org/10.1007/3-540-45496-9_25

20. Petitcolas, F.A.P., Steinebach, M., Raynal, F., Dittmann, J., Fontaine, C., Fates, N.: A public automated web-based evaluation service for watermarking schemes: StirMark benchmark. In: Security and Watermarking of Multimedia Contents III. Proceedings of SPIE, vol. 4314, pp. 575–584 (2001). https://doi.org/10.1117/12. 435442

21. Petitcolas, F.: Stirmark benchmark 4.0. http://www.cl.cam.ac.uk/~fapp2/ watermarking/stirmark/

22. Petitcolas, F.A.P.: Watermarking scheme evaluation. IEEE Signal Process. Mag. **17**(5), 58–64 (2000). https://doi.org/10.1109/79.879339

23. Petitcolas, F.A.P., Anderson, R.J., Kuhn, M.G.: Attacks on copyright marking systems. In: Aucsmith, D. (ed.) IH 1998. LNCS, vol. 1525, pp. 218–238. Springer, Heidelberg (1998). https://doi.org/10.1007/3-540-49380-8_16

24. Podilchuk, C.I., Delp, E.J.: Digital watermarking: algorithms and applications. IEEE Signal Process. Mag. **18**(4), 33–46 (2001). https://doi.org/10.1109/79. 939835

25. Solachidis, V., Tefas, A., Nikolaidis, N., Tsekeridou, S., Nikolaidis, A., Pitas, I.: A benchmarking protocol for watermarking methods. In: Proceedings of ICIP 2001, pp. 1023–1026. https://doi.org/10.1109/ICIP.2001.958300

26. Steinebach, M., et al.: StirMark benchmark: audio watermarking attacks. In: Proceedings of ITCC 2001, pp. 49–54. https://doi.org/10.1109/ITCC.2001.918764

27. Stütz, T., Autrusseau, F., Uhl, A.: Non-blind structure-preserving substitution watermarking of H.264/CAVLC inter-frames. IEEE Trans. Multimedia **16**(5), 1337–1349 (2014). https://doi.org/10.1109/TMM.2014.2310595

28. Vorbrüggen, J.C., Cayre, F.: The Certimark benchmark: architecture and future perspectives. In: Proceedings of ICME 2002, pp. 485–488. https://doi.org/10.1109/ ICME.2002.1035651

29. Wang, H., Ho, A.T.S., Zhao, X.: a novel fast self-restoration semi-fragile watermarking algorithm for image content authentication resistant to jpeg compression. In: Shi, Y.Q., Kim, H.-J., Perez-Gonzalez, F. (eds.) IWDW 2011. LNCS, vol. 7128, pp. 72–85. Springer, Heidelberg (2012). https://doi.org/10.1007/978-3-642-32205-1_8

30. Wang, K., Lavoué, G., Denis, F., Baskurt, A., He, X.: A benchmark for 3D mesh watermarking. In: Proceedings of SMI, vol. 2010, pp. 231–235 (2010)

31. Wang, K., Lavoué, G., Denis, F., Baskurt, A.: A comprehensive survey on three-dimensional mesh watermarking. IEEE Trans. Multimedia **10**(8), 1513–1527 (2008). https://doi.org/10.1109/TMM.2008.2007350

32. Zhu, X., Ding, J., Dong, H., Hu, K., Zhang, X.: Normalized correlation-based quantization modulation for robust watermarking. IEEE Trans. Multimedia **16**(7), 1888–1904 (2014). https://doi.org/10.1109/TMM.2014.2340695

SPOSE 2020

Nothing Standard About It: An Analysis of Minimum Security Standards in Organizations

Jake Weidman[1](✉) (iD), Igor Bilogrevic[2](iD), and Jens Grossklags[3](iD)

[1] The Pennsylvania State University, State College, USA
jakeweidman@google.com
[2] Google, Zurich, Switzerland
ibilogrevic@google.com
[3] Technical University of Munich, Munich, Germany
jens.grossklags@in.tum.de

Abstract. Written security policies are an important part of the complex set of measures to protect organizations from adverse events. However, research detailing these policies and their effectiveness is comparatively sparse. We tackle this research gap by conducting an analysis of a specific user-oriented sub-component of a full information security policy, *the Minimum Security Standard.*

Specifically, we conduct an analysis of 29 publicly accessible minimum security standard documents from U.S. academic institutions. We study the prevalence of an extensive set of user-oriented provisions across these statements such as who is being addressed, whether the standard is considered binding and how it is being enforced, and which specific procedures and practices for users are introduced. We demonstrate significant diversity in focus, style and comprehensiveness in this sample of minimum security standards and discuss their significance within the overall security landscape of organizations.

1 Introduction

Massive data breaches within corporations such as Target, Home Depot and Yahoo have become relatively commonplace, with numerous companies suffering millions of dollars in losses (and millions of consumers having data records exposed) in a widely publicized way. Though not as predominately focused on by traditional media outlets, academic institutions have also become increasingly popular targets for cyber attackers, with numerous universities suffering damaging security incidents over the past few years. Often, within either type of organization, data breaches are at least partly related to some form of employee (in)action, whether it be intentional or inadvertent [28,36].

Jake Weidman is now with Google. The work was done while the lead author was visiting researcher at the Technical University of Munich, Germany.

I. Boureanu et al. (Eds.): ESORICS 2020 Workshops, LNCS 12580, pp. 263–282, 2020.
https://doi.org/10.1007/978-3-030-66504-3_16

To build a first line of defense against data breaches, organizations strive for an effective *Information Security Policy* [15,47], which, in theory, can help educate and instruct users about how they should act on an organizational network. In reality, however, these policies can often be complex in their content and presentation, and intended audiences may struggle to identify relevant policy terms and to comprehend provisions within these policies. For instance, in our previous work we have encountered security policies in academic institutions that include dozens of individual lengthy documents covering a diverse range of technical and non-technical issues [47–49]. Further, policies need to account for diversity in the employee population [16]. Given this complexity, it is challenging to avoid non-compliance, thus placing organizational security at risk [41]. At the same time, we argue – when given a reasonable opportunity to do so – employees can be stalwart in assisting in the protection of organizational networks [6].

Our work focuses on one organizational approach, deployed in practice, which may serve to address the challenge of the overburdening complexity of security policies and resulting non-compliance. More specifically, we have observed the emergence of a user-oriented, sub-component of full information security policies: the *Minimum Security Standard*.

These minimum security standards are designed to target a specific audience, such as network administrators, or employees, and indicate clear requirements that should be followed by that individual within a technical system [24]. For example, end-users of a network may be instructed to enforce an automatic screen lock on mobile phones or computers after a certain period of time. Whereas businesses and academic organizations now almost always have some form of information security policy available within their system, minimum security standards are still less present, at least within the scope of the academic institutions we observed, which are the primary focus of this work.

Minimum (security) standards are not to be confused with separate organizational documents, referred to as procedures or guidelines. Rather, minimum security standards exist in a space between high-level, formal information security policies, and the low-level, and often simple procedures or guidelines, while simultaneously containing elements of both. For universities providing these standards, we seek to understand the general composition and formatting of these emergent documents, and to infer aspects related to their likely comprehension, implementation, and technological adequateness.

In particular, we describe our methods for obtaining and analyzing 29 minimum security standards from different universities. We evaluate these standards by first coding the documents (in seven categories) focused on end-user components, and then performing quantitative analyses on the resulting data. This included descriptive statistics, readability and tone measures, and cross-standards comparisons on features found within and across these documents. To the best of our knowledge, we provide the first analysis of the emergent policy document class of minimum security standards, and contribute to the sparse literature on the analysis of written security policies.

2   Related Work

Security Standards and Organizational Focus: Most, if not all, organizations seek to protect their digital assets primarily by following an information security policy [15], which is designed to provide mechanisms and rules to protect essential organizational data [4]. Although these information security policies are not novel, they are still regarded as difficult to construct and maintain, and thus various templates or pre-established guidelines are often used to assist administrators and policy developers in their writing of these documents [15,22]. A major component of (or, in some cases, parent of) an information security policy is generally known as a *Security Standard*, or something of a similar nomenclature.

The first standard and guideline in this space was the BSI Group's BS 7799 (published in the United Kingdom in 1995) [24,45]. It was designed to be a common information security framework that could be applied to many industry segments as well as to government agencies [24,42]. Several years after its original development, BS 7799 was adopted as an international standard, and became more commonly referred to as ISO/IEC 17799[1], which was defined as a code of practice for information security management [8,24,37]. In what may be even more recognizable to some, standards such as these led to further focused legal frameworks and guidelines from governments, including the National Institute of Standards and Technology's (NIST) FIPS 199, or Federal Information Processing Standards [12].

Each of these different standards had a similar objective, i.e., to provide organizations across different sectors with a common baseline of information security techniques and methods for protecting their own entities from digital threats. Although these standards are effectively being used worldwide [17], they are not without issues. Due to the generalizable nature of documents intended for an international community, these various standards are often difficult for organizations to implement without modification, as a result of individual organizational security concerns and requirements [29,39]. In particular, what aspects of ISO 17799 work for, and are compatible with the desired work flow of one organization may not be suitable for the size and scope of another organization. As a result, in many instances, organizations use these standards more as an inspiration or guiding principles, while attempting to account for their organizations' individual differences [20,21]. Thus, while studying published international security standards can yield some conclusions about the current state of information security standards in an abstract manner [38], the extremely high number of organizations throughout the world, combined with an unclear number of individual differences in policy-making, lead to a likely highly entropic state of information security policies, and standards as a result, making the space difficult (but interesting) to study.

Even further, once organizations establish set security standards, they are often very protective of them, citing security by obscurity (the idea of keeping

---

[1] ISO 17799 is now known as ISO 27002.

something secure by camouflaging it) [1,33], while academics continuously debate whether or not this is an effective option, with security through open sourcing being another suggested method [1,14]. In reality, at least with corporate organizations, some degree of security through obscurity seems to be the prevalent approach, with little cooperation given to academic researchers studying the space of written security policies [25].[2] In our work, we focus on organizations which share attributes with businesses and are more open to the study of information security standards: academic organizations [46,50]. We, thereby, also extend our previously published work on *Acceptable Use Policies* [48,49] and *Information Security Policies* [47] to the context of minimum security standards. Likewise, Doherty et al. studied a sample of information security polices from universities [9]; their investigation does not include minimum security standards.

Like many corporations, academic organizations employ hundreds, if not thousands of people, and are also eminent producers of intellectual property that needs to be protected [43]. Again, like corporations, academic organizations are also increasingly becoming victims of data breaches, partially due to the high amount of intellectual property being generated. Unlike corporations, however, academic organizations are far more open about internal operations, and many post (or are required to post) a majority of their internal policies and procedures on the Internet, which can be publicly accessed. A report funded by the U.S. Department of Justice from 2006, which is partly based on survey responses and interviews with representatives from academic institutions, provided early insights in this problem domain [7].

Technical Components: Standards, including ISO/IEC 27002, contain specific recommendations that organizations should introduce into their infrastructure to ensure a baseline level of security with a vast majority of these provisions focusing on technical components. Specific to our study, major technical components within ISO/IEC 27002 include access control, cryptography, physical and environmental security, communications security, operation security, and compliance [19]. Each of these components breaks down into smaller items, which can be used to understand how an organization implements security. When describing access control, the standard includes items such as password creation/management, device lock or screensaver settings, and more. Cryptography and communications security primarily focus on encryption techniques used within an organization for data at-rest (stored on a computer or server) or in-transit (via email, website etc.). Physical and environment security alludes to physical premises where computer equipment or servers are stored, as well as access control to these spaces. The concept of operation security generally is focused on backups, logging, malware protection etc. Lastly, compliance does not only consider state and federal laws (where applicable), but also matters within organizations themselves, including information security reviews [19].

---

[2] Interestingly, the paper by Kotulic and Clark was published even though the research was incomplete due to lack of corporate cooperation. The paper ultimately became more focused on talking about the difficulties of academics working with corporations in the space of information security policies and standards.

Security Minimum Standards: As indicated in the introduction, minimum security standards are a newly emerging phenomenon constituting a subcomponent of the broader policy framework of organizations. Our initial understanding of these subcomponents is that they are introduced to reduce the complexity of existing intricate organizational policy frameworks by providing item-by-item provisions about how to act on a network. To the best of our knowledge, no theoretical or empirical research exists studying this phenomenon beyond an industry report by Braun and Stahl from 2004, which provides a useful taxonomy of suggested must-do practices for a *Minimum Security Standard of Due Care* from a legal perspective [5].

3   Methodology

Selection and Pre-processing of Minimum Security Standards: The acquisition and analysis of the minimum security standards utilized in this study was a multi-step process. To begin our selection, we utilized the college ranking list constructed every year by U.S. News [44], which sorts and ranks the top national universities in America. Based on this list, at the time of searching for these documents, we were able to collect a sample of 30 university minimum security standards.

In searching for standards, we generally attempted to perform a Google search for the name of a given university, followed by keywords such as 'minimum security standards', 'security standards', or 'minimum standards' (e.g., "Stanford University minimum security standard"). However, in many cases, this strategy often did not yield direct results, requiring us to perform searches for the respective Office of Information Security or Information Technology, in order to locate information security policies and minimum security standards for a given university. In some instances the searches over subdivisions of university webpages provided accessible information security policies, minimum security standards, or both. In some cases, universities protected these documents behind firewalls, making them inaccessible to the public.

When ultimately identifying candidates for minimum security standards, we collected documents that were explicitly called as such, with only minor variances accepted (e.g., "Minimum Security for Computing Devices Rule" was acceptable, but "Cyberinfrastructure Standards Policy" was not). To further restrict our selection process, we only collected minimum security standards that explicitly mentioned, and were primarily focused on, end-user interactions. To clarify what we describe (or these standards describe) as an end-user, this is any individual in any capacity who connects to a given organizational network. This includes anyone from employees, students or guests. In many instances, additional parallel standards would exist for network or server administrators, and other technical administrative entities, and while these documents may also be interesting to study, our primary focus were standards that directly impacted end-users.

The minimum security standards discussed in this work were collected between July 24–25, 2017, and were archived to preserve the state of the standards at that time. After archiving 30 such standards, we converted each one of them to plaintext formats, and removed any extra content or formatting errors that may have been introduced when extracting content from the web. This allowed us to not only review the content of these security standards ourselves, but also perform automated analyses on them. After reviewing the minimum security standards documents we had collected, we chose to remove one document, as the content within the standard was drastically different than any of the others we had collected, and generally focused on different subject matter (not related to end-users), leaving us with 29 total minimum security standards to examine.

Research Ethics: Please note that we do not intend to pass any form of judgment upon individual organizations through this work. Rather, the collection of these *publicly* available documents serves to provide us, and the research community, with a overview of the state-of-the-art with respect to minimum security standards at a given point in time.

Coding of Minimum Security Standards and Analysis: The analysis we conduct in this work is based on the coding of these 29 minimum security standards. In developing our coding schema, we first referenced ISO/IEC 27002 [19], and then followed more focused work by Braun and Stahl [5], which provides seven key information security elements that should be contained in a minimum security standard (from a legal perspective). This list included executive management responsibility, information security policies, user awareness training, computer and network security, third-party information security assurance, physical and personal security, and periodic risk assessment. We based our coding on these seven primary categories, with certain relevant subcategories that were added for completeness. During the coding phase, a major issue we encountered was the appearance – in some of the 29 standards – of additional content beyond the scope of our current study. Specifically, a share of the minimum security standards that we collected contained standards not just for end-users, but for "Servers" and "Data/Applications" in the same document. As our focus for this work was primarily on end-users, any information focused on servers or data/applications found within any section was left for future study. In summary, our coding was based on 7 categories, with a total of 29 items across these categories for our analysis.

To analyze the minimum security standards we collected, we begin by performing descriptive statistics across all 29 universities and coded items. Frequencies, distributions, and examples for each item are provided. We then continue our analysis by reporting the Flesch-Kincaid readability scores of each minimum security standard document, which has been previously used to analyze consumer-oriented, online privacy policies [32] or End User License Agreements [13]. Continuing this theme of text analysis, we also conduct a language tone analysis utilizing IBM's Watson Tone Analyzer [18]. Specifically, we used the 2016 variant of the Tone Analyzer API (2017 is the most recent), as it breaks down analyzed text among a wider number of dimensions. At the highest level, these dimensions are based on three tonal categories: Emotion, Language, and Social tone(s). Within each of these categories are sub-items, which include:

anger, disgust, fear, joy, and sadness (Emotional tones); analytical, confident, and tentative (Language tones); and openness, conscientiousness, extraversion, agreeableness, and finally emotional range (Social tones). Each of the Social Tones are based entirely on the Big-Five personality model, which has been used by psychologists for many years [3], while the Emotional Tones are self-explanatory. The additional Language Tones are based on the following: Analytical tones are intended to describe a writer's analytical and reasoning attitude and ability; Tentativeness is intended to show the attitude of inhibition; and Confidence is designed to show the degree of certainty exhibited by the author of any text [18]. While a relatively straightforward series of metrics, demonstrating readability scores and tones is a necessary, albeit basic, foundational process of analyzing these documents. Next, we perform a simple cross-document text comparison to determine any similar language patterns, common phrases, or possible duplication of document text across university standards.

4   Results

We begin presenting the results by showing descriptive statistics and examples of each of the 29 coded measures.

Executive Management Responsibility. The role of Executive Management Responsibility is to define who, or what organization, in management has responsibility for the content of a minimum security standards document. To begin our analysis of this primary component, we determined whether or not each minimum security standards document clearly stated a person or entity who issued the standard, thus declaring ownership and responsibility. We found that 34.5% of the security standards contained this information. For example, Boston University provides this information through a statement at the top of their standard, which reads "Responsible Office: Information Services and Technology". This also contains a hyperlink which directs individuals to this respective office's webpage. In another example, UC Merced provides a responsible official and responsible office, which are referred to as "Responsible Official: Chief Information Officer" and "Responsible Office: Information Technology", respectively.

A second component of this category is whether the security standards clearly state who is affected or impacted by the standard. 82.8% provided such information. The University of Cincinnati, for example, provided a statement indicating:

"This standard outlines the responsibility of all university community members, including students, faculty, staff, agents, guests, or employees of affiliated entities. This includes (a) individuals who connect a device, either directly or indirectly, to the university data network or support infrastructure, (b) individuals who install, maintain, or support a critical server, and (c) individuals who develop, deploy, or maintain an application that resides or runs on a critical server."

Another example is found via Rochester Institute of Technology, which states: "This standard applies to any computers that access RIT information resources."

A third component we measured was whether or not our collected standards had an effective date, or a next review date, which would indicate when these policies were made active, and when they may be updated. In regards to the latter, only one university did so (UC San Francisco). Within the scope of effective dates, UC Merced provided two dates; an issuance and effective date, June 8th, 2015, and July 1st, 2015, respectively. Other universities, such as Iowa State, also provided effective dates in the format of "Effective: August 1, 2015".

Within the component "Executive Management Responsibility", we examined whether documents provided users with some form of high-level justification or purpose. We found that 69% contained such information. Boston University, for example, begins their security standard with a "Purpose and Overview" section, which states:

> "Protecting University Data is a shared effort. Individuals with access to University Data are responsible for accessing, storing, and processing data on systems that have appropriate security controls in place for the class of data."

Information Security Policies. The main goal of the information security policies component is to determine how management in an organization approaches compliance with security responsibilities by members of the network. We first briefly comment on the naming conventions of these minimum security standards. Due to our search and selection criteria, we only observe minor or subtle variations. For example, at Iowa State University the title of the document is "Minimum Security Standards and Guidance".

The next components that we measured were whether or not each minimum security standard classified itself as a mandatory document, including whether content within these standards can be enforced, and if sanctions for violators are provided. We found that 62.1% stated that the minimum standards were mandatory. For instance, Colorado State University stated the mandatory nature of its standard in a preamble: "The requirements in this section are mandatory, minimum requirements that shall be implemented on all IT systems associated with the University." Other universities, such as UT Austin, would specify further systems on which the standards should be mandatory, but – in this case – in less strict language: "This section lists the minimum standards that should be applied and enabled in Confidential, Controlled, Published data systems that are connected to the university network. Standards for Confidential are generally required." In the area of enforcement, 34.5% of the documents included some reference to rule enforcement. Similarly, 24.1% included some mention of sanctions for those who violated the standards. The University of Georgia, for example, included a "Consequences and Sanctions" section in their standard:

> "Non-compliance with these standards may incur the same types of disciplinary measures and consequences as violations of other University policies, including progressive discipline up to and including termination of

employment, or, in the cases where students are involved, reporting of a Student Code of Conduct violation. Any device that does not meet the minimum security requirements outlined in this standard may be removed from the UGA network, disabled, etc. as appropriate until the device can comply with this standard."

Iowa State followed a similar pattern by including a "Compliance" section in their standard, which read: "Non-compliance with these standards will result in revocation of access to the data, system, and/or network, as well as notification of superiors. All Iowa State University employees are required to comply with all applicable policies, standards, rules, regulations and laws."

As we were examining technical documents dictating how end-users should act on an organizational network, we measured whether universities included any form of technical definitions for content that may be discussed within a minimum security standard (e.g., what a firewall or anti-virus is). We found that 24.1% of universities provided terminology within the minimum standards themselves to assist in the reading of these standards[3]. Finally, we measured the percentage of universities that provided data (sensitivity) classifications. In some instances, we noted that a few institutions not only provided minimum standards for all devices, but also broke down the standards by how sensitive information stored on certain devices would be. In our sample, 34.5% of the universities provided this breakdown of information sensitivity, which was generally expressed in three categories, such as Public, Non-Public, and Confidential as with the University of Nebraska, but also Low Risk, Moderate Risk, and High Risk, such as at Stanford University.

User Awareness and Education. As one of the seven components of our analysis, we sought to determine which documents explicitly mentioned any form of user awareness training or education in regards to operating correctly on an organizational network. It should be noted here that it is very possible that these universities do offer training on these topics. However, for the sake of this work, we are only focused on what is contained in the collected minimum security standards. We found that 17.2% mentioned training for network administrators, while 10.3% mentioned anything about training for end-users. For instance, the University of South Carolina included a section on end-user training, which included: "Option(s): Security awareness videos recommended and available at no additional cost through Securing The Human". Iowa State University presented a section on "Training and Compliance", and provided two requirements: 1) "All system users must be notified of what protected data exists on a system and its protection requirements.", and 2) "At least annually all system users must sign the Protected Data Confidentiality Agreement."

---

[3] We do note that some standards included hyperlinks to other pages which contained technical definitions. However, as they were not explicitly mentioned in the documents themselves, they are not counted here.

Table 1. Technologies discussed in university minimum security standards.

Technology name	Universities that detail the technology (in %)
Patching	93.1%
Encryption	89.7%
Anti-virus	79.3%
Firewalls	79.3%
Passwords	75.9%
Access control	75.9%
Physical security	72.4%
Device locking	58.6%
System logging	51.7%
Backups	48.3%
Anti-malware	48.3%
System integrity	37.9%
VPN access	34.5%
University-provided security tools	24.1%
Two-factor authentication	20.7%
Third-party tools/Access	13.8%

Computer and Network Security and Third-Party Roles. Much of the information we collected for this study dealt with the computer and network security component of these minimum security standards. Specifically, we were seeking to understand the technical makeup of these documents; which features and technologies are discussed, and which ones are not. We break down the various technologies, and what percentage of universities explicitly mentioned those, in Table 1. We also include the percentage of universities which include any statements of third-party information security assurances or discussions.

Physical and Personnel Security. Within the physical and personnel security aspect, we sought to determine if physical device security or device locking policies were discussed. In the area of physical device security (e.g., keeping devices stored in locked offices), we found that 55.2% mentioned this topic. Duke University's minimum security standards document states, for example: "Locate workstations in an access-controlled environment. Keep laptops with you at all times or stored in a secured location. Use a lock to prevent laptop theft." Somewhat less comprehensively, Mississippi State University states the following about physical security: "Systems must be physically secure or encrypted with restricted access". For device locking (e.g., passcode requirements on a mobile device), we found that 58.6% mandated some form of additional security. The University of Alabama requires devices to be auto-locked, stating: "Devices shall be configured to automatically lock and require a logon, pin, or other means of authentication after being unattended or inactive for a predefined period of time." UCLA provides the following explanation and rule-set: "Unauthorized physical access to an unattended Device can result in harmful or fraudulent modification of data, fraudulent email use, or any number of other potentially dangerous situations. In light of this, where possible and appropriate, Devices must be configured to 'lock' and require a user to re-authenticate if left unattended for more than 20 min."

Periodic Risk Assessment. The final component we explored was the concept of Periodic Risk Assessment, or whether or not universities clearly specify their intention to continually review and update their pre-existing security documentation. In our data corpus, we found that only 6.9% clearly stated something reflecting this aspect in their security standards. The University of Cincinnati states: "OIS must review this document and must update or modify the standard requirements as necessary on at least an annual cycle." Similarly, UC San Francisco also mandates reviews on an (at minimum) annual cycle, stating: "The minimum standards in this document are reviewed, updated for applicability, and approved by the Information Security Committee (ISC) at least once a year or more often as determined by Security & Policy (S&P)."

Readability Analysis: Beyond the categorizations and quantifications of information from these minimum security standards, we also conducted readability analyses on these documents to be able to quantitatively discuss the makeup of these texts from a human-centered aspect. Utilizing the Flesch-Kincaid readability tests, we show the resulting readability scores for each university, along with the number of words in each standard to describe these documents.

We found that the mean readability score was 28.34 ($SD = 4.91$). According to the Flesch-Kincaid analysis, this places the average minimum security, plus or minus one standard deviation, at above a level of complexity necessitating a college degree (scores between 0 and 30). Mississippi State held the score for the most complex text, at 17.7 (college graduate or higher level), and Yale contained the most readable text at 38.1 (some college education). The average length of the minimum security standards was 1256.89 ($SD = 718.55$) words, with Duke University issuing the shortest minimum security standard, and UC San Diego publishing the longest.

Tonal Analysis: While readability scores can be one means of analytically describing text, we chose to analyze the tones of each minimum security standard to determine how these documents might be perceived by readers. The Watson Tone Analyzer tool allows for a tonal analysis across 13 dimensions, organized into three categories of high-level tones (Emotion, Language, and Social). The visualized results of this analysis can be found in Fig. 1. Beginning with Emotional tones, we found that the majority of the standards did not convey a significant degree of emotion. However, there were 6 individual standards documents which portrayed a distinct level of emotion (between 40% and 52%); specifically, Joy (2 standards) and Sadness (4 standards). For example, standards that were perceived as having sad language included the use of words such as 'failures', 'discouraged', and 'vulnerable'.

Although most of the examined minimum security standards were not inherently emotional, we found that the documents were very analytical in their nature. Only one standard was classified as being less than 40% analytical. Examples of statements classified as Analytical are: "Category I data is protected specifically by" or "Information Security Program Minimum Security Standards for Computer Systems". Within the Language Tone category, the concept of Confidence was the most disparate measure. In many instances, standards would be found to be 0% confident. In contrast, one standard was found to be highly confident at 80.85%. Examples of Confidence within this document included items such as: "Firewall rule changes must be documented and tracked." and "All vulnerabilities must be remediated within 30 calendar days.", among others. A number of standards also contained Tentative language. Generally, these classifications dealt with language that deflected responsibility away from a given standards document, and on to another authority. Examples of such language use included: "If you have questions, ask your supervisor, Departmental Security Administrator, or Information Security." or "Other countries may have requirements concerning access to data stored in or crossing their borders."

The third tonal category, Social Tone, was moderately applicable to nearly all examined standards. Concepts of Openness, Conscientious, and Extraversion were throughout well-represented. Examples of Openness included phrases like "The following standards apply to the use of Cloud Services provided by or arranged for by, the University:", while Conscientious concepts were extracted from phrases such as "You must read and understand the terms of use, including whether the provider has access to your data and what it can do with the data." Extraversion was also a predominant feature, represented by phrases such as the following: "Set up your system and applications to receive updates automatically except where specific business requirements prevent doing so." Many of the sentences classified as various Social Tones tended to show a certain directness in language, without being overly emotional or negative. Moreover, nearly all of the documents had a very low degree of Agreeableness. Lastly, based on the common occurrence of various Social tones through the examined security standards, we found that the documents had a high amount of Emotional Range, which is to say that the documents often expressed multiple sentiments throughout.

Standards Cross-Comparison: After determining the tone(s) and readability of each minimum security standard individually, we also compared each of the collected standards to each other. This ultimately yielded 807 document comparisons in total. Understanding potential commonalities between these documents can potentially provide insights about how these documents may have been created or where they might have drawn inspiration from.

We found that 86% of the compared standards shared less than 2% of content similarity between them. Examples of this would include simple, and common, phrase duplication such as "[...] the minimum security standards [...]". 7.8% of universities shared between 2% and 10% similar content to other documents.

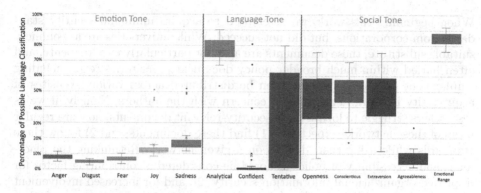

Fig. 1. Tonal analysis of minimum security standards

In these instances, longer, though still common phrases were duplicated including: "[...] may be made for patches that compromise the use of critical applications [...]", or "[...] devices must not provide an active SMTP service that allows unauthorized third parties [...]".

Only 3.45% of documents shared a high level of similarity with other security standards (>10%). In these cases, sentences and sections were very related, only distinct from others via additional or redacted components of sentences. We demonstrate this via the two text blocks below:

[...] apply high severity security patches within seven days of publish, medium severity within 14 days, and low severity within 28 days. Use a supported version of the application.

[...] apply critical and high severity security patches within seven days of publish and all other security patches within 90 days. Use a supported version of the application.

In this example, we can most likely see some form of duplication occurring, with certain words or phrases omitted or added to separate the two sentences slightly and to account for different requirements. We also find that in these instances, visual styles duplicated as well. Within this dataset, we found that a number of standards seem to be designed in a similar fashion to that of Stanford University, which structures its document via a series of tables. For example, the documents of Stanford University and Virginia Tech share 56% of their content with each other, and appear to be based on the same visual design. We also encountered highly similar documents from universities within the same school systems. Examples of this included UC Berkeley and UC Merced sharing 70% of their standards, as well as UT Dallas and UT Austin, which shared 80%.

5 Discussion and Concluding Remarks

As has been remarked in other works [25], creating a dataset of information security policies, including minimum security standards, is a daunting task.

When beginning this work, we attempted to acquire minimum security standards from corporations, but did not succeed. While universities are a seemingly suitable substitute, these documents are also not particularly easy to locate, and often buried within much broader policy document repositories (e.g., including employment policies) that may even be distributed across various websites of a university network. This raises a concern with the authors. Namely, if we as researchers struggle to locate these security-relevant documents, how are regular users of these networks expected to 1) find these documents, and 2) follow these standards while using their devices on a given network. Rethinking the placement and accessibility of policies should be considered a contributing factor for improved organizational information security [2], and for increased involvement of employees and staff within an organization as valuable security assets [35].

In the event that an individual finds these standards, there is still a persistent issue of readability that seemingly plagues many policy-type documents [34] considering the average Flesch-Kincaid score of 28.34. Lessons that have been learned in studies on consumer-facing policies still seem to be seldom implemented, questioning the cross-cutting impact that this literature generally has in practical environments. An additional problem that we find in this space is the lack of definitions or terminology within many of these technical documents, with less than 25% of standards containing this information. Knowing that end-users generally struggle with technical jargon [11], including these technical definitions could be a way to increase readability for those who are less technically inclined. This is consistent with other literature in the legal space, which suggests that simplified sentence structure and terminology lead to higher comprehension among non-experts [31].

How Do Similar Standards Differ? The cross-document comparison shows that most documents do not share common phrases, which could be considered somewhat surprising given the specific focus of the document corpus. However, there are also several pairs of documents with a high degree of consistency across standards. For example, based on an exact language comparison, Stanford University and Virginia Tech are 56.10% similar to each other; a significant overlap. Specifically, Virginia Tech shares 56.10% of its content with Stanford's minimum security standard, while Stanford shares 44.10% of its content within the Virginia Tech standard. However, these direct language comparisons alone offer an incomplete picture of what is within these standards.

Finally, we can explicitly compare the individual factors occurring within a set of security standards. In our example, we find for our 29 measured items, that Stanford University contains 2 items that Virginia Tech does not include, and Virginia Tech lists 4 items that Stanford does not capture. More specifically, Virginia Tech has an effective start date, definitions for data sensitivity levels, a device-locking standard, and a password construction/maintenance standard; Stanford does not. Inversely, Stanford presents definitions for technical terms within the standard, and mentions system integrity, which Virginia Tech does not. What is perhaps surprising about this result is that Virginia Tech has the shorter standard based on word count (i.e., 1004 vs. 1314 words), but contains more items that we measured, at least at a high level, than Stanford.

A further key difference between documents relates to details and actionability (i.e., the ability given to a user to take action on a given item). In our example, though these two university minimum security standards are very similar at a high level, Stanford's standard generally provided more comprehensive descriptions for each item within its standard, and often provided actionable instructions or hyperlinks that would allow anyone reading the document to learn more, or take immediate action to follow a given standard item. An example of this can be found regarding whole disk encryption, something both universities covered. Virginia Tech provided the following statement regarding whole disk encryption: "Use FileVault2 for Mac. Use BitLocker for Windows. Consider using Veracrypt if applicable." Stanford, for the same standard item, provided the following statement: "Enable FileVault2 for Mac, BitLocker for Windows. SWDE is recommended, option to use VLRE instead. Install MDM on mobile devices.", but also provided embedded hyperlinks for FileVault2, Bit-Locker, SWDE, VLRE, and MDM. Following any of these hyperlinks would display a highly detailed page describing how to implement each of these given technologies.

Actionability is an aspect that we did not consider in depth when running this initial document study. However, it is clear that even for similar standards, this hard-to-measure concept could be a critical factor in determining the effectiveness of these standards documents in practice. Standards that are able to provide immediate, actionable information should allow for a higher degree of understanding by readers of such a document, and ideally, of compliance as well.

How Different Are Dissimilar Standards? In the following, we discuss an example of low overlap according to our initial metrics. When directly comparing Boston University and the University of South Carolina based on text similarity, we observed a 0% match for each other; that is to say, that no exact duplicate sentences, statements, or short phrases were shared between the two documents. Again, beginning at a high level we analyzed the readability and length of both standards. The University of South Carolina was found to be 818 words long, while Boston University was 2,666 words long; a significant difference. In terms of readability, Boston University had a Flesch Reading Ease score of 31.3, while the University of South Carolina had a score of 24.6 (lower scores indicate a higher reading difficulty).

Focusing on the content found within the two standards, we also see a large number of differences between the two, with Boston University containing many more components than the University of South Carolina. Specifically, Boston University contained 14 measured items that South Carolina did not, while the University of South Carolina contained 4 measured items that Boston University did not include. Many of the similar items shared between the two universities were administrative features, such as including an effective date, and certain technical features, including logging, software patching, backups, 2FA, encryption, and anti-virus. Beyond this, however, a majority of the items were different from each other.

The differences continued when analyzing the visual format of the two standards. Boston University, for example, presented its standard in a semi-structured outline format, with large section headers and bullet points, with each point containing one or more sentences describing the elements of the standard. The University of South Carolina opted for a table-based design, organized with each standard as a row item, with goals and options for meeting those goals displayed in a corresponding column. Both of these formats were seen frequently when examining standards, so these differences are not unusual. However, similar to the example above, the main difference between these two documents in terms of presentation is that of added details. Boston University provides more content, not only in the items included in their standard, but with the explanations detailing the standard as well. While intuition might suggest that these added details might lead to readability problems, our results suggest the opposite, showing that the lengthier, more detailed standard was easier to read than the shorter standard. This presents an interesting outcome for standards authors, as this shows that brevity may not always be the best action when writing technical documents.

2020 Updates. As the sample of minimum security standards was accessed in July 2017, and at the time of publication, it is 2020, we decided to "check in" on the standards to see what, if anything had changed. In short, the magnitude and comprehensiveness of changes was rather limited: only 11 of the 29 minimum security standards had been updated since we had last accessed them. In many instances, these changes were small. For example, Virginia State's standard had been updated twice with only minor revisions. For example, we observed the following change (Policy: June 16, 2020 - Endpoints section): "Install antivirus (e.g. Windows Defender) and configure to automatically update and run scheduled scans" was changed to "install antivirus software if possible and configure to automatically update and run scheduled scans."

For other standards, although they had been "updated", this did not necessarily mean that they contained up-to-date information or standards. In one such instance, at the University of Colorado, the minimum security standard (last updated on February 20, 2018) still noted that devices on the network should "Enable Windows XP or 2003 firewall". Considering that end-of-life occurred for Windows XP in 2014, this standard is woefully out of date [10]. In most other instances, it was not inherently clear as to what changes had been made to the security standards, and they appeared to be nearly identical to their predecessors. Only two security standards had undergone any significant changes. In one instance, at the University of Wisconsin, a previously singular security standard was now found to be broken up into several smaller components. In a second instance, the University of South Carolina had removed public access to their minimum security standard, placing it behind a single sign-on service. In summary, while some updates to these security standards have been made over recent years, they are *minimal*, and for a majority of security standards that we analyzed in the study, they have not changed or been updated in comparison to our sample from 2017.

Concluding Remarks. Through our analyses, we find the key contribution of this paper: a very clear lack of consistency in the construction of minimum security standards, across a number of dimensions. Considering that these are all organizations within one business sector (i.e., higher level education institutions), we should expect to find a reasonable amount of similarity between security standards, as the issues and threats faced by each organization are related.

We also find that while university standards contained technical items with a degree of consistency, covering topics such as patching, encryption, anti-virus, and more, we still found several that were severely lacking in this area. This is an issue that should be addressed; namely, that all standards should be required to meet at least a base specification of technical requirements. This disparity is more clear when it comes to the lesser-discussed administrative components of these standards; specifically, who writes/is responsible for them, when their effective dates are, when they were last updated, and when they will be updated again. This, however, becomes especially important, as technological threats develop rapidly. To illustrate this point, only 48.8% of the universities we sampled discuss backups. Over the past years, ransomware attacks have crippled numerous computing systems, including transportation systems and hospitals [26,30]. One of the key defenses again ransomware attacks are consistent, secure backups [27,40]. However, without a standards group who regularly reviews and updates these standards, these potential gaps in security could be left unchecked for a long period of time, making organizations (in our case, universities) a softer target for cyber attacks. This combination of modest technological comprehensiveness, and a slower re-evaluation of standards, is a clear issue that should be addressed by many organizations.

Finally, we noted the largest amount of dissimilarity across all of the universities in the areas of technological comprehensiveness, readability, and managerial aspects, and it is worth highlighting that *no* two universities shared exactly the same items in their minimum security standards. In this vein, we also wish to briefly discuss the presentation of these standards. In some instances, the security standards we viewed came in the form of a formal outline, detailing categories, sub-categories, and then items. Others present their minimum security standards in a very visual way, utilizing tables with technical rules, with check-marks indicating which systems, and types of data, are affected by a specific rule. Work is needed in this area to determine which methods are most suitable to visualize and present this information, similar to research previously conducted on privacy policies [23]. Another set of inconsistencies we encountered involved the intended target audience of a given standard. A number of security standards not only focused on end-users, but also servers, and a third category which was generally titled data/applications. Some standards had all of these target audiences, while others only had end-user information. Inversely, others may only have standards for servers, or administrators, but not end-users. This lack of consistency in the addressed audience of these standards is yet another issue worth noting, and hearkens back to the general theme of this section, and the title of the paper: the minimum security standards that we analyzed are not standardized.

Acknowledgements. We thank the reviewers and the participants of the Second Workshop on Security, Privacy, Organizations, and Systems Engineering for their feedback.

References

1. Anderson, R.: Security in open versus closed systems - the dance of Boltzmann, Coase and Moore. Technical report, Cambridge University, England (2002)
2. Ashenden, D., Sasse, A.: CISOs and organisational culture: their own worst enemy? Comput. Secur. **39**, 396–405 (2013)
3. Barrick, M., Mount, M.: The big five personality dimensions and job performance: a meta-analysis. Pers. Psychol. **44**(1), 1–26 (1991)
4. Baskerville, R., Siponen, M.: An information security meta-policy for emergent organizations. Log. Inf. Manag. **15**(5/6), 337–346 (2002)
5. Braun, R., Stahl, S.: An Emerging Information Security Minimum Standard of due Care. Citadel Information Group, Inc., Los Angeles (2004)
6. Bulgurcu, B., Cavusoglu, H., Benbasat, I.: Information security policy compliance: an empirical study of rationality-based beliefs and information security awareness. MIS Q. **34**(3), 523–548 (2010)
7. Burd, S., et al.: The impact of information security in academic institutions on public safety and security: assessing the impact and developing solutions for policy and practice. Technical report, Project funded by National Institute of Justice, Office of Justice Programs, U.S. Department of Justice (2006)
8. Disterer, G.: ISO/IEC 27000, 27001 and 27002 for information security management. J. Inf. Secur. **4**(2), 92–100 (2013)
9. Doherty, N.F., Anastasakis, L., Fulford, H.: The information security policy unpacked: a critical study of the content of university policies. Int. J. Inf. Manage. **29**(6), 449–457 (2009)
10. Farhang, S., Weidman, J., Kamani, M.M., Grossklags, J., Liu, P.: Take it or leave it: a survey study on operating system upgrade practices. In: Proceedings of the 34th Annual Computer Security Applications Conference (ACSAC), pp. 490–504 (2018)
11. Felt, A.P., Ha, E., Egelman, S., Haney, A., Chin, E., Wagner, D.: Android permissions: user attention, comprehension, and behavior. In: Proceedings of the Eighth Symposium on Usable Privacy and Security (SOUPS). ACM (2012)
12. Grance, T., Stevens, M., Myers, M.: Guide to selecting information technology security products. NIST Special Publication 800-36 (2003). https://nvlpubs.nist. gov/nistpubs/Legacy/SP/nistspecialpublication800-36.pdf
13. Grossklags, J., Good, N.: Empirical studies on software notices to inform policy makers and usability designers. In: Dietrich, S., Dhamija, R. (eds.) FC 2007. LNCS, vol. 4886, pp. 341–355. Springer, Heidelberg (2007). https://doi.org/10.1007/978-3-540-77366-5_31
14. Hoepman, J.H., Jacobs, B.: Increased security through open source. Commun. ACM **50**(1), 79–83 (2007)

15. Höne, K., Eloff, J.: Information security policy - what do international information security standards say? Comput. Secur. **21**(5), 402–409 (2002)
16. Hudock, A., Weidman, J., Grossklags, J.: Security onboarding: an interview study on security training for temporary employees. In: Proceedings of Mensch und Computer (MuC), pp. 183–194 (2020)
17. Humphreys, E.: Information security management standards: compliance, governance and risk management. Information Sec. Tech. Report **13**(4), 247–255 (2008)
18. IBM: Watson Tone Analyzer - New service now available. IBM Cloud Blog, December 2016. Information available at: https://web.archive.org/web/20181206170813/ https://www.ibm.com/blogs/bluemix/2015/07/ibm-watson-tone-analyzer/
19. International Organization for Standardization (ISO): ISO/IEC 27002:2013 - Information technology - Security techniques - Code of practice for information security management (2013)
20. Johnson, M., Karat, J., Karat, C.M., Grueneberg, K.: Optimizing a policy authoring framework for security and privacy policies. In: Proceedings of the Sixth Symposium on Usable Privacy and Security (SOUPS) (2010)
21. Johnson, M., Karat, J., Karat, C.M., Grueneberg, K.: Usable policy template authoring for iterative policy refinement. In: Proceedings of the IEEE International Symposium on Policies for Distributed Systems and Networks, pp. 18–21 (2010)
22. Karat, J., et al.: Policy framework for security and privacy management. IBM J. Res. Dev. **53**(2), 4:1–4:14 (2009)
23. Kelley, P.G., Bresee, J., Cranor, L.F., Reeder, R.: A nutrition label for privacy. In: Proceedings of the Fifth Symposium on Usable Privacy and Security (SOUPS). ACM (2009)
24. Kenning, M.J.: Security management standard – ISO 17799/BS 7799. BT Technol. J. **19**(3), 132–136 (2001). https://doi.org/10.1023/A:1011954702780
25. Kotulic, A.G., Clark, J.G.: Why there aren't more information security research studies. Inf. Manag. **41**(5), 597–607 (2004)
26. Krebs, B.: Hospital declares 'internal state of emergency' after ransomware infection. Krebs on Security (2016)
27. Laszka, A., Farhang, S., Grossklags, J.: On the economics of ransomware. In: Rass, S., An, B., Kiekintveld, C., Fang, F., Schauer, S. (eds.) Decision and Game Theory for Security, GameSec 2017. LNCS, vol. 10575, pp. 397–417. Springer, Cham (2017). https://doi.org/10.1007/978-3-319-68711-7_21
28. Liginlal, D., Sim, I., Khansa, L.: How significant is human error as a cause of privacy breaches? An empirical study and a framework for error management. Comput. Secur. **28**(3–4), 215–228 (2009)
29. Ma, Q., Pearson, M.: ISO 17799: "Best practices" in information security management? Commun. Assoc. Inf. Syst. **15**, 577–591 (2005)
30. Mansfield-Devine, S.: Ransomware: taking businesses hostage. Netw. Secur. **2016**(10), 8–17 (2016)
31. Masson, M., Waldron, M.A.: Comprehension of legal contracts by non-experts: effectiveness of plain language redrafting. Appl. Cogn. Psychol. **8**(1), 67–85 (1994)
32. McDonald, A.M., Reeder, R.W., Kelley, P.G., Cranor, L.F.: A comparative study of online privacy policies and formats. In: Goldberg, I., Atallah, M.J. (eds.) PETS 2009. LNCS, vol. 5672, pp. 37–55. Springer, Heidelberg (2009). https://doi.org/10. 1007/978-3-642-03168-7_3
33. Mercuri, R., Neumann, P.: Security by obscurity. Commun. ACM **46**(11), 160 (2003)

34. Milne, G., Culnan, M., Greene, H.: A longitudinal assessment of online privacy notice readability. J. Public Policy Mark. **25**(2), 238–249 (2006)

35. Pfleeger, S.L., Sasse, A., Furnham, A.: From weakest link to security hero: transforming staff security behavior. J. Homel. Secur. Emerg. Manage. **11**(4), 489–510 (2014)

36. Richardson, R.: CSI computer crime and security survey. Computer Security Institute (2008). http://i.cmpnet.com/v2.gocsi.com/pdf/CSIsurvey2008.pdf

37. Saint-Germain, R.: Information security management best practice based on ISO/IEC 17799. Inf. Manag. **39**(4), 60 (2005)

38. Siponen, M.: Information security standards focus on the existence of process, not its content. Commun. ACM **49**(8), 97–100 (2006)

39. Siponen, M., Willison, R.: Information security management standards: problems and solutions. Inf. Manag. **46**(5), 267–270 (2009)

40. Sittig, D., Singh, H.: A socio-technical approach to preventing, mitigating, and recovering from ransomware attacks. Appl. Clin. Inform. **7**(2), 624–632 (2016)

41. Sohrabi Safa, N., von Solms, R., Furnell, S.: Information security policy compliance model in organizations. Comput. Secur. **56**, 1–13 (2016)

42. Susanto, H., Almunawar, M.N., Tuan, Y.C.: Information security management system standards: a comparative study of the big five. Int. J. Electr. Comput. Sci. **11**(5), 23–29 (2011)

43. Thursby, J., Kemp, S.: Growth and productive efficiency of university intellectual property licensing. Res. Policy **31**(1), 109–124 (2002)

44. U.S. News: National university rankings (2017). https://www.usnews.com/best-colleges/rankings/national-universities

45. von Solms, R.: Information security management: why standards are important. Inf. Manag. Comput. Secur. **7**(1), 50–58 (1999)

46. Weidman, J.: Policies, standards, and practices: an analysis of the current state of organizational security at universities and corporations. Ph.D. thesis, Pennsylvania State University (2018)

47. Weidman, J., Grossklags, J.: What's in your policy? An analysis of the current state of information security policies in academic institutions. In: Proceedings of the European Conference on Information Systems (ECIS) (2018)

48. Weidman, J., Grossklags, J.: The acceptable state: an analysis of the current state of acceptable use policies in academic institutions. In: Proceedings of the European Conference on Information Systems (ECIS) (2019)

49. Weidman, J., Grossklags, J.: Assessing the current state of information security policies in academic organizations. Inf. Comput. Secur. **28**(3), 423–444 (2020)

50. Willinsky, J., Alperin, J.P.: The academic ethics of open access to research and scholarship. Ethics Educ. **6**(3), 217–223 (2011)

The Bigger Picture: Approaches to Inter-organizational Data Protection Impact Assessment

Dimitri Van Landuyt[1]([⊠]), Laurens Sion[1], Pierre Dewitte[2], and Wouter Joosen[1]

[1] imec-DistriNet, KU Leuven, 3001 Leuven, Belgium
{dimitri.landuyt,laurens.sion,wouter.joosen}@cs.kuleuven.be
[2] imec-CiTiP, KU Leuven, 3000 Leuven, Belgium
pierre.dewitte@kuleuven.be

Abstract. Contemporary data processing activities rarely involve a single entity but, rather, rely on complex inter-organizational collaborations between (joint) controllers, processors, sub-processors, recipients, and third parties.

However, current approaches in support of Data Protection Impact Assessment (DPIA) traditionally address data protection risks through the perspective of a single entity. As a result, the assessment of complex, inter-organizational data processing activities is scattered across multiple isolated efforts conducted by different parties. This leads to mismatches between the factual descriptions of data processing activities among the concerned entities, but also dilutes the argumentation related to the general principles governing the processing of personal data.

In this article, we explore and discuss the benefits and downsides of approaches that foster inter-organizational collaboration when conducting a DPIA. We also highlight the main requirements, namely: (i) establishing consensus on and consistency in the descriptions of data processing operations and the legal argumentations, (ii) controlling the sharing of information between organizations, (iii) addressing data protection compliance from an end-to-end, holistic perspective and (iv) allowing for dynamism and continuous, flexible re-evaluation. Finally, we discuss and contrast two alternative approaches for inter-organizational and collaborative DPIA: a fully centralized versus a fully federated approach.

Keywords: GDPR · Data protection by design · Privacy by design · Data protection impact assessment · Inter-organizational privacy

1 Introduction

The General Data Protection Regulation (GDPR) [18] contains various provisions that oblige controllers and, to a lesser extent, processors to document their personal data processing operations. This follows, among others, from the principles of transparency and accountability (Art. 5, 24), the Data Protection by

I. Boureanu et al. (Eds.): ESORICS 2020 Workshops, LNCS 12580, pp. 283–293, 2020.
https://doi.org/10.1007/978-3-030-66504-3_17

Design (DPbD) paradigm (Art. 25(1)), the obligation to maintain a record of processing activities (Art. 30), and the need to conduct a Data Protection Impact Assessment (DPIA) when the processing is likely to result in a high risk to the data subjects' rights and freedoms. DPIA, as one of the cornerstones of the Regulation, involves substantiating data protection risks throughout the entire data processing life cycle. Not only does a DPIA contain a comprehensive description of the processing operations at stake, but it also include the necessary argumentation to justify and demonstrate compliance with the rules stemming from data protection law.

Contemporary personal data processing activities rarely involve a single entity (i.e. a single organization or actor). Cloud computing, for instance, involves the outsourcing of some aspects of computational processing and data storage to third-party cloud providers, typically acting as processors on belhalf of the controller. Furthermore, the increasing degree of inter-connectivity and integration of systems, such as in smart cities [10] leads to complex and dynamic interactions between services which are determined by very concrete events. Similarly, open data marketplaces allow for the dynamic trade of large-scale data sets based on specific characteristics and their business value.

In all these scenarios, personal data continuously cross inter-organizational boundaries. The underlying network of controllers, processors, recipients, and third-parties contributing to a single data processing operation can therefore be characterized as (i) complex, (ii) dynamic, and (iii) multi-layered. As a result, each of the involved parties might not necessarily aware of the entire data processing chain, be it in terms of entities, data sets, or processing activities. For example, a controller may outsource some processing steps to a processor, who, in turn, delegates parts of its tasks to another sub-processor, and so on. The complexity of the processing operations does not, however, absolve the involved organizations of their responsibilities under the GDPR.

In this article, we argue that current DPIA approaches and tools, which focus exclusively on documenting the data processing activities from the point of view of a single organization, fall short of ensuring and maintaining an accurate, end-to-end view of complex data processing operations. In turn, inconsistencies and misalignment in the system representation and overall legal justifications leads to fragmented risk identification and to the implementation of inappropriate or inefficient countermeasures, and weakens the overall quality and relevance of the legal argumentation contained in a DPIA.

We discuss the main requirements for approaches that support (i) the collaborative description of data processing activities and (ii) the end-to-end assessment and mitigation of the risks stemming from the processing operations. Based on these requirements, we contrast two fundamentally different approaches—centralized versus federated—and discuss the technical challenges, advantages and disadvantages of each of them.

The remainder of this article is structured as follows. Section 2 shortly discusses the state of the art in tools and methods to support DPIA and motivates the paper. Then, Sect. 3 outlines the main requirements and concerns at play in the context of inter-organizational collaborations. Subsequently, Sect. 4 presents two distinct and contrasting architectural approaches paving the way for more integrated collaborative DPIA. Finally, Sect. 5 concludes the paper.

2   Background and Motivation

The very first step of a DPIA is the systematic description of the processing operations (i.e. its nature, scope, context, and purposes) [8] which then serves as the basis for (i) allocating responsibilities and (ii) identifying and mitigating the risks to the data subjects' rights and freedoms [17]. Many tools and methods have been developed to assist controllers when conducting DPIAs. These vary widely and take the form of mere textual guidance documents, questionnaires, checklists, and templates offered by National Supervisory Authorities (NSAs) [2, 6,26], sometimes integrated in tool support [13]. In addition to these soft-law instruments, researchers have also proposed more systematic methodologies and approaches to conduct such assessments [1,4,9,16,19–21], often reflecting on the development of appropriate tool support [14,15,27].

Besides solutions that focus exclusively on DPIAs, several initiatives have put forward a principled model-based approach as a means to explicitly frame data protection concerns. One example is prOnto [22], an ontology developed to capture the main concepts stemming from the GDPR as well as their relations, and that supports legal reasoning and compliance checking. In the same vein, CARiSMA [3] and APDL [5] both leverage annotations inserted in UML design models to establish a mapping between software artifacts (classes, methods) and their role in the data processing activities. Torre et al. [25], Tom et al. [24], and Sion et al. [23] have all proposed meta-models that constrain the construction of the system representation and, in some cases, also support the identification and mitigation of a wide range of issues, ranging from model completeness and soundness to legal assessments traditionally deployed in DPIAs.

Motivation. The above-mentioned methodologies and tools mainly focus on the description of the data processing activities from the perspective of a single entity—i.e. the controller or the processor. However, while the need to capture the broader context in which a given set of processing operations takes place is emphasized in all of them, little effective support exists for describing and maintaining a comprehensive overview of interrelated processing activities. As a result, each organization that plays a role in a complex, inter-organizational or federated collaboration will: (i) conduct its own, isolated DPIA and (ii) make assumptions about other organizations that contribute to the same processing activities. Failing to consider the entire chain of processing operations across the involved organization raises several legal issues.

First, it hinders the proper qualification of the involved entities as controllers or processors, which relies on the identification of the relevant processing operations and the assessment of their respective role. This creates uncertainties as to the allocation of responsibility for compliance and liability in case of a breach of law. This has been illustrated by the recent case law of the Court of Justice of the European Union (CJEU) when clarifying the notion of controllership in multi-entity setups [11,12].

Second, it makes it difficult to comply with the many obligations governing the relationship between all the entities involved in the data processing chain. Article 28(1) of the GDPR, for instance, obliges controllers to only use processors that provide sufficient guarantees on their compliance with the Regulation. In practice, doing so requires controllers to have an accurate, comprehensive understanding of the processing operations performed by their processors. The same goes for the appointment of a sub-processor by the processor, in which case the latter remains liable to the controller for any mistake made by the former (Art. 28(4) GDPR). A controller might, for instance, assume that its processor does not transfer personal data across regional borders but may be unaware that this processor itself utilizes IaaS or PaaS platforms hosted outside these border.

Finally, it confines the relevance and efficiency of the countermeasures to the processing operations performed by a single entity. End-to-end compliance with the principle of purpose limitation, for instance, would require that any entity processing personal data it has not collected itself (i) inherits the original purposes of the collection, and (ii) performs the compatibility assessment using the criteria listed in Article 6(4) GDPR and developed by the Article 29 WP [7].

While in practice, the establishment of such inter-organizational collaborations is governed by exhaustive contracting between these organizations, this process is manual, rigid, slow, and error-prone. More advanced methods and tools are required to support DPIA as an inter-organizational and collaborative effort in which each involved entity explicitly contributes to the DPIA, both in terms of the descriptive aspects, the construction of the legal argumentation and the overall risk assessment.

3 Requirements

Based on the issues outlined above, we distill a set of essential requirements that any approach for supporting the conduct of collaborative, federated DPIAs should meet.

R1 Consensus and consistency. The involved entities should reach consensus on a common description of the data processing steps, as well as the complementary legal argumentations (e.g. the proportionality of the processing or purpose compatibility), and the overall outcome of the compliance assessment. To accommodate this, inter-organizational assumptions should be made explicit to streamline the allocation of responsibilities and the exchange of knowledge. An important step in this context is to reach an agreement between the organizations involved in the personal data processing operations about the allocation of their responsibilities and liabilities.

R2 Controlled information sharing. Conversely, the involved entities should only be required to share the information that is strictly necessary to allow the conduct of a collaborative, end-to-end DPIA. In that sense, an individual organization should, for instance, be able to extend only the parts that pertain to its activities. This requirement is especially relevant when interrelated data processing activities involve competitors or organizations pursuing incompatible or opposing purposes.

R3 Holistic perspective. Rather than performing isolated DPIAs from their individual perspectives, the involved entities should consider the entire chain of organizations that contribute to interrelated data processing activities when conducting a DPIA. This will improve the robustness and consistency of the legal, technical, and organizational countermeasures implemented by each individual actor.

R4 Dynamism. As inter-organizational federations are highly likely to be dynamic, the involved description of processing operations should be easily modifiable and extendable, with support for frequent re-evaluation and for automated reporting towards the affected entities (e.g. involved organizations) or other stakeholders (e.g. data subjects, authorities) when new risks emerge or when existing liabilities are insufficiently covered as a result of changes.

As discussed in Sect. 2, current approaches require each of the involved entities to perform or contribute to a DPIA from its own, isolated perspective. This falls short of meeting the above-mentioned requirements since: (R1) it does not ensure that interrelated processing activities are consistently or completely addressed; (R2) it does not endorse nor support the systematic sharing of information between the involved entities; (R3) it does not consider the broader data processing chain in which a given set of processing operations takes place; and (R4) it does not allow modifications to the description, legal argumentation or assessment outcomes made by one entity to be reflected in those by other organizations in the same processing chain.

4   Approaches to Collaborative DPIA

The degree of *centralization* and the consequential necessity for a trusted third-party or a coordinating entity is a determining factor. While the controller could be a natural candidate for such a coordination role, such approach is inherently centralized as it still requires the trust from the other involved organizations. Moreover, it does not resolve the complexity in the case of joint controllership where multiple organizations bear responsibilities for a given set of processing operations, nor in cases where a single entity plays different roles depending on the processing at stake.

As such, we identify two fundamentally different approaches to align organizations' isolated perspectives on DPIAs, each representing an extreme in the spectrum between entire centralization and entire decentralization (*federation*). Figure 1 visualizes the differences between these architectural approaches. It depicts how the involved organizations describe their data processing operations, augmented with their legal argumentation (both expressed within a *description*, graphically represented as rectangles). The subsequential assessement activities (represented with a gear icon) then act upon these descriptions to assess the residual risks to the rights and freedoms of data subjects. As a final step, appropriate documentation that represent the tangible outcome of a federated DPIA exercise can be generated.

4.1 Centralized Approach

As depicted in Fig. 1a, the first approach is entirely centralized, in terms of (i) the management of the description of processing operations, (ii) the legal argumentation, and (iii) the overall compliance assessment. Each organization involved in the processing contributes to a common, shared model by providing their perspective on the processing operations and the information necessary for the other parties to ensure, among others, the proper allocation of responsibilities. This central representation provides a global and consistent perspective on the processing operations which is then used to conduct an end-to-end DPIA and for eventual reporting.

4.2 Federated Approach

In contrast, the second approach depicted in Fig. 1b is entirely decentralized and fully federated. Each organization involved in the processing individually describes and motivates its role only in collaboration with its direct peers within in the broader graph of interrelated activities. To ensure consensus and consistency between the representations used by all entities, fragments of their interactions (represented as dashed rectangles in Fig. 1b) are shared with the relevant organizations. The assessment itself involves a partial assessment conducted from the limited peer-to-peer perspective. These are then collected and combined with joint federated assessment steps to reach a global result across the involved organizations. The benefit of this approach is that it gives each organization flexibility in constructing their own representation of the processing operations and provides more control over what data is exactly shared – there is less dependence on trust. Such an approach, however, icomplicates the performance of the joint federated assessment and the decentralized executiuon of a holistic assessment.

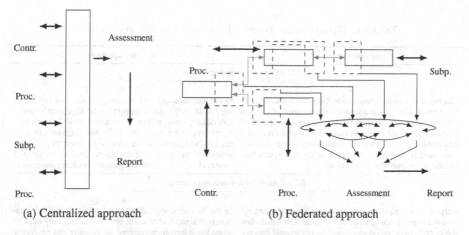

(a) Centralized approach   (b) Federated approach

Fig. 1. Overview of the range of approaches, ranging from central (Fig. 1a) to fully federated (Fig. 1b). The □'s denote both the description of the processing operations and the related legal argumentation, the Π's represent the involved organizations, the ı's and l's the data protection risk assessment, and the Ø's the resulting DPIA reports. The ı's represent the partial collaborative assessments by each of the involved organizations.

4.3   Requirement Coverage

This section revisits each of the requirements listed above in Sect. 3 and discusses how they are addressed in the centralized and federated approach. Table 1 presents our assessment and discusses a number of key trade-offs in terms of complexity and trust.

The centralized approach better addresses R1 and R3 because the adoption of a single model forces consistency and consensus and, as a result, the outcome of the DPIA assessment itself is less fragmented since it can be conducted on the entire description at once. The federated approach, however, is better suited for R2 and R4 as organizations only have to disclose the details that pertain to the inter-organizational interactions. Furthermore, changes to the descriptions can be kept local and will not necessarily affect the other involved organizations in the processing.

As highlighted, both approaches represent the extremes in the spectrum between a fully centralized and a fully federated approach. However, the trade-offs discussed above will—to a certain extent—also apply to hybrid approaches. For example, an approach in which the factual description of data processing activities is centralized does not necessarily imply that the legal argumentations will be constructed collaboratively taking into account the individual perspective of each of the involved entities.

Table 1. Requirement trade-offs involved in the approches.

Centralized approach	Federated approach
R1 – Consensus and consistency	
+	=
The use of a central representation forces the involved organizations to agree upon a shared understanding of the processing operations. Responsibilities between the involved parties can be explicitly captured and allocated in the shared description (e.g. in term or organization roles). Explicit agreement is required on the parts of the description that involve more than one organization.	In the federated approach, reaching a consensus and ensuring consistency requires support for the alignment between individual parties, as there is no central, shared description of the processing operations. Individual fragments on how the involved parties interact with their direct peers in the context of the processing operations have to be mapped onto each other and made compatible to ensure consistency.
R2 – Controlled information sharing	
=	+
Relying on a central description of the data processing operations requires fine-grained access control to ensure that the contributions of organizations do not exceed descriptions that are out of their scope of operations and to avoid organizations from sharing an unnecessary amount of information with other organizations (e.g., internal details on the concrete security and privacy measures in place). Managing and enforcing these access control restrictions involves some additional overhead to enforce.	In the federated approach, control of the shared information is straightforward as the involved parties only need to share the information required for aligning and analyzing the global data processing operations, and only with their direct peer organizations. Further details on their own processing operations do not need to be shared. Identifying and extracting the relevant information to share with the other entities can, however, require additional processing of the description of the processing operations.
R3 – Holistic perspective	
+	=
Since the centralized approach yields a single, shared representation of the processing activities, the compliance assessments traditionally deployed in a DPIA can be performed while taking the perspective of all the concerned entities into account. In turn, this supports the implementation of robust, cross-organizational countermeasures.	The federated approach requires coordination of assessment activities, as these first requires reconstructing a global view on the data processing operations from the fragments shared by the involved organizations. Alternatively, the involved parties can perform a federated analysis of the data processing operations and share the outcome of their own analysis to serve as input for the end-to-end DPIA.
R4 – Dynamism	
-	+
Any change in the modalities of the data processing operations has to be captured in the description shared between all the participating organizations. This may introduce additional overhead as smaller local modifications that do not affect any of the other organizations all need to be reflected in the central descriptions. Individual assessments by the participating organizations are not possible unless the organization duplicates some of its effort by re-creating the description of the processing operations locally.	The federated approach is very flexible, as it does not require any party to centrally collect the information on all data processing operations. Instead, any organization can locally extend and expand the description of its own processing activities. As long as such extensions do not impact the other parties, a global re-assessment is not needed. The federated assessment may involve interactions with new parties as (sub-)processors are introduced by any of the existing organizations involved in the processing chain.
Inherent complexity	
+	-
Simplicity in deployment (client-server system), centralized access control, centralized coordination, versioning, and conflict management of descriptions.	Complex deployment (peer-to-peer system), controlled information sharing, decentralized coordination, versioning, and consistency and conflict management.
Trust model	
-	+
Necessary dependency on a trusted third party (TTP) to manage the descriptions, impose access control, guarantee consistency and consus, and provide support for the DPIA.	No dependency on a TTP, but on shared and immutable data structures such as distributed ledgers and shared infrastructure to execute smart contract-based logic in support of assessment and generation of accountability documentation.

5 Conclusion

In this paper, we have adopted the stance that current approaches to DPIA, which rely on each of the involved organizations to perform their own assessment in isolation, are inherently suboptimal, especially as contemporary data processing operations increasingly involve a multitude of stakeholders acting in different capacities ((joint) controllers, processors, sub-processors, third parties, recipients, etc.).

Furthermore, we have argued that addressing this problem requires an integrated approach that explicitly considers the perspectives of all parties involved in the processing operations as well as more principled support for the coordination and alignment of these aspects. Despite the wide range of solutions available to assist in modeling and analyzing data processing operations, none of them explicitly considers the inter-organizational aspects of the processing operations and, hence, supports the performance of a comprehensive, end-to-end data protection impact assessment.

Against this backdrop, we have then elicited and discussed four key requirements inter-organizational approaches to DPIA should cover, and have provided an in-depth comparison between a fully centralized and a fully federated solution taking the above-mentioned criteria as well as their inherent technical challenges into account.

In contrast to current approaches that are heavily contract-based and thus rather static in nature, it is the main tenet of this paper that more dynamic assessment tools and platforms are needed to address the complexity of emerging distributed and federated systems such as smart IoT-based ecosystems, e-health applications, big data analytics, and data marketplaces. It is a key challenge in our ongoing work to establish and evaluate methods and techniques that implement this vision, on the interdisciplinary intersection between legal and software engineering research.

Acknowledgments. This research is partially funded by the Research Fund KU Leuven and the PRiSE research project.

References

1. Agarwal, S., Steyskal, S., Antunovic, F., Kirrane, S.: Legislative compliance assessment: framework, model and GDPR instantiation. In: Medina, M., Mitrakas, A., Rannenberg, K., Schweighofer, E., Tsouroulas, N. (eds.) APF 2018. LNCS, vol. 11079, pp. 131–149. Springer, Cham (2018). https://doi.org/10.1007/978-3-030-02547-2_8
2. Agencia Española de protección de datos (AEPD): Guía práctica para las Evaluaciones de Impacto en la Protección de los datos sujetas al RGPD (2018)
3. Ahmadian, A.S., Jürjens, J., Strüber, D.: Extending model-based privacy analysis for the industrial data space by exploiting privacy level agreements. In: Proceedings of ACM SAC 2018: PDP (2018)

4. Alnemr, R., et al.: A data protection impact assessment methodology for cloud. In: Berendt, B., Engel, T., Ikonomou, D., Le Métayer, D., Schiffner, S. (eds.) APF 2015. LNCS, vol. 9484, pp. 60–92. Springer, Cham (2016). https://doi.org/10.1007/978-3-319-31456-3_4

5. Alshammari, M., Simpson, A.: Towards a principled approach for engineering privacy by design. In: Schweighofer, E., Leitold, H., Mitrakas, A., Rannenberg, K. (eds.) APF 2017. LNCS, vol. 10518, pp. 161–177. Springer, Cham (2017). https://doi.org/10.1007/978-3-319-67280-9_9

6. APD: Recommandation n° 01/2018 du 28 février 2018 concernant l'analyse d'impact relative à la protection des données et la consultation préalable (2018). https://www.autoriteprotectiondonnees.be/sites/privacycommission/files/documents/recommandation_01_2018.pdf

7. Article 29 Working Party: Opinion 03/2013 on purpose limitation (WP203) (2013)

8. Article 29 Working Party: Guidelines on data protection impact assessment (DPIA) (WP248 rev.01) (2017)

9. Bieker, F., Friedewald, M., Hansen, M., Obersteller, H., Rost, M.: A process for data protection impact assessment under the European general data protection regulation. In: Schiffner, S., Serna, J., Ikonomou, D., Rannenberg, K. (eds.) APF 2016. LNCS, vol. 9857, pp. 21–37. Springer, Cham (2016). https://doi.org/10.1007/978-3-319-44760-5_2

10. Christofi, A., et al.: Smart city privacy: enhancing collaborative transparency in the regulatory ecosystem. In: 2019 CTTE-FITCE: Smart Cities Information and Communication Technology (CTTE-FITCE), pp. 1–5 (2019)

11. C.J.E.U.: C-210/16 Unabhängiges Landeszentrum für Datenschutz Schleswig-Holstein v Wirtschaftsakademie Schleswig-Holstein GmbH, June 2018

12. C.J.E.U.: C-40/17 Fashion ID GmbH & Co.KG v Verbraucherzentrale NRW eV, July 2019

13. CNIL: PIA: Analyse d'impact sur la protection des données (privacy impact assessment). Commission Nationale de l'Informatique et des Libertés (2018)

14. Coles, J., Faily, S., Ki-Aries, D.: Tool-supporting data protection impact assessments with CAIRIS. In: 2018 IEEE 5th International Workshop on Evolving Security & Privacy Requirements Engineering (ESPRE), pp. 21–27. IEEE, Banff, August 2018

15. Dashti, S., Ranise, S.: A tool-assisted methodology for the data protection impact assessment. In: 16th International Joint Conference on e-Business and Telecommunications-International Conference on Security and Cryptography (SECRYPT 2019), vol. 2, pp. 276–283 (2019)

16. De, S.J., Le Métayer, D.: PRIAM: a privacy risk analysis methodology. In: Livraga, G., Torra, V., Aldini, A., Martinelli, F., Suri, N. (eds.) DPM/QASA -2016. LNCS, vol. 9963, pp. 221–229. Springer, Cham (2016). https://doi.org/10.1007/978-3-319-47072-6_15

17. Dewitte, P., et al.: A comparison of system description models for data protection by design. In: Proceedings of ACM SAC: PDP (2019)

18. European Union: Regulation (EU) 2016/679 of the European Parliament and of the Council of 27 April 2016. Official Journal of the EU (2016)

19. Makri, E.-L., Georgiopoulou, Z., Lambrinoudakis, C.: A proposed privacy impact assessment method using metrics based on organizational characteristics. In: Katsikas, S., et al. (eds.) CyberICPS/SECPRE/SPOSE/ADIoT -2019. LNCS, vol. 11980, pp. 122–139. Springer, Cham (2020). https://doi.org/10.1007/978-3-030-42048-2_9

20. Martin, N., Friedewald, M., Schiering, I., Mester, B., Hallinan, D., Jensen, M.: The Data Protection Impact Assessment According to Article 35 GDPR - A Practitioner's Manual (2020). https://www.isi.fraunhofer.de/en/presse/2020/presseinfo-08-Handbuc-DSFA.html

21. Oetzel, M.C., Spiekermann, S.: A systematic methodology for privacy impact assessments: a design science approach. Eur. J. Inf. Syst. **23**(2), 126–150 (2014)

22. Palmirani, M., Martoni, M., Rossi, A., Bartolini, C., Robaldo, L.: Legal ontology for modelling GDPR concepts and norms. In: JURIX, pp. 91–100 (2018)

23. Sion, L., et al.: An architectural view for data protection by design. In: 2019 IEEE International Conference on Software Architecture (ICSA), pp. 11–20, March 2019

24. Tom, J., Sing, E., Matulevičius, R.: Conceptual representation of the GDPR: model and application directions. In: Zdravkovic, J., Grabis, J., Nurcan, S., Stirna, J. (eds.) BIR 2018. LNBIP, vol. 330, pp. 18–28. Springer, Cham (2018). https://doi.org/10.1007/978-3-319-99951-7_2

25. Torre, D., Soltana, G., Sabetzadeh, M., Briand, L.C., Auffinger, Y., Goes, P.: Using models to enable compliance checking against the GDPR: an experience report. In: 22nd International Conference on Model Driven Engineering Languages and Systems (MODELS) (2019)

26. ULD: The standard data protection model: a concept for inspection and consultation on the basis of unified protection goals (2017)

27. Zibuschka, J.: Analysis of automation potentials in privacy impact assessment processes. In: Katsikas, S., et al. (eds.) CyberICPS/SECPRE/SPOSE/ADIoT -2019. LNCS, vol. 11980, pp. 279–286. Springer, Cham (2020). https://doi.org/10.1007/978-3-030-42048-2_18

Systematic Scenario Creation for Serious Security-Awareness Games

Vera Hazilov[1] and Sebastian Pape[2,3(✉)] (iD)

[1] Intero Operations and Services GmbH (INOS), Munich, Germany
[2] Chair of Mobile Business and Multilateral Security, Goethe University Frankfurt,
Frankfurt, Germany
sebastian.pape@m-chair.de
[3] Social Engineering Academy GmbH, Frankfurt, Germany

Abstract. While social engineering is still a recent threat, many organisations only address it by using traditional trainings, penetration tests, standardized security awareness campaigns or serious games. Existing research has shown that methods for raising employees' awareness are more effective if adjusted to their target audience. For that purpose, we propose the creation of specific scenarios for serious games by considering specifics of the respective organisation. Based on the work of Faily and Flechais [11], who created personas utilizing grounded theory, we demonstrate how to develop a specific scenario for HATCH [4], a serious game on social engineering. Our method for adapting a scenario of a serious game on social engineering resulted in a realistic scenario and thus was effective. Since the method is also very time-consuming, we propose future work to investigate if the effort can be reduced.

Keywords: Serious game · Security awareness · Personas · Scenario creation

1 Introduction

Social engineering is older than the electronic age itself and is still a part of our life. The European Network and Information Security Agency, ENISA, defines social engineering as a technique that exploits human weaknesses and aims to manipulate people into breaking normal security procedures [21]. In most cases, maliciously motivated attackers aim to gain access to their victims' commercial, financial, sensitive or private information in order to use it against them or cause harm otherwise [2]. Social engineering's key elements are deception, exploitation and use of psychological tricks. Social engineering attacks represent a threat to individuals and organisations and often lead to some kind of financial losses.

However, most organisations have difficulties addressing this issue adequately. According to Kevin Mitnick – a former hacker who now works as an IT security consultant, most companies rather purchase heavily standardized security products, such as firewalls or intrusion detection systems, than considering potential threats of social engineering attacks [19]. Mitnick criticizes this approach

I. Boureanu et al. (Eds.): ESORICS 2020 Workshops, LNCS 12580, pp. 294–311, 2020.
https://doi.org/10.1007/978-3-030-66504-3_18

and argues that technology-based products simply create an illusion of security however, leave organisations disarmed towards attacks that are directed towards their employees. Peltier [22] supports this argument and states that technology-based countermeasures should be applied whenever possible. However, he also claims that no hardware or software is able to protect an organization fully against social engineering attacks. In addition to that, social engineering is highly interdisciplinary, however most defense strategies are advised by IT security experts who rather have a background in information systems than psychology [26,27].

Traditional trainings mainly focus on transfer of knowledge and often do not address employees' attitude towards security or raise their awareness sufficiently. While knowledge is a prerequisite to counter social engineering attacks, a successful defense also requires a sufficient security-aware culture among staff [1], which represents a challenge for many organisations. Mainly because security policies are often in a bad shape and rather inform employees about what not to do than providing any guidance about desired behaviour and outcomes. Penetration tests are attached to a lot of obligations and legal burdens that need to be resolved beforehand. They can demotivate employees, who as a consequence might give up on defending social engineering attacks at all, and usually can not be repeated regularly, because employees become aware of penetration testers [9]. Security awareness campaigns often fail because they evoke negative feelings such as anxiety, fear or stress and are therefore often ineffective. In addition to that, individuals generally dislike following advice or instructions because it is associated with losing control. Lastly, awareness campaigns often provide only information about risks, are often not engaging, interesting and entertaining enough and therefore fail to change individuals' behavior [3]. Serious games however, are more entertaining and engaging than traditional forms of learning and can influence individuals' behavior due to their use of pedagogy and game-based learning principles, such as motivation, cognitive apprenticeship and constructivism [10]. They have demonstrated a potential in industrial education and training disciplines [23,25] if respective organizations care for players' privacy and working atmosphere [16], do not use gaming data for appraisal or selection purposes and clearly communicate this to the employees [17]. Abawajy's observations [1], that trainings can be greatly enhanced through interactive content, support this statement and make serious games a strong candidate for overcoming issues of traditional training methods.

However, not only for security awareness campaigns, but also for serious games it is important to address the target audience as specific as possible. Therefore, in this paper, we aim to adjust a serious game to a specific target group by adapting it accordingly. For that purpose we chose the serious game HATCH [5] and developed a new scenario for one of its variants in order to be suitable for consulting companies. This approach tackles that problem, that although many serious games for IT security exist, it is still hard to find a accurately fitting serious game for a specific organisation or scenario.

2   Background and Related Work

This work is based on two concepts, personas and HATCH. Personas represent a popular technique that is often used in user-centered design in order to create services, products or software [24]. HATCH is a serious game on social engineering, for which we have developed a scenario as proof of concept. However, hardly any specific properties of the game were used, so it should be possible to generalise the results and develop scenarios for related games.

2.1   Personas

By definition, personas are imaginary however, realistic descriptions of stakeholders or future users of a service or product, who have names, jobs, feelings, goals, certain needs and requirements [11]. The concept was firstly introduced by Cooper [7] in 1999. Cooper argues that developers need to consider future users' needs, goals and wishes, instead of designing products for 'elastic users'. The latter term represents highly standardized descriptions of users, which are unrealistic and in many cases rather represent developers' own needs. According to Cooper, the use of elastic users therefore leads to products, which only partly satisfy real users' needs.

In 2011, Faily and Flechais [11] introduced a method for developing personas that is based on grounded theory. The latter is a "[...] systematic, yet flexible guideline for collecting and analyzing qualitative data" [6]. Faily and Flechais [11] collected necessary data through interviews, each of them lasting approximately an hour. All interviews have been transcribed and subjects to a grounded theory analysis using ATLAS.ti, a qualitative data analysis and research tool. The process of developing personas included three steps [11]: the first step includes reading all interview transcripts, identifying relevant text passages, assigning appropriate phrases (codes) to them and formulating them as propositions. The propositions are later summarized and as a result represent most significant concepts developed personas need to explore. As next, appropriate propositions are selected and stated as potential characteristic of a persona. The final step of this approach involves selecting relevant characteristics and writing a persona narrative. Faily and Flechais [11] used their approach successfully to derive accurate archetypes of their respective user communities (personas) from around 300 quotations and 90 thematic concepts.

2.2   HATCH

Hack and Trick Capricious Humans (HATCH) is a physical (tabletop) serious game on social engineering [4,5]. The game is available in two versions, a real life scenario and a generic version. Each version of the game pursues a slightly different objective: The real life scenario is aiming to derive social engineering security requirements of a company or one of its departments. Therefore, a real environment is modelled and players attack their colleagues in order to identify real attack vectors. The generic version of the game aims to raise players' awareness for social engineering threats and educate them on detecting this kind of attacks. In order not to unnecessarily expose and blame colleagues during a training session, it is based on a virtual scenario with personas as attack victims [16]. The scenario consists of a layout of a medium-sized office and ten personas, which are fictional descriptions of employees. All of which are printed on cards and contain information such as this employee's name, role, familiarization with computers and attitude towards security and privacy [5].

In both versions two deck of cards are used (psychological principles and social engineering attacks). When playing the game, each player draws one psychological principle card and three social engineering attack cards and reads the respective descriptions. Psychological principle cards state and describe human behaviors or patterns that are often exploited by social engineers, as for example: 'Distraction - While you distract your victims by whatever retains their interests, you can do anything to them'. On the other hand, the social engineering cards name and define some of the most common social engineering attacks, for example dumpster diving, which is 'the act of analyzing documents and other things in a garbage bin of an organization to reveal sensitive information'. Each player has then the task to choose a victim[1] which fits to the psychological principle card and elaborate an attack by using one of the social engineering attack cards which matches the victim and psychological principle best.

Players take turns to reveal their cards and describe the social engineering attack they came up with. Other players discuss the proposed attack and award points for attack's feasibility and viability and rate if it is compliant with descriptions of this player's cards. The total score of each player is calculated by the end of the group rating and the player with the highest score wins the game. At the end of the game, all players briefly reflect on proposed social engineering attacks and derive potential security threats.

Beckers and Pape [4] showed that the real life scenario was helpful to increase the security awareness of employees [5] and in the elicitation of context-specific attacks by utilizing the domain knowledge of the players and their observations and knowledge about daily work and processes.

3 Methodology

The data that was used to develop a consulting services scenario for HATCH was collected through expert interviews, which have proven to be of good practical value [18]. The interviews were executed as semi-structured interviews based on the interview guide described in Sect. 3.1. Section 3.2 describes the interviewees and Sect. 3.3 the subsequent coding and qualitative analysis.

3.1 Interview Guide

Meuser and Nagel [18] emphasize the importance of using an interview guide. In particular for semi-structured interviews they serve two purposed. On the one

---

[1] Depending on the version either a colleague or a persona.

hand, they help the interviewer to not get lost in irrelevant topics and focus on the goal of the interview [12]. On the other hand, they help the interviewer to organize and structure the interviews and adapt them to knowledge gained in previous interviews [20].

The interview guide was constructed taking following aspects into consideration:

- the appropriate number of questions – although a large number of questions might provide deeper insights, too many questions can also extend the interview to an inefficient level. In alignment the suggestion from Gläser and Laudel [13] to limit the number of questions to approximately fifteen, the derived interview guide consists of seventeen questions.
- appropriate format of questions – asked questions can be noted as fully formulated sentences which provides stability or stated vaguely which increases interviewer's flexibility to react ad hoc [13]
- appropriate content of questions, which means that asked questions can be based on existing theories, publications or interviewer's own experience or knowledge [12].

The interview guide was tested within two one-hour interview sessions. At the end of each session, interviewed experts were asked to provide feedback regarding the guide's length, format and content. The initial interview guide was adopted during the process based on received feedback: an explanation of this work's main objective and approach was added to the introduction section. The interview guide's second section was extended by a definition of the term social engineering for the purposes of general introduction. All remaining sections stayed unchanged and aim to uncover this industry's specifics, assets, communication channels, their physical location as well as existing roles, skills and attitudes towards security and privacy. Table 1 gives a brief overview of the interview guide's structure.

3.2   Interview Implementation and Participants

All nine expert interviews were conducted in January and February 2017 and lasted between 35 min and 61 min (cf. Table 2). All interviews were conducted in German –the experts' native language in order not to obstruct experts' thinking ability and allow them to provide complex and comprehensive answers. Most interviews were conducted face-to-face, only interview seven and eight were recorded over the phone. None of the participants received any printed information, such as handouts or printouts, before or during the interview in order to avoid any distraction. However, before the interviews, participants were informed about the study's approach and goal and asked for consent as indicated in Table 1. Table 2 presents an overview of all participants, their role, professional experience, corresponding business unit and the interview's duration.

Due to difficulties of cold calling professional consultants and requesting their help for creating a serious game scenario, all participating interviewees were approached based on existing contacts. Furthermore, none of the approached

Table 1. Interview guide

#	Section	Content
1	Introduction	• Greeting and opening • Statement of classification • Declaration of consent • Introduction to the research's approach and main goal
2	Social engineering	• General understanding • Definition • Previous experience with SE attacks
3	Industry's specifics	• General understanding • Associations • Characteristics
4	Assets & location	• Company's assets and employees • Asset's location
5	Roles & tasks	• Specific roles • Responsibilities and tasks
6	Communication channels	• Company's communication channels • Management process • Access rights • Relevant content
7	Personas	• Skills • Knowledge • Attitude towards security and privacy

employees of a 'client company' were willing to participate, since they were afraid of revealing sensitive information which could potentially lead to a social engineering attack. However, we do not think that this was a major drawback, since the developed scenario aimed to focus on consulting companies.As a consequence, all interviewed experts have in common that they are employed by a large consulting/auditing firm, however differ in their roles, business units, gender, age and level of professional experience. The experts' selection was done in order to introduce a certain level of variety, however contain a strong focus at the same time: We expected that a more unified selection of participants would have resulted in a highly specific scenario, while a too diverse selection of experts may have yielded unfocused results.

3.3   Data Analysis

All interviews were audio recorded, transcribed literally[2], and all transcripts were imported into MAXQDA, a professional software for qualitative text analysis, and coded in chronological order. The applied process of coding consisted of two rounds, open and axial coding. While open coding is the process of reading

---

[2] Pauses and certain sounds were neglected such as 'huh' etc.

Table 2. Participants overview

#	Role	Experience	Business unit	Duration
1	Consultant	1–3 years	Management consulting	61 min
2	Consultant	1–3 years	Risk consulting	54 min
3	Consultant	6+ years	Technology consulting	55 min
4	Consultant	3–6 years	Technology consulting	35 min
5	Assistant	1–3 years	Management consulting	37 min
6	IT	1–3 years	Technology consulting	60 min
7	Consultant	3–6 years	Technology consulting	35 min
8	Consultant	6+ years	Technology consulting	59 min
9	Consultant	6+ years	Technology consulting	46 min

Fig. 1. Process of axial coding

textual data line-by-line, identifying certain phenomena within it and attaching adequate phrases (e. g. codes) to it, axial coding represents the process of examining previously assigned codes, identifying certain relationships among them and summarizing them into concepts and categories [8]. This work's coding process is illustrated in Fig. 1.

The illustration above shows a fraction of all text passages that have been assigned with the code 'project work' and later formulated into propositions 'projects are limited in their duration and therefore can lead to time pressure' and 'revenues are generated through selling projects to clients'. All relevant propositions were later summarized to the concept 'project work' and assigned to the category 'industry's specifics'. Following this approach, 110 pages of interview transcripts were assigned with 509 codes.

3.4   Development of the Scenario

Since we took HATCH for granted, as it already existed before, we do not describe its development, however focus on the creation of a new scenario. Figure 2 illustrates the steps of the scenario development.

In the previous sections, we have already described the interview, transcript and coding phases (stage 1 to 3). Following Faily and Flechais' method [11] for developing personas, we developed propositions from codes (stage 4), such as '
more consultants are hired for project than clients', 'with the exception of client's assistants, consultants are generally younger' and 'generally, the consulting team consists of 4 to 5 people'. These propositions were summarized, assigned to concepts and categorized (stage 5). For example, previous propositions were assigned to the concepts 'role' and 'age' and categorized as 'personas'. Altogether 21 concepts were sorted into five categories, which represent the main components of the consulting services scenario for HATCH. Those categories are: industry's specifics, assets, communication channels, location and personas. The first four of them represent a consulting firm's working environment, while the last embodies personas' characteristics.

As the last step, appropriate propositions were selected and stated as potential characteristics of a persona to write persona narratives and develop the scenario (stage 6). For this purpose, all personas-related concepts and propositions were reviewed again, in order to identify most valuable and meaningful insights, and later embodied into future personas. For example, the propositions from the concepts 'roles' and 'age' lead to the decision of having more consulting personas (4) than personas of the client company (3). Furthermore, with the exception of the client's assistant, all consulting personas are younger than personas of the client. In the same manner, propositions were used to develop professional consultants' working environment and surroundings.

3.5 Evaluation

Note that this work focuses on creating a new scenario in order to adapt an existing game called HATCH, which has already been evaluated [4,5]. Therefore, we did not evaluate the game, its rules and elements itself, however rather focused on evaluating the consulting services scenario.

The developed consulting services scenario for HATCH was evaluated by five players and within two sessions: the first session was conducted on 30th of March 2017 and lasted roughly one hundred minutes, while the second session took place on March 31st, 2017 and continued approximately two hours. One moderator was present at both sessions and all players had an IT background, were employed by an auditing/consulting firm. None of the players was involved in the previous interview sessions.

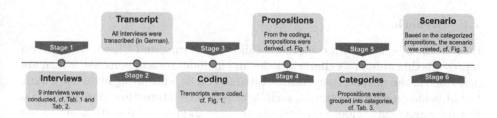

Fig. 2. Overview of scenario creation process

Table 3. Derived scenario related categories and concepts

#	Category	Concept
1	Industry's specifics	• Project work
		• Customer orientation
		• Change
2	Assets	• Information (sensitive, project-related, private)
		• Laptops
		• Phones
		• Emails
		• Prints, handouts
		• Documents (office)
3	Communication channels	• Face-to-face
		• Phone calls
		• Emails
		• Video conferences
		• Collaboration platforms
		• Prints, Handouts
4	Location	• Client's office
		• Remote locations
5	Personas	• Age
		• Roles and tasks
		• Skills and knowledge
		• Attitude towards security and privacy

4   Results

With the process described in the previous section, we derived five relevant categories with altogether 21 concepts as shown in Table 3. The industry's specifics, consultants' assets, communication channels and location are incorporated within the scenario, which represents working environment and surroundings of professional consultants. These companies' assets and communication channels are pictured at the top of the scenario, since their location might vary a lot between companies and we aimed to avoid a too strict mapping to an individual or a certain location (cf. Fig. 3a). The results from the personas category were used to create different persona cards as shown in Fig. 3b to Fig. 3d.

4.1   Scenario

Besides the layout of both companies, called Consulting and Client, the scenario represents this industry's characteristics and includes several personas, which are described in the next section. As illustrated in Fig. 3a, consulting firms use a number of communication channels, such as face-to-face interaction, phones, emails, instant messengers, video conferencing tools or Skype, collaboration platforms,

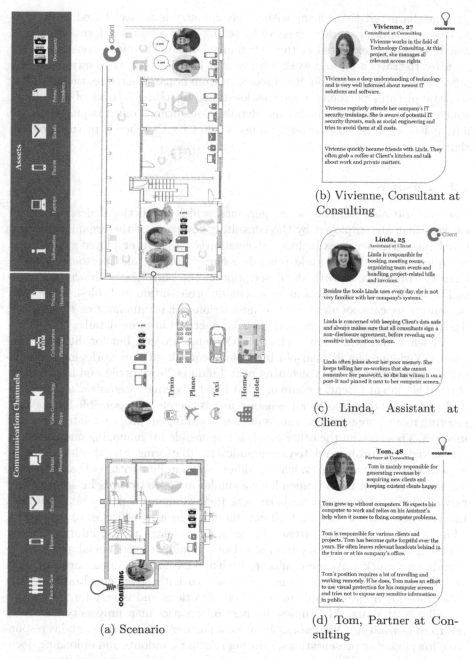

(a) Scenario

(b) Vivienne, Consultant at Consulting

Vivienne, 27
Consultant at Consulting

Vivienne works in the field of Technology Consulting. At this project, she manages all relevant access rights.

Vivienne has a deep understanding of technology and is very well informed about newest IT solutions and software.

Vivienne regularly attends her company's IT security trainings. She is aware of potential IT security threats, such as social engineering and tries to avoid them at all costs.

Vivienne quickly became friends with Linda. They often grab a coffee at Client's kitchen and talk about work and private matters.

(c) Linda, Assistant at Client

Linda, 25
Assistant at Client

Linda is responsible for booking meeting rooms, organizing team events and handling project-related bills and invoices.

Besides the tools Linda uses every day, she is not very familiar with her company's systems.

Linda is concerned with keeping Client's data safe and always makes sure that all consultants sign a non-disclosure agreement, before revealing any sensitive information to them.

Linda often jokes about her poor memory. She keeps telling her co-workers that she cannot remember her password, so she has written it on a post-it and pinned it next to her computer screen.

(d) Tom, Partner at Consulting

Tom, 48
Partner at Consulting

Tom is mainly responsible for generating revenues by acquiring new clients and keeping existent clients happy.

Tom grew up without computers. He expects his computer to work and relies on his Assistant's help when it comes to fixing computer problems.

Tom is responsible for various clients and projects. Tom has become quite forgetful over the years. He often leaves relevant handouts behind in the train or at his company's office.

Tom's position requires a lot of travelling and working remotely. If he does, Tom makes an effort to use visual protection for his computer screen and tries not to expose any sensitive information in public.

Fig. 3. Scenario and personas "consulting company"

prints, handouts and posses assets that are mostly focused around information: laptops, phones, emails, prints or handouts and Word, Excel or PowerPoint documents.

One characteristic of firms within this industry is project-based work. Consulting companies generate revenues by selling their services in form of projects, which are mostly executed at their customers' office. Therefore, consultants are required to travel a lot and work from various locations e.g. their own or client's office, public transportation, hotel rooms or from home. Therefore, the presented scenario pictures personas in various locations, including layouts of two offices, which contain several elements and details. Consulting's office is placed on the left, it has a kitchen and several rooms, while Client's office is pictured on the right.

4.2   Personas

The scenario also contains seven personas, which are fictional descriptions of workers that are employed by the consulting company or the organisation that hired them. All personas include information such as an employee's name, age, occupied role, tasks, attitude towards security/privacy and personality traits. Players will get cards with the description of the personas as shown in Fig. 3b to Fig. 3d. We also provide a more schematic presentation in Table 4. Since both presentations can not describe the interactions, the remainder of this section describes developed personas and their interactions in more detail.

Vivienne and Linda are working on the same project, but for different companies: Vivienne is a 27-year-old technology consultant and works for 'Consulting', a large auditing and consulting firm. Linda is 25 years old and has recently started her job at Client, a company that hired Vivienne's organization for a limited period. Linda works as an assistant and is therefore responsible for booking meeting rooms, organizing team events and handling all project-related bills and invoices. Vivienne, on the other hand, is responsible for managing and assigning access rights to project-related communication platforms. She also has a deeper understanding of technology, while Linda is only familiar with tools and systems she uses every day. Both women have a similar attitude towards IT security and privacy and are concerned with keeping their company's data safe. Therefore, Linda always makes sure that all consultants sign a non-disclosure agreement, while Vivienne regularly attends IT security trainings to get informed about potential IT security threats and risks. Both women are very social and became friends very quickly. As a consultant, Vivienne has strong communication skills and is comfortable with starting conversations with strangers. Linda, on the other hand, is friendly, tends to trust her co-workers and is very forgetful.

Niko is 21 years old, studies business informatics at a university and is an intern at Consulting. Niko works for Tom, a partner at Consulting, and is responsible for preparing presentations, printing relevant handouts and uploading documents for his boss. Niko loves computer games, currently learns how to program and is very ambitious. He wants to get everything right and on time, which often stresses him out. Whenever Niko is stressed, he tends to leave his computer unlocked and forgets to shred Tom's documents that often include sensitive information. As an intern, Niko is not required to travel and works form Consulting's office. Tom is often gone and Niko gets bored easily. In that case, he socializes with other interns and loves to chat about Tom's projects.

Table 4. Developed personas with a description of their (T)asks, (S)kills, (A)ttitude towards security and (P)ersonality

	Vivienne, 27, Consultant at Consulting
(T)	Works in the field of Technology Consulting, manages relevant access rights at this project
(S)	Has a deep understanding of technology, well informed about newest IT solutions and software
(A)	Attends her company's IT security training regularly, aware of potential IT security threats, such as social engineering, tries to avoid potential security threats at all costs
(P)	Communicative and open minded, quickly became friends with Linda, often grabs a coffee at Client's kitchen to catch up with Linda

	Linda, 25, Assistant at Client
(T)	Responsible for booking meeting rooms, organizing team events and handling project-related bills and invoices
(S)	Familiar with tools she uses every day, not very familiar with any other of her company's systems
(A)	Concerned with keeping her company's data safe, ensures all consultants sign a non-disclosure agreement
(P)	Forgetful,trustworthy towards her co-workers, tells her co-workers that she cannot remember her password

	Barbara, 44, Project Lead at Consulting
(T)	Plans, coordinates and controls the project at Client, responsible for informing the sponsor of the project about its current state
(S)	Has 16+ years of experience
(A)	As a project lead, she has access to every room at Client's office, concerned with keeping any client or project-relevant data safe
(P)	Required to travel a lot, spends four days a week on a project at her client's office, works from home or at her company's office on Fridays

	Hans, 56, Head of IT at Client
(T)	Ensures Client's systems run smoothly, updates security features, checks if access rights are assigned correctly
(S)	Knows his company's systems very well
(A)	IT security has the highest priority, spends hours getting informed about potential IT risks and how they can be prevented
(P)	Passionate about his job, launched an anti-social engineering campaign at Client, informs his colleagues about adequate security behavior

	Tom, 48, Partner at Consulting
(T)	Responsible for generating revenues by acquiring new clients, makes sure existent clients are happy, supervises various clients and projects
(S)	Grew up without computers, expects his computer to work, relies on his assistant's help when it comes to fixing computer problems
(A)	Tries not to expose any sensitive information in public or while working remotely, makes an effort to use visual protection for his computer screen
(P)	Forgetful, often leaves relevant handouts behind, travels a lot due to his position

	Gabriele, 64, Project Sponsor at Client
(T)	Responsible for allocating resources efficiently, ensures projects are executed on time
(S)	Familiar with the tools she uses a lot, not very familiar with the tools she doesn't use regularly
(A)	Careful about revealing her company's information to any of the consultants
(P)	Not very trusting towards consultants, often has a hard time understanding their recommendations

	Niko, 21, Intern at Consulting
(T)	Responsible for preparing presentations, printing handouts and uploading relevant documents online
(S)	Studies business informatics, has a good understanding of IT due to his studies at a university, is learning how to program
(A)	Not aware of potential IT security threats, not very concerned with revealing sensitive data or information
(P)	New to the consulting industry, ambitious and therefore often stressed and forgetful

Tom has been with the company for more than eighteen years and is 48 years old. As a partner at Client, he is responsible for generating revenues by acquiring new projects and clients and making sure that existing clients are happy, which requires him to travel a lot. He just left his office and is currently on his way to Client. Over the last couple of years, Tom has become forgetful and started to leave printed documents behind. Tom often works remotely and always tries to get as much work done as possible. He often participates in conference calls with his colleague Barbara and employees of Client, Hans and Gabriele. Barbara is 44, has more than 16 years of professional experience and works at Consulting as a project lead. She takes her role very seriously and is responsible for planning, coordinating and reporting this project's current status to Gabriele. Barbara is concerned with keeping any client or project-relevant data safe and, like most professional consultants, spends four days a week at Client's office. On Fridays, she either works from home or her company's office.

Gabriele is 64 years old and the CFO of Client. She is responsible for allocating her company's resources efficiently and ensures that all projects are executed on time. Due to her background in finance, Gabriele knows everything about Client's financial IT tools and systems. However, she is not very familiar with any other tools at Client. She is also very cautious about revealing her company's information to any of the consultants, especially after she started working with Hans. Hans is 56 years old and Client's Head of IT. He has dedicated his life to his department and makes sure that all systems run smoothly and Client's security features are up to date at all times. Hans knows all of his company's systems very well and often checks if all access rights were assigned correctly. IT security has the highest priority for Hans, he spends hours researching potential IT threats and how they can be prevented. He has just launched an anti-social engineering campaign at Client and uses every chance to inform his colleagues about adequate security behavior.

Today, Vivienne is not required to take part in this meeting. She often works from Client's kitchen and grabs a coffee with Linda. The two have been getting along great. Linda is always excited to catch up with Vivienne, grab a cup of coffee and have a chat about work and personal matters.

5   Evaluation

In this section, we describe the evaluation process of the scenario. It was used to evaluate our methodology's outcome, since the quality of the developed scenario and personas is the main goal of the proposed method.

The evaluation sessions were structured as follows: the participants of the session were introduced to this work's main goal, the development of a consulting services scenario for HATCH, and shown a video about social engineering in order to clarify the term social engineering, its key elements and techniques. Subsequently, any emerged questions were answered and all participants were introduced to HATCH, the game's rules, scoring sheet, scenario and personas. Next, HATCH was played according to its rules, ensuring that each player at least takes three turns. At the end of each session, all participants were first briefly asked about the game itself to prevent that a misunderstanding of the elements and rules of HATCH would influence scenario's evaluation. We then asked the players to evaluate the scenario, particularly in regards to its comprehension, completeness and closeness to reality. The provided feedback was audio recorded and subsequently analyzed.

We did not aim to evaluate HATCH's rules, game elements or mechanics and wanted to ensure that participants of the evaluation session are not distracted from the consulting services scenario. Therefore, HATCH was not elaborated any further after the participants claimed that its rules and key elements were clear and easy to understand.

In regards to HATCH's scenario, all participants agreed and stated that the represented consulting services scenario and personas are intuitive[3], easy to understand[4] and very realistic[5]. When asked for an extension of the scenario, participants suggested that the presented scenario could be extended by additional personas. While participants of the first evaluation round suggested to include an office administrator or a receptionists, members of the second session argued for adding an external service provider such as security or a cleaning personnel[6].

6 Discussion

In this section, we first discuss the results of the evaluation, followed by considerations how the presented approach can be applied in future scenarios. At the end of this section, we discuss limitations of our research.

6.1 Scenario

Reflecting the feedback of the evaluation session, it is necessary to discuss if the created consulting services scenario should be extended by additional personas, such as an office administrator, receptionist, cleaning or security personnel. On the one hand, additional personas could potentially enrich the scenario and make the serious security-awareness game more engaging and fun. On the other hand, too many personas within the scenario increase its level of complexity, make the game more difficult to play, since players need more time to go through the persona descriptions.

---

[3] [ES1: 1:38] "The description of the different people is very intuitive and very simply [...] modeled, also because of the figure. You could recognise it [...] very clearly".

[4] [ES2: 2:46] "Persons were described clearly and very realistic. I am able to imagine exactly how the person might be in real life, because these different types of people really exist".

[5] [ES1: 5:35] "The scenario was definitely realistic and also the [...] markers are intuitive".

[6] [ES2: 04:10] "if I am an outsider and I somehow sneak into the office, I still have to pass some [...] security guard or receptionist, that is still an upstream step, which should also be considered, I think".

Therefore, firstly we recommend including a justified and reasonable number of personas within a scenario. For example, a guard and a cleaner both represent employees of an external service provider over whom the two companies have only limited authority. Including these personas within the scenario might not contribute too much to raising employees' awareness, however will likely result in requests for establishing a security policy for externals (if not already in place). However, if they are included, it might be a reasonable trade-off to only include one or the other.

Secondly, we suggest summarizing similar roles, tasks, skill sets and attitudes towards security or privacy in one persona wherever possible. For example, receptionists and office administrators perform very similar tasks, such as handling incoming calls, arranging meetings, planning events, organizing meeting rooms and handling invoices and expenses, and therefore might resemble in their daily tasks and IT skills. However, it is also very likely that administrators/receptionists of different companies differ in their attitudes towards privacy and security. Considering all arguments, for the next version, we would extend the presented scenario by two additional personas: an administrator/receptionist who is employed by each of the respective companies, Consulting and Client.

As our study was done in 2017, we also considered the changes within the consulting industry, for example that the number of female consultants has increased [15], which is already at a reasonable level within our scenario.

6.2   Methodology

The feedback of the evaluation sessions also allows a second conclusion: the applied method for creating a scenario for a serious security-awareness game was successful, since all participants agreed that the scenario and its personas are intuitive, easy to understand and very realistic. However, since the applied method is very time-consuming and requires a lot of effort, it only makes sense under certain circumstances. One use case is, if the respective company plans to play the game on a regular basis or with a large number of players. Another use case of the derived scenario is, while being specific being generic enough to be used by other organization within the same industry (here: consulting).

6.3   Threats to Validity and Limitations

All participating interviewees were approached based on existing contacts, which could lead to a selection bias. The latter was a consequence that trials to attract 'external' consultants for interviews without payment failed, since we did not have any funding. However, the participating interviewees still had diverse properties such as position, age, gender, etc. Furthermore, it could be argued that only nine interviews were conducted. However, even within nine interviews, we could observe some satiation manifesting in a repetition of answers and similar views and statements of the experts. In the same manner, since there is no clear definition of the term 'expert' in this context, one could question our sampling. However, according to the definition of Meuser and Nagel [18], experts are individuals who carry specific knowledge, emphasizing with the term 'specific' that the knowledge should not reflect everyday knowledge or common sense. Thus, despite experts were chosen purely based on the judgement of this work's authors, since they all work in an consulting company, they share specific knowledge about day-to-day work and processes, and therefore can be considered as experts and appropriate participants for our study.

In addition to that, it could be argued that this work's findings are not reliable, since the interview and coding process (open and axial coding), was done in two different languages: Interviews and open coding was done in German, all propositions were later summarized in English. However, we still assume that executing the interviews in the interviewees' native language is beneficial for the outcome and the translation at the end does not harm the result.

Furthermore, received answers during interviews and evaluation sessions might be subject to response biases, since we can not rule out that interviewed participants answered what they assumed the interviewer wants to hear or is socially acceptable. We tried to address that by not using any triggering terms and did not push for a response, allowing the interviewees a way out by not answering the questions.

6.4   Future Work

We suggest further validation of our method and its results to investigate if it can be transferred to another organization or domain. Additionally, we suggest to investigate if in the same manner or with which changes, a scenario and personas could be derived for a similar serious games on social engineering.

Additionally, we think that as future work it should be evaluated if the effort can be reduced, for example by conducting less or shorter expert interviews. In addition to that, we believe that the process of deriving an interview guide can be shortened and based on the interview guide presented in this paper, since all questions are directed towards the game's key elements, which are the industry's specifics, assets, communication channels, location and existing personas.

Hill et al. [14] showed that the use of multiple photos (of males and females) for a single persona to avoid gender stereotypes did not reduce project designers' engagement with the personas. Thus, another interesting question, far beyond the scope of this work, is if the use of multiple photos for a single persona would change players' engagement with HATCH's personas.

7   Conclusion

In this paper, we added to addressing the problem that many firms do not address social engineering security threats adequately or only apply ineffective defense mechanisms, such as traditional trainings, penetration tests or standardized security awareness campaigns or serious games. We proposed to create specific scenarios considering the the organisation's specifics and based on the work of Faily and Flechais [11] proposed a method to develop a new scenario for HATCH.

The result of our research is that our method for adapting a serious game on social engineering was effective, since all participants of the evaluation sessions agreed that the derived scenario and its personas are realistic. However, the proposed method is also very time-consuming, requires a lot of effort and only makes sense if the scenario can be used several times by an organization or can be transferred to another, similar organization. We propose future work to investigate if the effort can be reduced.

Acknowledgements. This work was supported by European Union's Horizon 2020 research and innovation program from the project CyberSec4Europe (grant agreement number: 830929) and from the project THREAT-ARREST (grant agreement number: 786890). We are grateful for image services of Pixabay, Pexels and Unsplash.

References

1. Abawajy, J.: User preference of cyber security awareness delivery methods. Behav. Inf. Technol. **33**(3), 237–248 (2014)
2. Alexander, M.: Methods for understanding and reducing social engineering attacks. SANS Inst. **1**, 1–32 (2016). https://www.sans.org/reading-room/whitepapers/critical/methods-understand-ing-reducing-social-engineering-attacks-36972
3. Bada, M., Sasse, A.M., Nurse, J.R.C.: Cyber security awareness campaigns: Why do they fail to change behaviour? CoRR abs/1901.02672 (2019). http://arxiv.org/abs/1901.02672
4. Beckers, K., Pape, S.: A serious game for eliciting social engineering security requirements. In: Proceedings of the 24th IEEE International Conference on Requirements Engineering, RE 2016. IEEE Computer Society (2016)
5. Beckers, K., Pape, S., Fries, V.: HATCH: Hack and trick capricious humans - a serious game on social engineering. In: Proceedings of the 2016 British HCI Conference, Bournemouth, United Kingdom, 11–15 July 2016 (2016)
6. Charmaz, K.: Constructing Grounded Theory. Sage, Thousand Oaks (2014)
7. Cooper, A.: The inmates are running the asylum. indianapolis, ia: Sams. Macmillan (1999)
8. Corbin, J., Strauss, A.: Basics of Qualitative Research: Techniques and Procedures for Developing Grounded Theory. Sage publications, Thousand Oaks (2014)
9. Dimkov, T., Van Cleeff, A., Pieters, W., Hartel, P.: Two methodologies for physical penetration testing using social engineering. In: Proceedings of the 26th Annual Computer Security Applications Conference, pp. 399–408 (2010)
10. Donovan, L., Lead, P.: The use of serious games in the corporate sector. A State of the Art Report. Learnovate Centre (2012)
11. Faily, S., Flechais, I.: Persona cases: a technique for grounding personas. In: Proceedings of the SIGCHI Conference on Human Factors in Computing Systems, pp. 2267–2270 (2011)
12. Flick, U.: An Introduction to Qualitative Research. Sage, Thousand Oaks (2014)
13. Gläser, J., Laudel, G.: Experteninterviews und qualitative Inhaltsanalyse: als Instrumente rekonstruierender Untersuchungen. Springer, Heidelberg (2009)
14. Hill, C.G., et al.: Gender-inclusiveness personas vs. stereotyping: can we have it both ways? In: Proceedings of the 2017 Chi Conference on Human Factors in Computing Systems, pp. 6658–6671 (2017)

15. Huang, J., Krivkovich, A., Starikova, I., Yee, L., Zanoschi, D.: Women in the workplace 2019. McKinsey & Company and LeanIn.Org (2019). https://www. mckinsey.com/~/media/McKinsey/Featured%20Insights/Gender%20Equality/ Women%20in%20the%20Workplace%202019/Women-in-the-workplace-2019.pdf

16. Kipker, D.K., Pape, S., Wojak, S., Beckers, K.: Juristische bewertung eines social-engineering-abwehr trainings. In: Rudel, S., Lechner, U. (eds.) State of the Art: IT-Sicherheit für Kritische Infrastrukturen, pp. 112–115. Universität der Bundeswehr, Neubiberg (2018). https://www.itskritis.de/_uploads/user/IT-Sicherheit %20Kritische%20Infrastrukturen%E2%80%93screen.pdf#page=112

17. Malheiros, M., Jennett, C., Seager, W., Sasse, M.A.: Trusting to learn: trust and privacy issues in serious games. In: McCune, J.M., Balacheff, B., Perrig, A., Sadeghi, A.-R., Sasse, A., Beres, Y. (eds.) Trust 2011. LNCS, vol. 6740, pp. 116–130. Springer, Heidelberg (2011). https://doi.org/10.1007/978-3-642-21599-5_9

18. Meuser, M., Nagel, U.: The expert interview and changes in knowledge production. In: Bogner, A., Littig, B., Menz, W. (eds.) Interviewing Experts, pp. 17–42. Springer, Heidelberg (2009). https://doi.org/10.1057/9780230244276_2

19. Mitnick, K.D., Simon, W.L.: The Art of Deception: Controlling the Human Element of Security. John Wiley & Sons, Hoboken (2003)

20. Naderer, G., Balzer, E., Batinic, B., Bauer, F., Blank, R., David, J.: Qualitative Marktforschung in Theorie und Praxis. Springer, Heidelberg (2007). https://doi. org/10.1007/978-3-8349-6790-9

21. Papadaki, M., Furnell, S., Dodge, R.: Social engineering: Exploiting the weakest links. European Network & Information Security Agency (ENISA), Heraklion, Crete (2008)

22. Peltier, T.R.: Social engineering: concepts and solutions. Inf. Secur. J. 15(5), 13 (2006)

23. Petridis, P., et al.: State of the art in business games. Int. J. Serious Games 2(1) (2015)

24. Pruitt, J., Adlin, T.: The Persona Lifecycle: Keeping People in Mind Throughout Product Design. Elsevier, Amsterdam (2010)

25. Riedel, J.C., Hauge, J.B.: State of the art of serious games for business and industry. In: 2011 17th International Conference on Concurrent Enterprising, pp. 1–8. IEEE (2011)

26. Schaab, P., Beckers, K., Pape, S.: A systematic gap analysis of social engineering defence mechanisms considering social psychology. In: Proceedings of the 10th International Symposium on Human Aspects of Information Security & Assurance, HAISA 2016, Frankfurt, Germany, 19–21 July 2016 (2016)

27. Schaab, P., Beckers, K., Pape, S.: Social engineering defence mechanisms and counteracting training strategies. Inf. Comput. Secur. 25(2), 206–222 (2017)

Analysing Simulated Phishing Campaigns for Staff

Melanie Volkamer[1], Martina Angela Sasse[2(✉)], and Franziska Boehm[1]

[1] Karlsruhe Institute of Technology, Karlsruhe, Germany
{melanie.volkamer,franziska.boehm}@kit.edu
[2] Ruhr-Universität Bochum, Bochum, Germany
martina.sasse@rub.de

Abstract. In an attempt to stop phishing attacks, an increasing number of organisations run Simulated Phishing Campaigns to train their staff not to click on suspicious links. Organisations can buy toolkits to craft and run their own campaigns, or hire a specialist company to provide such campaigns as a service. To what extent this activity reduces the vulnerability of an organisation to such attacks is debated in both the research and practitioner communities, but an increasing number of organisations do it because it seems common practice, and are convinced by vendors' claims about the reduction in clickrates that can be achieved. But most are not aware that effective security is not just about reducing clickrates for simulated phishing messages, that there are many different ways of running such campaigns, and that there are security, legal, and trust issues associated with those choices. The goal of this paper is to equip organisational decision makers with tools for making those decisions. A closer examination of costs and benefits of the choice reveals that it may be possible to run a legally compliant campaign, but that it is costly and time-consuming. Additionally, the impact of Simulated Phishing Campaigns on employees' self-efficacy and trust in the organisation may negatively affect other organisational goals. We conclude that for many organisations, a joined-up approach of (1) improving technical security measures, (2) introducing and establishing adequate security incident reporting, and (3) increasing staff awareness through other means may deliver better protection at lower cost.

Keywords: Social engineering · Phishing · Security awareness

1 Introduction

Although phishing attacks are not a new phenomenon, they are still a major threat to many organisations: small or large, national or international, public or private sector. There are a number of definitions of what a phishing attack is; in this paper, a broad definition. Phishers try to

I. Boureanu et al. (Eds.): ESORICS 2020 Workshops, LNCS 12580, pp. 312–328, 2020.
https://doi.org/10.1007/978-3-030-66504-3_19

- either steal the (digital) credential of their victims to harm them directly, or
- use stolen (digital) credentials to carry out attacks on others, or
- install malware on the victim's system, that can then be used to steal credentials or other information, or make files unaccessible and extort payments to have them restored.

A single employee who falls for a phishing attack can cause significant damage to an organisation, for instance if files that are needed for daily business are no longer available. Sometimes, it can also be the starting point for further attacks on customers or suppliers.

To prevent their staff falling victims to phishing attacks, organisations resort to running simulated phishing campaigns. In a simulated phishing campaign, email messages with malicious links or attachments are sent to staff to see if they are 'vulnerable' to this form of attack, and then present those who are with education or training measures that aim to help them recognise this form of attack - and thus not fall for them in again. Given the plethora of security vendors offering toolkits or service for simulated phishing campaigns, many organisations are under the impression that this is an essential measure to defend against such attacks. In this paper, we will examine the different objectives and forms of phishing campaigns, and point out the challenges associated with with conducting them in practice; we also present the associated costs and potential side effects organisations should consider before deciding whether to implement such a campaign.

We first present various elements and types of phishing attacks (Sect. 2). In Sect. 3, we examine the objectives an organisation has when conducting simulated phishing campaigns. Section 4 presents the different forms of phishing campaigns, and what choices an organisation can make when implementing them. In Sect. 5, we examine phishing campaigns from security, legal, and human perspectives, to highlight the side effects and longer-term consequences for an organisation. Finally, in Sect. 6 we discuss to what extent the data collected during simulated phishing campaigns are a valid reflection of how vulnerable, or not, an organisation is to this form of attack.

2   Different Forms and Types of Phishing Messages

In this chapter we define the types of phishing messages attacker send[1]. Phishing messages can be sent via different channels, be it by email, via messages and/or posts in social media or social networks, via direct messages in messengers, or as text message. It is important for organisations to be aware that attackers increasingly use other channels - such as text messages - to trick staff into make contact with the attacker, and that in addition to malicious links or attachments,

---

[1] Some phishing messages are also referred to as spam. Spam includes any kind of unsolicited messages, so phishing messages are a sub-set of spam messages - and indeed many staff do not distinguish and use the "spam messages" instead of phishing.

attackers may use media files, for instance voicemails that seem to come from the chief executive officer (CEO).

The contents of phishing messages can be dangerous in different ways. In a phishing message, the recipient is usually asked to perform one of the following actions:

1. disclose sensitive data such as access credentials, confidential documents, or credit card data,
2. transfer money or make calls, e.g. to supposed friends or business partners (e.g. in connection with the so-called CEO fraud),
3. disable or circumvent security measures, e.g. deactivate virus protection or install a (malicious "update",
4. click on links or go to go websites, which
   (a) either lead to a genuine-looking but fraudulent website, where sensitive data such as login details have to be entered, or
   (b) lead to a website that attempts to install and distribute malware on your devices (just clicking on the link can cause immediate damage), or
   (c) open dangerous attachments that contain malware or dangerous links.

The sophistication of phishing messages - and thus the difficulty involved in detecting them - varies considerably:

- Very easy to identify phishing messages contain noticeable spelling and grammatical errors[2] and/or incorrect presentation.
- Phishing messages that are moderately difficult to identify may look credible in terms of content and presentation, but may come from an implausible sender (e.g. sender's email address[3] or sender's phone number). In some email clients, only the sender's name may be displayed, and checking the sender's address requires an extra action from the user - e.g. to hover the mouse over the name.
- Phishing messages that are difficult to identify are plausible in terms of content, presentation, and sender. Accordingly, depending on the type of response desired by the phisher, the message can only be recognised by the account or telephone number, the URL behind the link, or the attachment type. Such messages can be sent because, for example, real message content is copied from large providers (so-called clone phishing), the email address is spoofed (faked), the salutatory address is replaced accordingly, and the corresponding information is exchanged.

---

[2] Note that on the other hand, not all message with incorrect spelling and grammatical errors are phishing messages - with increasing digitalization and widespread use of social networking, and increasing awareness of conditions such as dyslexia, much non-malicious written communication contains such errors; when attackers impersonate some senders, it can even be interpreted as a sign of authenticity.

[3] It is important to check the sender's e-mail address and not just rely on the sender's name, because the latter is very easy to alter.

– Phishing messages are very difficult to identify if the phisher has access to a genuine email account, and uses that to send plausible-sounding phishing messages - and sometimes even referring to a previous email communication. The email account is usually that of a person, e.g. a colleague, or another employee of a customer or supplier. Attackers have also managed to gain access to the email accounts of genuine service providers and sent phishing messages from there.

Phishing messages lead the recipient to believe that there is a - more or less plausible - reason why she should carry out the requested action. Attackers often add psychological triggers - such as creating time pressure, threatening punishment or promising gains - are used[4,5]. The triggers steer the recipient towards carrying out the action, and away from checking for signs that of a phishing message.

Attackers pursue a range of different strategies: They either try to reach as many potential victims as possible with the same message, or they target their message at a specific person: In the case of *'classic' phishing*, the attacker sends the same message to all recipients available to him (i.e. not just to one organisation). Usually, the salutatory address is 'Dear customer, dear ladies and gentlemen'. The message is personalised only if this can be done automatically, e.g. because the attacker attempts to derive the name from the sender's information (such as the email address), or because the name or the gender are known in addition to the email address (e.g. because this information is also available on websites and can be read automatically). From the attacker's point of view, such a phishing attack is successful even if not all recipients react to the message, but only a few to whom the message appears plausible at the time - e.g. if a (phishing) message from Amazon one day after having placed on order. Classic phishing is mainly based on phishing messages with dangerous links and attachments, as these are likely to be clicked/opened by many recipients. Phishing messages of varying degrees of simplicity or difficulty are used in case of 'classic' phishing. *Spear phishing* is a form of phishing where attackers specifically attack an organisation or even a person. The attackers first collect information - either purely via the information freely available on the Internet about the organisation (e.g. customers, service providers, cooperation partners, or newsletter), or via the staff or even additionally via phone calls. Based on this bunch of information, organisation-specific phishing messages (e.g. from a customer, service provider, or cooperation partner) are then written. Due to the message's reference to the organisation, and possibly to one's own position and function in the organisation, spear phishing is generally much more difficult to identify than classic phishing.

---

[4] Stajano, Wilson: Understanding Scam Victims: Seven principles for system security. Communications of the ACM 2011, 54(3):70–75.

[5] Again, the same tactics are used by senders of legitimate messages .

3   Objectives of Simulated Phishing Campaigns

In conducting a simulated phishing campaign, an organisation may pursue one or more of the following objectives:

Objective 1: To determine how vulnerable – or resistant – the organisation currently is to phishing attacks (and how many identified phishing attacks are being reported). Security staff may do this to obtain more budget for IT/information security and/or data protection activities, or to make the case that a mandatory security awareness campaign and/or security training should be introduced.

Objective 2: To demonstrate to staff who click that they vulnerable, and create a so-called "teachable moment". Here it is assumed that someone who falls for a (simulated) phishing message is particularly receptive to security awareness training immediately afterwards. At the exact moment when they recognise they might have potentially fallen victim to such an attack, staff are presented with information on how to recognise phishing messages, and on how to report them. Creating a "teachable moment" - as opposed to providing this information as part of general awareness campaigns or training - is supposed to be more effective because the awareness that one is vulnerable is supposed to focus attention and increase motivation[6]. The security training delivered at this point can be optional or mandatory. There are two types of settings:

- (objective 2a) In this case, the number of staff who fell for messages, or reported a messages, are not collected and reported. In this setting, the purpose of the simulated phishing messages is purely to raise awareness of the organisation's vulnerability.
- (objective 2b) In this case, the number of staff who fell for the message or reported a message are counted to evaluate the security awareness measure, and (hopefully) show that the campaign has decreased the organisation's level of vulnerability. This is typically measured as a percentage how many simulated messages resulted in a link or attachment are being clicked on.

Objective 3: (Scientific) evaluation of a security awareness measure deployed by the organisation (or parts of it) - e.g. an awareness campaign or training module. In this case, the simulated phishing campaign serves only to evaluate the effectiveness of the security awareness measure - which may be a new product, or a new security awareness measure created by researchers. Such quasi-experimental evaluations are often limited to subsets of staff.

Some organisations conduct campaigns purely for compliance reasons simply to be able to report to an auditor or regulatory authority that the organisation has "run awareness campaigns" or "trained staff". Indeed, some audit procedures do not ask for more evidence than that. However questionable, there is sometimes also the assumption that by virtue of having conducted a simulated phishing campaign, the organisation can 'offload' the responsibility in case of a breach

---

[6] Kumaraguru, Sheng, Acquisti, Cranor, Hong: Teaching Johnny not to fall for phish, ACM Transactions on Internet Technology 2010, 10 (2):1–31.

on the staff member who fell for an attack, despite "having been made aware" of the risks. Since this is not a responsible approach, we will not consider this objective in this paper.

4 Simulated Phishing Campaign Designs

Simulated phishing campaigns involve sending various fraudulent messages to the staff of the organisation over a certain period of time. There are different ways of designing and conducting such campaigns .

As outlined in Sect. 1, phishing campaigns can cover different message channels, different types of dangerous content, different levels of difficulty of phishing attacks, with or without the use of psychological triggers, and different attack strategies. When we refer to a simulated targeted spear phishing campaign, we use that term "spear phishing campaign", and "phishing campaign" for general ones. In addition, different types of message content and sender type (e.g. the message comes from a person or organisation) can be used. Messages can be sent with or without reference to recent events - the former increases the plausibility of the message, and hence the difficulty of recognising it as phishing[7,8].

Campaigns can be carried out by the organisation itself - usually security staff, who may use an off-the shelf product they can configure, or by creating messages and the delivery mechanism from scratch. Alternatively, the organisation can commission an external service provider, who may then sent simulated phishing messages from within the organisation, or externally.

Phishing campaigns can be one-off or send repeated message over a period of time; they can target all employees or a subset, and the same messages may be sent to all, or messages may be targeted at subsets of employees. If a campaign involves multiple messages, the order may be random, or the campaign may start with the easiest or most difficult message, and increase or decrease in difficulty, respectively. Additionally, the level of difficulty of the next message sent may depend on whether the previous message was identified as a phishing one, or not.

Finally, there are several ways of how the organisation deals with the fact that such campaigns involve deception:

– The victim is informed once fallen for a simulated phish. In addition, the victim may or may not receive some information about phishing or explanations. If an explanation is provided, it can provide a form of "training by explaining", e.g. which signs in the specific messages could have been recognised as indicators of phishing.

---

[7] Burns, Johnson, Caputo: Spear phishing in a barrel: Insights from a targeted phishing campaign. in Journal of Organizational Computing and Electronic Commerce 29(1):24–39.

[8] Benenson, Gassmann, Landwirth: Unpacking Spear Phishing Susceptibility. Financial Cryptography Workshops 2017: 610–627.

- The organisation issues a general statement or message to staff that makes them believe that there has been a problem with the email service, but that does not disclose that they have fallen for a simulated phishing message.
- The victim does not realise that he/she has fallen for a phishing message, e.g. because he/she is redirected to a legitimate website.

In the last two cases, all staff or those who fell for the deception can be informed at a later date that they received phishing messages, and possibly be directed to further explanation or training.

In general, the organisation can inform staff that a campaign has taken place, with or without explanation. To do this by email is the most common form at the moment, but some organisations have provided explanation and results via departmental meetings or general staff meetings. This allows staff to engage and ask questions, and start a dialogue on how simulated phishing campaigns are perceived.

Phishing campaigns can be announced – beforehand – more or less prominently and in more or less detail. There may even be contexts where no information at all is given to the organisation's staff.

As for the survey of the current state (Objective 1), the evaluation of the teachable moment (Objective 2b), or the evaluation of (newly developed) security awareness measures (Objective 3), different parameters are considered and collected either individually or in combination.

- The number of persons who per phishing message perform the relevant insecure action (e.g. click on the link/disclose sensitive data/open the attachment).
- The number of persons who report/delete an identified phishing message.
- The number of persons who, after having noticed it, report that they have fallen for a phishing message.
- The number of persons who are unsure and inquire about the received message.

Reporting can also be done at different levels of detail - for example, for all staff or for individual groups, or per phishing message or message type.

5   Problems with, and Obstacles to, Simulated Phishing Campaigns

First of all, we will consider reasons against organisations carrying out a simulated phishing campaign - irrespective of what the specific objectives of the campaign may be. The organisation may think about it as testing how resilient it is against such attacks, but staff may perceive it as being tested individually - and if they fall for a simulated phishing email, found wanting. The perception that they are being attacked by their own organisation while working to deliver its productivity goals can have a negative impact on staff trust in the organisation, and the security and error culture. This in turn can create a range of security problems. Furthermore, some aspects of simulated campaigns may not be compatible with national employment or data protection laws, or local agreements with labour organisations. All three aspects are discussed below.

5.1   Security Aspects

Simulated phishing messages try to reproduce messages sent by attackers, and do so with varying degrees of accuracy. Of the phishing messages mentioned in Sect. 2, those calling on their victims to make cash transfers or phone calls and those asking for security measures to be disabled or circumvented are more difficult to simulate. While the message itself is easy to send, it is difficult to verify whether an employee who received it thought it was genuine. Attackers sometimes send messages asking the recipient to deactivate or circumvent organisational security measures - simulated campaigns tend not to replicate this aspect because asking staff to do so poses a security risk. This has however a negative effect on how well the collected data reflects the organisation's actual vulnerability. An organisation needs to consider carefully what type of messages it considers a threat, and whether simulating those messages, and the actions some staff may take in response, create additional risk to the organisation.

Security Problems Caused by Simulated Phishing Campaigns. Several security problems can arise while conducting a simulated phishing campaign. First of all, the infrastructure must be configured so that all simulated phishing messages reach the staff that is being targeted. In the case of emails, the simulated phishing messages must end up in staff's inboxes - if messages end up in junk or spam folders, staff will not see them. This can happen especially if the messages are sent by an external provider of such campaigns.

There are a number of obvious questions: How can configurations be changed? Will the messages be tailored to each employee (considering his/her salutation) and will exactly these tailored messages then be whitelisted?[9]. Or can only individual senders or individual names of attachments or domains/URLs be whitelisted?[10]. In addition, the campaign provider usually has very limited knowledge of the infrastructure and can therefore only propose very general measures to make phishing campaigns possible. Thus, the risk of generally lowering the security level is correspondingly high. Is it technically possible to use whitelisting prior to the actual security audit of messages?[11]. Should the security audit itself be adapted?[12] .Organisations may end up creating configurations

---

[9] Wholesale general whitelisting means that phishers can take the same approach and can be sure that their phishing messages reach the recipient.

[10] This can still be used by phishers if this information is leaked.

[11] After the security audit, whitelisting is not helpful, because with an adequate security level of the security audit, most of the phishing campaign messages would be blocked and thus would present no risk to the organisation and its staff. This, again has a negative effect on how well the collected data reflects the organisation's actual vulnerability.

[12] If an external email service provider is used, this change may not be possible at all.

that reduce their level of protection in general. This is particularly risky because genuine phishing messages will still be sent - and now are more likely to end up in staff inboxes.

Explanatory notes: (1) Whitelisting does not reflect reality - the following information would be missing: Are the phishing campaign emails really that ones that staff need to identify, because the security measures in place would not recognise and remove them? Or does the campaign mainly contain messages which, without whitelisting, would not reach the staff (and this would completely question the campaign's effectiveness)? (2) If the argument is that, for the simulated phishing campaign, one does not at all change the configuration, it must still be clear which of the campaign's messages actually reached which employee - otherwise, the effectiveness of the campaign again is questionable. If the argument is that almost all messages reach staff, one could argue that the organisation needs to improve its technical countermeasures to reduce its vulnerability. In addition, there is a productivity cost associated with staff with dealing with those messages, and running a campaign requires further resources, and is not without risks - so both in terms of security and economics, investing in better countermeasures makes more sense. (3) A change or reduction of the security measures for campaign purposes might violate organisations' security policies, and lead to significant problems during security audits.

An additional risk associated with a simulated phishing campaign is that attackers may use as a basis for a phishing attack. For example, the phisher can pretend to be the campaign organiser, and send a phishing email to all known email addresses. This email, for example, can contain a link or an attachment that is supposed to inform the recipient about his/her own performance in the campaign. Such attacks are possible, even if the staff have not been informed in detail in advance, since some staff end up alerting colleagues - either with the best of intentions, because they think it is an actual attack, or because they want to warn colleagues not to fall for the "same trick". If the campaign is run an external provider, the provider may name customer organisations in their advertising, and thus, staff may be forewarned, and attackers alerted to a possible opportunity. Organisations who use external providers should consider this carefully.

Explanatory note: Even if attackers have no concrete evidence that an organisation is running simulated phishing campaigns, they may try this because, as simulated phishing campaigns have become commonplace, staff are likely to have heard of them and thus believe that their organisation is, even if there has been no announcement.

Security Problems Associated with Informing Staff About Simulated Phishing Campaigns. Security problems can arise if staff cannot distinguish between simulated phishing messages, and real phishing messages that are sent by attackers, because staff might interact with a real phishing message (e.g. open the attachment, follow the link, etc.) - in most cases, they do it they feel invited to interact with the messages and learn more about them. Some staff may click on every link they see as a form of protest, because they feel it is unreasonable for the organisation to "trick" them in this way. No organisation can rule out that real phishing messages will reach their staff during the campaign - unless they stop delivering all external emails and only send simulated ones. If the organisation has promised there will be no negative consequences employees who fall for simulated phishing messages, they have to do the same for staff who fall for real ones. It is very difficult to communicate that, on the one hand, staff will not be punished for falling for simulated phishing, but at the same time, they are requested to be alert at all times, and try their very best to recognise and report phishing messages. The fact that it is not possible to distinguish between realistic, simulated and real phishing messages during a campaign means staff are faced with an impossible task - and we will return to the wider implications of this in the Human Aspects section below. If the organisation puts staff in that position, punishing staff who "fail" is from a legal and ethical point of view indefensible. Also, it reduces reporting, which plays an important role in reducing the damage of real phishing messages, because it enables the organisation to adjust its email filter and communication to staff.

A further problem is what happens after staff realise that they have fallen for a real phishing attack may not report it, because uncertainty or fear of negative consequences causes them to try to hide their failure and hope for the best. Others realise they have failed, but then assume it is part of the campaign, are be annoyed for a moment, but then don't report because they assume that their "failure" has already been logged.

Finally, whilst many staff are aware that distinguishing all simulated from real phishing messages is an impossible task, some are not. Such staff may be happy to have himself/herself identified a "simulated" phishing message, but may not report it because they have experienced a common side-effect of campaigns in the past: overwhelmed help-desks and IT security staff who respond with (with varying degrees of exasperation) "thank you, but it's a training message, no need to report but please don't tell anyone else". Negative experiences of reporting will lead staff to think twice before reporting again.

Explanatory notes: (1) Of course an organisation could point out that it is actually impossible to always distinguish between simulated and real phishing messages, and request staff to report all suspicious messages. But explaining why it is subjecting staff to training that has limited efficacy is challenging. (2) If the organisation is willing to this, the reporting and investigation processes must be clearly regulated, communicated, and integrated into everyday work. Staff must be given information on what to do, and to whom they should report if:

- they are unsure about a message
- they identify a phishing message, simulated or real
- they have fallen for a phishing message, simulated or real

Assuming the organisation has established such reporting and investigation protocol, and that in the run-up to the campaign, it made clear that distinguished between simulated and real phishing messages is not always possible, and thus reporting and investigation is mandatory.

Assuming a reporting and investigation protocol is in place, and staff understand and accept it, a phishing campaign will result in more reports and investigations. The situation can also become more complex because (a) it is now possible for staff to get feedback on which messages were simulated and real, (b) simulated and real phishing messages identified in time can be reported, and (c) staff who have fallen for a simulated or real phishing message can be told[13]. Rules for handling messages will be amended accordingly. Depending on the objective of the phishing campaign, documentation tasks will be added. To deal with this added load, the organisation has to either add staff to deal with these properly, or there will be longer waiting times. Longer waiting times will be frustrating for staff waiting to hear whether or not to proceed with a message, and increases the risk that they do interact with it. And again, delays in responses to reporting will reduce the likelihood of reporting in future. A reporting and investigation system that struggles to manage reports to real phishing messages will not be made better by the additional load created by simulated ones.

Explanatory notes: (1) We have witnessed several cases of simulated phishing campaigns in organisations being aborted or significantly scaled back because IT helpdesks and IT security staff were overwhelmed. In theory, the organisation should increase the number of staff for reporting and investigation during the campaign to be prepared for this. In practice, most organisations do not have suitable staff "on tap", and the administrative workload and financial implications of hiring temporary staff are off-putting - so some providers of simulated campaigns are reluctant to raise the issue, and play down the importance of reporting and investigation instead. (2) If there is any omission or ambiguity in the reporting and investigation protocol, there will be more enquiries because staff are unsure about how to deal with these messages and/or incidents.

Regarding Objective 2b (Measuring if the Combination of Phishing Campaign and Subsequent Security Awareness Measures has an Effect). In order to measure the exact effect of the phishing campaign, no other security awareness measures should be provided to the staff at the same time. So, if the phishing campaign does not have the desired effect, the organisation has also lost the opportunity for other security awareness measures related to phishing.

In order to achieve the objective 2b, the campaign should last as long as possible, or even carry on permanently (to keep reminding staff of the risks of phishing). However, running campaigns on an ongoing basis would also require regularly reducing the level of protection (see above) - which most organisations will not want to do.

The level of difficulty of the simulated phishing messages can also have a negative impact on security. Messages that are easy to identify as phishing - e.g. with bad spelling and/or grammar, an unknown sender, or attachments with

---

[13] Burns, Johnson, Caputo: Spear phishing in a barrel: Insights from a targeted phishing campaign. in Journal of organisational Computing and Electronic Commerce 29(1):24–39.

suspicious data types - lead staff to believe that they can detect phishing. This makes them more vulnerable to sophisticated attacks.

5.2 Legal Aspects

Organisations have to pay attention to the specific laws of the countries in which they operate and employ staff. In most cases (for Objectives 1 and 2b presented in Chap. 3), phishing campaigns will also measure work performance. This gives rise to legal questions in the context of employment protection and data protection. In Germany, for instance, the organisation's works council needs to be consulted on any measures to covertly assess staff. Data protection requirements may not allow identification of individual staff, in particular in European countries.

In addition to law pertaining to staff, legal limits may arise from trademark law. Messages pretending to be from other organisations, or clone phishing, may only look credible if they include the logos of the providers (e.g. of SAP or Paypal). It is only possible to do this without trademark infringement if campaigns are run purely in-house, on the organisation's own infrastructure, and do not express a business purpose of their own. However, all phishing websites created are then restricted for use within the organisation. It is also necessary to check whether the use of such logos conflicts with the organisation's code of conduct or other rules - imitating a trademark can be seen as a form of undermining that company's reputation, and make staff doubt it's trustworthiness in future. Intellectual property laws and copyright protection of such logos must be considered. All this needs to be clarified before phishing messages are sent. If clone phishing messages or messages from certain providers cannot be used, this limits the significance of the phishing campaign, as it is not possible to send the kind of phishing messages that are common otherwise.

5.3 Human Aspects

In most organisations, security is not a particularly popular topic with staff. Most organisations have many security policies, which staff may have heard or read about, but often find impossible to understand or follow. Staff feel justified in ignoring security policies and training that they find impossible to follow and/or that noticeably reduce their productivity. With simulated phishing campaigns, staff are taught to check many aspects of each message they receive - one campaign commissioned by a UK bank literally tells people to "take 5" - min - before acting on a message. Since most staff in modern organisations receive dozens or hundreds of emails per day, the productivity reduction that would result from following this advice would be enormous. Many organisations have security policies create impossible tasks, with serious side effects: unsurprisingly, it creates resentment, and creates the perception that IT security is "impossible" and best ignored. Yet staff do not happily breach the rules - they do worry about enabling a breach and being blamed for it, after having failed at the impossible task. Simulated phishing campaigns contribute further to this unhappy state of affairs.

In a phishing campaign, the organisation "attacks" its own staff. In particular, if the campaign is conducted internally, one group of staff (usually from the IT or security department) attacks all others - though they may not attack the organisation's management. Depending on the design of the phishing messages, all staff attack each other to a certain extent: since it is impossible for staff to distinguish whether the received message is part of the simulated phishing campaign, a real phishing attack, or whether the colleague wrote the message based on a message he/she received within the campaign. As soon as word of the latter possibility has spread among the staff, distrust among staff increases, and already difficult relationships will deteriorate further. This, in turn, also leads to reduced productivity, and in the worst case, mediation talks will become necessary.

If a campaign is announced, the sender will receive questions. If the sender is a member of the IT or security department, and does not have a good relationship, they might misinterpret those questions, which again would lead to new conflicts. If the campaign has not been announced, and a simulated phishing message is identified as a phishing message, staff members may feel tricked, in which case resentment and potentially conflicts may follow. Phishing campaigns, in which messages from other staff - e.g. the CEO or Head of Human Resources - are simulated, it may affect the perception of those staff members, trust in the organisation. Staff who fall for (poorly designed) phishing messages might be perceived as stupid or careless, and treated with disrespect. This also has a negative effect on the culture of the organisation.

Launching a phishing campaign without first instructing staff (i.e., explaining how to identify phishing messages, where to report if they are unsure, how to deal with phishing messages they have identified, and where to report if they fell for such messages) is simply unfair. Simulated phishing campaigns are not likely to increase staff' trust in the organisation's management - particularly if the campaign is not widely announced. Simulated campaigns are supposed to improve the security awareness and skills of staff, but those who fall for a simulated message experience failure. Self-efficacy has been shown to be the key factor in changing security behaviour: staff who are confident in their ability to perform a new security task are significantly more likely to change behaviour than those who are not. Making staff experience failure a security task can lead them to conclude they cannot reliably detect messages anyway, and thus resort to reporting any message they are not absolutely sure of.

If the campaign has not been announced officially, but rumours are circulating through the organisation, further problems arise if the reporting and investigation processes have not been clearly communicated in advance of the campaign: Staff are unsure of how to proceed if they have identified or fallen for a phishing message. Does the same reporting process apply to simulated phishing? Why do I get this message and others do not? Who knows now that I have made a mistake? What is the consequence of this? Often, staff feel unsettled and controlled by phishing campaigns. Both will have a negative impact on the organisation's reporting culture. Another problem of not announcing the campaigns officially and in detail is that false information then spreads quickly and is difficult to correct. Simulated phishing messages have to be treated in the same way in the reporting and inquiry process. This not only requires a great deal of effort and resources, but deceiving staff. Deception does not create trust in the reporting and investigation system. This can even have a negative effect on the level of protection if the consequence is that people generally do not want to ask questions or do not want to report anything because they do not want this kind of behaviour. Accordingly, phishing campaigns also have a negative influence on the organisations' error culture.

If the phishing campaign is widely announced, staff will look critically at many more messages, and may try to verify the sender, e.g. by phone. This again reduces productivity, and being asked several times an hour whether I really sent that messages will not improve working relationships. organisations cannot expect work to continue as normal during a simulated campaign - staff must be given time to deal with the extra work of scrutinising messages and reporting them. If this is not the case, it increases pressure and has a negative effect on the perception of the organisation's leadership.

Further productivity losses can result staff becoming overly cautious, and treating legitimate messages as phishing messages. This means invoices are not paid, job applications not considered, and queries by customers or suppliers ignored. Message from any 3rd party - e.g. an external travel or survey company - now have a hard time getting responses from staff in many organisations. A responsive reporting and investigation process that can quickly provide responses can help, but it requires significant resource.

The level of difficulty of the simulated phishing messages can also have a negative influence on staff' mood. If they are too easy, the impression can quickly arise that the management thinks that staff cannot be identify obvious phishing attempts. If an employee receives a second phishing message of the same type (after one has fallen for the first one of that type), she gets the impression that the management suspects that she still does not understand. Again, this does not have a positive effect on staff' trust in the management.

Regarding Objective 2b (Proof was Given of the Fact that the Combination of Phishing Campaign and Subsequent Security Awareness Measures has an Effect). From the point of view of the phishing campaign alone, this would mean that staff would only have access to the information from the security awareness measure if they had made a mistake. This easily leads to irritation and uncertainty. It leads to the situation that if you want to know more (because you think you do not know enough) you have to interact with phishing messages, which, as one knows, should actually not be done. This has a negative effect on the self-efficacy of staff and reduces the level of protection.

Regarding Objective 1 (Assessing the Current Situation and then Motivate for a Subsequent Security Awareness Measure) and Objective 2b). These cases entail another problem: Nobody likes being confronted with his/her own weaknesses. Being told what you do wrong makes you feel bad. However, that's exactly what may happen if phishing campaigns are designed in such a way that sooner or later one finds out that one has fallen for a phishing message. Very well-designed phishing messages are very likely to have many victims, and they initially go through a negative experience. It is questionable whether and how the willingness to learn how to identify phishing messages in the future will increase as a result of a negative experience; it has been shown several times that a lack of self-efficacy has a negative influence on security behaviour[14]. In the case of Objective 2b, it is particularly important to find out whether the staff who became victims were so shocked and surprised by their own failure that they closed the document or exited the website quickly, so that no one else will notice that they have fallen for a phishing message. Accordingly, the victims would not notice that information on how to recognise phishing messages in the future is provided in the message.

6   What Do the Numbers Collected During the Simulated Phishing Campaign Tell Us?

Data regarding the people having fallen or having (not) reported are collected in case of Objectives 1, 2b), and 3. To achieve theses objectives, different data types - individually or in combination - can be considered, i.e.:

1. the number of staff who perform the corresponding unwanted action per phishing message (e.g. click on the link/open the attachment); this needs to be defined more precisely (e.g. clicking on a link only, or entering access data or other sensitive data[15],
2. the number of people who report a detected phishing message,
3. the number of people who report that they have fallen for a phishing message after they have discovered the deception,
4. the number of people who respond with inquiries about messages.

The question is what can cause high or low numbers of people who fall for a simulated phishing attack.

The (external) validity of the results is strongly influenced by several facts. First of all, the external validity depends on the amount of information about the phishing campaign distributed to the staff. A (large) part of the staff will be more sceptical about the relevant messages than usual, will ask or inform colleagues, or generally talk about it having discovered a phishing message. Others are so against "attacking" staff that they intentionally interact with every phishing message.

All this is especially true when the time frames for campaigns are short. At the same time, short campaigns only increase the security risk for a short period

---

[14] https://www.enisa.europa.eu/publications/cybersecurity-culture-guidelines-behavioural-aspects-of-cybersecurity.

[15] The latter quickly becomes another security problem. Because these sensitive data must not be transferred.

of time. All these influencing factors should at least be considered as a limitation of the validity[16].

It is also assumed that there is a well-established reporting and inquiry process even before the phishing campaign starts. It would also be necessary for the process to provide for the reporting of detected phishing messages, and not for how many have been deleted. Otherwise, phishing messages cannot be distinguished from other spam messages or other messages that are deleted. Part of the reporting and inquiry process must also include the reporting of phishing messages that are already known to have been reported by other staff (e.g. a colleague working in the same office).

Explanatory note: It is strongly recommended to first critically analyse one's own reporting and inquiry processes before considering a simulated phishing campaign.

In case you are wondering why it is not sufficient to record the number of staff who perform the relevant unwanted action per phishing message (e.g. click on the link/open the attachment), please consider the following explanations.

Non-interaction can have many reasons and therefore cannot be interpreted as a clear indicator that the message was identified as a phishing message: The message was not seen at all because the person concerned was on vacation or sick, had no time or was not relevant, does not have a corresponding account, or because a colleague has already drawn attention to the phishing message. The latter does not mean that the respective colleagues would have automatically identified the message as a phishing message. It is not possible either to tell staff not to inform other staff, because this is exactly what you want in the case of real phishing messages: Staff are supposed to react and help others to protect themselves and the organisation.

Ultimately, the false positives would also have to be counted, i.e. messages that were legitimate but were reported as a phishing attack and were therefore not processed for the time being. To put it bluntly: A phishing campaign that has the consequence that all phishing messages are reliably detected, but that also has the consequence that every second legitimate message is deleted because it is considered to be a phishing message, is not effective either.

The external validity of the results of a phishing campaign also depends on the simulated phishing messages. The rule of thumb is: The easier they are to detect, the "better" the results. Simulated phishing messages that are extremely difficult to identify would hardly be recognised as such by anyone. Actually, the simulated phishing messages would have to represent those from real attacks (and thus a multitude of different ones), but for this purpose, messages from staff and external providers would also have to be used, which would have a number of disadvantages (including the relationship of trust between colleagues and the fact that one might have to check trademark law aspects). All in all,

---

[16] This is particularly true in the case of Objective 3, and any other evaluation would also have limitations. Here, it may make sense to use different study forms for the evaluation.

the external validity should always be seen in relation to the simulated phishing messages as well as in relation to changes in the infrastructure.

The results' validity of the collected data also depends on whether or to what extent other influencing factors, e.g. media reports, can be controlled during the period of the survey.

If Objective 2(b) is pursued, the following should be considered in addition:

Additional data would need to be collected. For the evaluation, it would be necessary to know whether and how long the subsequent security awareness measures have been dealt with. For this purpose, the data could only be collected in a pseudonymised but not in an anonymised way. This must be checked for admissibility under data protection law.

7   Conclusion

The external validity of results for simulated phishing campaigns in general, and especially for some particular forms, is a matter of debate. Security experts and service providers selling the services equate a reduction in click rates with reduction in vulnerability, while human factors experts point to the futility of training staff on what is essentially an impossible task, and economists - and some organisational leaders - count the mounting productivity losses caused by this countermeasure.

Our analysis has shown that creating a simulated phishing campaign that minimises additional security problems and is legally compliant is extremely difficult and costly. Even if an organisation is willing to invest this much, the combined negative impact of simulated phishing campaigns on the self-efficacy of individual staff, and the reduction of inter-personal trust and trust in the organisation, and the reduced productivity of all staff involved are enormous. The cost and negative side-effects clearly outweigh the low external validity of a such a campaign, and the limited reduction in vulnerability that results. We therefore recommend that organisations invest time and money in (1) an improvement of technical measures. In addition, (2) appropriate awareness measures should make staff aware of the type of phishing messages they can reach despite all technical measures and of how they can identify them. Finally, (3) the reporting and inquiry process should be improved. As a result, the effort for each individual employee is comparably low and can be implemented. The level of protection increases without negative effects on trust relationships and self-efficacy.

Author Index

Printed in the United States
By Bookmasters